God's Eagles,
Athletes and Pilgrims

Those who hope in the Lord will renew their strength. They will soar on wings like eagles; they will run and not grow weary; they will walk and not be faint. (Isaiah 40v31, NIV)

God's Eagles, Athletes and Pilgrims

A weekly devotional with real stories of real people

Revised Edition

HAIDE S. SANCHEZ

authorHOUSE®

AuthorHouse™ UK
1663 Liberty Drive
Bloomington, IN 47403 USA
www.authorhouse.co.uk
Phone: 0800.197.4150

Published by AuthorHouse 01 June 2015

ISBN: 978-1-5049-3975-1 (sc)
ISBN: 978-1-5049-3976-8 (e)

Print information available on the last page. This book is printed on acid-free paper.

This Revised Edition is a more compact, updated and edited version of the 2012 edition.

The author had underlined some portions of scripture quotations in this book and
capitalised pronouns referring to God for emphasis and clarity.

Acknowledgments

It would not have been possible for me to produce this book without the help or input of so many people to whom I owe my deepest gratitude. To them I say, "THANK YOU SO MUCH!"

To those who contributed testimonies or stories which form the major part of this book. Appendix 5 lists their names and the titles of their stories.

To my main proof-readers, Lou Mosey and Máire Byrne, who painstakingly spent so many hours checking the manuscript. Also to Marcus, Heather, Gill, Esther, Maria-Louisa and Arthur who helped with some proof-reading.

To Tarun who patiently helped me by sharing his computer expertise.

To Gerry Villegas for capturing on paper the mental image of the book cover art work that the Lord showed me.

To my pastor, Marcus Mosey, to my home group and to the rest of the congregation at Christians Alive in Lancaster, for their support, encouragement, advice and prayers. Many of the stories in this book are from people of this church.

To my Internet prayer partners Shirley, Linda, Gayle and Máire, who inspired and encouraged me to begin working on this book and helped me to birth it through their prayers.

To Leo and Emma for being bold and for taking the time to declare the Lord's prophetic message to me.

To the many teachers and preachers from whom I have learned a lot over the years since I became a Christian in 1973, people who shared their experiences and insights from the pulpit or through books, television and the Internet, particularly the authors A.W. Tozer and John Bevere.

To my husband Arthur, daughter Maria-Louisa, and brother Joey, for their help with this project, and most especially for their love and support.

To Jesus, my Lord, who gave the vision and the provision for this book. To You I owe my utmost gratitude. I can never thank You enough!

Dedication

This book is dedicated to my beloved husband Arthur, precious daughter Maria-Louisa, faithful mother Haide, and my loving siblings.

I also dedicate this book to all of God's eagles, athletes and pilgrims, especially in the Philippines and in Lancaster and Cumbria in England.

Most of all, I dedicate this book to my God, Lord and Saviour Jesus Christ, who makes possible the impossible and sets our hearts ablaze with the fire of His Holy Spirit (symbolised by the colours of the book cover) as we soar, run and walk with Him.

To my brothers and sisters in Christ, this is the message of the artwork on the cover of this book:

God is waiting for His eagles, athletes and pilgrims to lead people on the right path, the path of *Jehovah Tsidkenu*[1], because the old is passing away and a new day is dawning[2].

---

[1] *Jehovah Tsidkenu* = "God is my Righteousness"

[2] 2 Corinthians 5v17 (TM): *The old life is gone; a new life burgeons! Look at it!* The direction to which the eagle, runner and walker are facing represents the "right" path. The colours of the cover are that of a sunrise and sunset. The sunset symbolises the end of the old world, old life, old mind-set; and the sunrise represents the new life in Jesus, the One who is "making everything new" (Revelation 21v5, NIV).

Contents

Section 3: Walking like Pilgrims on Earth

Introduction: The Story Behind this Book

Those who hope in the Lord will renew their strength. They will soar on wings like eagles; they will run and not grow weary; they will walk and not be faint. (Isaiah 40v31, NIV)

This book was not conceived in my own mind, but was written in obedience to a prophetic word. The story behind it began in 2001 when I was in the Philippines, my native land, for a short holiday. For the first time in my life I received prophetic words, and these from several prophetic ministers. One of them was Emma, the wife of a Filipino pastor, who prophesied to me that I would soon stop editing the magazine of the church my family and I were attending at that time, and that I would one day write a book containing stories that Christians would give me. A few months later I had to quit as editor of the magazine, but years passed and I did not hear anything again about the book. I had wondered if it was a true word from the Lord, or if the Lord had forgotten! ☺

In June 2010, my family and I vacationed in the Philippines. I had a chat with Leo, a Filipino pastor I first met in 2001 and who had since mentored me in the prophetic. I believe I had not mentioned to him the prophecy recounted above so I was stunned when he told me the same thing nine years later – that I would be writing a book containing stories or testimonies from Christians. Leo also added one detail – that the book would be "a devotional".

I came home to Lancaster having no idea what to do or what the devotional was going to be about, so I again shelved the prophetic word. One day, I chanced upon Isaiah 40 verse 31 while reading my Bible and remembered what I read from an Internet site many years ago about the passage. The author said that it means that God gives us the strength to "soar like eagles", metaphorically speaking. If we cannot soar, He will help us to "run without getting weary"; and if we cannot run, then He will help us to "walk without fainting". This explanation did not satisfy me, so I asked the Lord for revelation about the passage. Finally it came. God wants us to receive revelation from Him so that we can 'soar' like eagles above our circumstances (soaring is a metaphor for receiving revelation). We then 'run' with the revelation that we have received[1]. There are many references to athletes running races in the Bible because 'running' prophetically stands for doing what God tells us to do so that we can fulfil

---

[1]   Habakkuk 2v3 (NIV): *Write down the revelation and make it plain on tablets so that a herald may run with it.*

our life's purpose. The Bible also tells us that Christians are pilgrims here on earth[2]. 'Walking' in Isaiah 40 verse 31 pertains to this. Therefore, God wants His children to be all three: spiritual eagles receiving divine revelation, athletes running the race He sets before us, and pilgrims walking this earth with a heavenly perspective on the way to our eternal destination.

I did not connect, however, what I learned about Isaiah 40v31 with the prophecy about the book until my blogging friends, after hearing a totally different story I narrated, suggested to me that I write a book! It was then, in August 2010, that I realised that the Lord wanted me to collect stories and write a devotional about "eagles, athletes and pilgrims".

I sent out letters to people I know and to people they know with a request for testimonies or stories. I decided to make this a weekly devotional (52 stories for the 52 weeks in a year would be easier to collect than 365 for a daily devotional), but I had no idea what to do with the stories. I only knew that as I worked on this project, God would direct my steps. To connect the stories with the 'eagles, athletes and pilgrims' theme, I realised I had to write forewords for each week. In writing the forewords, I was mindful of the fact that the Lord wanted me to produce a devotional that would speak not only to Christians, but also to those who are not yet believers in Jesus (this is why I included Bible verses in the footnotes). He wanted a devotional that would not only encourage, edify and exhort the reader, but also teach from His word.

The stories you will find in this book are by Christians from different parts of the world and of different backgrounds. I grouped these stories under three headings, hence the three sections of this devotional. You may want to spend seven days on each week's entry, or read through it in one sitting. It depends on you. However, whatever day, week or month you begin reading this book, **please start with Week 1 and read progressively to the end of Week 52**.

It is my prayer that just as I have been so blessed in working on this devotional, you will also be so blessed in reading it. May it help you to grow in Jesus as an eagle, athlete and pilgrim!

- Haide Sanchez

---

[2]   Hebrews 11v13b (NKJV): [They] *confessed that they were strangers and pilgrims on the earth.*

Section 1

Soaring on Wings like Eagles

(Week 1 to Week 17)

Week 1: God Wants to Communicate with You

Where there is no revelation, people cast off restraint.
(Proverbs 29v18, NIV)[1]

The Bible says this about God's people: "They will soar on wings like eagles..." (Isaiah 40 verse 31, NIV). It is in the nature of eagles to "mount up"[2] to the sky with their powerful wings and to soar. As stated in the Introduction, this is a metaphor of people receiving divine revelation which is a message or communication from God. God, the Creator, gave each of us a spirit[3]. Therefore, in each of us is a spiritual eagle that longs to soar and communicate with the Divine, whether we acknowledge this or not.

Proverbs 29 verse 18 above illustrates the importance of revelation. Without this, people "cast off restraint"[4]. When a person casts off restraint, he wanders away from God and travels his own path. He will eventually suffer ruin or destruction because only God's way leads to life; any other way leads to spiritual death[5] (separation from God). We need God to communicate His guidance to us so that we can know the right way.

In other versions of the Bible, "perish" takes the place of "cast off restraint"[6] (the word in the original Hebrew text, *para*, can mean both). Without revelation, a person will not be able to live in the peace and joy that is not affected by circumstances. He will eventually perish under their weight. We need God to communicate comfort to us so that we can overcome.

We need God's revelations. The good thing is that He wants to communicate these to us!

---

[1] Each Bible quotation in this book was taken from the version that gives more clarity to the message of the story. Refer to the Copyright page for the different Bible versions used.

[2] Other versions of the Bible (e.g., KJV, NASB, ESV) for Isaiah 40v31 read: *"They shall [or will] mount up with wings as [or like] eagles".*

[3] We were created as tripartite beings – each with *body, soul* (mind, will and emotions) and *spirit.* This is implied in 1 Thessalonians 5v23 (NIV*): "May God Himself, the God of peace, sanctify you through and through. May your whole spirit, soul and body be kept blameless at the coming of our Lord Jesus Christ."*

[4] Or "are unrestrained" as in the NASB.

[5] Proverbs 14v12 (NKJV): *There is a way that seems right to a man, but its end is the way of death.*

[6] As in the KJV.

The Bible is full of stories of people with whom God communicated. One of them was Moses before whom God appeared as a burning bush in order to catch his attention (Exodus 3 verses 1-5). Do you know that God wants to communicate with you? Does He need to show you a burning bush just to catch your attention?

Below is a story of a homeless man who received revelation from above through a "strange voice in his head", the voice of One who had been waiting for him to come home, the same One who did amazing things in his life years before.

Welcome Home, Owen!

In December 2009 I was homeless and living on the streets, sleeping in the open air in such diverse places as Williamson's Park, on the river bank beneath the motorway bridge, or even beneath the aqueduct bridge – anywhere that was quiet and out of sight. I got free meals at Edward Street[7], The Ark and Mustard Seed[8]. Over the winter period I stayed at the shelter at St. Thomas' Church and at Christ Church. I visited The Olive Branch[9] and was given not only advice but also a small tent to keep out of the worst of the weather, so at least I was not waking up with an inch of snow covering my glasses any longer. During this time I was informed by another homeless person that I could get out of the cold and have a hot drink and some biscuits if I went to Christians Alive Church on a Sunday morning. Being cold and hungry, I decided to try it, thinking that if they start preaching to me, I could always walk out.

So one Sunday morning I approached the main door of the church. A hand reached out to shake mine and a friendly voice greeted me, "Good morning and welcome. Come in, put your pack down and take a seat near this radiator." At that moment I forgot about the tea and biscuits. Also at that very same time I heard a strange voice inside my own head, one that I did not recognise. I think I felt it more than heard it. This voice said, "Welcome home, Owen!"

These words were still echoing in my head when another voice offered me a hot drink. It was a voice I recognised. It was Sally who, along with JC, Jess, Dan G., Amy and others from Christians Alive, had for the past few weeks been giving me and other needy people a hot drink and sandwiches most evenings in the middle of town. These people already knew that I was not a religious person, that I had turned my back on

---

7   Lancaster and District Homeless Action Service runs a day centre based in Edward St. in Lancaster (www.ldhas.org.uk/homeless-action.html).
8   The Ark and Mustard Seed are Christian ministries in Lancaster that provide hot meals to the homeless or needy.
9   The Olive Branch (www.the-olivebranch.org.uk) is a Christian charity serving and helping the socially disadvantaged in Lancaster. You will read about it in Week 17.

God forty or so years ago. You see, I was brought up in a Church of England family. I was not given a choice and was told, "You will go to church! You will go to Sunday school!" But the strangely comforting voice or sound or feeling in my head would not go away. It gradually dawned on me that I was not alone.

I have been going to Christians Alive every week since and have found peace and happiness there[10]. I started to think, "Should I return to God?" Maybe, just maybe, I could find in Him an end to my pain and problems. I was invited to spend some nights sleeping on a couch belonging to a person whom I didn't know but now count as one of my closest friends. Then suddenly, out of the blue, I got a place of my own in March 2010 and received furniture and household goods from many people. I also started having treatment for my painful kidneys and people prayed for me. These prayers were answered!

One Wednesday in September I was admitted to the Royal Blackburn Hospital for an operation to remove a significant number of kidney stones. That went well. The following day my intravenous drip was removed along with the catheter. I had no pain from either. Later that day the first of two drains in my right kidney was clamped. No pain. Later still this drain was removed. Again no pain. I started to get big-headed, thinking that I had overcome the pain barrier. Friday night came and the second drain was clamped. I thought, "This is going to be easy!"

Boy was I mistaken! The pain was so massive I thought I had been shot in the kidney with an elephant gun! I tried to put on a brave face but the nurse saw right through me and immediately released the clamp. Oh, such bliss and blessed relief! On Saturday morning the drain was flushed out with saline solution and was again clamped. This time I knew I could handle the pain. Well, I was wrong again. I stuck it out for about an hour but the pain was so bad the nurse had to give me morphine. This only left a terrible taste in my mouth and did nothing to relieve the pain. By this time I was ready to pass out because of the agony. So the clamp was removed again. Sunday morning came along and I was visited by one of the hospital chaplains. I was offered and received Holy Communion, during which I (the devout agnostic) prayed to God for help with the pain I was expecting to come.

Later that day the nurse arrived at my bedside and asked, "Should we try again?" I reluctantly agreed. (How could I walk around with a plastic tube sticking out of my back?) As soon as the nurse started to flush it out again, a strangely familiar voice came into my head saying, "This time Owen, it will work!" The nurse turned and walked away so I asked her when she was going to clamp it. She answered that it was already clamped and was looking good. Three hours or so later I was still not in

---

[10] www.christians-alive.org.uk

agony. It then dawned on me that God has a sense of humour. I had got big-headed and God put me in my place. How cool is that?

Monday arrived and still no pain. I prayed again, this time thanking God for the restful, pain-free night, the first I'd had for ages. The nurse came to my bedside again and asked if I would lie on my tummy so that she could inspect the drain. As I turned over I thought, "Here comes the flushing fluid again!" Sure enough that weird feeling in my kidney kicked in again. It was neither pleasant nor painful, just strange. Then the nurse said, "All done Owen! You can get up now, thank you." Puzzled, I asked, "When will you be attempting to take it out?" She replied, "Take what out? This?" She pointed to the narrow plastic tube on the tray and said, "It's out already!"

I have heard many people, myself included, say, "If there is a God, prove it! Give me a sign. Give me a miracle!" Well, what about my life?

I was born in the year 19-hundred-and-frozen-stiff. I was the last of seven children. My mother had a difficult pregnancy (I've been difficult ever since) and I survived a very bad childbirth. Eight years later I suffered a green stick fracture to my left thigh. My parents were told that I would never be able to walk without a calliper (leg irons), that I would walk with a pronounced limp and that my left leg would always be shorter than my right one. At age eleven or so I suffered severe burns to my face and both arms and was expected to be disfigured for life. At thirteen I had a brain haemorrhage caused by a crushed temple (I had been in a fight like a typical teenager, you see) and my parents were told to "expect the worst" – that I would either not survive the operation or would be permanently and severely handicapped.

Well, I don't walk with a calliper. I am no oil painting, but I don't think that I am disfigured. I might not be a brain surgeon but I am not brain dead either. Despite the fact that my heart apparently stopped three times during the operation on my head, I obviously survived. I used to believe that I had beaten the odds by myself, but could I have been the subject of at least four miracles? I like to think so. As for my left leg, it used to be shorter. I was asked if I believed in God's healing by the power of prayer[11]. I said I wasn't sure but would like to try it. I now believe in God's healing and the power of prayer as my legs are now more or less equal in length.

For many years I had been trying to walk away from God, but He had stayed at my side, waiting for me to come back when I was ready[12]. Now I'm back!

---

[11] Exodus 15v26b (NIV): *I am the Lord, who heals you.*

[12] Isaiah 30v18 (NLT): *So the Lord must wait for you to come to Him so He can show you His love and compassion.* God doesn't force Himself on us!

During my adult life I had served in the Reserve Army and had sworn an oath of allegiance to Her Majesty the Queen on three occasions. Now I swear a new oath of allegiance to the Father, Son and Holy Spirit[13]! Amen!

- Owen (Lancaster, Lancashire, England)

April 2011

God, help me to believe that You are there and want to communicate with me. When (not if!) You do, please help me to recognise Your voice. Amen!

---

[13] The doctrine of the Holy Trinity is foundational to the Christian faith. Although the word 'Trinity' is not found in the Bible, there are lots of scriptures that point to this truth. One is Matthew 28v19 (NIV): *Therefore go and make disciples of all nations, baptising them in the name* [singular] *of the Father and of the Son and of the Holy Spirit...* This verse implies common essence (the Father is God, the Son is God, the Holy Spirit is God) and both plurality and unity (three in one).

Week 2: God Wants to Reveal Himself to You

.... like an eagle that flies toward the heavens. (Proverbs 23v5, NASB)

Have you seen an eagle flying toward the heavens? It is a spectacular sight! Its long wingspan and broad wings enable it to soar effortlessly by using rising currents of warm air (thermals) and updrafts generated by mountain slopes, edges of valleys and other terrains similar to these. Some cultures believe an eagle soars higher and higher to touch the face of God.

God created you to soar like an eagle that flies toward the heavens and receive revelations from Him. Almighty God, the One who has measured the waters on earth in the hollow of His hand, who marked off the heavens using the tip of His thumb to the tip of His pinkie, who has held the dust of the earth in a basket and weighed the mountains on the scales and the hills in a balance[1], and called the whole universe into existence by the word of His mouth[2], is interested in you and wants you to know Him. He wants to reveal Himself to you!

Many people have discovered throughout history that God reveals Himself in various ways, but more clearly through the reading and study of Scripture, the Holy Bible. In it we read that the ultimate revelation of Himself that He has given us is through His Son, Jesus Christ[3]. The apostle Paul wrote: "I keep asking that the God of our Lord Jesus Christ, the glorious Father, may give you the Spirit of wisdom and revelation, *so that you may know Him better*" (Ephesians 1v17, NIV). God desires to reveal Jesus to us personally and progressively so that we can know the Father better.

Do you want to know Him better? Do you want to touch the face of God?

Below is a story of how a Chinese girl's concept of God changed through revelation, and how this transformed her life and gave her the passion to tell others about Him.

---

[1] Isaiah 40v12 (NIV): *Who has measured the waters in the hollow of His hand, or with the breadth of His hand marked off the heavens? Who has held the dust of the earth in a basket, or weighed the mountains on the scales and the hills in a balance?*

[2] The account of creation in Genesis reflects this. For example, in Genesis 1v3 (NIV): *And God said, "Let there be light", and there was light.*

[3] Hebrews 1v1-2 (NLT): *Long ago God spoke many times and in many ways to our ancestors through the prophets. And now in these final days, He has spoken to us through His Son.*

A Chinese Girl's Conversion

My English name is Muriel and I come from Guangzhou (formerly Canton) near Hong Kong in Southeast China. As in other places in China today, there are Christian churches in my city. They are required by law to be registered with the government as 'Three Self Churches'[4]. Regulated by the Chinese Communist Party which decides who can preach and what can be preached, these churches focus on social rules and the social benefits of Christianity. Preaching outside the church as well as evangelism is forbidden. Government officials, school teachers, soldiers, police officers and minors (below eighteen) cannot be Christians. Obviously, these policies try to restrict the influence of Christianity in my country.

I was born in 1987, the only child of hard-working parents. Because they were unable to care for me, I lived with my grandmother until I was eleven years old. As a young girl, I remember listening to her fascinating stories about Guangzhou when she was a teenager during the Japanese occupation[5]. It was through her stories that I first heard about Christianity. This was when Grandma told me about a group of Christians from a church in Hong Kong who came to Guangzhou to provide aid, clothes and food to scores of people left homeless by the Japanese bombardment of the city. The visitors started a fellowship and organised parties and lessons for the children. Grandma received help from them, volunteered her services and sang in the choir. She said that she also got baptised. Unfortunately, the situation in Guangzhou got worse and the Christians from Hong Kong had to leave. With this group gone, Grandma's infant church was left with no support. The lack of discipleship may account for her lack of understanding of God's nature and of the Christian faith.

By and large, I grew up being influenced by the secular society in which I lived. In keeping with the ideology of the Chinese Communist Party, I received no religious education in school. (Politics and some philosophy took its place.) Like other school children, I was taught that there is no God, eternity and life after death. We accepted what we were taught.

Since the Qin dynasty[6], Guangzhou has been an important commercial port for international maritime trade. It is probably for this reason, aside from its remoteness to the central government, that Guangzhou has been quite open to western influence. In my teens I could watch TV programs from Hong Kong, then under British rule. One such program was a weekly Christian production in Cantonese called 'Amazing

---

[4]   The "three selfs" are self-governance, self-support and self-propagation. This means that foreign church leadership, foreign financing and foreign missionaries are rejected.

[5]   1938-45

[6]   Third century before Christ

Grace'. It featured people relating the changes which had happened to them after they had committed their lives to God.

Dad watched this program with me every week and sometimes he would even remind me that it was on. I suppose the reason for this interest was Dad's respect for Christians because of their reputation for friendliness and helpfulness. Although we didn't get the theology of Christianity through these programs, we did get the concept that there is in fact a God. Unfortunately, that concept was marred not only by our background, but also by an article written by a Chinese writer which influenced us greatly. In this article the author explained that God controls half of one's life and the other half is controlled by oneself. (He seems to equate God with fate.) He asserted that one's goal should be to get total control of one's life. Dad liked this article because it reflected Chinese life and philosophy (i.e., the desire to control one's life). Although I was intrigued by the sincerity of the Christians I saw on TV, I accepted the theology Dad was happy to adopt. Nevertheless, I'm sure that program sowed seeds in my young mind.

Perhaps it was these seeds that caused me to be so fascinated by another article I chanced upon on the Internet. It was in fact a Chinese translation of the poem, 'Footprints in the Sand'[7]. It had such a powerful effect on me because it gave me a revelation that challenged the theology I accepted – the revelation of a personal and loving God[8]. I was so touched by this because of the problems I was having at school. I was fifteen and had no friends since the bullies kept them away from me. As I read the poem and imagined myself being carried in God's arms, I felt I was not alone, that a Person called God was giving me the strength to face the rejection I was suffering.

I graduated and moved on to senior middle school. After a year of getting along well with other students, another round of bullying came which was worse than before. The bullying however paled in comparison to the betrayal by my best friend. It was at this time that I made a connection with a politics teacher six to seven years older than me, something unusual in our culture. Ellen's heartache over the break-up with her boyfriend probably led her to look for a friend and she found me. I believe she was one of those people God put in my life because my relationship with her played an important part in my walk with God.

When the time came for me to choose a major, I chose Physics which turned out to be a bad decision considering the maths in the course. Because of the emphasis put

---

[7]   'Footprints in the Sand' was written by Mary Stevenson in 1936. You can read the poem and the story behind it in www.footprints-inthe-sand.com.

[8]   1 John4v16 (NASB): *We have come to know and have believed the love which God has for us. God is love, and the one who abides in love abides in God, and God abides in him.*

on good grades in Chinese schools, my math (and head-) teacher was not happy with me. I worked hard, but she and Dad thought I was not doing enough. This led to big arguments with Dad, especially when I told him I wanted to study abroad, something he considered a crazy idea. Upset over his lack of support and encouragement, I ran away from home. I stayed with Grandma for a few days and then went back home. This was the start of a pattern of running away and then coming home after a few days. There were times I stayed with people I hardly knew, just to get away from the feeling of helplessness and isolation. I would recall the God I read about in 'Footprints' and tried to find comfort in churches, but they wouldn't accept me as a member because I was only seventeen.

Ellen eventually met a Christian guy, became a Christian herself and got married to him. I was the bridesmaid in her Christian wedding which was attended by a few relatives and closest friends. A Korean evangelist officiated at the wedding through an interpreter. I sat at the same table with him during the meal. He then spoke about family relationships from a Biblical perspective. I agreed with what he shared because I was having family problems at this time. When this evangelist asked if there was anyone who wanted to become a Christian, I declared that I was ready. Right there and then, he baptised me with water from a teapot! Everybody was excited especially when someone pointed out that my name in Mandarin is pronounced the same way as the Mandarin for 'priest'. After this, Ellen organised Bible studies but I only went a few times.

After graduation, I left home and despite not having a university degree, God provided me with a job and I was able to support myself, thus gaining the respect of my family and peers. After two years, Dad gave me permission to follow my dream of studying abroad. I don't know how I got accepted at Lancaster University to read Psychology, but I believe God opened that door. I came to the UK feeling that something was waiting for me.

Once in Lancaster, I didn't intend to look for Christian friends, but the Lord sent them to me and I found myself accepting an invitation to attend a service at Christians Alive Church. I was moved by the words of the worship songs being sung and although I was thousands of miles away from Guangzhou, I felt at home, that finally I belonged. Sarah, an English girl at this church, befriended me and helped me to study the Bible. I also went to Christian Union[9] events where I learned more about Jesus, the Bible and Christianity. I took the opportunity to attend the New Word Alive Conference in Wales as well as the Edinburgh International Outreach. My experience in doing

---

[9]   Christian Unions are mission teams operating in universities and colleges. For more information about Christian Union, visit www.uccf.org.uk

friendship evangelism on the streets of Edinburgh among international students there gave me confidence to talk to strangers about God.

In the summer of this year, I went back to Guangzhou for a short visit and had the opportunity to talk to Grandma (who's now over ninety) and my parents about Jesus. I don't know how much they understood, but I trust God will continue to reveal Himself to them. My discovery at this time that Grandma's father was actually a Christian gives me hope for my family! I also organised a bite-size course on Christianity with a small group of friends. I pray that my family and friends will one day come to know the One who walks with me through the sands of time.

- Muriel (Guangzhou, China)
Sent from Lancaster, England
September 2011

Dear God, thank You that You want to reveal Yourself to me. Please help me to get to know You better! Amen.

Week 3: God Wants to Unveil Spiritual Truths to You

Like an eagle that rouses her chicks and hovers over her
young, so He spread His wings to take them up and carried
them safely on His pinions. (Deuteronomy 32v11, NLT)

The Book of Revelation, the last book of the Bible, is also known as the Apocalypse of John. 'Apocalypse' is from the Greek *apokálypsis* which means 'revelation' or 'unveiling'.

In the scripture above, God is described as an eagle that spreads its wings and carries its young up in the air in order to teach them to fly and soar. It is God's desire to carry you on His wings and lift up your spirit so that you may see the spiritual truths He is unveiling to you. He wants you to receive revelations from Him. Why? Because He wants to be in *relationship* with you: He as your Father, and you as His child.

John 14v6 (NIV) reads: "Jesus answered, 'I am the way and the truth and the life. *No one comes to the Father except through Me*'". That Father-child relationship that Almighty God offers is therefore only possible through Jesus, the One who bridged the sin-gap between you and your Creator through the cross.

In the following stories, you will read about how God, the Spirit of revelation[1], unveiled spiritual truths to Gareth and Shirley to help them come to a decision to become followers of Christ. In the second story, you will also see how God, the Spirit of wisdom[2], imparted wisdom to Shirley so that she could unveil spiritual truths about Jesus to others.

Gareth's Story

I was born in May 1986 in Leytonstone, East London and am blessed with a good Dad. He and my mum divorced when I was six. I did not like living with Mum and preferred to live with Dad after the split. It was a relief when Dad was awarded custody of my younger sister and me, with Mum having access rights. Dad worked very hard to provide for us for the ten years he looked after us even though he wasn't in employment until 2004. From January 2001 until September 2008, contact with Mum was pretty much non-existent.

---

[1]   Ephesians 1v17 (NIV): *I keep asking that the God of our Lord Jesus Christ, the glorious Father, may give you the Spirit of wisdom and revelation, so that you may know Him better.*
[2]   Ibid

While in my early days at university here in Lancaster, I had been to a church a couple of times with a friend, but this didn't last long as my friend had stopped coming and I didn't have the desire to keep going. Then at the end of November 2008, I was invited by my friend Louise to a Mission Week meal and a talk. At the end of the meal, I signed up to a bite-size course[3] on the Gospel of Mark which was being planned by the Christian Union (CU). I enjoyed the course as it was very relaxed and I was able to contribute, which felt good. After this, I started to attend weekly CU meetings on a Thursday night.

I was given a Bible by another friend, Ruth, and I was really touched by the gesture as she had written a really nice inscription in it for me as well. I had also begun to attend one of CU's small groups to study the word of God and to meet up with my friend John on some afternoons to study the book of Romans.

I graduated from University in July 2009 and spent a couple of months with Dad over the summer. I returned to Lancaster in September and resumed attending small group with the CU. Come October, things really started to happen. One weekend, I spent some time with a friend who was troubled and we began to study the book of Matthew. We were looking at Matthew 8 when I had a revelation from Matthew 8 verses 21 to 22 (NIV): "Another disciple said to Him, 'Lord, first let me go and bury my father'. But Jesus told him 'Follow Me, and let the dead bury their own dead'". As a good Jewish guy, Jesus was not speaking disrespectfully of the dead. Among His own people, these words would have been understood to mean, "Let those in your family who are spiritually dead in their sins bury the physically dead." Jesus was in effect telling the man not to make excuses for not choosing the highest calling, which was to follow Him.

I was going to comment about this man not following Jesus when I was struck with the thought: "Who am I to speak against this man when I am doing exactly the same thing?"

The following Monday, I spoke to my older sister, Bronwen, who had become a Christian a couple of years beforehand, and asked her if there was anything I needed to change about myself before coming to Jesus. She answered, "Nothing!" That was

---

[3]   The CU's bite size course is an opportunity for people to come to a course to investigate Jesus' life and claims. It discusses the basic doctrines of Christianity.

another revelation I received. I did not have to change a thing about me to come to Jesus[4]. It's He Himself who will make the change in me after I decide to follow Him![5]

That evening, I joined my small group and we looked at the birth of Jesus in Luke 2. Afterwards I went to my friend's place for a while. As I was walking home, I turned my phone back on to find a text from Ruth asking me how I was as she thought I'd been a bit quiet at the small group meeting. I texted her back with the message that I was OK and that I had been thinking and had decided to give my life to Jesus. I then said out loud that I had become a Christian and felt a real excitement! I can still remember when I sent that text. It was at 01:23 AM on Tuesday, 13 October 2009. Praise God!

- Gareth (Lancaster, England)
March 2011

Sharing the Good News

Long, long ago and far away (in Dallas, Texas), when I was about twenty-one, I went to a Young Life Camp in Colorado as a cabin mum to nineteen teenage girls. I was also responsible for vespers each night. Since I had no clue what I was doing, I asked the Lord if He would be so kind as to let me know what He wanted me to do regarding vespers. On the first night, the idea came to me to ask them, "What is a Christian?" I did, and there were as many answers as there were kids. Then, in response to the "believe in God, believe in Jesus" answer, I said, "The book of James[6] says, 'You believe in God? You do well. Even the devils believe and tremble.' So tell me, are the devils saved? Noooooooo! Well then, what is a Christian?" Then I didn't give them any answers (a heart instruction from the Lord), and it drove them crazy.

Before week's end, I gave them the "rest of the story": "Romans 10 verse 9 says that if we confess with our mouth the Lord Jesus and *believe* in our hearts that God raised Him from the dead, we shall be saved. What's the difference between the 'devils believe' and 'if YOU believe'? The Greek word for *believe* in both verses (James 2v19 and Romans 10v9) is the same[7]. The difference is 'the heart', meaning to accept personally, to take the gift and unwrap it, making it your own."

---

[4] John 6v37 (AMP): *.... and the one who comes to Me I will most certainly not cast out [I will never, no never, reject one of them who comes to Me].*

[5] Philippians 2v13 (NCV): *God is working in you to help you want to do and be able to do what pleases Him.*

[6] James 2v19

[7] Greek *pisteuo.*

At the end of the week, about five of the nineteen stood to receive Christ. They had come thinking they were Christians because they knew ABOUT Jesus, but realised that they were not when the gospel was presented. I was on Cloud Nine about that. Now they knew Him!

I had told the teenagers I would meet with them for Bible study any time after the Young Life camp ended, which I did with the few who were interested. I had to ride the bus to downtown Dallas, get off and connect with another that went across viaducts to their side of town. Coming home, it was after 11 pm and I was standing on a downtown street corner, sooooo tired and wondering why the bus had not come. I had already waited an hour. A man who had just arrived was also waiting along with a few others and he and I struck up a conversation. I don't remember how we got around to "religion" (maybe because I told him I was coming from a Bible study with some teenagers), but I heard myself explaining the difference: "Religion is a system of works and rules and regulations whereby one attempts to gain the approval of God and heaven, whereas Christianity is a relationship with God through Jesus Christ, His Son[8]." He said to me, "I never heard that explanation before! You see, I'm a psychologist, and relationships are my business."

He thanked me for talking to him, at which time I looked up again to see if the bus was coming and saw the street sign. I WAS WAITING ON THE WRONG STREET! However, I believe with all my heart that it was a God-ordained meeting. Scripture says, "One man plants, another waters, but it is God who gives the harvest!"[9]

As a nine year-old girl, I was at a children's retreat when I decided not to listen to the preacher because in my opinion he was arrogant. So I didn't. But at the end, he explained our guilt before a holy God and that Jesus had taken the punishment we deserved, and all we had to do was to receive His gift of forgiveness, since He had already paid for our offenses[10]. I practically ran down the aisle! In an instant, I felt like the guiltiest sinner in the world – at age nine! I actually felt the weight of my sins on my shoulders. When I told the Lord I understood what He had done for us and received Him into my heart as my very own sin sacrifice[11], *instantly* the weight lifted and I felt light and as clean as I could be. Then I had to go home and learn how

---

[8]   John 1v12 (NIV): *Yet to all who did receive Him, to those who believed in His name, He gave the right to become children of God.*

[9]   1 Corinthians 3v7 (NLT): *It's not important who does the planting, or who does the watering. What's important is that God makes the seed grow.*

[10]   Jesus paid the penalty for our sins on the cross so we will not have to suffer the "second death", which is hell (Revelation 20v14). But this gift has to be received personally.

[11]   1 Peter 3v18a (NIV): *For Christ also suffered once for sins, the righteous for the unrighteous, to bring you to God.*

to grow in my faith[12]. But it really was that simple, with times of hunger for more along the journey.

The Gospel really IS good news[13]!

-Shirley (Houston, Texas, USA)
April 2011

God in heaven, please help me to respond positively to what You are revealing to me about Jesus at this time. Please help me not to make excuses for ignoring this revelation. Thank You that You want me to relate to You as Your child. Help me to receive You as my Father, and Jesus as Your gift who makes this possible. Amen.

---

[12] 2 Peter 3v18 (NIV): *But grow in the grace and knowledge of our Lord and Saviour Jesus Christ.*

[13] 'Gospel' is from 'Godspell' = God + spell, a story or tale. It means 'Good News', especially concerning the Kingdom of God and salvation through Jesus Christ.

Week 4: The Greatest Revelation

For God so loved the world that He gave His one and only Son, that
whoever believes in Him shall not perish but have eternal life.
(John 3v16, NIV)

God created you to be a spiritual eagle and gifted you with the capacity to know Him. Through creation, He makes known His power and majesty. That is not enough to the Creator, however, because He wants each person to also know His love. This is why He reveals Himself personally.

The truth stated in the Bible passage above is the greatest revelation God wants to give you. It is the greatest revelation from Him because the greatest expression of His love for you is Jesus' death on the cross on your behalf so that you do not have to suffer eternal death in hell, but enjoy eternal life with Him in heaven.

If you have not responded to this revelation before, God is giving you the chance to do so now. As with other revelations, you have the choice to receive it or not. However, you will not be able to receive it if you do not do so with humility, for "God opposes the proud but shows favour to the humble" (1 Peter 5v5, NIV). Receiving this revelation with humility means acknowledging the fact that you have sinned before a holy God, that you need Jesus as your Saviour, and that you are willing to give the reins of your life to Him as your Lord.

Below is the story of a man's revelation of Jesus as his Saviour and Lord and how he finally responded to the invitation to go "the right way".

A Man Finds the Right Way

I was born in Nigeria into a Muslim family of six children. My parents are God-fearing and instilled this into my siblings and me since our childhood. My mother is a very committed Muslim who usually observes prayers and other Muslim religious activities. My father, on the other hand, is not a devout Muslim. Although he generally observes Muslim religious festivals, he also likes to celebrate Christmas.

As a boy, I observed that the religious festivals in Nigeria, either Islamic or Christian, were very special as these were usually associated with new clothes, presents, lots of food and parties. Everyone would always join in irrespective of their religious persuasion. We were all happy to be what we were.

Things however began to change for me when I was a teenager. I would see visions of myself preaching in a Christian church congregation. The visions were so real that I was afraid to lose God's favour because of something I did. I believed in God but was not sure if I was serving Him in the right way. I began searching for the true God since the world presented me with many versions of Him. I eventually narrowed my search to two main religions – Christianity and Islam. I delved deeply into the origins of the two religions. Islam was started by Mohammed, a warlord prophet. Mohammed was inspired by an angel whom he alone met in a cave. He would get back home and in a trance dictated certain aspects of the Quran as we know it today. Jesus, on the other hand, was openly baptised by John[1] and a voice was heard saying that Jesus was the Son of God[2]. This difference baffled me for years. I noted as well that Christianity existed before Islam which started 500 years later. It didn't make sense to me that God would start one religion to replace it with another five centuries later. I remember also watching films about Jesus and crying at what people did to Him. I felt He was unjustly killed and could not understand why He had to die. Gradually, I was leaning towards believing Jesus as Christ, God's Son. However, my religious upbringing suggested that God does not have a Son.

In my quest I asked my mother why we were Muslims, and she replied that it was because we were born that way. I remember thinking that my mother would not have been an animist even if she had been born into an animist family. This single incident made me believe one must search and find God for himself rather than leave it to one's family.

Around the age of seventeen my family life was turned upside down. Two years earlier, my younger brother became a Christian and started going to a fellowship. I noticed a profound change in his life. He would come to the dinner table and pray before eating. But about a year afterwards, he began to suffer from an incurable illness that defied medicine. The doctors and herbalists could not help him. My mum was at his side throughout the period of his illness, which was almost a year. This led to my mum's business suffering. My brother eventually died at thirteen years of age.

---

[1]   From John 1v32-34 (NIV): *Then John gave this testimony: "I saw the Spirit come down from heaven as a dove and remain on Him. And I myself did not know Him, but the One who sent me to baptise with water told me, 'The Man on whom you see the Spirit come down and remain is the One who will baptise with the Holy Spirit.' I have seen and I testify that this is God's Chosen One."*

[2]   Matthew 3v16-17 (NIV): *As soon as Jesus was baptised, He went up out of the water. At that moment heaven was opened, and He saw the Spirit of God descending like a dove and alighting on Him. And a voice from heaven said, "This is My Son, whom I love; with Him I am well pleased."*

As a family we were distraught. I was very confused because up till then I believed that if one treated people justly and nicely, God would ward off evil from that person. My dad was told by certain people that my brother died as a result of evil people. This led my dad to seek protection for his family in whatever way he could find. We were taken to herbalists and churches to ward away the evil, and being the first-born, I would usually get "double protection". I was also afraid of the devil as I believed that he could do anything he wanted and get away with it. I needed the help of Someone bigger than the devil so I became more religious and started attending the mosque regularly, even observing fasts and five-times-a-day prayers. I was soon off to university where my quest for meaning in life continued.

Bewildered over the things that had happened to my family, I read books about esoteric religions while at university. I also tried astral travel and other spiritual quests. They were not fulfilling, but led to more questions, so I decided not to follow organised religion but start a new one. My philosophy of "Godism" was born! When people asked me who a Godist is, I would reply that a Godist believes in God and in doing good to his neighbours, but would not follow any of the organised religions. I did my best as a Godist to please God and be good to everyone, but I failed miserably. On the surface, I was a nice person, but inwardly I felt the opposite. The hardest was trying not to live in sin and I did not succeed in that effort. I eventually came to the understanding that I could not help myself. So I began praying to God to help me find Him in the 'right way'. I must have done this for about a year.

In my search for the right way, I was haunted by these words of Jesus, "By their fruit you will recognise them" (Matthew 7v16, NIV). I felt that my Christian friends and associates lived lives that truly bore witness to their faith. I also noticed that whereas others speak of God as if they knew about Him, the Christians spoke of Him as if they knew Him in a deeper and personal way, something I coveted for myself. This then left me with only one choice – Christianity. I started reading and collecting Christian tracts and listening more to my Christian friends. I was invited to watch a film called 'Burning Hell' by a Christian group on campus. The film frightened me considerably. I learned straight away that I would go to hell if I didn't have Christ[3]. Still I resisted giving my life to Jesus. I thought about it more seriously when I had a dream, which I now know to be apocalyptic.

---

[3] John 3v18 (NLT): *There is no judgment against anyone who believes in Him* [Jesus]. *But anyone who does not believe in Him has already been judged for not believing in God's one and only Son.* Revelation 20v15 (NLT): *And anyone whose name was not found recorded in the Book of Life* [which contains the names of all believers] *was thrown into the lake of fire.* This was written in the past tense because John, the author, was describing a vision or revelation he saw.

In the dream I saw what seemed like the world passing away. Everything was getting destroyed; there were earthquakes, lightning, and other indescribable horror. I woke up and wrote down what I saw. My roommate would later tell me how my narrative frightened him when he read it. After this time I became more composed and thoughtful about life, but the rigours of life and studying still prevented me from becoming a Christian. I resorted to being even nicer, hoping God would notice!

Soon after this, a renowned evangelist came to my campus for a crusade to which I was invited by a friend. The message hit me so hard that when the altar call was made, I finally decided to give my life to Jesus. However, the reality of the Christian life was still not very obvious in me at this time. I eventually dedicated myself to Christ almost a year later at another campus fellowship which nurtured me. My life was completely turned around. I developed a passion for wanting to know God more. I came to dislike sin and every appearance of it. I felt like a new person altogether! My previous mischievous nature was turned to sober reflection and care and concern for others to come to know Christ as I had done. By this time I fully understood that Christ came and died for me and the whole world to save us from our sins[4]. The greater understanding of God's love for me made me feel liberated[5]. I wanted to know so much in a short time that I read the whole Bible through within three months! I burned all my pop records, read every Christian book I could lay my hands on and saw a lot of miracles which the Lord worked through me. Then the Lord used me to bring some of my friends to Christ.

To God's glory I've been a born-again Christian for over twenty-one years and have witnessed numerous mind-boggling miracles. I now feel such richness in my life that I fail to understand why some Christians choose to backslide. Having found the right way[6], I prefer to stay on it!

- Abdulahi (Lagos, Nigeria)[7]
Sent from Lancashire, England
June 2011

---

[4] John 3v16-17 (NIV): *For God so loved the world that He gave His one and only Son, that whoever believes in Him shall not perish but have eternal life. For God did not send His Son into the world to condemn the world, but to save the world through Him.*

[5] John 8v36 (NIV): *So if the Son sets you free, you will be free indeed.*

[6] In its early days, Christianity was called 'the Way' (Acts 19v9 and 23, NIV).

[7] Abdulahi's four siblings in Nigeria are now all Christians. In answer to one sister's prayer, God sent a man in his seventies to their father to talk to him about Jesus. The two became friends and the father started reading the Bible. Because the father was no longer anti-Christian and allowed himself to be prayed for by his new friend, Abdulahi and his siblings believe their father became a Christian before he died in March 2012.

1 John 5v9-13 (NLT) says: "Since we believe human testimony, surely we can believe the greater testimony that comes from God. And God has testified about His Son. All who believe in the Son of God know in their hearts that this testimony is true. Those who don't believe this are actually calling God a liar because they don't believe what God has testified about His Son. And this is what God has testified: He has given us eternal life, and this life is in His Son. *Whoever has the Son has life; whoever does not have God's Son does not have life.* I have written this to you who believe in the name of the Son of God, so that you may know you have eternal life."

The apostle John wrote the above to assure anyone who believes in Jesus as Saviour and Lord that he or she has eternal life, a life of intimacy with God, a life as God's child whose name is written in His Book of Life. If you haven't received Jesus into your life as your Saviour and Lord, here's a prayer you can use:

Father God, thank You for sending Jesus to die for my sins so that I can be saved from eternal death in hell and receive eternal life with You in heaven. I don't fully understand this, but with the little that I understand now, please help me to respond to Your invitation. I confess I have sinned against You and I believe that Jesus came, died on the cross and rose again so that I can be forgiven of all my sins. I receive Him now as my Saviour and turn my life over to Him as my Lord. I receive Your gift of eternal life. Thank You that I am now Your child! Amen!

Week 5: Experiencing God

"But you are My witnesses, O Israel!" says the Lord. "You are My servant. You have been chosen to know Me, believe in Me, and understand that I alone am God. There is no other God – there never has been, and there never will be. I, yes I, am the Lord and there is no other Saviour". (Isaiah 43v10-11, NLT)

In the previous readings, we have noted that the soaring eagle is a symbol of revelation and that God gives us revelations that we might *know* Him. In the Bible, the word 'know' implies more than receiving or acquiring knowledge. It has a more intimate connotation. In the original Hebrew of the text above, the word for know is *yada* which means not only *to perceive, understand* and *believe*, but also *to experience*[1].

As Isaiah's words indicate, 'you' refers to the people of Israel. God by His grace chose Abraham to be the father of the nation He would create, and He chose to relate to this nation to reveal Himself to the world. He revealed His character and His power to the people of Israel so that they would get to *yada* Him, and through them, the people of the world would come to *yada* God as well[2]. Brave Jewish men who came to *yada* God in the ultimate way He could be intimately known – through His Son, Jesus Christ[3] – did take that mandate outside Israel with the Good News of Jesus. Since then, countless 'yous' through the ages have experienced God's love and are sharing it with others as God's witnesses.

Could it be that you are reading this because God has chosen YOU to *yada* Him, the only true God and Saviour? Could it be that He is inviting you to personally experience His love in a greater way? Will you accept His invitation?

Romans 5 verse 8 (NIV) declares, "God demonstrates His own love for us in this: While we were still sinners, Christ died for us." God had demonstrated His love at the cross of Christ 2000 years ago. Now God wants us to personally experience His love because

---

[1]   In Genesis 4v1 (KJV), the intimate connotation is obvious: *And Adam knew* ['yada'] *Eve his wife; and she conceived, and bare Cain...* 'Yada' means to know intimately.

[2]   Genesis 12v2-3 (NIV): *I will make you* [Abraham] *into a great nation and I will bless you; I will make your name great, and you will be a blessing. I will bless those who bless you, and whoever curses you I will curse; and all peoples on earth will be blessed through you.*

[3]   God ultimately revealed Himself through His Son, Jesus – Hebrews 1v1-3a (NIV): *In the past God spoke to our forefathers through the prophets at many times and in various ways, but in these last days He has spoken to us by His Son, whom He appointed heir of all things, and through whom He made the universe. The Son is the radiance of God's glory and the exact representation of His being, sustaining all things by His powerful word.*

He wants us to love Him in return. The more we realise God's love for us, the more we will love Him. As 1 John 4v19 (NKJV) says, "We love Him because He first loved us."

This is the story of a Finnish family who experienced firsthand the love of the God of miracles when He answered a prayer and provided for a need. As usual, it was the children who were convinced from the beginning that God would provide…..

A Bed from Heaven

We are a quite normal Finnish family: I'm the father, my beautiful wife and three smart and talented boys. My wife and I have often wondered where our boys inherited their gifts from. They are very good at music and in drawing pictures as well, whereas my wife and I can't draw at all!

We pray for our boys a lot, since they were little. When they were younger, we used to read stories to them from the children's Bible every day and we taught them how to pray. Like other children growing up in Christian households, our boys believed these Bible stories and in their minds, I'm sure they had no doubt that God is a God of miracles. Adults find it more difficult to believe in miracles, although every second of our lives, miracles happen inside our body. (You know what I mean!) My wife and I had always known that God can do miracles, but we had never tested this because we never asked for one for our lives, until God surprised us when a need arose!

We were missionaries many years ago in southern Europe in a small French-speaking area. The children went to the local school and my wife and I worked at a Christian radio station. Our salary was not huge but we had everything we needed. Our pastor used to say that as regards the hymn 'Great is Thy Faithfulness'[4], we sing, "All I have <u>needed</u> Thy hand hath provided," and not, "All I have <u>wanted</u> Thy hand hath provided." Needed and wanted – there is a great difference.

Our home was small at the time when we had only two children and the boys had one small room for the two of them. Our oldest son was about six or seven years old when he asked if we could buy a bed and a table for him because his bed was by now too small for him and he needed a table for his school work. We went to the shopping mall to see if they had anything for a good price. We found a bed that had a table under it. It was nice and practical. The price was 2400 French francs[5]. We didn't have the money but we promised our son that when the money would come, we would buy the bed and table for him. After a few weeks he asked again, but we still didn't have

---

[4] This is a popular Christian hymn written by Thomas Chisolm in 1923 and set to music by William M. Runyan in Kansas, USA.

[5] This was before the Euro was adopted as the currency in France.

the money. After a few months we told the boys we should pray together and tell the Lord that if He wanted to give the bed to us, it would be a great thing.

Some weeks after we prayed that prayer, I came home from work and our boys ran to welcome me home saying with absolute conviction that the Lord had sent the money to us! They showed me a letter from Antwerp in Belgium with our name on the envelope. The letter was from our friend whom we had not seen for ten years. In this letter she said that she had been keeping Dutch guldens for bad days. She and her husband lived in Holland before and this was why she had money in Dutch currency. She wrote that God asked her to send it to us. She took half of the money and put it in the envelope, but God said: "All of it!" At first she didn't want to write her name, but changed her mind because she wanted us to tell her if we had been praying for that amount of money. She could not have obtained the information about our need by reading something we posted on Facebook or sent by email (we had no computer then and this was before Facebook) so she believed, as we did, that she got the information from the Lord.

I went to the bank the next day and my surprise was huge after the lady at the desk counted the French francs equivalent of our Dutch guldens. It was 2402 francs! Crazy ideas came to my mind like, "God, we prayed for only 2400 francs. You made a two francs mistake!" ☺ I know that our God understands humour much more than we do and forgives our crazy thoughts!

At home my wife and I prayed with our boys, thanking God for His provision and for the many lessons we had been learning through this experience. We went to the store as soon as we could and discovered that they had only one unit left of that particular bed and table we saw before and liked, and it was the one that was assembled and on display. Not only were we spared of the need to assemble it, we also paid less than we anticipated because the price of the display unit was only 1700 francs. Praise the Lord! He supplied our need, with extra to spare. Apparently, the two francs 'mistake' was a sign that God was going to bless us with more than enough![6]

For grown-up people, it is not easy to believe that God can do miracles. For children, it is more natural. Of course God sent the money! This was what we prayed for. I wish that one day I would trust our Lord the way little children do.

- Matti (Espoo, Finland)
May 2011

---

[6] One of the Old Testament titles of God is *El Shaddai*, the name He used in Genesis 17v1. It is usually translated in English Bibles as 'God Almighty', but which means more literally, 'The Pourer of Blessings' or 'The More-Than-Enough God'. *El Shaddai* gives more than enough! Appendix 1 lists more of these names or titles.

God of miracles, my heavenly Father, thank You for loving me! Thank You for Your invitation to know and experience You more intimately and deeply. Help me respond to Your invitation. I do want to know You and love You more. Please help me to see Jesus in my experiences. Help me to trust Him more and more. In His name I pray, amen!

Week 6: Our Direct Line to God

Whoever dwells in the shelter of the Most High will rest in
the shadow of the Almighty. (Psalm 91v1, NIV)

Most eagles are large and powerful hunters with light bodies and long wings made for soaring[1]. These wings and short tails help these birds to effortlessly glide on air currents, but make it a bit difficult for them to take off from and land on the ground. This is one reason why an eagle lives in a high place[2], a vantage point which gives it a greater field of view for hunting. With its amazing visual acuity and binocular vision (for accurate judgment of distance), the eagle is able to spot a rabbit hiding in the grass as far as two miles away. It can even see a fish in the water from high up its perch[3]. Then it simply falls and swoops down on the unsuspecting prey.

When one stands on a high place, he will see more of what is below. God has given all who put their trust in Jesus a high vantage point where we can see our circumstances from His perspective and get a revelation from Him about our situation. On this vantage point, prayer is transformed from a mere recitation of our needs, to an expression of our trust in God to meet our needs according to His will, not ours. (After all, He knows what is best for us.) Prayer is simply communicating with God, the One who knows us best, warts and all, yet loves us the most. It is so much easier than using a mobile phone, email, Facebook or Twitter, and the line is open to us 24/7! We can live or dwell on our vantage point, the "shelter of the Most High", 24 hours a day, 7 days a week.

God of course knows everything. He knows what we will tell Him before the thought comes to our head. So why pray? Our prayer affirms God's importance in our life and invites Him into our situation. It opens the door for Him to act on our behalf in the way that He knows best. Knowing this should free our mind from anxiety. And when we see the prayer answered, our trust and confidence in Him grows. Philippians 4v6-7 tell us more: "Do not be anxious about anything, but in every situation, by prayer and petition, with thanksgiving, present your requests to God. And the peace

---

[1] There are 59 different species of eagles in the world. The majority are found in Asia, Russia, and Europe. Two species live in North America and two in South America.

[2] Eagles generally live in the mountains near the seacoast or lakes. They build their nests high up in the trees, around 75 feet or more above the ground. This height gives security for their nests.

[3] Job 39v28-29 (NIV): *It* [the eagle] *dwells on a cliff and stays there at night; a rocky crag is its stronghold. From there it looks for food; its eyes detect it from afar.*

of God, which transcends all understanding, will guard your hearts and your minds in Christ Jesus" (NIV).

Here are stories of two women who discovered that they do not have to be anxious about anything because they can bring it to God in prayer, our direct line to God.

It Was Important to Him

One day in January 2011, I read the following devotional entry from *The Word for Today*[4] posted on an Internet forum:

The 4-year old son of a missionary family in Africa spotted a picture of a little pink dinosaur in a magazine and set his heart on having one. His mum knew it was impossible (the magazine was 3 years old), but he never doubted God would come through for him.

Ten months later, on Christmas Eve, a box from home arrived. At first glance it seemed to contain something special for everyone, except for a 4-year old boy. Then they reached to the bottom – and they were stunned. The lady who sent the box had no way of knowing God would use her to answer a little boy's prayer. Before taping up the box, at the last minute, she tossed the one item impossible for his parents to provide, something so insignificant no rational adult would ever have been foolish enough to ask God for – a pink plastic brontosaurus from a fast food restaurant promotion!

Sometimes we feel foolish bothering God with little things, but we shouldn't. The Bible says, "...pray about everything"[5]. God is interested in every detail of your life. If something is important to you, it's important to Him. In Bible times, two sparrows were sold for a penny, yet Jesus said, "....not a single sparrow can fall to the ground without your Father knowing it. The very hairs of your head are all numbered" (Matthew 10v29-30). When you learn to trust God in little things, you'll be able to trust Him in big ones.

These words particularly stood out for me: "Sometimes we feel foolish bothering God with little things, but we shouldn't. The Bible says, '...pray about everything.'

---

[4] The extract is from the 30 January 2011 reading of *The Word for Today*, a daily devotional published by United Christian Broadcasters, Westport Road, Stoke-on-Trent, ST6 4JF, UK. Free copies can be obtained within the UK and Ireland. Telephone 0845 3040401 or visit ucb. co.uk/wft. This extract was used by permission of UCB.

[5] Philippians 4v6 (NLT): *Don't worry about anything; instead, pray about everything. Tell God what you need, and thank Him for all He has done.*

God is interested in every detail of your life. If something is important to you, it's important to Him."

I needed to be reminded of that truth! I had been feeling bad about a missing pet, but didn't pray about it as it seemed so trivial compared to missing and exploited children and other horrors people have to endure. But reading those words made me realise that my great big God does not mind me praying for my pet cat who had been missing for three days. And so I decided to say a little prayer for Snoball. I also posted in the forum a photo of Snoball, informing the pray-ers in that forum thread about my missing pet.

After I'd done that, I went out of the house to take care of my cat brood. Something or someone ☺ impressed on me to walk around the farm and call Snoball's name. Mind you, I had been outside calling her name a lot, but I hadn't walked around like I should have. Well, I came to the outer reaches of the farmyard and heard many loud "meows" in response to my calling. Snoball was up in an old farm building on narrow two by four rafters and couldn't get down! Thank You Lord I finally found her!

I couldn't reach her so I ran to the shop and found a little footstool that I placed on a snowdrift and I was able to get to a second layer of rafters. From there I was able to reach her. She seemed okay after three days and nights, except for being hungry.

I came back to the Internet forum a few hours after reading that devotional and posted that God had answered my prayer and that Snoball was back in a heated barn with her sister and step-sister, eating and drinking. I ended my post with these words: "I'm crying with relief for I love Snoball, and for the lesson God and you guys taught me today! Thank you!"

- Kathi (in a farm in SW Minnesota, USA)
June 2011

A Praying Woman

My mother has been a Christian for many years and is a praying woman. She was a working woman as well, sewing to help augment Dad's income. I remember one time Mum wanted to change direction from sewing for a living to doing something different. She prayed about this and God gave His answer through the sermons Mum heard over the next few weeks.

On the Sunday following her prayer, the sermon preached in our church was on David and Goliath[6]. David decided to face the giant Goliath. King Saul wanted David to wear the king's armour, but it was cumbersome for David. Instead of the king's armour, David would rather use the weapon he was familiar with and skilled at using – his slingshot. Despite his smaller size, David prevailed over the giant with his slingshot. The message of the sermon was for God's people to use the gifts, talents and skills God had already given them. Mum came home thinking about that message.

The holiday season soon came and Dad and Mum went away to Tenby in Wales for a short holiday. They attended a local church there. The preacher's sermon was on David and Goliath! After returning home from their holiday, Mum and Dad went to church on the Sunday. That day a visiting preacher came. Guess what he preached on. David and Goliath!

Mum felt that the three sermons she heard on the same theme meant that God was telling her to stick with the skills she had gained sewing.

Time came when both Dad and Mum retired. Due to the economic climate and their retirement, Mum was concerned she would not be able to manage the household budget. For a few months during the Christmas period, she struggled to buy food and presents. So she prayed to God for provision.

One day she found a £20 bill on the ground outside our house. Another time God provided through the Line Dancing group that Mum attended every week at our local community centre. Everyone had a membership number. The numbers were put in a draw and her number came up! She got the prize money, enough to get by on.

When she ran out of money, Mum asked God again. This time it came through an elderly man (with whom Mum had conversations about Jesus). He was grateful for the help and care he had received from Mum in his time of need. He gave Mum a card and inside was a £20 bill! Mum had not mentioned her need to him, but God knew her need and supplied it.

Through experiences like these, Mum learned that she could take all her worries to God in prayer, as the old hymn[7] says:

What a friend we have in Jesus,
All our sins and griefs to bear.
What a privilege to carry

---

[6] From 1 Samuel chapter 17.
[7] 'What a Friend We Have in Jesus' by Joseph M. Scriven, 1855.

Everything to God in prayer!
Oh, what peace we often forfeit,
Oh, what needless pain we bear.
All because we do not carry
Everything to God in prayer!

My Mum through the years had discovered that as long as she stays close to the Lord and does His will, she does not need to worry about anything because she can pray about it. And He answers!

- Vivienne (Lancaster, England)
October 2011

Thank You Father God that because of Jesus I have direct communication line to You 24/7. Help me to see my circumstances, no matter how difficult they may be, from Your perspective. Help me to remember that I don't need to worry about anything because I can pray about it. In Jesus' name, amen.

Week 7: On Wings of Faith

Depend on the Lord; trust Him, and He will take care of you.
(Psalm 37v5, NCV)

With eyes designed for long distance visual clarity, an eagle perches on a high place to get a commanding view of the terrain for its next meal. It tries to get to this vantage point with minimal flapping of its large wings to conserve energy, especially if it needs to fly over large distances to follow seasonal food supplies. The six slotted feathers at the tip of each wing which curves upward reduce the drag on the wind and this helps the eagle to minimise the need to flap its wings. It soars or hitchhikes on a thermal convection current, letting the rising air take it upward with very little effort. Then it just glides through long distances until it finds the next column of rising air. Because soaring conserves the eagle's energy, it is an important survival skill for the eagle.

In the same way, it is vital for every person to surrender to the wind of God's Spirit and soar above his fears, circumstances, difficulties and low expectations with wings of faith. It is vital because if you do not overcome these things, they will overcome and defeat you. To the one who puts his trust in God's Son, He gives wings of faith so he can prevail over the things that prevent him from living life to the fullest[1]. It cannot be done without these wings of faith; God made sure of that because He created us to be dependent on Him[2].

Spread your wings and let the wind of the Spirit take you to a vantage point where you can communicate with God through prayer and His word and where you can view from God's perspective your life on earth. You will see and experience that He can be completely depended on to take care of you because "the Lord is faithful, and He will strengthen and protect you from the evil one" (2 Thessalonians 3v3, NIV).

Here is a story that hopefully will help you to confront your fears and to take off on wings as eagles. With your wings of faith in Jesus, you are more than a conqueror![3]

---

[1] 1 John 5v4 (NLT): *For every child of God defeats this evil world, and we achieve this victory through our faith.*

[2] Acts 17v28 (NLT): *For in Him we live and move and exist.*

[3] Romans 8v37 (ESV): *…. we are more than conquerors through Him who loved us.*

Sleepless in Seattle
=

In the 1980s I registered as a PhD student at the University of Washington in Seattle, Washington, USA. The time came when I had to take the first of a series of three courses in biochemistry/molecular biology. I was already warned by a friend that these were difficult subjects and this was why the number of students (over 400 of us at the start) would progressively get smaller. So it was with great apprehension that I began the course.

The first course in the series was 'Proteins and Enzymes'. As a foreign student, it took some time for me to get used to the accent of the professor, although he was a really good lecturer. As I listened to him, I took down notes and even taped his lectures on my mini cassette recorder. Soon the date of the first of three exams in the subject was announced. I was distressed when I found out it was on the same day as my first exam in another course.

I prepared myself for the two exams by reviewing (or revising) way ahead of the exam date. However, on the night before my exams, I was so uptight because of the fear of failure (I had never failed a course before) that I developed a tummy ache. To make matters worse, I couldn't sleep at all. Not a wink! I was feeling rather ill in the morning so I missed my exam in biochem. I didn't want to miss two exams in a day so I took the exam in the other course. By God's grace I did well although I'm sure I could have done better if I wasn't feeling so light-headed.

There were three exams in each of the biochem courses, the last one being the finals. A student was allowed to miss any of the first two and the grade in the part of the finals which had the same subject matter as the missed exam was doubled to make up for the missing grade. Because I already missed the first exam, I felt more tense as I reviewed (revised) the more difficult course material for the second exam, so much so that sleep eluded me, not for one night before the exam, but for the entire week! The night before was the worst, but I had to go the following morning and take the dreaded test.

I was feeling so light-headed and anxious as I took the exam paper. As soon as I looked at the first question, my mind went blank! I had never suffered a mental block before an exam prior to this so for a moment I panicked. Praise God He reminded me that I could pray about the situation, so I closed my eyes and just whispered, "Help Lord!" After a few seconds, I opened my eyes and looked at the exam paper again. This time, I could understand every question.

After a few days, the exam results came out. My hands shook as I took my graded paper from the professor. I could not, really could not believe what I got – a 3.9! (A grade of 4 was the highest possible grade and 0 the lowest, with increments of 0.1. Grades were based on the average score of the class.) I knew without a doubt that it was only by God's grace I got this. After all, I had a week of sleepless nights and my background in molecular biology was inadequate.

The time to prepare for the finals came and the same thing happened to me: I got no sleep for the entire week before the exam! I had no problem in my other subjects, but this course was the most difficult subject I had to take. The finals covered the entire course content. This and the fact that I missed the first exam made this a very important exam for me. Hence, my stress level.

I didn't experience any mental block the day of the finals. However, it didn't help when a few of my classmates stood up and left the exam room because the questions were "too difficult"! But praise God He was with me. Despite the fact that many could not finish the exam, I was able to answer all the questions. I had no idea, however, if my answers were correct!

Then the day of reckoning came when all students had to get their graded exam papers. The grade given was for the course itself, not just the finals. Can you believe what I got? A 3.9! Unbelievable? The proteins and enzymes in my brain could not believe it either!

You'd think by this time I would rest on my laurels and relax a bit in the next quarter of the school year. I believe I couldn't because the next course in the series, 'Intermediary Metabolism', was worth four credits, compared to just three for the others. To pass the course, one needed to memorise countless molecular formulas, several metabolic pathways and the enzymes involved, and to understand how the atoms interact in the biochemical reactions. Therefore, one needed to be clear-headed and focused during the exams.

As I prepared for the first exam of the course, my fear of failure transformed into fear of not being able to sleep. Job says, "What I feared has come upon me; what I dreaded has happened to me" (Job 3v25, NIV). The dreaded week-long sleeplessness happened again. No wonder Jesus told His followers many times, "Fear not!" I did attempt to do something about the insomnia. My brother sent me some pills which I tried days before the first exam in Intermediary Metabolism. However, although I was able to get some sleep, I would wake up from terrible nightmares. One day as I was walking to the university, the Lord asked me, "Will you trust Me?"[4] I received Jesus into my life in 1973 and have experienced God's faithfulness since. I knew that

---

4   Proverbs 3v5 (NLT): *Trust in the Lord with all your heart; do not depend on your own understanding.*

I could trust Him completely even though I didn't understand what was happening. I said yes and threw away all the pills. I thought this 'act of faith' would remove the problem, but the sleepless nights didn't go away. I went through a week of sleepless nights before every long exam in this course!

But again, through it all, God was with me. No, this time I didn't get a 3.9. In all three exams I got a whopping 4.0! How was that possible? By this time I had metabolised the fact that with God, indeed nothing is impossible![5]

In the following quarter, I enrolled for the last course in the biochem series, 'Molecular Genetics'. Because I practically didn't have any background on the subject, I chickened-out and opted to take the course on a 'pass or fail' (ungraded) basis. I soon forgot my apprehension in taking the course for I found the subject so fascinating.

I thought that because of my interest in the subject as well as my goal of just passing the course, I would have no sleep problems. I was wrong! I had exactly the same sleep problem as before. It was as if my mind, laden with Molecular Genetics information, had suffered a mutation and would not rest at night. I often asked God why this was happening to me. Then I would hear the same answer, "Will you trust Me?" I didn't like what was happening nor fully understand why God was allowing me to go through it. All I knew was that although I needed to do my part (study), I should put my total dependence on Him.

To cut the story short, I regretted opting for a pass or fail because I didn't only get 4.0 in all the exams in the course, I also got the highest total score among the just over 200 students who survived this biochem series! I realised that if I trusted God enough, I would have gone for the grade.

The Lord didn't remove my sleeping problem as I asked Him to. Instead, He took me through it, through three quarters (about nine months) of biochemistry and nine gruelling exams. He did this because He wanted to deal with the root of my problem which was fear, fear of failure and fear of not being able to sleep. On hindsight, the only way for that to happen was for me to go through the experience and come out victorious in Jesus!

When I finally realised after those nine months that His grace was sufficient for me and that His strength would manifest in my weakness as I trusted Him[6], those fears

---

[5] Luke 1v37 (NKJV): *For with God nothing will be impossible.*

[6] 2 Corinthians 12v9 (ESV): *But He said to me, "My grace is sufficient for you, for My power is made perfect in weakness." Therefore I will boast all the more gladly of my weaknesses, so that the power of Christ may rest upon me.*

finally left me. God truly meant what He said when He promised, "Don't be afraid, for I am with you. Don't be discouraged, for I am your God. I will strengthen you and help you. I will hold you up with My victorious right hand" (Isaiah 41v10, NLT). This precious truth prepared and helped me go through the storms in the years that followed. More importantly, it is also helping me in the fulfilment of God's call on my life.

I wholeheartedly agree with these words of Paul from 2 Corinthians 4v17 (NLT): "Our present troubles are small and won't last very long. Yet they produce for us a glory that vastly outweighs them and will last forever!"

- Maria-Corazon (Manila, Philippines)
September 2011

In John 10 verse 10, Jesus declares: "The thief [the devil] comes only to steal and kill and destroy; I have come that they [Jesus' followers] may have life, and have it to the full" (NIV).

Father God, thank You that I can depend on You to help me overcome all my problems and fears. Thank You for sending Jesus so I can live life to the fullest and soar above difficult circumstances with the wings of faith that You give me. Thank You that You are completely trustworthy. I praise You for who You are!

Week 8: Use Your Wings

I am crucified with Christ: nevertheless I live; yet not I, but Christ liveth in me: and the life which I now live in the flesh I live by the faith of the Son of God, who loved me, and gave Himself for me. (Galatians 2v20, KJV)

When a person receives Jesus into his life as his Saviour and Lord, he truly becomes a spiritual eagle because he also receives 'wings of faith'. This faith is the supernatural kind that is not limited by our human senses. It is the God-kind of faith.

The King James Version rendition of the verse above is different from those of other versions in which this verse reads, "I live by faith *in* the Son of God". The KJV rendition is similar to that given by the Online Greek Interlinear Bible[1] (which gives the original Greek to English translation): "I live by *the faith of* the Son of God". (Other versions like Wycliffe, Young's and Darby render this passage in the same way.) These words imply that God gives to every believer the faith of Jesus! This is why Peter could write to the scattered Christians of his time, "To those who *have received a faith of the same kind* as ours, by the righteousness of our God and Saviour, Jesus Christ" (2 Peter 1v1, NASB). He also said: "By His divine power, God *has given us everything we need* for living a godly life. We *have received all* of this by coming to know Him, the one who called us to Himself by means of His marvellous glory and excellence" (2 Peter 1v3, NLT). God has provided everything we need to live the Christian life, including all the faith we need to do what He calls us to do[2]. It is the faith of Jesus, the "measure of faith" that is given to all who believe. There is therefore no reason for some to think they have more faith than others[3].

Most of the time, however, we tap into our own human faith which is little or weak and then quit, rather than tap into the faith supplied to us by God, Jesus' faith. What we need to pray, therefore, is not for more faith, but for God's help for us to believe we have already been given all the faith we need, and to understand how to use it according to God's will, as Jesus always did.

---

[1] www.scripture4all.org/OnlineInterlinear/Greek_Index.htm

[2] As in Romans 12v6-8 (NIV): *We have different gifts, according to the grace given to each of us. If your gift is prophesying, then prophesy in accordance with your faith; if it is serving, then serve; if it is teaching, then teach; if it is to encourage, then give encouragement; if it is giving, then give generously; if it is to lead, do it diligently; if it is to show mercy, do it cheerfully.*

[3] Romans 12v3 (KJV): *For I say, through the grace given unto me, to every man that is among you, not to think of himself more highly than he ought to think; but to think soberly, according as God hath dealt to every man the measure of faith.*

An eagle does not need more wings than the two he already has to fly and soar. He only needs to spread them out and learn to use them to their *fullest potential*. We have God's word to help us use our wings of faith in increasing measure. Romans 10v17 (NIV) says: "Consequently, faith comes from hearing the message, and the message is heard through the word of Christ". The original Greek word for 'word' in this verse is *rhema*, a 'word in season', a 'now word' that is relevant to our situation and which proves that God's *logos* (His written word[4]) is alive because it comes from the *Logos*, the living Word of God[5]. If we let God's *logos* (the Bible) fill our lives with its wisdom, comfort and instructions, we will receive a *rhema* from Him regarding the situation or circumstance we are praying about. Acting on this *rhema* exercises our wings of faith, the faith of God's *Logos,* Jesus. The more we act on a *rhema*, the more we exercise our wings until the time comes when we are using our God-given faith to its fullest potential[6]. So 'hear' God's *logos* and *rhema* and use your wings!

The parents in the story below received a revelation (a *rhema*) from God's *logos* about their baby. They did not allow their human faith to overcome their God-given faith. Therefore they could say, "Our faith assured us". It was Jesus' faith!

Something Happened to Our Baby

We were going to have a baby, our first! What better news could there be? From the day we realised we were having a baby, we prayed each night, placing our hands over the bump. We prayed for the development of our baby as it formed inside the womb as well as for its health and future.

Filled with excitement and anticipation, we went along to the maternity unit at the hospital for the final routine scan of our baby. The scan followed the same format of all the previous ones, but at the end of the examination we were asked to wait for one of the doctors to come and talk to us. The wait seemed endless as we sat in the cubicle. Then the doctor arrived with some unexpected news. He said that an abnormality had appeared on the scan that showed our baby's kidneys were enlarged and bright. We were stunned and probably didn't take in everything that was said on that day. The doctor said that he would arrange a more detailed scan to take place at St. Mary's Hospital in Manchester. We left the hospital a little less excited than when we arrived and with a strong feeling that we needed to find out what this might mean for our unborn baby.

---

[4]   Colossians 3v16 (NKJV): *Let the word* [Greek 'logos'] *of Christ dwell in you richly.*

[5]   Jesus is the living Word or *Logos* of God: "*The Word* ['Logos'] *became flesh and made His dwelling among us. We have seen His glory, the glory of the one and only Son, who came from the Father, full of grace and truth*" (John 1v14, NIV).

[6]   As in spiritual warfare (Week 26) and for "signs, wonders and miracles" (Week 46)

The following month we went to Manchester to have the scan. The scan equipment appeared to be more high-tech than the machines at our hospital and the detail of the new scan was much clearer. However, the second scan confirmed the first one – one of the baby's kidneys was much larger than the other. We went home with heavy hearts, but not without hope.

Our son was born the next month and everything appeared to be fine. We named him Joel Peter and started to pray for his healing.

When he was a month old, Joel had an appointment to go back to St. Mary's for a scan and x-ray to check his kidneys and bladder function. He wasn't impressed with the ordeal as he lay on a couch in the x-ray suite waiting for his bladder to work. We, the parents, were both scanned at the same time to check for any abnormalities in our kidneys. We finally got Joel dressed again and went to see the consultant in his office. The consultant discussed various possible treatments and left us with the bombshell of the probable need for a kidney transplant for Joel. He requested us to bring Joel for a scan every year and to take him to the hospital at Manchester at age five when his kidneys would be fully developed. According to the doctors, the health of our son was looking uncertain and we left the hospital in a state of shock! We shed a few tears that day, and yet we had an inner peace and renewed determination to trust and believe God for Joel's healing.

In the weeks that followed, Joel's skin would often appear yellow in colour. The information the consultant gave us was always at the back of our mind as we took care of our baby.

About a month after the visit to St. Mary's, we took Joel to a healing service at our church despite the fact that the service was in an evening and we didn't normally take him out at night especially as it was a rough winter's night. Towards the end of the service, we brought Joel in front of the congregation and as a church family we prayed for him. As we prayed, we were reminded of this Bible verse[7]: "For You formed my inward parts; You covered me in my mother's womb. I will praise You, for I am fearfully and wonderfully made. Marvellous are Your works, and that my soul knows very well".

Something happened that night! We took this revelation (*rhema* word) as a promise that God was re-creating Joel's abnormal kidneys. All anxiety and fear left us. Our

---

[7]   Psalm 139v13-14, NKJV

faith assured us[8] that Joel had been healed. Joel's colour improved almost right away and his general health got better each day!

For the next two years Joel had his blood pressure checked every six months by our GP and for four years we took Joel for health checks and scans to the hospital where we saw the consultant. On each of the annual visits the consultant would assess our baby's health, but said he would wait until Joel was five before deciding upon any form of treatment, or if his health started to suffer.

Then just after Joel's fifth birthday we received an appointment to attend the Manchester Children's Hospital for various tests, x-ray and scan to assess his kidneys. During all the time that had passed we kept our trust in God and never doubted that Joel had been healed. We spent most of the morning at the hospital undertaking the various tests.

We will never forget being called into the consultant's office and we will always remember what he said to us on that day. He announced to us, "Joel's kidneys are perfectly normal. There is no trace of any abnormality and whatever the problem was has now gone". The consultant couldn't provide us with a medical explanation for this complete change of events. We were thrilled and left with such thankful hearts!

Joel is now fifteen and has grown into a healthy five foot seven inches teenager, exceeding the expectations of the paediatricians. He plays drums in the church and high school worship groups as well as in the school jazz band and local brass band.

We will remain thankful to the Lord for healing our son and we praise Him for this amazing miracle!

-Peter and Fiona Collins (Lancaster, England)
July 2011

Father God, thank You that You have already given me everything that I will ever need, including the faith of Jesus that I require to face and overcome any situation or problem. Help me to fill my life with Your precious logos and help me to act on Your rhema. Enable me to use the wings You gave me for Your glory. In Jesus' name, amen!

---

[8]   Hebrews 11v1 (NASB): *Now faith is the assurance of things hoped for, the conviction of things not seen.*

Week 9: Where is Your Focus?

So, faith comes from listening, but it's listening by means of Christ's message. (Romans 10v17, CEB)

Apart from its upper and lower eyelids, the eagle also has special eyelids that move sideways. These are the transparent nictitating membranes which enable the eagle to see even whilst blinking. These membranes also act as built-in sunglasses that allow the eagle to look directly at the sun for some time if it needs to. The eagle also has a skull that gives it unique eyebrows. These offer protection against injury as well as shield from the blinding glare of the sun.

The eagle uses its ability to look directly at the sun to escape from an enemy, the condor, the largest flying land bird in North America. The condor will try to attack the eagle, but the eagle does not stay and fight a claw-to-claw combat with the bigger condor. Instead, it turns to the sun and flies directly towards it. The condor tries to follow the eagle, but is blinded by the sun and has to turn away.

Our enemy, the devil, is powerful and cunning. We cannot win over him in a 'hand-to-hand' or close combat. Our battle strategy is not to fight him, but to turn our focus off the temptation, fear or worry that he is throwing at us, and onto Jesus, the Son of God. This does not mean ignoring the problem. (If the eagle merely ignores the condor, guess what will happen!) So how do we do this?

Romans 10v17 above shows the importance of what receives the attention of our natural and spiritual ears. We must not empower those words that do not align with what the Bible says by focusing on them. Rather, we must tap into the faith that God has already given us by focusing on what Jesus, the living Word of God, the *Logos* (Week 8), says in His written word, the Bible. He will surely 'quicken'[1] a specific scripture for us, making it a *rhema* word that we can speak over our situation. Yes, speak out the *rhema* word because "the tongue has the power of life and death"[2]. By choosing to believe what He says despite our circumstances and by speaking God's *rhema* over our situation, we fly towards the Son of God. Then our enemy, like the condor, will have to back off from his pursuit.

---

[1] John 6v63 (KJV): *It is the Spirit that quickeneth... The words that I speak unto you, they are spirit, and they are life.* The word 'quicken' in Biblical parlance means to make alive, to give life or vitality.

[2] Proverbs 18v21, NIV.

I pray that my own story below will help and encourage you not to focus on your problems, but on the Son of God. Turn to the Son and fly to Him!

"Don't Look at the Situation and Circumstances"

At the time of writing this, a month has passed since I sent out a request to all my contributors for their signed permissions to publish their stories in this book. I learned about this requirement the day after I submitted the manuscript to the publisher. I am distressed because of the failure by the contributor of this week's designated story to respond to my pleas that she send me her signed permission. Should I wait longer? What if she says no? It is logical not to drop the whole project just because of one story, but I have been dreading the thought of deleting that story and writing a replacement which is about the same theme and length and which incorporates all the footnotes of the original story. The most distressing aspect for me is that replacing the original story means withdrawing the original manuscript and submitting a revised one, and that this is likely to cost me much more than I anticipated. By writing this story, I am taking the step of faith that the Lord will guide me in my writing and that He will either supply the additional money I need to publish this book, or grant me favour with the publisher – or perhaps, favour with the said contributor.

Looking back, I realise that the Lord had actually prepared me to face this current obstacle in the completion of my project by giving me three blessings which reminded me of His love and faithfulness.

The first blessing is connected with the artwork for this book. About a month ago as I was praying about the cover design, a picture flashed across my mind's eye. It lasted only for about a second, but I could tell that there were three figures in the picture – an eagle soaring, a man running below the eagle, and a man walking behind the runner. All figures were black silhouettes. I also saw shades of yellow and orange. That day I emailed my brother in the Philippines to ask if he knew anyone who could design the book cover for me with these details incorporated in the artwork. He responded that he would ask his former colleague who is into graphic design. Two days later, my brother emailed me with the artwork of Gerry Villegas as an attachment. I was amazed when I opened this because Gerry's design captured what I believe the Lord showed me in the vision! I had forgotten to tell my brother that in the vision, all three figures were facing towards the right, but Gerry nevertheless depicted them in this way. I really believe that this was an answer to my prayer that God would direct the hand of the designer of the cover artwork. What you see on the cover of this book is Gerry's design concept.

The discussions I had with my Internet friends Shirley, Gayle, Linda and Máire about Gerry's artwork confirmed to me that there was a message in this picture (that it is prophetic). I have included that message in the Dedication page. I pray that it will speak to you as it did to me!

The second blessing God gave me is connected with a message I received many years ago. When I learned about the need to ask all my story contributors for their signed permissions, I became very apprehensive because of the number of people I needed to contact and the fact that many of them lived abroad. But I did what I had to do. Hoping to find the address of one of my contributors in the Philippines, I had to look through several of my old notebooks. One particular notebook was one I had not opened in years. I turned towards the back and noticed the small piece of paper that I had glued onto the last page. It was a print-out of the prophetic words sent to me by email in 2002 and 2003 by Yoly, one of the seven prophetic people in the Philippines who prophesied to me in 2001 (see "Rainbow Connection", Week 15).

The message given to me in November 2002 was this: "Fear not, My child, for I am with you in the things you have started to do for Me. I am the One who will give you the strength to overcome the hindrances the enemy is placing before you. Trust in Me. Look towards Me and I will make a way for you to continue what you have begun. Do not be dismayed at the things you see that may cause you to lose faith. Do not stop or loosen your hold because what you are doing is according to My will. Continue and you will be amazed at the things I will do in your life. Trust Me in all things and My hand will be the one that will work and move for you... Be strong for Me. I am with you always. I will never leave you nor forsake you. You don't have to fear or worry about anything for as long as it is My will you seek to do. I will not fail you. I will be the One who will guide you until you accomplish what I want you to do." I know I can believe that this was indeed a *rhema* from the Lord because those words agree with what God says in the Bible.

On the back of the paper was another message that Yoly sent in May 2003. It contains these precious words from the Lord: "Do not fear. Have faith! Stand on My words and promises. All is well! Don't look at the situation and circumstances. Look up to Me for I am the author and the finisher!"

Those words given in 2002 and 2003 are indeed *rhema* to me for this September 2012 because they are so relevant at this time when I am experiencing the agonising frustration caused by the delay in the production process of this book. I was reminded not to focus on my situation, but on my Lord's promise that He would finish what He had begun. Because this book was really His idea (see Introduction), that makes Him its "author". Therefore, He will also be its "finisher". Although my faith is as small as a mustard seed[3], I was reminded that to "have faith" means to use the faith that Jesus has already given me to overcome any situation I face (Week 8). I was reminded to practise what I preach and not to agree with the devil by saying the negative words he wants to hear from me, but to agree with what God has said to me and to declare His words over the distressing situation in which I find myself – that God would not fail me in this project which was His idea in the first place and that He would bring it to completion!

The third blessing I received from the Lord was to be reminded of my experiences in 2004 and 2005. In 2004, the Lord told me to study the eagle and its prophetic symbolisms (much of what I include in this book is an outcome of that study). In 2005, my family and I visited the Philippines. A day before we flew back to England, I spent some time with a couple whom I had first met in 2001 (they are two of the seven people in my story in Week 15). They promised to return the next day to pray for me and to anoint me with oil before I leave. As Emma was talking to me, I saw a vision in my mind of the wing feathers of a big bird. The experience was actually more than a vision because for a few seconds I was not aware of anything but of those feathers. I felt like I was sitting on the back of that big bird as it was soaring in the air. I soon realised that the bird was an eagle! Suddenly, the vision ended and I was back with Emma. I told her and her husband Jonathan about the vision and they smiled. Emma's response amazed me. She said that the Lord had instructed them to anoint me with oil and to pray for the "eagle anointing" on me. The Lord had now brought me back to my conversation with the couple and my eagle vision and made me realise that not only am I an eagle who has been anointed to soar over the difficulties that hinder me in completing the assignments God has given me, but also that God is the great Eagle who carries me on His wings so that I can overcome these difficulties.

I have had amazing experiences (such as those mentioned here) which prove God's love and faithfulness to me. Many hands have been laid on me[4] in order to anoint me to do what the Lord has assigned me to do. These recollections and the messages given to me in 2002 and 2003 are helping me to focus on my Lord and on His

---

[3]   Jesus says in Matthew 17v20 (NIV), *"Truly I tell you, if you have faith as small as a mustard seed, you can say to this mountain, 'Move from here to there,' and it will move. Nothing will be impossible for you."* The size of our natural faith does not really matter even if it is as small as a mustard seed as long as we believe in and receive the supernatural faith of Jesus that has already been given to us to face our problems. We do this by focusing on what His word says rather than on our situation. Habakkuk 2v4 tells us we are to "live by faith". To live by faith is to focus on the Son. Do not focus on your own human faith or the lack of it. Focus on the Son who is faithful and full of faith!

[4]   There are many references about the practice of the laying on of hands in the Bible, such as Acts 28v8 (NKJV): *Paul went in to him and prayed, and he laid his hands on him and healed him.*

promises and not on the problems I now face regarding the completion of this book. I have come to the understanding that the Lord is not just interested in this book, but also in me. He wants me to grow into a mature eagle. He wants me to learn how to rest in Him. For these reasons, I must experience the trials that I am now facing.

At this time I still do not know how my problem will be resolved, but the fact that you are reading this book is a testimony that the Lord is indeed faithful to His promises! I pray that my story will encourage you not to look at your situation and circumstances, but on the Lord and what He says in His word. He is faithful and He has anointed you to be His eagle!

- Haide (Lancaster, England)
September 2012

Turn your eyes upon Jesus,
Look full in His wonderful face,
And the things of earth will grow strangely dim,
In the light of His glory and grace.[5]

Father God, thank You for the gift of Your Son Jesus and for His words that are recorded in the Bible. When the problems of life come against me, help me not to empower them by focusing on them. Help me instead to turn my eyes upon Jesus by believing His words and speaking these words over my situation. Greater is He who is in me than he who is in the world[6]!

---

[5] From the hymn 'Turn Your Eyes upon Jesus' by Helen H. Lemmel, 1922.
[6] 1 John 4v4 (NIV): .... *the One who is in you* [Jesus] *is greater than the one who is in the world* [the devil].

Week 10: Learning to Fly

... like an eagle that stirs up its nest and hovers over its young, that spreads its wings to catch them and carries them aloft. (Deuteronomy 32v11, NIV)

Parent eagles take very good care of their young and feed them well.[1] The eaglets grow rapidly and soon they begin to lose their fluffy down and develop flying feathers. When they are fully feathered, the parents would hover over the nest and flap their wings. The fledglings mimic the parents. This helps to develop strength in their wings.

The parents would then begin to 'stir the nest', tearing out with the beak the animal skin and fur that make the nest cosy and exposing the twigs and thorns underneath. The nest would become so uncomfortable that the eaglets would not want to stay in it much longer, especially if the parents withhold food at times to force the babies out of the nest. It's time for the eaglets to learn to fly!

The mother eagle would eventually coax an eaglet to the edge of the nest and push it out while the father circles nearby. If the eaglet is so paralysed with fear that it doesn't open its wings and is in danger of splattering on the ground, the mother swoops down, catches it, carries it on its wings and returns it to the nest. Sooner or later, the little one gets kicked out of the nest again. It may have to be carried on the mother's back and shaken loose in mid-air thousands of feet high to force it to spread out its wings and fly. The next eaglet then goes through the same training until all eaglets have been taught to fly on their own and soar as effortlessly as the parents do.

The Bible says that those who receive Jesus as Saviour and Lord become God's children[2]. God loves His children, but His love for us is not the pampering kind because He is more interested in the growth of our character than in the increase of our comfort. He wants us to grow into mature believers who know how to use the faith of Jesus that He has given us. He wants all those who have been made right with God through Jesus' death and resurrection to live by faith[3]. This is why He must 'stir the nest' to force us out of our comfort zone and teach us to use our wings of faith so that we can fly and rise above our difficulties, obstacles, limitations and fears. God is glorified when we do!

---

[1]   Eagles lay between 1 to 3 eggs per year. It is rare for all 3 to survive.

[2]   John 1v12 (NIV): *Yet to all who did receive Him, to those who believed in His name, He gave the right to become children of God...*

[3]   Habakkuk 2v4 (NCV): *But those who are right with God will live by faith.*

Just when we think we have failed, He catches us and carries us on eagle's wings[4]. With His loving affirmations and encouragements, He lifts us up to try again!

Is God stirring your nest?

Below is a story of a woman who could have opted out of a very challenging position, but decided to believe God's word and to rise above her fears and limitations.

I Will Be With You!

I came to Lancaster in 2004 with my husband Graham after we got married in Malaysia. I was often left on my own during the daytime in the flat we rented. I felt very lonely in my new surroundings, but soon made friends with the owners of an Oriental shop in the city. Then I began to talk to God about my desire to find a job.

One day I was told about a supplier's need for a Malaysian lady to man a display of Malaysian products in a three-day exhibition in London. I took this stint and won the praise of my employers who then encouraged me to apply for the position of sales representative for this same big supplier of Oriental products from Malaysia, Thailand, Japan, Indonesia and the Philippines. The job description implied the need not only for the usual business and communication skills, but also for basic computer skills, familiarising oneself with the company's catalogue of ten thousand products, as well as driving to different places in the UK. Because the job would be based in Reading, I wasn't interested. However, after a few days, I was told I could be based in Lancaster if I wished! The company seemed very eager to hire me, but I hesitated to take the offer.

You see, I did not know how to use a computer, and could not even type! Maths would easily rob me of my confidence. Besides, I had lived in the UK for less than a year and I would have to drive to places I had not seen or even heard of before. But these were nothing compared to this: for twenty years I feared driving on the motorway. I wondered if it was wise for me to take the job knowing that I inevitably would have to take the motorway to the north, south, east and west of the country. I asked myself, "What will I do if it happens again, a panic attack on the fast lane?"

The memory of that time in 1984 when I was still a teenager was enough to cause my body to tremble with fear. My friend and I were travelling up north from my home city of Kuala Lumpur in Malaysia. My friend was driving and I was in the front passenger seat. We were on the Karak Highway, on a particularly dangerous stretch of motorway with a history of accidents. Driving at high speed, my friend foolishly

---

4   Exodus 19v4 (NIV): *…. how I carried you on eagles' wings and brought you to Myself.*

tried to overtake the lorry in front of us. To our horror, we saw another lorry coming straight towards us! We could not brake in time because of the speed my friend was driving at. We could not pull off the motorway to the left because that meant falling off a cliff. We had to quickly pull back into our lane, slamming the car onto the rear of the first lorry. Our car got smashed, but surprisingly, no one was hurt, not even I. The lorry's huge metal bumper came crashing into our car, but stopped inches from my stomach! This was when I realised that God's saving hand was on me.

However since then, I never ventured on motorways again, only feeling comfortable and safe on the city roads of Kuala Lumpur. A few years later, I had to drive to Malacca, another city, and found myself on the motorway for the first time since the accident. It was a short journey so I thought I'd be okay. However, panic attack overcame me. My blood pressure rose, my head ached and my vision blurred. All of a sudden, it looked as if the road ahead of me disappeared and I thought my car would topple over. I called on God and talked myself into being sensible. How did I finally get to my destination? It could only be God! That incident was a miracle, as was the story of how I escaped death the day of the accident on Karak Highway.

As I knelt on the floor of our flat in Lancaster agonising whether or not to accept the job offer, it dawned on me that God must be opening this door for me; for despite the fact that I had no sales experience and higher education to boast of, and not even a résumé to send with my application, I was being offered the job based in Lancaster! But would I cope driving up and down the UK on roads I had not driven on before? As I wrestled with my fear, I heard the Lord say, "I will be with you! I will be with you!"[5] With that assurance, I accepted the job.

The training period as sales rep proved to be quite an embarrassment and a challenge to me. I had to ask simple questions like how to turn on the laptop the company provided. I struggled typing with one finger as I looked for the correct letters. No wonder the other sales reps were secretly laughing at me, betting that I wouldn't last a month in the job!

To help me with the driving, Graham taught me some of the things I had to know about the roads and signs in the UK (like what 'junction' means). Before I would hit the road, we would sit down together, study the maps and sketch a route that I would take to get to the place where I would meet up with a customer. (Sometime later, the company gave me a car with satellite navigation, but that at times proved quite useless!)

---

[5] This promise appears several times in the Bible, such as in Exodus 3v12, Joshua 1v5, Isaiah 43v2.

As I took to the road, praying became a must even as I drove. On the country lanes, I would wonder if I was on the right road. And on the motorways, I would drive with fear and trembling. My objective was not only to get to where I needed to go, I also had to be there on time for the appointment. Sometimes, I would lose my way (even after following the sat nav's direction!) and had to stop and call Graham for advice. Once I reached the place, I had to tackle another challenge, that of finding a parking space. And after all that, I had to face the customer who may be too busy to leave the till and to sit down with me while I opened the thick catalogue of ten thousand products. With pen in hand, I would take the orders, and would then email the orders to the company, making sure I entered the right details and double-checked the calculations.

Contrary to expectations, I did not quit after a month! A few months later, I called my boss and informed him that he had mistakenly deposited more than my salary in my bank account. He told me he had not made a mistake. In fact, he had given me a pay rise because the company was very pleased with my performance! After nearly a year in the job, I was not only able to retain all my customers, but I was also able to open eight new accounts for the company.

With regards to my fear of driving on motorways, I did pretty well considering that despite myself, I was able to get to London, Reading, Sunderland, Leeds, Scotland, and other places. One day after a long drive back to Lancaster, I realised that I could drive on the motorway with no more fear. My phobia had been broken – and in a foreign country! I fell on my knees on the same floor of our flat, this time worshipping and thanking God.

Ultimately, I had to decide not to accept the promotion which required me to be away from home for longer periods. So after a year in the job, I decided to resign to start a family. However, I will always be grateful to God for the experience. Through the job, God not only gave me a good sum of money, He also helped me gain more confidence and broke my phobia. I discovered through my experience that indeed the One who gave me this promise is faithful: "I will be with you!"

- Christina (Lancaster, England)
March 2011

Father God, forgive me for the times I was timid to take risks when I could tell that You were stirring my nest, nudging me to try my wings. Help me to step out in obedience to You and with confidence in the faith of Jesus that You have given me. Thank You that You can be trusted to help me overcome my fears and limitations. Each time You stir my nest, help me to step out and use my wings. My desire is to use the faith Jesus gave me to its fullest potential so that Your name may be glorified through me. Amen!

Week 11: At Rest in the Storm

I sought the Lord and He answered me; He delivered
me from all my fears. (Psalm 34v4, NIV)

The eagle is a symbol of power, freedom and transcendence. One reason for this is the eagle's response to storms. They don't frighten the eagle! Most animals will hide during a storm, but not the eagle. Like other animals, it can sense a storm coming. It perches on the highest point it can find. There it gathers information about the storm's speed and direction. It then adjusts its feathers and flies right into the midst of the storm. Using the wind to its advantage, the eagle stops flapping its powerful wings and allows the strong winds to lift it higher where it can soar above the storm clouds. With wings at rest as it soars, an eagle can reach great heights (up to ten thousand feet or more). This is especially useful when the eagle has to traverse great distances during migration or seasonal flights.

Storms of life come against us, but we do not have to be frightened and be overcome by them. If we choose to look at them through God's perspective, we will see these crises as opportunities to train ourselves to use our wings of faith (the faith of Jesus) to their fullest potential. We can make these storms work for us by using them to transcend our fears and limitations and to move on to a new level of maturity. With the wind of the Holy Spirit beneath our wings, we can soar above the storms of life with the tranquillity that faith in God can bring.

In the English rendition of Psalm 91v9-10, many versions say about those who make God their 'dwelling place': *no evil shall befall you*[1]. This does not mean that the believer will not face storms or troubles in life. It means that his troubles have been screened by God's love and allowed by Him for his ultimate good (Week 52), much like the parent eagle that stirs the nest and pushes the eaglet out so that it will learn to fly, a skill that is important for its survival. The New Living Translation of Psalm 91v9-10 is easier to understand: "If you make the Lord your refuge, if you make the Most High your shelter, *no evil will conquer you*." How can evil conquer you if, through God's love, the troubles satan throws at you become your stepping stones to being all that God wants you to be? Having this mindset helps us to be at rest even in the storm.

Here is a story of how God used a literal storm to deliver a lady in Texas from fear, torment and trauma. May it encourage you to be at rest in your storm!

---

[1] Psalm 91v9-10 (NKJV): *Because you have made the Lord, who is my refuge, even the Most High, your dwelling place, no evil shall befall you...*

Shirley's Story

Twenty years ago a man broke into my house and tried to rape me and murder me while I slept. To make a long story short, I came out of sound sleep screaming the name of Jesus. I knew I would either get a miracle or go be with Him in an instant. His name prevailed – praise the Lord! As I screamed "Jesus" over and over and over, the man kept saying to me, "Shut up or I'll kill you. Shut up or I'll kill you." In addition to having his hands tightly around one side of my throat, he was also stabbing at me with a very large knife he had gotten from my kitchen. The miracle was, he didn't hit me, but the pillow had so many stab holes in it, it had to be thrown away. When terrified, humans cannot talk. They can scream a word or just scream, but cannot speak in sentences. God strengthened me to say a sentence: "Devil, I bind you in this man in the name of Jesus!"[2] .... and went right back to screaming "Jesus" over and over.

When I did this, the man snapped out of his drugged state, asking, "How did I get in here? Oh my God! I'm trying to rape and murder you! How did I get here?" I took that opportunity to jump out of bed, run down the hall into the den and went to the kitchen to wash the blood off me. It wasn't mine. It was his. He had cut a major artery in his wrist when he broke the glass in the back window of my house, and had bled heavily all the way through my house as he proceeded first to the kitchen to get a knife and to wrap his wrist with a lot of paper towels. Then he walked down the long hall to my bedroom to do his dastardly deed.

Once in the kitchen, while washing my hands and arms, I heard myself, like listening to another person speaking, say, "Johnny, Johnny! Jesus loves you so much. He died for you so you don't have to live like this"[3]. Then I remember thinking, "Who is that stupid woman saying such things to this man?" That was the only time in my life I have experienced the division of the soul and spirit. The Holy Spirit through my spirit was issuing a statement of love to this criminal, while my soul was condemning him.

I discovered during the ordeal in the dark that this was a man named Johnny who was visiting relatives who lived next door to me. As he and I sat in the den for a little while after I had washed my hands and arms, I talked to him about Jesus and receiving Him as Saviour and Lord. Then I felt impressed to get him out of the house. As long as I talked to him, he would follow me, so as I spoke to him, I walked backward through

---

[2] There is power in the name of Jesus! Philippians 2v9-11 (NIV) says: *Therefore God exalted Him to the highest place and gave Him the name that is above every name, that at the name of Jesus every knee should bow, in heaven and on earth and under the earth, and every tongue acknowledge that Jesus Christ is Lord, to the glory of God the Father.*

[3] Romans 5v8 (NIV): *But God demonstrates His own love for us in this: While we were still sinners, Christ died for us.*

the den, out the front door, down the sidewalk and across the driveway to the fence and convinced him to go back next door and go to sleep.

It was now about 11:30 or midnight. I called a good friend and calmly told her what had happened, that I didn't feel like staying alone, and asked if she would come over. She yelled over the phone that she would be at my house as soon as she could drive there. On the way, she picked up a woman I barely knew, who has since become a good friend, and as we sat in my den and talked about this, they asked when the police were coming and had I called them. I was in shock and had not called the police; so, they did it for me. The police erroneously thought it was a crime in progress and sent SIX policemen and a forensics team! They said they got more DNA evidence from my house than they have in most crimes, that the state would prosecute him for me and I would not have to go to court. He went to jail for only two years because he hadn't killed me, and although he almost bit one of my fingers off and gave me huge bruises on one side of my neck, I was not otherwise physically harmed.

I was understandably so nervous after this that I started walking with a friend for exercise. Thirty days after the attack, I was walking with this friend on a high school track in the area at dusk when a man grabbed me from behind and tried to drag me off the field. This time I just screamed. Thirty days after that, someone woke me by trying to take the screen off my bedroom window. I phoned a neighbour who came over and scared whoever it was away.

I lived in torment after these events for another three months. I was so afraid I burned every light inside and outside my house day and night. I would also push a heavy piece of furniture in front of my bedroom door before retiring to sleepless and anxiety-laden nights. In those three months, I asked God daily when was He going to deliver me from this fear and torment. I reminded Him that David had said, "I sought the Lord…. and He delivered me from ALL my fears" (Psalm 34v4, ESV).

At the end of those three months, a hurricane struck my part of Texas. I could tell it had hit when I was awakened by the extreme quiet and darkness (due to power failure). I got up and felt my way to the bedroom door, pushed the furniture out of the way, felt my way down the dark hall to the kitchen, felt for the drawer with the matches, lit my kerosene lamps (for decoration until they were needed), let my dog in from outside and sat on the couch and waited. All of a sudden I realised I had been paddling around in a pitch-black dark house – AND I HAD NO FEAR! To this day, it has never returned. Praise the Lord!

God has creative ways of setting us free, and afterward, I found it amusing that He would use a hurricane. I do indeed know by experience what trauma is, and I can say, "Thanks be unto God who ALWAYS causes us to triumph in Christ Jesus![4]"

- Shirley (Houston, Texas, USA)
September 2011

"Whoever dwells in the shelter of the Most High will rest in the shadow of the Almighty. I will say of the Lord, 'He is my refuge and my fortress, my God, in whom I trust'" (Psalm 91v1-2, NIV).

My loving heavenly Father, thank You for Jesus who made it possible for me to come to You as Your child. Thank You that in You I can be at rest in the storm because You are my refuge and my fortress. Thank You that You are able to deliver me from all my fears and cause all storms in my life to work for my benefit in the end. I put my trust in You!

---

[4]   2 Corinthians 2v14 (NASB): *But thanks be to God, who always leads us in triumph in Christ.*

Week 12: Eagle's Eye – Hindsight, Insight and Foresight

I will pour out my Spirit on all kinds of people. Your sons and daughters will prophesy, your old men will dream dreams, and your young men will see visions. (Joel 2v28, NCV)

The large front-facing eyes (placement that gives good binocular vision) of the eagle are densely packed with sensory cells, about one million light-sensitive cells per square millimetre of retina, five times more than in humans. An eagle can see five basic colours due to its five classes of cones (compared to three types of cones, hence three basic colours, in humans), allowing it to spot even camouflaged prey a long distance away. The eagle also has two foveae in each eye (the fovea is the part of the retina where vision is sharpest), compared to only one in humans.

Another interesting fact is that although an eagle cannot move its eyes as much as humans can, it can twist its head to about 270°, just a quarter short of a full circle. These and other facts account for the eagle's acute depth perception, telescopic sight, amazing peripheral vision and a keen awareness of what is in front of it, to its left and right, and behind it. It is as if the eagle can see the past, present and future.

Besides its ability to soar, perhaps it is because of the above that the eagle has been associated with revelation and the prophetic. Revelation (communication or message from God) is related to prophecy (the proclamation of God's revelation). Just as the prophetic book of Revelation, the last book of the Bible, is the revelation of Jesus in the past, present and future, the prophetic has to do with proclaiming a hindsight (past), insight (present) or foresight (future) message from God. This proclamation is a prophetic or *rhema* word from the Lord (Week 8)[1].

A hindsight revelation from God looks at the past and interprets it. It highlights the lessons that must be learned from past events to help us develop deeper spiritual roots. It also gives us understanding of what God had done to give us guidance for the present and the future.

Insight revelation gives us insight into the will of God and supplies us with an interpretation of current events from God's perspective. It reveals to us what God is saying now to enable us to respond properly to the present and to keep in step with what God is doing.

---

[1]   A *rhema* word must always be tested and we need discernment to do this. If the message is really from the Lord, it will never contradict God's written word or *logos*.

Foresight revelation gives us foresight into the plan of God. It predicts future events to help us prepare for them. It tells us the direction God wants us to take based on what He intends to do. It gives encouragement by showing that God knows the future and is in control of it. If necessary, it also gives warnings of coming judgment or disciplinary actions of the Lord.

Joel 2v28 above implies that we would hear prophetic words from other believers. God sends us these words to bring us closer to Him and to aid in maturing us in Christ. But they must be viewed with wisdom, something that we get as we pray and study the word of God ourselves.

The story below reflects the hindsight, insight and foresight aspects of prophecy, the 'eye of the eagle' gift of the Holy Spirit.

In the Right Place at the Right Time

Have you ever wondered if you've made the right decision about something, or if you are in the right place, the place where God wants you to be? I want to share with you stories of two specific times the Lord gave my family His assurance in very special ways that we were in the right place at the right time.

In 1993, my wife, daughter and I moved to semi-rural England from the sunny Cote d'Azur region of southern France. It was a job that brought us to Monaco, where our daughter was born. For almost seven years, we lived in France just outside Monaco, and when my contract finished, God answered our prayer and gave me a job in an ecological centre based at Grange-over-Sands in Cumbria (England). The contrast in sights and smells between our new surroundings in Grange-over-Sands (houses near farmlands and quaint village shops) and that of southern France (heavily-built up areas with lots of shops nearby) was so stark that we wondered if we would end up having sheep for neighbours!

I remember the day we arrived at the centre to get the key to the cottage which the secretary found for us to occupy temporarily. When the secretary told us she lived in the village of Allithwaite, I inquired if she knew the person to whom a letter we were carrying was addressed, a letter which a couple from our church in Monaco asked us to post once we arrived in the UK. During their trip to Israel, our friends in Monaco met a young couple from Cumbria, a Dr. and Mrs. Gray who lived in Allithwaite. Our friends struck up a friendship with the Grays especially because they too were Christians. We were thrilled to be informed by the secretary that Dr. Gray was actually a staff member at the centre. It was very reassuring to know that God brought us to a place where there were Christians like us! Through the Grays, we met other Christian staff members at the centre, and through them, Christians in the town and the surrounding villages. Several months later, one of the Christian ladies at the centre told me that for some time, she and the other Christian staff had been praying that God would bring another Christian family to the centre. She believed we were God's answer to that prayer! How could one not be moved by this? To us, it was confirmation from the Lord that indeed, we were in the right place at that particular season of our lives.

We lived in Grange-over-Sands (no, our neighbours were not sheep!) for about ten years, then moved to Cockermouth in north Cumbria when I took another job. Sometime after we moved to our new house, my wife received a word from a prophetic man she met in the Philippines that God was going to give us an "ideal house". At that time we thought the message was quite late so we didn't think much of it. Our new house was newly built, nice and spacious so we thought that it was certainly ideal for us. Sometime later, we got another word via email from a prophetic lady in the Philippines. In her email she said that as she was praying for us, God gave her a 'vision' (a picture in her mind) of "a little brown house with a pathway through the garden". She then asked if this described our new home. Well, our house was red-brown, but it could hardly be called little, and there was a pathway around the house, but not through the garden. So we thought her vision was not accurate.

After two years, our daughter left home to attend Lancaster University. When she did, our ideal home didn't seem ideal anymore; it felt too big and lonely for just two people. When my contract finished the next year, my wife and I decided to move and we felt that God was calling us to Lancaster. Although our daughter thought at that time that we were moving to Lancaster because she was there, my wife and I strongly felt that Lancaster was indeed the place the Lord wanted us to move to.

After a long and tiresome process of viewing houses, we finally found a house in Lancaster. Because a good amount of work was needed to improve the house (refurbishing the kitchen and bathrooms, new floors for the living and dining rooms, not to mention a new boiler), we wondered if we made the right decision. One day, not long after we had settled in the house, my wife happened to look out of the dining room glass door, taking in the details of the garden, particularly the small brown wooden shed and the concrete paving slabs that were lined up to make a pathway from the shed through to the end of the garden. She recalled the vision of the lady from the Philippines, that of "a little brown house with a pathway through the garden" and this thought came to her: Could it be that the Lord gave the lady a vision of our garden in Lancaster with the brown shed (which looks like a little brown house!)?

We also remembered the other prophetic word about the 'ideal house'. We then realised that the Lord was referring not to our house in Cockermouth, but to the house in Lancaster because the refurbishments done to this house were according to our own specifications, making it ideal for us! Actually, the same person who gave us the 'ideal house' message also told us about a vision he saw of a canoe in the water when he learned about our plan to leave Cockermouth. We were reminded of this much later when we saw people canoeing up and down the Lancaster Canal as well as the River Lune. (Our house is not far from both.) We concluded that the Lord gave us those prophetic words and pictures because He knew we would not stay long in Cockermouth and that we needed encouragement and confirmation that we were indeed in the centre of His will when we moved to Lancaster.

We moved to Lancaster unsure what the future held for us, but through those confirmations, we came to know that God indeed orders the steps of the "godly"[2], those whose sins are forgiven because they have placed their faith in the finished work of His Son, Jesus, at the cross. Therefore, we can trust that God meant what He said in His promise, "For I know the plans I have for you, plans to prosper you and not to harm you, plans to give you hope and a future" (Jeremiah 29v11, NIV). Part of that plan is to bring us to the right place at the right time!

- Arthur (Lancaster, England)
September 2011

Thank You Father that You are interested in every detail of my life. Thank You that You have a good plan for me. Please grant me hindsight into the things You've done for me in the past so that my roots in You can grow deeper. Grant me insight into what You are doing now so that I can keep in step with You through my obedience, not going ahead of You and not lagging behind. Grant me foresight into Your plan for my life so that I can prepare for it with the help of Your Holy Spirit. In Jesus' name I pray, amen.

---

[2]   Psalm 37v23 (NLT): *The Lord directs the steps of the godly. He delights in every detail of their lives.*

Week 13: Speak Lord, I Am Listening

My sheep hear My voice, and I know them, and they follow Me.
(John 10v27, NKJV)

As we have noted before, the eagle is often a symbol of revelation and the prophetic. To a large part, the prophetic is about 'hearing' from God.

In the reading in Week 1, we learned that God wants to communicate with us. The stories in this book tell us how the storytellers heard from God, such as through dreams, visions (mental pictures or images), impressions, prophetic messages given by other believers, and most importantly, through the written word of God.

It is exciting to receive prophetic words from others, but we need to hear God ourselves. John 10 verse 27 (see above) reveals that all believers in Jesus (Jesus' 'sheep') should hear His voice in their spirit. In this sense, all believers are prophetic. However, because of the cacophony of voices trying to get our attention, we must learn to recognise God's voice so that we can discern correctly if the voice we hear is really His. The more we know Him, the more we will recognise His voice. We get to know Him better by spending time in His presence through worship, prayer, studying the Bible and meditating on His word, and fellowship with other believers.

John 10v27 also says that God's children follow or obey Him. Our obedience may involve telling someone what we heard from God, nothing less and nothing more, in love and without compromise.

Below is a story of what John heard from God and how his obedience blessed many. It is a good illustration of the purpose of prophecy: to strengthen, encourage and comfort God's people[1].

God Doesn't Only Talk to Big Shots

I'd just flown in from Manila. It was late and I was glad to be in Singapore again with old friends after the dusty roads and dodgy hotels. Everything seemed to be going well with the spiritual and humanitarian projects I had visited in Taiwan and the Philippines. The workers I had visited were all doing well and this was my last but one call before heading for home in the UK. Four hectic weeks away from my

---

[1] 1 Corinthians 14v3 (NCV): *But those who prophesy are speaking to people to give them strength, encouragement, and comfort.*

family was quite enough and a couple of days here in Singapore to get my breath back would be wonderful.

My host and friend was a rural evangelist and editor of the Singapore Assemblies of God magazine. When I informed him that my last call was to be a day in Kuala Lumpur to set up a conference for the next year, he told me that the next day, all of their ministers were going up to a mountain resort near Kuala Lumpur in Malaysia for their annual conference and suggested that I might like to join them as a guest. This didn't sound like a very good idea to me as I wanted to get the job done in KL and then head home, so I declined his kind offer.

The next morning I saw them off to the airport and began writing my director's report of my trip. By mid-morning this was completed and I was taking some time out to be quiet and contemplative. It was then that I heard the voice. Not an audible voice as I had once heard a year or two before, just a compelling conviction that I should be at that conference. I was familiar with that feeling from past experiences when God had directed me in ways I had not planned. One friend of mine calls it "a nudge from God". Obeying it had always ended up with something wonderful happening. I hadn't a clue what it was all about this time, but I certainly wasn't going to miss out on something special. The scripture came to mind, "You will hear a voice behind you saying, 'This is the way, walk in it'"[2]. I called Changi Airport to bring my flight forward by one day and was told that there were no seats available at all on any flights up to KL that day. There were even a number of people on a waiting list.

The voice wouldn't go away so I called another friend who drove me to the airport where they confirmed that there were no seats available and that there were people waiting hopefully ahead of me. My friend offered to drive me back to my digs but I told her that I would hang around and see what would happen. I bought a coffee and a magazine and sat tight. After a while the Singapore Airlines desk called me over. They had a seat for me on the next flight out which was in about twenty minutes. One booked passenger had failed to show up and there had been three people waiting for seats ahead of me. One of them had given up and gone home a few minutes earlier and the other two were a married couple who needed two seats. So-oooo, I got on that plane!

The Genting Highlands resort is high up in the hills about an hour and a half from KL so I took a taxi from the airport. The road twists and winds ever upwards out of the oppressive heat of the city into the cool mountain air. I asked the driver if he could pick me up the next morning to take me back to KL and he agreed. Then he asked me why I was going up there for just one night and I found myself saying that I was going to speak at a conference.

---

[2]   Isaiah 30v21 (NIV): *Whether you turn to the right or to the left, your ears will hear a voice behind you, saying, "This is the way; walk in it."*

"Mosey, you're a liar." The almost audible voice inside my head embarrassed me, but I was so convinced that I had spontaneously and unwittingly spoken the truth that I began to put some thoughts on paper as we wound our way up the mountain.

I arrived just as the conference delegates were going in for their first evening, pre-meeting meal and was greeted with some surprise and joy by my friends who found me a seat at their table. The General Superintendent of their churches came over and welcomed me and began to chat. Now, Singaporeans seldom come straight to the point and this man was no exception. He went on and on with inconsequential pleasantries until I began to wonder if I had made a mistake. I have found that such doubts are often a part of the deal when seeking to be obedient to the voice of God.

Then it came. Their main speaker had missed his flight in Bangkok and wouldn't be there until the next morning. He was due to give the keynote opening address that evening and would I be so kind as to take his place. I replied that God had already spoken to me and I had come prepared to do just that! I was given a bedroom and spent a little time getting myself physically and spiritually ready after my long and very sticky day.

Of course, the Lord had omitted to tell me (or hadn't I been listening?) what the theme of the conference was. "Oh, well, that was too bad!", I thought. "They would just have to have what God had given me." I walked into the conference hall through a door at the side of the platform and gazed nervously on the couple of hundred faces in the congregation. The Superintendent beckoned me over to sit on the front row next to him. As I sat down and faced the platform, I looked up and saw a huge banner announcing the theme of the conference. It was exactly what I had prepared whilst sitting in the back of the taxi on the way up – "WALKING IN THE SPIRIT"!

The sense of God's presence in the place was almost tangible. I have seldom been in a place where it was so easy to minister God's Word. The thoughts that had come to me in the taxi formed the basis of the message and from them flowed others. I can't remember exactly what I said now but the anointing of God's Holy Spirit was heavy upon me[3]. At the end of the meeting I appealed to the people to leave behind

---

[3] The Bible doesn't define 'anointing'. In Old Testament times, the kings and priests of Israel were anointed with oil as a sign of their consecration for God's service. Since all believers are consecrated ('set-apart') to God, they are all 'anointed'. We see, however, another aspect of the anointing in Acts 10v38 (NIV): *"... how God anointed Jesus of Nazareth with the Holy Spirit and power, and how He went around doing good and healing all who were under the power of the devil, because God was with Him."* From this we can deduce that 'anointing' also refers to the manifest presence of the Holy Spirit in a person as well as His supernatural enabling upon that person to do what God wants to be done for His glory.

their secure, human, fleshly, journey as they sought to serve the Lord and to embark on this awesome, sometimes scary, adventure with God. Unknown to me, there had been considerable tension between some of the leading brethren in the movement. As I concluded, I was amazed to see some of these mature, godly men prostrate on their faces before the Lord, asking for forgiveness. My friend told me later that a real work of grace had been done that day.

The next morning, my driver took me down to Kuala Lumpur. I quickly concluded my business there and I was soon on my way home. At the time I had just got on with doing what I had to do, but as I looked back I realised that God had been most gracious in using a very ordinary chap like me in a rather special way to achieve His purposes. I'm glad that this sort of thing doesn't happen every day; it would be somewhat stressful. But I'm equally glad that God doesn't only talk to big shots. I'm looking forward to the next time!

- John Mosey (Arnside, Cumbria, England)
May 2011

"Speak, Lord. I am Your servant and I am listening" (1 Samuel 3v10, NCV).

Father God, teach me to recognise Your voice when You are speaking to me. Help me to receive whatever You tell me, even if it is a word of correction. If it's something You want me to do, help me to be obedient to You. Grant me discernment especially when the message comes to me through dreams, visions or prophetic words spoken by others. If these are really from You, then please send me confirmation, understanding and wisdom so that I can act according to Your will. Speak Lord Jesus, for Your servant is listening!

Week 14: In the Shadow of Your Wings

Keep me as the apple of Your eye; hide me in the
shadow of Your wings. (Psalm 17v8, NIV)

Psalm 91 verse 4 gives a beautiful metaphor of God's protection over His children, as a parent eagle protects its young with its wings: "He will cover you with His feathers, and under His wings you will find refuge; His faithfulness will be your shield and rampart" (NIV). To the Jews, the *tallit* or prayer shawl represents the 'wings of God'. They drape it over them as a sign of being "under the shadow of His wings", that is, under God's protection.

One way God protects His people is by exposing the devil's deceptions. Light exposes things that are hidden, hence why light is used as a symbol for revelation. Through the light of revelation, God's prophetic people are able to discern correctly and make right judgments. This is why 1 Thessalonians 5v20-21 admonishes us: "Do not scoff at prophecies, but test everything that is said" (NLT). We need to test every hindsight, insight and foresight message we hear to see if it is from God. How can we tell?

Revelation 19v10 declares that "the testimony of Jesus is the spirit of prophecy" (NKJV). This means that a true *rhema*[1] or prophetic word from God ultimately points people to Jesus. This is because the Holy Spirit, who gives the true gift of prophecy[2], always exalts and glorifies Jesus[3]. It also means that a true *rhema* word from God reflects and does not contradict the teachings of Christ (His testimony) as they appear in God's written word or *logos*, the Bible (Week 8).

2 Corinthians 13v1 (NIV) states that "every matter must be established by the testimony of two or three witnesses". A true *rhema* from God does not contradict His *logos* and He also confirms it. To discern correctly, we therefore need to ask God for 'witnesses' to confirm a personal *rhema* word or any revelation we received. One of the "two or three witnesses" may be the Holy Spirit impressing on us that the message is really from Him. In any case, He will decide how to confirm the message to us and when.

---

[1] *Rhema* (Greek) means 'a now word' or 'a word in season'. See Week 8.
[2] 1 Corinthians 12v4 (NLT): *There are different kinds of spiritual gifts, but the same Spirit is the source of them all.*
[3] John 16v14 (NIV): *He* [the Holy Spirit] *will glorify Me* [Jesus] *because it is from Me that He will receive what He will make known to you.*

The fact that God wants to confirm His *rhema* words helps to free us from the fear of getting a misleading word, and even from the fear of giving a wrong one! The fear of making mistakes stops many Christians from stepping out in faith to share with others what God had revealed to them. To succumb to such fear is to disobey God and to give in to satan's intimidation. If God tells us to share a message with someone ('if', because sometimes the revelation we receive is a matter for us to pray about and not to share with anyone), we need to be both bold by stepping out in obedience, and humble by admitting we could be wrong and by advising the person we address to pray for wisdom, understanding and for confirmation of the message.

Here is a story of a woman who received a true and encouraging *rhema* word, but which the devil twisted. When the Spirit of wisdom and understanding gave her the correct interpretation, she finally realised the message was a great blessing for it spoke of God's love and protection over her.

Burdened by God's Love

It's astounding how we can believe the lies of the devil. Even though I have personally experienced God's overwhelming love multiple times, in January 2010 I fell prey to one of the worse lies I've believed, a rather bizarre lie: God loved me TOO much! One evening during a prayer service, our pastor encouraged the congregation to form small groups and listen prophetically for what God was saying to us about others in the group. Having grown up in a more traditional environment, at age twenty-five this would be the first time anyone would prophesy over me and also the first time for me to listen for what God wanted to say to others through me. I had no expectations, but didn't want to hinder what God wanted to do so I prayed with an open mind.

What I remember most from that night were the words spoken over me, "Men reject you, but you are the apple of God's eye." I should have asked for clarification, but instead I took that as the least encouraging word anyone could have given me! God loves everyone equally so how could I be the "apple of His eye", His favourite? I was twenty-five, single and had just spent the beginning of that week praying about a boy I liked because I didn't know whether he liked me too.

Somehow I felt the word I received implied that because I was God's favourite, He would not allow that guy to ever reciprocate my feelings because God loved me too much to share me. I would therefore not be allowed to experience the joy of falling in love with someone who would reciprocate. What God had intended to be an encouragement became this twisted lie that led me to feel God's love was burdensome!

For the rest of that week, I tried to shake it off, knowing it sounded ridiculous. I told myself that the person likely lacked experience in the prophetic as I did and perhaps she misheard or misspoke what she heard. I told myself that it was ridiculous to believe God loved me more than others. But it was too late; I had allowed my feelings to dictate what I believed, overriding the knowledge of God's truth. Looking back, I now know it was my pride and fear that enabled that lie to take root – pride from a belief that I could do more for God than others could (and hence be loved by God more than He loves others), and fear that this therefore meant I'm disqualified from partaking in the other pleasures of life including marriage. Oh the mess of sin! It's embarrassing to even admit it.

Over the next few months I lived in a state of defeat, feeling burdened by God's love. Eventually I shared this with two close Christian friends who immediately said I was believing a lie. They spoke His words over me: God's love is not burdensome[4], His love is unconditional[5], He does not show favouritism and loves all His children equally[6], and God withholds no good thing from those who do what is right[7]. This was a great turning point for me because truth liberates. As soon as these words of truth were spoken, the burden I had felt for the past few months simply vanished. At once I could smile again earnestly. Although these were all verses I'd read before, truths I had at one point known and understood, being freshly reminded of them dismantled the lie which had been holding me captive.

What sweet revelation! Yet, one year later, I was back in the same pit, believing the lie that God's love is burdensome. This time, it was attached to a different situation.

I spent about one and a half years working at a job I did not like. I was not growing, it was not utilising my skills, I was not passionate about the end result, and I didn't connect with the people I worked with. The only reason I didn't quit was because I knew God had given me that job and I wanted to allow Him to accomplish His purpose for it. Even so, I did occasionally apply for other jobs and felt God was going to give me a specific one. When I didn't even get selected for an interview, I became disappointed in God. I asked Him what in the world was His purpose for me in the

---

[4]   1 John 5v3 (NKJV): *For this is the love of God, that we keep His commandments. And His commandments are not burdensome.*

[5]   Romans 5v8 (NIV): *But God demonstrates His own love for us in this: While we were still sinners, Christ died for us.*

[6]   Acts 10v34 (NIV): *Then Peter began to speak: "I now realise how true it is that God does not show favouritism..."*
     Romans 2v11 (NIV): *For God does not show favouritism.*

[7]   Psalm 84v11 (NLT): *For the Lord God is our sun and our shield. He gives us grace and glory. The Lord will withhold no good thing from those who do what is right.*

job I didn't like. The only reason I could think of and the only thing others seemed to be affirming was that God had placed me there so I could make a difference in the lives of the other employees (whom I didn't connect with!). While that is a great and noble reason and I love pouring His truth into others, I was dissatisfied that this was my only purpose there. I felt cheated! I felt that because I knew God's love and was faithful to respond to it, my hopes and dreams of a meaningful career encompassing my passions were crushed because I had a duty to pour into the people at this job-site. Once again, I felt burdened by God's love, this time for others.

Eventually, a series of events led me to feel God was opening a door for me to quit my job. While some of these were difficult to face, I was in all honesty extremely relieved! God showed me three trees side by side: one had a regular amount of leaves, the second had only dry branches, and the third had abundant leaves. I believe this was a picture of my journey through the past two years. I had started out with many leaves, full of hope for the future. But as life went on, I became disappointed in God and lost my leaves. I went through a wintery period of drought, dry of the Holy Spirit because I wasn't placing my hopes in Christ. I had placed my hopes in a career and when I could not see how a meaningful one could emerge, I started to doubt His love and kindness for me in placing me at that job. I had been unable to see His purpose so I had become overwhelmed with anxiety because I could not trust God's wisdom. However, the third tree showed that the wintery period would come to an end! Up ahead would be a very fruitful and life-filled stage. Life-filled because oh so kindly, God told me it was Him who placed in me my passion for a career in international development and He would be faithful to fulfil it[8]. God's plans for me are magnificent, not because I deserve them, but because He is kind and faithful. He promises good to His children!

Only weeks after my last day at that job, I went to church on a Saturday morning to hear Steve Backlund, a guest speaker from Redding, California, who'd come to Fort Worth for the weekend with his prophetic team from the School of the Supernatural. After his message, my friend and I went to speak with the people in his prophetic team. One of them prophesied first to my friend and then to me. Everything he said to my friend was precisely correct. Then he spoke to me and exclaimed, "Woa!!! God wants you to know that you are the apple of His eye!" He went on but I remember only the intensity of the "woa" because following was the exact wording I'd received one year earlier! I still thought it was a very strange message, but since two strangers gave me that word, I decided to google it.

---

[8] Psalm 37v4 (NASB): *Delight yourself in the Lord and He will give you the desires of your heart.*

I discovered that to be called, "the apple of God's eye" means: 1) When He looks at me, He sees a reflection of Himself[9], and 2) He protects me intensely[10]. The eye is one of the most protected areas of the body (eyebrows, eyelashes, blinking capability, etc.). What a fun word for God to give me AGAIN!

Unfortunately I missed it the first time around. This time though, it meant so many things and it was also confirmation that I was where God wanted me to be. Unemployed and lacking hopeful prospects, God was speaking to me that He would protect me, that His eyes were focused on me. I received this truth and began to rest in the promises of God, submitting my will and my anxious thoughts to the One whom I know is working on my behalf. I'm trusting in the Lord to direct my path[11]. Trusting is nowhere near as difficult as it used to be because I finally believe God delights in giving me good things[12].

- Evelyn (Fort Worth, Texas, USA)
May 2011

My dear Father in heaven, thank You that I am the apple of Your eye! Thank You for the promise of protection You give under the shadow of Your wings. Thank You that when You look at me, You see Jesus who lives in my heart. Help me to submit to the transforming work of Your Holy Spirit in me so that I can become more and more like Jesus[13]. Please help me to get rooted and grounded in Your word so that I can discern better the enemy's deceptions. Confirm to me any rhema word You want to give me through others, and help me to be bold and humble to share with others any message You want them to receive through me. I pray these things in Jesus' name, amen.

---

[9] In Hebrew, this idiom literally means 'little man of the eye' in reference to the tiny reflection of oneself that one can see in another person's pupil. God already sees Jesus in every believer, but we are also becoming more and more like Him in character through the transforming work of the Holy Spirit.

[10] Psalm 17v8 (CEV): *Protect me as You would Your very own eyes; hide me in the shadow of Your wings.*

[11] Proverbs 3v5-6 (NKJV): *Trust in the Lord with all your heart, and lean not on your own understanding; In all your ways acknowledge Him, and He shall direct your paths.*

[12] Matthew 7v11 (NLT): *So if you sinful people know how to give good gifts to your children, how much more will your heavenly Father give good gifts to those who ask Him.*

[13] 2 Corinthians 3v18b (NLT): *And the Lord – who is the Spirit – makes us more and more like Him [Jesus] as we are changed into His glorious image.*

Week 15: Resting in God's Promises

The Lord is faithful to His promises. (Psalm 145v13, GNT)

The eagle seems to understand wind currents and aerodynamics. It waits patiently on its perch for the right wind to come along. When it does, the eagle takes off and lets the wind take it forward and higher. Surrendering itself to the wind, it is at rest high up in the sky.

There was a man who flew his glider over the mountains in the US. He hit an updraft and decided to ride it as high as he could. When he got to about 15,000 feet (very high altitude for a glider), he saw eagles. With wings locked as they rode the wind so effortlessly, it looked like they were asleep in mid-air!

In the Hebrew language of the Old Testament, the word for wind is *ruach,* the same word used for 'spirit'. In the Greek language of the New Testament, the word used for wind is *pneuma*, which is also the word for 'spirit'. To spiritual eagles, the Holy Spirit is the wind beneath their wings. This was true even of Jesus, as the Gospel accounts of His life on earth show us.

One gets the impression on reading the Gospels that Jesus never acted independently of the Father, but waited for the Father's directions and only moved with the Holy Spirit. Even when it meant going through the horrible suffering of crucifixion, Jesus surrendered to the Father's will because He was sure the Father was able to fulfil and would do what was promised long before Jesus was born: "Therefore My heart is glad and My tongue rejoices; My body also will rest secure, because You will not abandon Me to the grave, nor will You let Your Holy One see decay" (Psalm 16v9-10, NIV). Jesus knew that the Father watches over His word to accomplish it[1]. He could therefore rest in the promise that the power of the Holy Spirit would raise Him from the dead and will also one day raise from the dead those who have made Jesus their Saviour and Lord[2] (Week 51).

God fulfils His promises according to His timetable and the fulfilment of God's promises to you requires your partnership with Him. He will do His part, but you also need to do yours: to believe and obey.

---

[1] Jeremiah 1v12 (NCV): *The Lord said to me, "You have seen correctly, because I am watching to make sure My words come true."*

[2] 2 Corinthians 4v14 (NIV) ... *because we know that the One who raised the Lord Jesus from the dead will also raise us with Jesus and present us with you in His presence.*

The story below relates how God reminded His daughter about His promises using a natural phenomenon in the sky – the rainbow, a symbol of God's covenantal promise[3].

Rainbow Connection

I consider 2000 and 2001 special years because very significant *kairos*[4] moments happened to me. I got saved in 1973, but only got baptised in the Holy Spirit[5] in 2000 because I rejected teachings about it and about the gift of speaking in tongues[6]. My baptism in the Spirit happened when an illness that caused multiple chemical and food sensitivities brought me to my knees. Sick of being sick, I begged God to reveal Himself to me in a new way. I was alone in my bedroom in the summer of 2000 when the Holy Spirit came and poured Himself on me and for the first time, I spoke in a language I didn't understand. I just knew I was praising and worshipping God.

This put me in a predicament (albeit a happy one). Months before, I complained to the vicar of our church about Nicky Gumbel's videos on the Holy Spirit and on the baptism in the Spirit and speaking in tongues, teachings that were included in the first Alpha Course[7] our church was running. I even wrote to Rev. Gumbel himself! Then I experienced those same things which catapulted me closer to the Lord and His purpose for my life.

It was in a training session for the church's second Alpha course when God gave me the chance to make good my repentance (about turn). Before those who had volunteered to help in the course, I shared my testimony of my baptism in the Holy Spirit. As if to make sure what I said would not be forgotten easily, the Lord interrupted the little demonstration my friend, Denise, and I did afterwards on how to pray for someone to receive the Holy Spirit. We were just pretending, my friend

---

3   Genesis 9v13 (NLT): *I have placed My rainbow in the clouds. It is the sign of My covenant with you and with all the earth.*

4   *Kairos* is a Greek word that means the right or opportune time. To Christians, it means God's appointed time.

5   Acts 2v4 (NIV): *All of them were filled with the Holy Spirit and began to speak in other tongues as the Spirit enabled them.* This recounts the story of Pentecost when the Holy Spirit baptised the believers after Jesus' ascension. Some speak of the baptism of/in the Holy Spirit as the first time a believer gets filled with the Holy Spirit. The Lord baptises us in the Holy Spirit so that we can be empowered to do His work.

6   When someone 'speaks in tongues', he lets the Holy Spirit speak through him in a human language unknown to him, or in a heavenly prayer language unknown to humans. See Appendix 3.

7   The Alpha Course, developed by Holy Trinity Brompton in London, is a course that presents the basics of the Christian faith. In 1990, Rev. Nicky Gumbel headed the program and expanded it. Today it is offered in several countries by many denominations.

ministering to me, and I receiving prayer. A few seconds after she laid hands on me and prayed in tongues, something like a bolt of electricity struck my feet and travelled up my body and onto my hands. I fell to the floor, my hands and body trembling. After a few minutes, I recovered and got up, more stunned than the others in the room. Acts 1v8 (NIV) says, "But you will receive *power* when the Holy Spirit comes on you; and you will be My witnesses in Jerusalem, and in all Judea and Samaria, and to the ends of the earth." I never thought God's power could be so *electrifying*!

I believe these experiences prepared me for my *kairos* of 2001. My family and I went to see relatives in the Philippines before visiting my husband's sister in Australia. We stayed in the Philippines only ten days, but the Lord made sure I would receive a download of revelation that would change my life forever! In those ten days, seven prophetic people prophesied to me on separate occasions. I knew I had to take them seriously after I heard them say things about me no one had told them before. I marvelled at the fact that no one's word contradicted another's; all messages were in agreement. I received corrections, affirmations, prophetic words about God's calling on my life, as well as words of God's precious promises to me. Before we left the Philippines, Leo, one of the seven and a pastor in his late twenties who eventually became my mentor in the prophetic, prayed for me and said, "When you see the rainbow, remember God's promises to you!"

We flew to Perth in Australia where we stayed for two weeks. While there I recalled the words spoken over me in the Philippines. On the day before we were to fly back to the UK, my sister-in-law's husband took my family and me for a drive. On the drive back, it started to rain, but the sun was still shining and I saw a bright rainbow in the sky. Behind it was another one, but less vivid. I was in awe because I had never seen a double rainbow before. As I stared at this phenomenon, someone startled me with the question, "Do you know what the rainbow stands for?" I looked at those with me in the car and I realised none of them had said anything to me. It seemed no one else heard the question. Then I thought it must be the Lord. I remembered the story of Noah in Genesis 9 and Leo's words and I answered, "A promise, Lord!" I will never ever forget what my Saviour then whispered to my heart, "Remember My promises to you!" What a precious moment that was!

That day, God showed me a double rainbow – rainbow to symbolise promise, and two of them to signify agreement between two parties making a covenant (my part is to believe and obey, His part is to empower and to bless). Since then, He draws a rainbow in the sky especially when I need His encouragement. I praise Him for the rainbow and for the fact that He's faithful to all His promises to me, some of which pertain to this book! (See Introduction for the story behind this book.)

(By the way, before I went to Penrith to attend the 2004 Alpha Conference, I wrote a letter of apology to Nicky Gumbel with the story of my experience.)

- Haide (Lancaster, England)
September 2011

The next story is from a young Dutch man who believed a promise in the Bible that the Holy Spirit impressed on his heart to claim as God's promise to him. Armed with the promise and the faith God had given, he stepped out to do his part.

A Promise Fulfilled

In the Bible we find an incredible promise about salvation: "Believe in the Lord Jesus, and you will be saved, you and your household" (Acts 16v31, NIV)[8]. Another scripture, Luke 19v9 (NLT), reads, "Salvation has come to this home today, for this man has shown himself to be a true son of Abraham." I believe this means that when one person in a family shows himself/herself to be a true son/daughter of Abraham (a true believer through faith in Jesus), then salvation comes to the whole family or 'household'[9]. This has become true in my life.

Four years ago, I accepted Jesus as my Saviour. One year later, I made Him the Lord over my life, my decisions and my plans. From that point onwards, He has not only changed my life, but also the lives of my siblings and my parents in incredible ways.

Shortly after I became a believer, my elder sister Johanna[10] also became a Christian. Two years later, the Holy Spirit urged me to talk to my family about the fact that Jesus welcomes children[11]. This was after we had eaten a meal together and we were still sitting at the table. As soon as I started talking, the Holy Spirit took over. I found myself in tears, begging my siblings to give their lives to Jesus. I believe that the Holy Spirit touched all of my siblings that day. On top of that, Jacob and Anna received Jesus into their lives.

---

[8] Also Acts 11v13b-14 (NIV): *Send to Joppa for Simon who is called Peter. He will bring you a message through which you and all your household will be saved.*

[9] But what about Jesus' words in Matthew 10v35 (NIV): *"A man's enemies will be the members of his own household"?* Jesus here is giving a warning to prepare people for what is inevitable when they decide to follow Him. It is not a promise because a promise demands faith as a response. You do not need faith to believe that you will encounter opposition from your own family when you turn to Jesus, but you do need faith to believe Acts 16v31.

[10] All names of Bart's siblings have been changed in this story.

[11] Matthew 19v14 (NIV): *Jesus said, "Let the little children come to Me, and do not hinder them, for the kingdom of heaven belongs to such as these."*

About six months later, my younger brother Peter and I were the only ones at home because the rest of the family was on holiday. It was a Sunday morning and he came with me to church. The sermon was about the importance of obedience to God. In his talk the preacher highlighted what the prophet Samuel said in 1 Samuel 15v23 (GNT): "Rebellion against Him [God] is as bad as witchcraft…" By that scripture I was motivated to be more obedient to God and to therefore listen to Him more radically. I soon heard His voice in my spirit when, as I was talking to Peter after the service, the Holy Spirit started to tell me what to say to my brother. So I said the things I heard the Spirit saying and soon Peter accepted Jesus as his Saviour and Lord.

At this point, all my siblings had given their lives to Jesus apart from my youngest sister, Lydia. I praise God that in a healing service in June 2011, she responded to an altar call and finally turned her life over to Jesus. That was the day God fulfilled His promise that salvation would come to my 'house'. In less than four years, all six of us siblings became members of God's family. Age didn't seem to matter since some of us were twelve years old and others were nineteen years old when we came to know Jesus. Was this coincidence? I don't think so! To me it was an answer to my prayer that was anchored on the promise in Acts 16v31 and Luke 19v9.

I believe that the salvation of all my siblings after my own is just the beginning of God's work in our family. I have dedicated my life to Jesus and will seek to work in His Kingdom here on earth, and so has my younger brother Jacob who is currently applying for a place in a Bible school. My father is showing a renewed interest in telling unbelievers about God. My mother is being used by God to revive her friends' relationships with Him and to help others fear God more than people or tradition. My sister Anna has shown that she is more concerned about what God thinks about her, than about what people think of what she does.

I praise God for what He has done and is doing in my family, and I am certain that He will complete His work just as He promised![12]

- Bart (Alblasserdam, The Netherlands)
August 2011

"I will worship toward Your holy temple, and praise Your name for Your loving kindness and Your truth; for You have magnified Your word above all Your name. In the day when I cried out, You answered me, and made me bold with strength in my soul" (Psalm 138v2-3, NKJV).

---

[12] Philippians 1v6 (NCV): *God began doing a good work in you, and I am sure He will continue it until it is finished when Jesus Christ comes again.*

Father God, because You have magnified Your word even above Your name, then I must take it seriously. Teach me what promises in the Bible are for me and help me to do my part in the fulfilment of those promises. If I need to do or say something, then make me bold with strength in my soul. Help me to trust You as to how and when You will fulfil Your promises. You may not be early, but You are never late; You are always on time! I praise You in the name of Jesus.

Week 16: The Word of God

Your word is a lamp to my feet and a light to my path.
(Psalm 119v105, NKJV)

Revelation is spiritual light. The very first recorded words of God are "Let there be light"[1]. In effect, He was saying, "Let there be revelation!" Revelation is an act of God, His act of communicating to us what otherwise we would not know: who God is, His hindsight, insight and foresight about events in our world, and His will and direction for His children. He has communicated these to us mainly through His written word.

Universally, God has revealed Himself through creation, but at various times and in different ways, He also spoke through the Jewish patriarchs and prophets. Their accounts are recorded for us in the Hebrew Scriptures (collectively called The Old Testament by Christians) which laid the foundation for the coming of the Messiah who would offer Himself as sacrifice for the atonement of our sins. Later on, God's revelation came to us through His Son, Jesus Christ, and through His disciples who wrote under the inspiration of the Holy Spirit[2]. The Gospels and the writings of these disciples constitute the New Testament which reveals Jesus as the One the Jews were waiting for, the Messiah or the Christ or Anointed One[3] of God, who was crucified, died and raised again for the salvation of mankind.

The thirty-nine books of the Old Testament and the twenty-seven books of the New Testament make up what is known as The Bible (from the Greek *ta biblia* which means, 'the books'). These sixty-six books of the Bible, the written word or *logos* of God, disclose to mankind the Holy One who must condemn sin, but who made a way for man's sins to be forgiven through and only through faith in God's one and only begotten Son. Undoubtedly, the Bible from Genesis to Revelation points to Jesus[4], the Living Word or *Logos* of God, "the Lamb of God who takes away the sin of the world"[5]. Reading the Old and New Testament books helps us to understand man's

---

[1] Genesis 1v3 (NASB): *Then God said, "Let there be light"; and there was light.*
[2] 2 Timothy 3v16 (NASB): *All Scripture is inspired* [literally, 'God-breathed'] *by God and profitable for teaching, for reproof, for correction, for training in righteousness.*
[3] 'Messiah' is from the Hebrew *Mashiah* (or *Mashiach, Masshiach, Massiach*) and 'Christ' is from the Greek *Khristos*. Both mean 'the Anointed One'.
[4] John 5v39-40 (NLT): *"You search the Scriptures because you think they give you eternal life. But the Scriptures point to Me! Yet you refuse to come to Me to receive this life."*
[5] John 1v29 (NIV): *The next day John* [the Baptist] *saw Jesus coming toward him and said, "Look, the Lamb of God, who takes away the sin of the world!"*

history through God's perspective. It makes us see the spiritual reality that actually, history is His-story, the story of Jesus, the only Messiah, the Saviour of the world.

However, mankind is not able to grasp the spiritual realities in the Bible with his cognitive skills. Not even a genius would be able to understand the spiritual truths revealed in the Bible without the direct illumination by the Holy Spirit[6]. This is His ministry which is available to those who humbly ask for it, the illumination of God's progressive revelation contained in the 66 books of the Holy Bible.

The following is a story about a man's discovery of God's progressive revelation of Jesus in the pages of the Old and New Testaments.

Lord of Life, Send My Roots Rain

A thousand or more men gathered at the Kotel, one of the most famous walls in the world. Once called the Wailing Wall, it is now known simply as the Kotel (Hebrew for wall) and it exercises a virtually irresistible gravitational pull to prayer. The centripetal spiritual force of this few metres of white Jerusalem stone draw Jewish people from all over the city and the world.

A few years ago I was part of that praying crowd. I had been visiting two brothers who have a wonderful little shop called *Shorashim* (Hebrew for roots) in the Old City when the call to pray came. Even though they knew that I was a Gentile[7] from Ireland, they invited me to join them in prayer for Israel as she faced yet another crisis. Over a thousand voices cried out as one, "*Adonai, hu elohenu!*" *Adonai* means 'Lord' and is the reverential way Jews address God, without pronouncing the divine name revealed to Moses at the burning bush[8]. *Hu* simply means 'he' and *elohenu* is a plural of majesty referring to our great God. As the cry went up, the truth sunk in: this was my God too! Creator, Liberator and God of the patriarchs was the One whom I believe had revealed Himself to me and to many other Gentiles in the person of *Yeshua Ben Joseph* ('Jesus, son of Joseph').

---

[6]   1 Corinthians 2v14 (NIV): *The man without the Spirit does not accept the things that come from the Spirit of God, for they are foolishness to him, and he cannot understand them, because they are spiritually discerned.*

[7]   Gentile = a non-Jew

[8]   Exodus 3v14 (NKJV): *And God said to Moses, "I AM WHO I AM." And He said, "Thus you shall say to the children of Israel, 'I AM has sent me to you.'"* The name "I AM" in Hebrew is transliterated YHWH. The vowels are not given because the Jews consider the divine name of God as too sacred to be uttered. See Appendix 1.

The Bible tells us that the person of Yeshua was the word made flesh and the fullness of deity in a human body[9]. A mystery indeed! Words of the late Abraham Joshua Heschel, a leading twentieth century rabbi, come to mind. Writing about God's glory in his book *God in Search of Man*[10], he said that the whole earth is full of His glory but we do not perceive it; it is within our reach but beyond our grasp. This could well be applied to the revelation of God's glory in the person of Yeshua who in the days of His earthly life was within the reach of people, but always beyond their grasp.

That moment at the Kotel marked a significant milestone for me, but the journey had started many years before, thanks to an inspiring Hebrew teacher at Westminster Seminary in Philadelphia, USA. Ray Dillard, who died prematurely at the height of his teaching and writing career, incarnated enthusiasm as well as embodied a wealth of knowledge. Every class, while intellectually stretching, was an eye-opening and fire-igniting experience. He followed the curriculum instituted by the risen Lord on the Emmaus Road (Luke 24v13-35) and guided us through the Hebrew scriptures (collectively called the Old Testament of the Christian Bible) that make up the *Torah* ('The Instruction'), the *Nevi'm* ('The Prophets') and the *Ketuvim* ('The Writings')[11], emphasising that Yeshua Himself was the interpretive key to the text. Unlike so much rather spurious Christian preaching that seems to jump from the third chapter of Genesis to the third chapter of John's Gospel, Ray taught us to value the progressive revelation of God in His historical covenantal relationship with Israel down through the centuries.

While Ray taught us, I imagined the Risen One walking me through the Scriptures that He knew so well. Marinated with the *Torah*, Yeshua was eminently well qualified to teach. I felt the thrill of being guided through the Genesis account by the One without whom nothing was made, and then I went through the saga of the patriarchs with the true seed of Abraham and the ultimate child of the promise[12]. In my mind I heard a "greater than Moses"[13] explaining how the historical liberation from Egypt was but the prototype of an even greater 'exodus' that He would accomplish, vanquishing

---

[9]   John 1v14 (ESV): *And the Word became flesh and dwelt among us, and we have seen His glory, glory as of the only Son from the Father, full of grace and truth.*

[10] *God in Search of Man: A Philosophy of Judaism*, 1955. Published by Farrar, Straus and Cudahy.

[11] *Torah* – Genesis, Exodus, Leviticus, Numbers, Deuteronomy; *Nev'im* – Joshua, Judges, Samuel, Kings, Isaiah, Jeremiah, Ezekiel, and the "12 Minor Prophets"; *Ketuvim* – Psalms, Proverbs, Job, Song of Songs, Ruth, Lamentations, Ecclesiastes, Esther, Daniel, Ezra and Nehemiah, Chronicles. The three collections make up the *Tanakh*, which is an acrostic of *Torah, Nevi'im* and *Ketuvim*.

[12] Yeshua (Jesus) is the true seed of Abraham (Galatians 3v16) and the ultimate child of the promise (Genesis 3v15, Isaiah 9v6-7, John 3v16).

[13] Hebrews 3v3 (NIV): *Jesus has been found worthy of greater honour than Moses, just as the builder of a house has greater honour than the house itself.*

the great enslaver, death, and setting His people free as the Passover Lamb[14] who died in place of His people.

The book of Leviticus, which many Christians consider boring, came to life as God's kindergarten, while Yeshua, the final High Priest and perfect offering[15], guided me through the intricacies of this exciting book. The whole wilderness experience recorded in Numbers took on deeper meaning for me. While the rabbis had taught that the *midbar* (Hebrew for wilderness) was the place Israel went to hear the *dabar* (Hebrew for word), I was taught to expect the guidance of the incarnate Word[16], Yeshua, who was lifted up like the serpent in the wilderness[17]. Our lessons from the *Torah* concluded with a penetrating insight on the nature of the divine-human covenantal relationship outlined in Deuteronomy and consummately expressed in the New Covenant cut in the blood of Yeshua.

As I apprehended the timeless truths of the books of the *Nev'im* being applied to our modern world by the ultimate exegete of existence Himself, I listened to the voice of God echoing in the words of the unique Man, Yeshua. Hence, history took on a new value to me. It is interesting to observe that Biblical Hebrew does not have a word for 'history' in its vocabulary. Instead, the word for 'memory' is used. 'History' is about what happened to other people in other places at other times in the past, but 'memory' is our story. In other words, when followers of Rabbi Yeshua open their Jewish Scriptures (from Genesis to Malachi), they are reading their story and not merely someone else's. I therefore discovered that the grand story of God's dealings with Israel is OUR story, and that our DNA is not pagan, but Jewish!

The Christian believer's roots are firmly embedded in Jewish soil. Isn't it truly striking that Paul, writing to the early believers in Gentile Corinth, spoke of *our* "fathers" who had been under the cloud, passed through the waters and had been

---

[14] 1 Corinthians 5v7b (ESV): *For Christ, our Passover Lamb has been sacrificed.*

[15] Hebrew 7v27-28 (NLT): *Unlike those other high priests, He does not need to offer sacrifices every day. They did this for their own sins first and then for the sins of the people. But Jesus did this once for all when He offered Himself as the sacrifice for the people's sins. The law appointed high priests who were limited by human weakness. But after the law was given, God appointed His Son with an oath, and His Son has been made the perfect High Priest forever.*

[16] John 1v1 (NIV): *In the beginning was the Word, and the Word was with God, and the Word was God.*

[17] Numbers 21v9 (NIV): *So Moses made a bronze snake and put it up on a pole. Then when anyone was bitten by a snake and looked at the bronze snake, he lived.* John 12v32 (NIV): *"And I [Jesus], when I am lifted up from the earth, will draw all people to myself."* The bronze snake of Moses was an Old Testament symbol of Jesus who would be lifted up on a cross as our sin-bearer.

baptised into Moses in the cloud and in the sea[18]? I'm sure Yeshua would transform a boring history lesson into an incredible trip down memory lane and provide us with an awesome sense of the big story that we are in. He would provide a timely reminder that salvation is not simply a one-night stand but being drawn into the rich texture of a grand unfolding story that started with Abraham and has not yet reached its climax. I truly believe that today, as never before, believers need that affirmation that they are actually part of this sweeping meta-narrative in which every individual story has its place.

As I imagined walking with Yeshua on the Emmaus Road, He guided me through the third and final section of the Hebrew Scriptures, the *Ketuvim*, and He grounded revelation from heaven in the realities of life on earth. Rooted in reality, the Writings consist of books like Ruth, Job, Psalms, Proverbs and Ecclesiastes. Here I found startling honesty in the face of harsh experiences. I envisioned standing outside Bethlehem with a woman who has lost her husband, her sons and her land (Ruth 1v1-11). No wonder Naomi wants to be renamed "Bitter" (the Hebrew word is *mara*). And yet Naomi and her daughter-in-law, Ruth, form vital links in the chain that leads to the birth of Yeshua (Matthew 1v5-6)[19]. I wondered what Yeshua would make of that story highlighting the essential roles of 'little people' in the 'big picture'.

Regarding the Book of Job, I could not think of any person better qualified than Him to sit beside Job to ponder why innocent people suffer. As the incarnation of wisdom itself, Yeshua can lead us through Proverbs and elucidate the skills for the good life while pondering the deeper meaning of existence itself with Qoheleth, the preacher who wrote Ecclesiastes (Week 44).

In a sense, the class which Yeshua started on the Emmaus Road is still open. The exciting thing is that we can be part of it. Geographically we may live in another part of the world, but the journey of discovery is something that we can join. As we travel, we learn to listen to the revelation of the God of Israel as He speaks to us 'in stereo' (through both the Old and New Testaments). From what I have learned and from my experience at the Kotel, I have come to understand that through the Hebrew

---

[18] 1 Corinthians 10v1-2 (NKJV): *Moreover, brethren, I do not want you to be unaware that all our fathers were under the cloud, all passed through the sea, all were baptised into Moses in the cloud and in the sea...* God appeared as a pillar of cloud to the Hebrews as they crossed the Red Sea under Moses' leadership. This crossing was a kind of baptism to the Hebrews. Paul implies that these Jews were the "fathers" of the Gentile believers in Corinth to whom he was writing.

[19] Matthew 1v5-6 (NIV): *"... Boaz the father of Obed, whose mother was Ruth, Obed the father of Jesse, and Jesse the father of King David..."* Jesus' human lineage was that of David's.

Scriptures, God has revealed 'so much' and then 'so much more' in the record and interpretation of the Christ event in the pages of the New Covenant.

It is very much to our detriment if we listen only 'in mono' when, in fact, we have 'stereo' available. As the writer of the letter to the Hebrews observed, it is the one God who is speaking throughout the ages. In the past, in preliminary and partial ways, He spoke to the patriarchs and the prophets, but now, in these last days, that same God has spoken definitively to us in Yeshua: two ages, one revealing 'so much', and the other 'so much more', but one and only one God speaking.

We do well to listen, whether we sit before the open Book or stand beside the ancient wall. This is the God of Abraham, Isaac and Jacob. He, too, is my God, the One who alone can send my roots rain!

- Desi Maxwell (Lisburn, Northern Ireland)
www.xplorations.org[20]
August 2011

As regards the Old and the New Testaments, someone succinctly stated: "The Old is the New concealed, and the New is the Old revealed". The two are inseparable and complementary.

We read these words in 1 John 5 verses 14-15: "And this is the confidence that we have toward Him, that if we ask anything according to His will He hears us. And if we know that He hears us in whatever we ask, we know that we have the requests that we have asked of Him" (ESV).

Knowing God's word helps us to know His will in matters that concern us. When we pray according to His will, then we are assured that our prayers will be answered.

Father God, help me to read, study and meditate on Your word. Help me to set aside daily time for Your word so that it becomes an everyday part of me. Teach me Your will as You teach me Your word. Thank You for Jesus, Your living Word who lives in me! Amen.

---

[20] Visit this website for more of Desi's insightful teachings modelled on the risen Lord's instruction of His disciples on the Emmaus Road.

Week 17: Engaging with the World

*And so, from the day we heard, we have not ceased to pray for you,
asking that you may be filled with the knowledge of His will in all
spiritual wisdom and understanding, so as to walk in a manner worthy
of the Lord, fully pleasing to Him, bearing fruit in every good work and
increasing in the knowledge of God. (Colossians 1v9-10, ESV)*

God wants us to be spiritual eagles soaring to receive progressive revelation that will grow our knowledge of His character, ways and will and bring us to increasing intimacy with Him. The revelations we receive ultimately testify to what Jesus has done in the past for us (hindsight), is doing in the present in us (insight) to prepare us for what He will do in the future through us (foresight). They help us not only to transcend our circumstances, but also to engage with a world that needs salvation, healing and transformation.

God has a specific plan or calling for each believer[1] concerning our engagement with the world. You may hear about this call through a prophetic word from someone, but you need to hear God for yourself to get deeper insight into His plan for your life, as well as the strategies to fulfil it. If you do not find out God's specific purpose for your life, how will you hear the Master's "Well done, My good and faithful servant"[2]? He is eager to reveal it to you more than you think! Usually, God does not show a believer all the details concerning His plan for the person so as not to overwhelm him/her, but as the person, in obedience, steps into what God has already revealed, then He reveals more.

Whatever God's unique plan is for each of His children, it is in keeping with His foremost vision: our progressive transformation so that we become more and more like Jesus in our character[3]. By being Jesus to the people we encounter, we bring His light into their world[4]. God gives us revelation, the understanding of that revelation and the wisdom to apply it so that we can engage with the world and be conduits of God's love and transforming grace. In this way we "bear fruit in every good work".

The final story in this section tells us how a woman's contacts with homeless people like Owen of Week 1 touched her heart strings. Then God gave her a vision of

---

[1] Jeremiah 29v11 (NIV): *"For I know the plans I have for you," declares the Lord, "plans to prosper you and not to harm you, plans to give you hope and a future."*
[2] Matthew 25v21 and 23
[3] Romans 8v 29 (NLT): *For God knew His people in advance, and He chose them to become like His Son, so that His Son would be the firstborn among many brothers and sisters.*
[4] John 1v4 (NIV): *In Him was life, and that life was the light of all mankind.*

bringing hope to the hopeless in the city where she lives, as well as the wisdom to bring the vision into fruition.

The Story of The Olive Branch

Before becoming a follower of Jesus, I had been through a difficult, dark and troubled time. Then at fifty I discovered that God indeed restores "the years the locusts have consumed"[5] and that we can have a living relationship with Jesus. In my early experience as a Christian, the Parable of the Sower (in Matthew 13) and the account of Peter stepping out of the boat (in Matthew 14) inspired me to begin a journey that is not yet complete.

Listening to the Parable of the Sower one Sunday morning, a determination stirred in my heart not to let the Word of God fall on stony ground, be eaten by birds of the air or be strangled by weeds of the world. I wanted it to bear fruit in my life and in the lives of others. As Peter stepped out of the fishing boat in response to Jesus' invitation, I prayed God would give me the courage to take the step of faith. But what would that be? Joining a small group of women meeting regularly to pray, I believed God would give the answer.

I began volunteering in different places in the city asking God where He wanted me to serve. Receiving a new identity as a child of God, I was presented with opportunities that took me out of my 'comfort zone' and helped equip me for God's purpose and plan.

Direction and inspiration came while volunteering at Edward Street for the Lancaster and District Homeless Action Service (LDHAS) which offers practical support to the homeless. Standing at the counter serving cups of tea and coffee, I listened to their stories. I watched people slowly dying in despair and hopelessness without knowledge of Jesus as Saviour, Healer and Friend. These experiences had a profound and lasting impact. My eyes were opened and I saw what God was showing me. A passion was ignited in me to see them set free. I witnessed the tragedy of addiction, childhoods destroyed by abuse, the human cost of family breakdown and the festering wounds of rejection. Believing no one cared, they saw themselves as social outcasts, the "lepers" of our time, "treated like dirt beneath the shoe" and beyond hope. A history of rejection often led to self-rejection, self-harming and suicide. They seemed powerless and voiceless.

How could such desperate needs be met and deep heart-wounds healed? Two separate conversations with John and his brother Stephen (now sadly deceased) brought deeper insight and recognition of the deep yearning and emptiness behind the mask. As a Christian, I knew Jesus was the answer. He had rescued me, healed my pain and given me new life and hope. How could I share this precious gift with them before it was too late?

---

[5] Joel 2v25 (NIV): *I will repay you for the years the locusts have eaten.*

During one memorable prayer meeting in the Welcome Centre, St. Thomas' Church, I had a revelation. If there was to be life transformation and justice for people like John and Stephen, action had to follow prayer. The time to 'step out of the boat' had come. Before my courage failed and fear and doubt rushed in, my prayer partner and I went to ask permission to use the centre as an outreach. The seed vision of The Olive Branch was planted – "to proclaim the gospel to the poor, bind up the broken-hearted and to set the captives free" (Isaiah 61v1)[6].

My heart's desire was to see the people I met at Edward St. healed and set free by the power of Jesus' love. Reading Romans 11, it had struck me that there was hope for the outcast and rejected through the grace of God.

I was asked to write down my proposal for consideration. This was new ground for me and I did not know how to do it. But it was an essential stage of "writing the vision and making it plain"[7]. I asked others to pray with me for wisdom.

The details came clearly and rapidly following prayer for guidance. The vision's strategy was simply to invite people to the Lord's table (the parable of the Wedding Feast[8]). The gospel message would be shared with a meal round one table just as Jesus sat down with sinners, prostitutes and tax collectors. The name "The Olive Branch" (TOB) came one morning while I was filling the kettle to make a cup of tea. From the beginning it seemed important to be overtly Christian, hence the gospel message and prayer before the meal, an all Christian team, music, literature and visual symbols of our faith around us. The provision and setting were to be of high quality so that our guests would feel welcomed, accepted and valued. There would be flowers on the table and the colours of the table setting would be those God chose for the Tabernacle: red, blue and purple[9]. Everyone who came would receive one clear, consistent message of love, faith and hope.

Several months of prayer, research and preparation followed, a time of 'waiting on the Lord', pushing doors and seeing them open. Encouragement, support and advice came from LDHAS, the community police, local churches and individual Christians. Then on Monday, 15 November 2004 at 4:30 PM, The Olive Branch opened its door for the first

---

6   Isaiah 61v1 (ESV): *"The Spirit of the Lord God is upon Me, because the Lord has anointed Me to bring good news to the poor; He has sent Me to bind up the broken-hearted, to proclaim liberty to the captives, and the opening of the prison to those who are bound..."* This prophecy was written about the coming Messiah about 500 years before Jesus. Just as He was anointed to do God's work, God's children are likewise anointed to do the same.

7   Habakkuk 2v2 (NIV): *"Write down the revelation and make it plain on tablets so that a herald may run with it."*

8   Matthew 22v1-14

9   See Exodus 26. The Tabernacle was a tent God told Moses to construct after the Hebrews left Egypt. It was God's dwelling place with His people on earth at that time.

time at the Stepping Stone, Lancaster Free Methodist Church, to bring the good news to the 'lepers' of our community – the homeless, the addicted, the impoverished and the broken.

The volunteer team, representing five Lancaster churches, were fundamental to our effectiveness in establishing strong relationships over the first three years. Sharing the Lord's table with our guests confirmed that building trust through friendship evangelism laid the foundation of our future success. We served our apprenticeship during these years. In many ways it was a personal baptism of fire, pushing through the fear barrier to proclaim the gospel despite opposition, challenge and shaking knees. The gospel message was given explicitly in 'word' and testimony before every meal, and implicitly through gentle witness of faith in action. Many conversations around the Lord's table planted seeds of salvation watered by our prayers.

It was a small but eternally significant beginning[10]. I believe that God blessed our unity as we reached out to win the hearts of our guests. A year later, following an opportune meeting with a Christian fundraiser, our vision's strategy changed. Instead of being just a place for fellowship with a hot meal, TOB became a registered charity (September 2006). We then rapidly raised the first year's rental for a shop (location as yet unknown) near the city centre, a place of our own at the heart of the Lancaster community. The three-year tenancy for an empty shop in Thurnham Street was signed October 2008 (another leap of faith). We opened first three then five days a week the following year, committed to spreading the message of Jesus' love, salvation and healing.

Many more people have sought help since the opening at Thurnham Street. Often they feel invisible, ignored and excluded with nowhere else to turn, having exhausted more formal community provision. We are increasingly becoming the first port of call and are supporting people who would not look to church for help. People come burdened and leave lighter. We see from their expression and tears that they have been touched by Jesus. The change is often remarkable as they experience the peace of His presence. As well as praying for everyone, we also listen, offer encouragement and hope, long-term support, advocacy, information and guidance, practical help (including Christian Against Poverty's[11] money budgeting courses, emergency food and more), referral to professional agencies, and of course, the gospel message.

---

[10] Zechariah 4v10 (NLT): *Do not despise these small beginnings, for the Lord rejoices to see the work begin...*

[11] Christians Against Poverty is a national debt counselling charity with a network of UK centres based in local churches. CAP offers hope and a solution to anyone in debt through its unique, in-depth service. See www.capuk.org for more information.

It has been far from being a smooth journey. There were many obstacles to overcome and giants to face, including the giants of fear, disappointment, opposition and discouragement. Every aspect of the ministry had been challenged, especially those aspects pointing to Jesus. From the beginning, The Olive Branch has been openly evangelistic in purpose, reaching out to people bound and crushed by addiction, homelessness, poverty, rejection, abuse and family breakdown. With emphasis on excellence, integrity and professionalism, we lift them high enough to bring hope.

Now after seven years we have moved to 1 Westbourne Road, a place "flowing with milk and honey"[12]. (This prophecy was given to us by someone who didn't know that above the front door of this new place is a relief sculpture of a honeycomb!) Our Isaiah 61 vision will surely be fulfilled. Our mission remains unchanged: to create a safe space for change to take place, to open the door of hope and to enable life transformation. The Olive Branch keeps stepping forward while trusting God, standing firm on His truth and holding fast to God's purpose and vision.

- Barbara (Lancaster, England)
The Olive Branch, www.the-olivebranch.org.uk
September 2011

Almighty God, thank You for transforming me and making me more like Jesus! Please help me to submit to Your Holy Spirit in this, His work. I know You have created me and put me on earth for a unique purpose, that through its fulfilment I may glorify You. Please help me to soar on wings like an eagle and reveal to me who I was born to be so that I may know what I must give myself to. Grant me a clear vision of Your vision for me and give me wisdom that I may be able to set my priorities right and make the right choices. One day, when my time on earth is over and I finally see You face to face, I pray that I will hear Your "Well done, My good and faithful servant!" I pray in the mighty name of Jesus, amen!

In Section 2 of this devotional, "Running like Athletes for God", you will encounter through their stories people who received revelation from God and ran to complete the course He set before them.

---

[12] Exodus 3v8 (NIV): *So I [God] have come down to rescue them from the hand of the Egyptians and to bring them up out of that land into a good and spacious land, a land flowing with milk and honey.*

Section 2

Running like Athletes for God

(Week 18 to Week 34)

Week 18: Press On and Enjoy the Race

Not that I have already obtained all this, or have already been made perfect, but I press on to take hold of that for which Christ Jesus took hold of me. Brothers, I do not consider myself yet to have taken hold of it. But one thing I do: Forgetting what is behind and straining towards what is ahead, I press on towards the goal to win the prize for which God has called me heavenwards in Christ Jesus. (Philippians 3v12-14, NIV)

As stated in the Introduction, we receive revelation from God as spiritual eagles so that we can 'run' with it as athletes. Running in scripture often relates to fulfilling God's purpose for our lives. In a sense, we are running a marathon because it will practically take our whole life to fulfil our purpose. But we also run sprints – assignments the Lord may give us for a season which will be related to our overall purpose and calling.

The verses above were written by the apostle Paul in his letter to the Christians in Philippi which was a Roman colony in Macedonia. The word for 'press on' in the original Greek text is *dioko* and it means 'to run as in a race in order to win a prize'. Whether you realise it or not, you are racing against time to fulfil God's call on your life. If at life's end it can be said that you have fulfilled God's purpose for your life, then you are a winner of the heavenly prize, God's "Well done!"

Before you were born, God already devised a plan of transforming you into the character of His Son, Jesus[1], "the Last Adam"[2], so that you can enjoy intimate fellowship with Him, as the first Adam did before the fall[3]. Despite the state of bliss he enjoyed, the first Adam succumbed to satan's temptation and fell. In contrast, the last Adam remained faithful to the Father despite the horrific torture he experienced (Weeks 40 and 41). This is the kind of person anyone, even God, would want to be intimate with. And we become this kind of person through this process of

---

[1] Romans 8v29 (NASB): *For those whom He foreknew* [those He knew would come to Him through Jesus] *He also predestined* [planned before they were born] *to become conformed to the image of His Son.*

[2] 1 Corinthians 15v45 (NIV): *So it is written: "The first man Adam became a living being"; the last Adam, a life-giving spirit.* 'Adam' is a term for man in Hebrew. Jesus is referred to as "the last Adam" because there would be no man after Him who would affect the destiny of the human race to the same degree as He and the first Adam did. The first Adam brought sin and death to mankind through his disobedience; the last Adam brought salvation and eternal life through His obedience to the Father.

[3] The account of the fall of Adam and Eve is in Genesis 3.

transformation (or 'sanctification'[4]). The amazing thing is that, God already chooses to look at the end product even while we go through the process. He already wants to be in intimate relationship with YOU because Jesus took hold of you for this very purpose!

God is making you perfect like Jesus if you are heaven-bound[5] (Week 51). But He also wants you to be of earthly good and this is why He also planned for you to do things for Him while you are on earth. Whether you accept this or not, you have a unique role to play on earth as God's witness by word and deed[6], and no one else can fulfil it but you with the help of God's Holy Spirit.

Are you willing to fulfil God's purpose for your life, to become like Jesus and to be His witness? Will you press on?

Scottish Olympic athlete Eric Liddle knew God called him to glorify His name as a runner. In the movie *Chariots of Fire*[7], his famous words are articulated: "I was made to run and when I run, I feel God's pleasure!"

Those who press on toward the goal of fulfilling God's plan for their lives will no doubt encounter opposition from their adversary, the devil, who will do everything he can to prevent them from fulfilling their purpose. But God is with them to help them and they <u>will</u> feel His pleasure. Because of this, they can enjoy the race!

The following story is literally about running a marathon, being a witness for Jesus in the race, finishing it, and enjoying the whole process.

My Challenge from God

"Are you going to do one then?" This was about the third time someone had said this to me.

---

[4] To sanctify means to set apart or to consecrate to God. Sanctification is the process by which a born-again believer in Jesus is progressively transformed into His character through the work of the Holy Spirit as he surrenders and consecrates his life to Him.

[5] That is, if you have been 'born again' by receiving Jesus into your life: *I tell you the truth, no-one can see the kingdom of God unless he is born again* (John 3v3, NIV).

[6] Acts 1v8 (ESV): *But you will receive power when the Holy Spirit has come upon you, and you will be My witnesses in Jerusalem and in all Judea and Samaria, and to the end of the earth.*

[7] *Chariots of Fire* is a British movie made in 1981 about the true story of two athletes in the 1924 Olympics: a devout Scottish Christian named Eric Liddell who runs for the glory of God, and an English Jew named Harold Abrahams who runs to prove that Jews are not inferior.

My husband was working for the church charity Help International (a Christian relief and development agency) and we were manning a display at the Welsh Bible Week. We were encouraging as many as possible to sign up to run a marathon and get sponsors to help with the funds. Most who responded were young people in their twenties or thirties, but the question kept coming, "Are you going to do one?"

I knew Ron would not be able to train and run a marathon, but what about me? I was not in my twenties or thirties or even forties. I was fifty-nine and a half and would be sixty before I would be ready to do one. When I spoke to Ron about it, he replied, "At your age? You must be joking!" I was fit, but had never done any running or jogging, so what was I thinking of? I tried to put it out of my mind but it would not leave me. Eventually Ron said if I went to the doctor and got the okay from him, he would back me all the way. This I did and was soon beginning on a programme to prepare me to run the New York Marathon in eight months' time!

Training was hard as I was doing it on my own. During this time I learned a lot not only about discipline and perseverance, but also about the faithfulness of God. I was sick of seeing miserable-looking runners and joggers so I had determined that I would smile and say "Hi" to everyone I passed. Everyone I knew who was training either lived far away or was much younger and quicker than I. However, I plodded on and increased my training time and my speed until I suffered an injury and had to have physiotherapy. Although I could not train for about four weeks, it did give me the opportunity to tell the physio why I was training for a marathon and that God had challenged me to do it. I was back training just before the Bible Week and found that week particularly tough. Running and power walking up and down the Welsh hills in the heat of an August day was hard going, but I found that when God calls you to do something for Him, He gives you all you need to get on and do it.

However, I was nervous! I had never done more than twenty miles before and the marathon was going to be just over twenty-six miles. "Please God! I don't want to be the first one to drop out!", I prayed.

The day finally arrived when we flew to America. "Business or pleasure?" asked the lady at passport control. "That's debatable", I answered. "You see, I have come to run the marathon!" "Then you go and enjoy it," she said. I did not know at the time that was a word from God. The man who had organised the trip for us also told me to enjoy it and to take my time. "You are not aiming to win (cross the finish line first), but to FINISH it, so pace yourself and enjoy it!," he advised.

As we met with the more than thirty-thousand runners, there was a real air of excitement. We were called to the starting point. The professionals must have been at least half a mile in front of us, but we eventually crossed the starting line and began to cross over the bridge. Two of the girls from our church were with me. I knew I was holding them back and they were putting pressure on me to try to go quicker. I eventually told them to go on at their pace and leave me. "There are too many people going my way. Go ahead! I won't get lost", I assured them. Along the way I spoke to so many people from different parts of the world doing the marathon for a variety of reasons. We were cheered on all the way!

At about twenty miles I caught up with a young girl from Texas. She was running on her own and was ready to give up. We walked and talked a bit and then I told her how I was helped in training by singing some songs to get me into a rhythm and invited her to join me. We set off at a good pace singing, "You shall go out with joy and be led forth in peace[8]." As we went on together, I told her how my life had been changed when I asked Jesus to be my Lord and Saviour. She responded saying she went to church, but had not got a personal relationship with Jesus. And so we talked some more. At last we approached Central Park for the last leg of the marathon. I then went on ahead as I had promised Ron that if I had any difficulties I would stop. I wanted him to see I was still strong!

My young friend came up behind me at the finish line. She told Ron that I was her guardian angel and she would not have finished but for me. Looking back then, I realised that God had sent her to help me too in the last six miles of the race. It was a tough challenge, but just as God was with me in difficult times, He was with me all the way in this race even though I was not always aware of it.

As regards to the message about enjoying the race, I must say I did enjoy every minute of it!

- Barbara (Lancaster, England)
Sent from Malaga, Spain
March 2011

You may feel you are now too old to do anything worthwhile for God. You may think it is too late for you to fulfil God's purpose for your life. Barbara ran the New York marathon when she was sixty. God called Moses to deliver His people from Egyptian bondage when he was eighty. Abraham became a father when he was a hundred. No, with God it is not too late[9], but do not wait any longer!

---

[8]   The song 'You Shall Go Out with Joy' (1975) was composed by Stuart Dauermann based on Isaiah 55v12.

[9]   Luke 1v37 (NIV): *For nothing is impossible with God.*

Or perhaps you feel your life has no meaning or purpose, or that you are 'good for nothing'. Your Creator does not think so! You are precious in His eyes. This is why He sent Jesus to die for you and why you are reading this book. Reach out to Him and make this day the first day of the rest and the best of your life!

Here I am, Lord! Take me as I am and change me as You will. I want to fulfil Your purpose for my life. Help me to press on. With Your Spirit's help, I know I can enjoy the race and finish it. In Jesus' name, thank You!

Week 19: Called to Be and Called to Do

For we are God's masterpiece. He has created us anew in Christ
Jesus, so we can do the good things He planned for us long ago.
(Ephesians 2v10, NLT)

To modern man, life is a race because of the fast pace, busyness and competitiveness that mark today's society. A large part of daily life is taken up by work. It is as if to work is to live and to live is to work.

Many in today's society believe that it is a man's work that gives him identity and sense of purpose. If this is right, then we might as well call ourselves "human doings"! The fact that we are called "human beings" suggests that God the Creator calls us 'to be' before He calls us 'to do'. His most important calling for each person on earth is *to be* in an intimate relationship with Him. You may not be proud of the circumstances of your birth, but God wanted YOU to be born and calls you to be in relationship with Him. Irrespective of how you view yourself, you are His masterpiece as the verse above says, and He wants to enjoy YOUR company, and you to enjoy His. To enter into this relationship, one must accept God's condition: to repent of one's sins[1] and receive Jesus Christ as one's Saviour and Lord (Week 4).

Secondary to your main calling is God's call for service. He calls you *to do* good deeds as His partner in His work of redeeming the world He created. As the verse above suggests, God had planned the good works He wants you to do even before you were born, good works that will testify of His love, grace and glory and that will give you true satisfaction. If you accept His invitation to be His "fellow worker"[2] on earth, then He will equip you with the talents, abilities, resources and relationships you need to be able to do these good things[3].

Your call for service is a call to use your God-given talents and abilities in the various roles you have in life: in your home, your workplace, your church and your community. These roles provide the context in which you can live out your calling 'to be' and 'to do'.

---

[1] Because sin separates us from God: *But your misdeeds have separated you from your God. Your sins have hidden His face from you so that you aren't heard* (Isaiah 59v2, CEB).

[2] 1 Corinthians 3v9 (NIV): *For we are God's fellow-workers...*

[3] Hebrews 13v20-21a (NIV): *May the God of peace, who through the blood of the eternal covenant brought back from the dead our Lord Jesus, that great Shepherd of the sheep, equip you with everything good for doing His will....*

As you work on developing your special relationship with God (through prayer, reading God's word and fellowship with other believers) and perform the tasks He wants you to do, you are progressively transformed into Christ's character, into the person God created you to be in the first place[4].

The story below recounts David's call to serve God as a minister of the gospel in Wanchai and how, through his ministry, Chinese men answered God's call 'to be' and 'to do'.

The Christ of Wanchai

In my early twenties, when I had not long committed my heart to the Lord, I was sent to Hong Kong (a British colony at this time) on National Service (1958-59). Our army barracks bordered a district in Hong Kong called Wanchai – a place of the most appalling human degradation. By this time, a million refugees had poured in from China to escape the atrocities of the Chinese Civil War. Some lived on the sampans which brought them, vast floating cities without sanitation. Others filled the hillsides with homes built of whatever they could salvage from the sea. Still more slept on the streets. It was impossible to walk out in the evening without having to step over them where the trams constantly rattled by. Every morning at dawn, a lorry travelled the streets to collect the dead.

In the heart of such suffering, my new-found faith might have been knocked to pieces. How could a gracious God allow such scenes as these? In fact the opposite happened. I had a profound sense that God was in some strange way suffering with these people. A voice repeatedly said to me, "You are walking where Christ walks. What are you going to do about it?" The Jesus I had come to know became more real. But without knowledge of the difficult language of Cantonese and coming from an entirely different culture, what could I do?

I noticed an advertisement in the South China Morning Post seeking teachers for refugees in a night school called the New Method College. My commanding officer allowed me to swap around my night guard duties to enable me to teach simple English two evenings a week. That way I came to know and love my class of thirty students in their early twenties. All had fled from China carrying virtually nothing. They warmed to my sharing of the love of Jesus, though many were full of questions. Without English they could only hope for jobs that earned a pittance.

---

[4] 2 Corinthians 3v18b (NLT): *And the Lord – who is the Spirit – makes us more and more like Him as we are changed into His glorious image.*

One late morning I was staring up at the dark trees on Victoria Peak (replaced today by forests of tower blocks) when the Lord called me to full time ministry. It came out of the blue. My calling was specifically to teach young people – to impart to them the love of Christ and to encourage them to share that love with others. So entranced was I by this vision that I arrived late for lunch at the cookhouse and sat down for my meal alone. The cook rested his elbows on the serving hatch and to my astonishment he asked, "Are you a padre, mate?", using the army word for a chaplain. "It's just you look as though you ought to be!", he explained. Christian ministers don't seem to me to have a certain look. They come in all shapes – tall, short, fat, thin, bald or bearded. This could only be the Lord's way of confirming my calling!

As soon as I returned to the UK I started my training for ministry. The first thing my college did for me was to find me a wife, so I was sent to her church to encourage the youth fellowship of which she was a leader. As we fell in love, I talked to Barbara incessantly about Hong Kong. A few years after we were married in Liverpool, we were on a flight to Hong Kong where I was to be chaplain of the Diocesan Boys' School, a mission school established in 1868.

I was introduced to Danny, a student who had passed through the school and gone on to university to study Chinese history and philosophy. His years as a boarder had warmed his heart, but he was uncertain about committing his life to Christ and he wanted to discuss it with me. Our discussion lasted for six months on Saturday mornings. Finally he said to me, "If I've got it right, to become a Christian I would have to surrender my life to Christ and think His thoughts and go His way? Well, my Chinese heritage prevents me from doing that. We are conditioned to get by in our own strength. To become a Christian would make me a beggar and beggars are to be despised because they have given up the struggle. I am sorry to tell you that whenever I pass a beggar on the street, my inclination is to spit on him!"

We parted as good friends and I thanked him for the many aspects of Chinese culture he had taught me. But the following Saturday he was back asking whether, after all, he could be baptised! He told me that when he left me, his bus journey took him as usual through the district of Wanchai. He looked down from the upper deck and saw a poor man covered in sacking, lying with one arm outstretched with his begging bowl. "Something came over me," he recalled. "In spite of what I had said to you, I had the compelling urge to get off that bus and help that man[5]. But I was jammed in like a sardine in a tin. I struggled to push my way to the lower deck, but by the time I got off, the bus had moved on several stops and taken several turns in the maze of backstreets. I spent ages trying to find my beggar, but failed. That night when I flopped down by my bed, floods of tears came. Your

---

[5]   Luke 10v33 (NIV):... and w*hen he saw him, he took pity on him....*

Jesus became so real to me and told me that as my heart longed to help that beggar, His heart had been burning to help me all my life. There and then I made the surrender I told you I could never make and instead of being weak, I am suddenly wonderfully strong!"

Danny was baptised with great joy. After he completed his university course, he joined a Hong Kong governmental agency for combating corruption. When Hong Kong returned to China, Danny, happily married, emigrated to Toronto where he has an important role within the YMCA interviewing asylum seekers. His whole family, including married son and daughter, are very active members of their church.

One of my main objectives in the Diocesan Boys' School was to involve the boys in serving their own community. Community service became an alternative to sports on Tuesday afternoons. We divided the Christian Union into groups who went out in various directions. One group went to teach children in a hospital; another was engaged in translating sponsorship letters; and yet another helped in various ways at the fledgling St. James' Settlement in Wanchai, mainly engaged in those days in caring for orphaned children. By being involved in works of compassion, these boys saw the connection between what they were doing and the compassionate work of Jesus in the Gospels which they studied as part of the school curriculum. One after another, those boys asked for baptism. Sometimes they met with a refusal from Buddhist or ancestor-worshipping parents.

Michael was one of our Wanchai helpers. In the midst of a class discussion, the Lord spoke to Michael. He was already a church member, but in the course of that discussion on compassionate caring, his relationship with Christ was warmed into life. He went on to take a degree in Social Science and for some years now has been working at the completely modernised and rebuilt St. James' Settlement in Wanchai, called upon to train workers in a similar role in Guangzhou in mainland China.

Michael with his army of Christian helpers has the language and the culture to do what I never could, but I believe that the Lord, who has the power to break down every barrier, called me to be His agent to carry His Spirit to those Chinese boys. Today, the work of St. James' Settlement is widely acclaimed as a shining beacon of the love of Christ in Hong Kong. The entire district of Wanchai has become a business centre, transformed beyond all recognition from the Wanchai over which I wept fifty years ago.

One final note: Another member of the same class who was deeply influenced by those Christian discussions is now principal of the vastly enlarged Diocesan Boys

School. Of all the hundreds of schools in Hong Kong, he got there via a headship at the New Method College, the same place where I first learned to love the Chinese people.

- David Ellis (Grange-over-Sands, Cumbria, England)
April 2011

Almighty God, You created me so it's only You who have the right to define who I am and what my life is for. Thank You that my life is important to You! Help me to hear Your call every day of my life, Your call to be in Your presence, and Your call to do good things for You, so that I can be the kind of 'Jesus' representative' that You want me to be, here where You have placed me at this time of my life. For Jesus' glory, amen.

Week 20: What is Your Purpose? (1)

We will not boast about things done outside our area of authority. We will boast only about what has happened within the boundaries of the work God has given us, which includes our working with you.
(2 Corinthians 10v13, NLT)

In Week 17 you read about Barbara's God-given vision of helping the homeless and the hopeless in Lancaster and how she is "running with the vision"[1] to see it fulfilled. In her particular case, God gave her the vision to establish The Olive Branch in Lancaster as her way of testifying by word and deed of the grace of God.

In Matthew 28 Jesus declared the over-all mission of the Church, His Body on earth – to make disciples of all nations[2]. God never intended, however, for every Christian or every local church to go to all the nations on earth. Each of us has a part to play in this "Great Commission". This is where God's specific and unique vision for you comes in.

In the text above, Paul uses the Greek word *kanon* (from which 'canon' is derived) to refer to his assigned area of responsibility in the work of spreading the gospel (i.e., he was called to the Gentiles). It is possible that he was thinking of a race track with lanes ("boundaries") marked out for the different runners. The visions God gives to His children (and the local churches) are like boundary lines that define a runner's field. Without these boundary lines, we will find it difficult to have focus and strategies. We will be running here and there and into other people without making much progress toward the goal. This leads to conflicts, discouragement and burn-out. Hence the warning: "Without a vision, the people perish[3]."

Our God-given vision of our purpose or calling, therefore, not only directs us toward the finish line, but also defines our area of responsibility, constraining and restraining our call to do things for God within a specific ministry and place because "without a vision, the people cast off restraint[4]." Vision allows us to concentrate on the work we are given and to measure our progress

---

[1] Habakkuk 2v2 (NIV): *Write down the revelation and make it plain on tablets so that a herald may run with it.*

[2] Matthew 28v18-20 (NIV): *All authority in heaven and on earth has been given to Me. Therefore go and make disciples of all nations, baptising them in the name of the Father and of the Son and of the Holy Spirit, and teaching them to obey everything I have commanded you. And surely I am with you always, to the very end of the age.*

[3] Proverbs 29v18. See Week 1.

[4] Ibid

God gives the vision and supplies the provision as well as the passion to run with the vision. Passion encourages focus, builds courage and inspires us to persevere against the obstacles that stand in our way. God's vision is often long-term and there will be times when He will clarify it, or even redefine and enlarge it as in the story below.

Have you asked God for His vision for you? Ask Him also for the passion to press on and see it fulfilled. May the story below stir your heart to do this.

The Story of Shepherd of the Hills Children's Foundation

In 1976 my parents, Rev. Jose and Fe Mejica, who were commissioned as missionaries, were heading for Cyprus in the Mediterranean with their four children. But then civil war erupted in that country, cancelling the travel indefinitely. The planned trip certainly created a lot of questions in the minds of my parents as they just made major decisions regarding leaving their home country, only to be in an unexpected scenario. While in Manila, a major calamity struck the Philippines. It was brought about by a very powerful typhoon that wrecked the city of Manila, causing hundreds of people to become homeless. Tragically, many children living in the city streets were abandoned, a situation my parents could not ignore. My father felt such a great burden for them that he and my mother decided to pick them up and bring them to their rented apartment for shelter.

To bring some relief to the children's pain, my parents listened to each of their stories. Having heard their stories and believing that God had given them a new vision which they wanted to obey, my parents became more determined to save homeless children and set up a bigger location. They contacted their friends abroad and shared their vision with them. In a short time these people started responding to the immediate and long term needs of the children. By God's grace and guidance, the act to rescue children evolved into the establishment of a children's home. My parents decided to legalise its existence under Philippine laws and Shepherd of the Hills (SOTH) Children's Foundation then came into being.

When my parents went to be with the Lord, the ministry which they had started was passed on to me, their second child. In 2003, my wife Ruth and I took over the management of the ministry, now in its thirty-second year. The vision became bigger, stronger and more challenging. As a result, the ministry has transitioned through the years from being an orphanage into a Christian child care and child development organisation focusing on children and youth who are in need, abandoned, neglected, orphaned, dependent, and underprivileged. The children in our care are no longer called "clients" but "sons and daughters". Yes, Ruth and I are the "nanay" (mother) and "tatay" (father) of the kids living with us and our own biological kids are growing with them. It is a structure we chose to adopt in order to effect change in the lives of the children. It's a change that gives a strong message to the children that they are part of a family, that someone cares for them and that they are loved.

This approach created a different atmosphere within the home. It paved the way to 'order in the house', unity and respect for each other. This wasn't an easy path as there were risks to consider in rearing our biological and spiritual children together based on their growing and changing needs. But these risks were not hindrances in achieving what was best for the children. By seeing God's perspective and trusting in His wisdom and guidance, we were able to come up with the right decisions on how to raise the children. We home school them until high school, train them in music and the arts, disciple them that they may become mature Christians, and provide those who are potential leaders with leadership training. We also expose them to people outside their comfort zones so that they may testify to what the Lord has done and is doing in our family and with their personal lives. Praise the Lord for their transformation!

Today, as a child care organisation, SOTH shelters children for short and long term care. As a developmental organisation, SOTH employs developmental programs adopted and designed to specifically address changing needs of children and youth in crisis. Currently, we are running three facilities in Manila, Zambales and Baguio and have one hundred spiritual children and teens. The children live in small family units headed by married couples serving as surrogate parents to a group of eight to ten children aged two to twelve, while the teenagers are grouped together and live separate from the younger children. Within this familiar environment, children and youth experience normal and healthy family structure, practical home-life work and training. They are mentored and discipled in the Christian faith based on their individual backgrounds and experiences. Through music lessons, the children learn to express themselves creatively, gaining not only skills in playing musical instruments, but also discipline through the training required. They love to perform in different places. They enjoy sports and recreation and gain practical skills in carpentry, livestock-raising, gardening and aquaculture and other relevant livelihood and day-to-day skills.

Our passion to build children's lives does not emanate from ourselves. It comes from the love of God streaming through us to them. I praise God that our biological kids, Danielle, Kenneth, Asiane and Selina, share this love for the underprivileged children and are one with us in serving the Lord at SOTH.

Jose and Fe Mejica were intending to leave the Philippines to go as missionaries to Cyprus, but God interrupted their plans and showed them a different vision. Today, that vision lives on because we believe that our children are the future leaders of our nation. We will therefore continue to hold on to what the Lord had promised in Jeremiah 29v11 (NIV): "I know the plans I have for you, plans to prosper you and not to harm you, plans to give you hope and a future." By God's grace and through our obedience to the vision, these children now have hope and a future!

- Nathan Mejica (Manila, Philippines)
www.shepherdofthehills.org.ph
August 2011

My Father, give me a vision of Your vision for my life! Direct me where You want me, and give me the wisdom, strength and resources to do what You want me to do. When there is a need for clarification and even a change of direction, help me to respond the way You want me to. In Jesus' name, amen!

Week 21: What is Your Purpose? (2)

Each one should use whatever gift he has received to serve others.
(1 Peter 4v10, NIV)

In ancient Greece there were four athletic events: the Pythian (Delphic) Games, the Isthmian (Corinthian) Games, the Nemean Games and the Olympic Games. The Pythian Games happened at Delphi. The Isthmian or Corinthian Games took place in the narrow part of the Isthmus of Corinth, to the north of the city. The Nemean Games were conducted at Nemaea, a town of Argolis. The Olympic Games were celebrated in Olympia, a town of Ellis on the Alphias River. The last were the most popular and prestigious and were attended every four years by people from all parts of Greece and from other countries. In all four games, the athletes competed mainly in running, jumping, horse racing, discus throwing, boxing and wrestling.

The 2012 Summer Olympic Games, officially known as the Games of the XXX Olympiad, were held in London, the first city to host the modern Olympiad three times, having done so previously in 1908 and 1948. Athletes from 204 independent countries and territories attended and there were competitions in twenty-six sports which were broken down into thirty-nine disciplines. For example, Gymnastics[1] had three disciplines: artistic, rhythmic and trampoline. Athletics included track events (100 to 10,000 metre races), road events (marathons and race walks), field events (throwing and jumping events) and combined events (pentathlon, decathlon for men and heptathlon for women) mostly consisting of running, jumping and throwing.

Athletes who enter the Olympic Games need to know what they are good at. Can you imagine the Jamaican sprinter Usain Bolt competing in Artistic Gymnastics[2]? In the same way, it is good for God's children to know what they are good at. God gives the necessary gifts, talents and abilities to enable us to do the good things He is calling us to do, and so your gifts, talents and abilities give an indication of God's purpose for your life. You may like to sing and you dream of becoming a recording artist, but if you do not have a good voice, then your dream is actually a fantasy and is not God's purpose for you.

---

[1] The word 'gymnastics' comes from the Greek for 'naked' because the early gymnasts used to perform with no clothes on!
[2] Even the modern Pentathlon does not cover gymnastics but fencing, swimming, horse riding, shooting and running. These sports were chosen for the Pentathlon based on skills required of a 19th century soldier.

Unfortunately, there are lots of people who use their gifts, talents and abilities to fulfil *their vision* and not God's vision for their lives. Take your gifts, talents and abilities and offer them to God, then ask Him to reveal to you how and where He wants you to use them to serve others and for His glory. Your life will become fulfilling and satisfying. That is a guarantee!

Here is a story of how God brought a Norwegian-American lady to a far-flung village in East Africa to discover that she could use the administrative and organisational skills God gave her to bring hope to the hopeless. The Ilula Orphan Program she established in Tanzania may well be a model for many.

Great Needs – Great Possibilities!

In 1986 I visited the Iringa Region of Tanzania in East Africa with the Girl Guides (Girl Scouts) and fell in love with the place. Several years later, I campaigned in the United States and Norway (where I originally come from) for the extension of the water line in this region. In 1998, as volunteer Chairman for Mission for the Algiers United Methodist Church in Indiana, I went back to Iringa, specifically to Ilula, a village of 6000 people, to see to the completion of the church's mission program of putting a water line to this village. During my stay I was approached by five Tanzanian orphans[3] who requested assistance in continuing their education after the seventh grade. I accepted the call to be a sponsor as a way of tithing[4] for the good Lord's children. Then I went home to Indiana and did not think much more of the consequences. But God had a secret plan! What started as a little support for five orphans escalated into a huge mission for Education and Care in the village of Ilula, Iringa Region in the Kilolo District of Tanzania.

The number of orphans I was supporting quickly grew from five to eighty, something impossible for just me to handle. The Christ United Methodist Church's Mission Committee was asked to adopt the sponsorship of these children, or it had to stop. The church accepted the call and the Ilula Orphan Program (IOP) was born in 2000. By this time, IOP was supporting about one hundred orphans.

---

[3] James 1v27 (NIV): *Religion that God our Father accepts as pure and faultless is this: to look after orphans and widows in their distress and to keep oneself from being polluted by the world.*

[4] The 'tithe' is a tenth of one's annual produce or earnings. Many Christians today give their tithe to God's work based on Malachi 3v8-10 (NIV): *"Will a man rob God? Yet you rob Me. But you ask, 'How do we rob You?' In tithes and offerings. You are under a curse – the whole nation of you – because you are robbing Me. Bring the whole tithe into the storehouse, that there may be food in my house. Test Me in this," says the Lord Almighty, "and see if I will not throw open the floodgates of heaven and pour out so much blessing that you will not have room enough for it."*

Because of the difficulty of communication with the staff in Tanzania (no telephone, fax or email), it was suggested that if IOP had a person on site, the work could progress easier. I was asked to volunteer as I had started the whole thing and knew the area (I had been there six times before) and I accepted! A small support fund was created for me to survive on. At the age of fifty-six, I sold my house, my business, my car and half of my belongings to be able to survive in Africa for a year or two. I left Indiana on 28 September 2001, three weeks after '9-11'.

I arrived in Ilula, Tanzania a few days later with my two suitcases. I was offered an apartment at the local hospital and quickly got started on the work I had come to do. As I began to explore the area, the people, the poverty, the lack of just about everything (schools, teachers, nutritious food, medication, doctors, water, HOPE!), I was stunned by how little support it would take from our well-to-do communities in America and Europe to develop an area like Ilula. Amazing!

In 2003, IOP was recognised as an NGO (non-government organisation) by Tanzania's Ministry of Home Affairs. The four volunteers had grown to eight (mostly teachers), but all paperwork and day-to-day administrative work was in my hands. I was supposed to be back home by this time, but this seemed impossible. It never entered my mind to stay longer, but I was asked to continue and I agreed. I had to use my own savings and the money from the property I sold so that I could continue my work. I thank God that He had something in His back pocket, and that many of my private friends supported me.

IOP's initial work was a great success, but so much more could be done, not only for the people, but also with the people and by the people. Christian mission and aid is not about handing out survival kits and letting people die when the kits become empty. Villagers have to be involved in forging their own future, grasping the opportunities presented to them with the means that they have, and creating something for themselves based on everyone's needs and possibilities[5]. Thus, IOP orphans in all secondary schools were asked to put in about forty to fifty hours of work in their local community in return for a sponsorship for school. Anyone in need was asked, "What can you do yourself?"[6] Sharing the burden became the key for IOP's work in an African village.

A troop of more than twenty Girl Scouts learned how to "always be prepared" and a group of twenty women met weekly to learn how to develop small businesses for

---

[5] 2 Thessalonians 3v10 (NLT): *Even while we were with you, we gave you this command: "Those unwilling to work will not get to eat."*

[6] Exodus 35v10 (NIV): *All who are skilled among you are to come and make everything the Lord has commanded.*

themselves, along with basic life skills, child care and other family-related skills. I received from the Norwegian YWCA Girl Guide Association half of the funds needed for building a planned Orphanage for Girls in Ilula and the Royal Norwegian Embassy in Dar es Salaam (Tanzania's capital city) provided the other half. In 2005, the nine thousand square feet building opened, having been built by only local village carpenters, masons and labourers. The foreman was an experienced leader, but there was no engineer, and the architect was me!

I developed a good relationship with scout friends in Norway, Netherlands, and Luxembourg, countries which established their own IOP committees. We forged partnerships between community volunteers and supporters in the United States and Europe. One of the first great donors who supported IOP's work was US President Bill Clinton through his HIV-AIDS Initiative. Other great donors are the Norwegian Church Aid, USAID, Tanzania's Rapid Funding Envelope, Norway's Gaiabarna Foundation, etc.

The work of IOP, starting with sponsorship for only five orphans, exploded in front of my eyes! Today, IOP touches the lives of thousands of children and those who care for them through the sponsorship program and the foster family program. In 2009 and 2010, the Norwegian Church Aid awarded IOP as the best of their programs for orphans and children in Tanzania!

IOP currently has many other on-going projects including the program for counselling and testing for HIV-Aids which is being funded by USAID/John Hopkins University. It's been eleven years since IOP's birth and by God's grace I'm still working as its coordinator and daily leader.

I believe the reasons for IOP's success are simple: (1) A person went in the name of Christ to support a mission program created in a simple way based on hands-on work and honesty; (2) The people who requested help with their education and future are themselves involved; and (3) We put our trust in the Lord. God created us with two hands – one to receive with and one to give with. Being a receiver, each IOP student above elementary school takes on the role of a giver when completing his/her education – giver to the community, to family, to orphans, or to others in need. The needs of the people were, and still are, so extremely, tremendously great, but the possibilities are equally great, and the people able to assist, numerous. We have so much to share and it takes so little to get great things done!

No human planned the birth of IOP. It just came along because God had a plan of using someone for a special purpose. Together, we can change the world to be a better place!

- Berit Skaare (Ilula, Kilolo District, Tanzania)
Ilula Orphan Program
www.ilulaorphanprogram.org
May 2011

Paul wrote this in the book of Romans chapter 12 verse 3 (AMP): "For by the grace (unmerited favour of God) given to me I warn everyone among you not to estimate and think of himself more highly than he ought [not to have an exaggerated opinion of his own importance], but to rate his ability with sober judgment."

Father God, help me to judge my own talents and abilities with sober judgment so that I can really know what I'm good at. I don't want to live in fantasy, trying to fulfil my vision, and not Yours, for my life. Close the wrong doors and open the right ones for me, doors that will lead me to the place You want me to be, to do the things You created me to do, in both ministry and profession. I give and commit my life to You. In Jesus' name, amen!

Week 22: Running Away from God's Call

Many are the plans in a man's heart, but it is the Lord's
purpose that prevails. (Proverbs 19v21, NIV)

God may send someone to speak a prophetic word to you regarding your purpose, or to say something that will give you confirmation of your calling. (Remember 'Padre' David of Week 19?) Whatever revelation you receive should not contradict what the Bible says. If it does, the word is not from God. (For example, if you are told you have been called to pray against the Jewish people, this cannot be from God![1]) God may not give you all the details of His vision for you, but as you obediently step into what God has already revealed and as you run the sprints He calls you to run for a particular time or season (i.e., do the assignments He gives), then He will reveal more or clarify the vision for you (Week 20).

If you refuse to learn God's vision for your life, or if you know what it is but refuse to fulfil it, you will end up fulfilling either your personal selfish ambition, the dictates of society, or the devil's plan for your life. All these may reward you with popularity, influence and financial success, but in the end regret will come and this will last for all eternity.

God has a unique purpose for each person born on earth because He wants to give to everyone the privilege of partnering with Him. Nevertheless, as the verse in Proverbs above indicates, His plans for the world will not be thwarted despite the fact that some people did not and will not fulfil God's purpose for their lives. He already knew how people would decide even before they made the decision and He has planned accordingly[2]. Believers who obstinately refuse to obey God's directions will find themselves in painful situations that God will allow in order to put them back on track. Remember Jonah, the one who got swallowed by a big fish?[3]

---

[1] Genesis 12v2-3 (NLT): *I* [God] *will make you* [Abraham and his descendants through Jacob] *into a great nation. I will bless you and make you famous, and you will be a blessing to others. I will bless those who bless you and curse those who treat you with contempt. All the families on earth will be blessed through you.*

[2] Isaiah 46v9-10 (NIV): *Remember the former things, those of long ago; I am God, and there is no other; I am God, and there is none like Me. I make known the end from the beginning, from ancient times, what is still to come. I say: My purpose will stand, and I will do all that I please.* Verse 11b: *What I have said, that will I bring about; what I have planned, that will I do.*

[3] His story is recorded in the Book of Jonah in the Old Testament.

God told Jonah to go to Nineveh, the capital of the Assyrian Empire, to warn the people about God's impending judgment if they did not repent. But Jonah refused this assignment because he did not want the Ninevites, enemies of Israel, to repent and escape God's judgment[4]. Perhaps he was also afraid that he would be treated badly or even killed in that wicked ancient Iraqi city[5]. So instead of going east from Israel to Nineveh as God had told him to, Jonah boarded a ship bound west for Tarshish in present day Spain. Why? Because Jonah thought that if he went as far from Nineveh as possible, he could run away from God and His call on his life. But he soon realised he could not![6] To help Jonah align himself with God's will, God sent a storm that rocked Jonah's boat and a big fish that swallowed him up[7]. In the belly of the fish, Jonah could do nothing but evaluate his situation and pray. Sense finally came to him and he concluded: *The best place to be is in the centre of God's will.*[8]

In the next story, Vic was heading for Saudi Arabia when an accident reminded him of God's plan for his life, a plan which turned out to be bigger than pastoring a congregation.

Pastor Vic's Story

When I was twelve years old, I observed that my father was ill. His belly was swelling and he had difficulty breathing, but the doctors could do nothing for him. We had seven carabaos[9] which we used to till our land and these were sold to raise money so he could see several specialists. However, they told us he did not have long to live.

---

4 Jonah 4v2b (NIV): *I* [Jonah] *knew that You are a gracious and compassionate God, slow to anger and abounding in love, a God who relents from sending calamity.*

5 The sins of Nineveh are not described in the book of Jonah, but in the book of Nahum. These sins include prostitution, witchcraft, commercial exploitation and brutality to prisoners of war like torture and mutilation.

6 Psalm 139v7-10 (NIV): *Where can I go from Your Spirit? Where can I flee from Your presence? If I go up to the heavens, You are there; if I make my bed in the depths, You are there. If I rise on the wings of the dawn, if I settle on the far side of the sea, even there Your hand will guide me, Your right hand will hold me fast.*

7 Jonah 1v17 does not specifically say it was a whale, but a "great fish" (NIV).

8 Jonah 2v7-10 (TM): *"When my life was slipping away, I remembered God, and my prayer got through to You, made it all the way to your Holy Temple.... I'll do what I promised I'd do! Salvation belongs to God!" Then God spoke to the fish, and it vomited up Jonah on the seashore.* Jonah 3v1-3 (TM): *Next, God spoke to Jonah a second time: "Up on your feet and on your way to the big city of Nineveh! Preach to them. They're in a bad way and I can't ignore it any longer." This time Jonah started off straight for Nineveh, obeying God's orders to the letter.*

9 Carabao – a subspecies of water buffalo indigenous to Southeast Asia and used as a farm animal for pulling a plough and a cart.

We tried to feed him his favourite food, but we were frustrated to see him suffer and saddened that we would lose him.

One day we heard a loud announcement from someone in the street about a crusade that was going to take place nearby. The announcer told people to bring the sick with them for healing. My father was glad to hear that there was a Doctor of all doctors who could heal the sick[10]. He was eager to go so we accompanied him to the crusade. When the people saw him being prayed for, some joked that in his condition, nothing could be done for him. But this did not stop him from believing what the speaker was saying, that the Lord could heal him. As the speaker prayed for him, he began to feel better. Several days later, the swelling of his belly started to decrease and from that point on, he received complete healing! Because of this, the whole family joined a church. My father testified about his miraculous healing and many people joined us in church. I thank the Lord that our whole family became believers, including our neighbours who witnessed my father's healing.

The whole family became very active in church activities and my father was made Sunday school teacher. One time, a foreign missionary visited our village and prophesied that there was a young man who would be used by God and would become a pastor. As there was no other young man there, I stood up and claimed the prophecy, and the church prayed over me.

When the school year began, I hoped in my heart that I could go to high school. This would require going to the nearby city of Surigao on a small boat. I also had to look for work to support myself through school, as the family money was all spent on father's illness. I found work in Surigao City as a live-in houseboy, but this work prevented me from going to school. However, I did not lose hope. Sometime later, I met the pastor from my village of Burgos, Surigao del Norte. It must have been a divine appointment because through this pastor, God answered my prayer to attend high school!

Mindful of God's desire for me to become a pastor, I attended the Berean Bible School in Surigao City after finishing high school. After a year in that school, the missionary who prophesied over me gave me financial help when he heard about my desire to also get a college degree at the Surigao del Norte School of Arts and Trade. Eventually, I graduated from Bible school and college. I also met Gloria in college who later became my wife.

---

[10] One of the names of God is *Jehovah Rapha* (Appendix 1) which means "God, the Healer". God introduces this name for the first time in Exodus 15v26.

After graduation, I was hired by the nickel company in our area and I was happy to be able to help my parents financially. I got promoted several times at work until I got recommended to work in Saudi Arabia. My parents were elated by this as my new wage would be a big financial help for the family. When my paper work was completed and I was ready to go, I went to say goodbye to my pastor and the church. They were not happy for me because I would not be able to attend church in Saudi Arabia. Nevertheless with heavy hearts they prayed for me.

Next morning, I got on the bus to start the trip, not expecting the accident that was about to happen. The bus got involved in a collision! Being on the front seat, I was among the critically injured. I was taken to hospital where the damage to my left leg was discovered. The doctor informed me that in order to walk again, I needed a stainless steel rod in my leg, but I refused this and prayed to the Lord that if He enabled me to walk normally again, I would not go to Saudi Arabia and instead go into ministry. I prayed this after it dawned on me that the accident happened because I interrupted God's plan for my life, that which was prophesied by the foreign missionary who visited our village when I was a boy.

The doctor just put my leg in a cast as I had requested and for some time I exercised it by walking with crutches. Even before I got better, I started getting myself into 'ministry' by distributing Bible tracts while doing my walking exercises on crutches. I thank God that Gloria was not embarrassed to do this with me. In less than a year, I was able to walk without crutches and my left leg went back to normal!

Grateful for this miracle from God, I no longer desired to take a secular job and so I decided to go into fulltime ministry and registered it as Surigao Holistic Ministries, Inc. here in Bislig, Surigao del Sur. Eventually, Gloria and I got married and were blessed with four children, all involved in our church's praise and worship ministry: Vic (who's now with the Lord), Glorivic, Gloriavic and Vincent.

When our eldest son Vic died in an accident, we were overcome with grief. At eighteen years of age, he was a very responsible son and was my ready helper whenever I travelled. At church he played the drums, taught the children at Sunday school and led the young people in praise and worship. He was hospitable to visitors at our church and most of all, very obedient to his parents. While we were at the cemetery for his burial, I noticed a young man named Junjun who came to help. He told me that he was always around to help when someone was going to be buried because he knew there was going to be food after the burial. I learned that Junjun came from a broken family. His mother worked as a housemaid but did not earn enough.

As Junjun told me his story, I felt compassion for him. I learned that he was one of those who attended my son Vic's evangelistic meetings in his community. We offered

Junjun our home to live in and to send him to school. Sometime later, we heard of four children left in the care of a man dying of heart disease. This man told me that his wish before dying was that I would take his children into my care because his wife worked as a housemaid and could not look after the young children. I felt sorry for him and granted his request. He was happy about this and within a few days, he died.

And so our home became the new home of five children after Vic's death. In the following months we met other homeless children who were orphans or victims of broken homes. I became the 'pastor', the father and shepherd, to these lost and abandoned sheep, as well as the pastor of our church here in Bislig and overseer of the outreach to the tribal people in the nearby villages.

Today, we have several children in our orphanage. We send them all to school and teach them to live as Jesus would like them to live. Some of those who have come of age have now become pastors and teachers who minister to the various tribal groups in our province. Recently, a woman who was abandoned by her husband left her one-month old baby with us since she could barely look after her eight other children. We did not anticipate the orphanage taking on babies as well. Trying to meet the children's needs for food, clothes, school materials and medicines can be quite a struggle especially because we do not have a steady source of income or on-going support from Christian ministries. Only the Lord's promise that He would send people who would meet the needs keeps us going.

I thank God for all those who have contributed to the work of the orphanage, particularly Christians Alive Church in Lancaster, UK who helped us finish the orphanage building. The Lord will not forget their good deeds because He promised in Genesis 12 verse 3 that He would bless those who bless His children[11]. I'm sure that includes the children in our orphanage!

> - Vic (Bislig, Surigao del Sur, Philippines)
> Surigao Holistic Ministries Inc.
> surigaoholisticministries@yahoo.com
> August 2011

Isaiah 6v8 (NLT): "Then I heard the Lord asking, 'Whom should I send as a messenger to this people? Who will go for us?' I said, 'Here I am. Send me!'"

My prayer for you:

---

[11] Genesis 12v3a (NIV): *I will bless those who bless you...*

My Father in heaven, for any reader who had not been interested in finding out Your purpose for his/her life and had been happily going about his/her own business and own affairs without even asking what You want the reader to do, please bring conviction towards repentance.

If You had given the reader some indication of Your call on his/her life, or given him/her an assignment to do but the reader was not interested or refused to do it, please also bring conviction that leads to repentance.

Whatever fear the reader may have that prevents him/her from obeying You, please remove that fear. Grant the reader love, passion and ability for the work You have planned for him/her to do. And as the reader takes the step of faith into Your calling, give all that he/she needs to complete each task and to finish the race for the glory of Your Son, our Lord and Saviour, Jesus Christ. Amen!

Week 23: The Blessing of Obedience

If you love Me, you will obey what I command. (John 14v15, NIV)

The best place to be is in the centre of God's will (Week 22). We get to this 'place' by receiving Jesus as our Saviour and Lord, and we stay in this place by obeying Him. Christians obey not to get saved; they obey because they are already saved! Our act of obedience demonstrates our gratitude to all that Jesus did for us.

According to the Online Greek Interlinear Bible[1], the word for love in the verse above in the original Greek is *agapate,* a form of the verb *agapao* (noun, *agápē*), and it implies a continuous action. God wants us to *keep on being in loving fellowship with Him.* Disobedience separates us from this fellowship. *Agápē* itself goes beyond having warm sentimental feelings of affection for God. It is love that moves one to obedient action!

The Greek word for obey in the verse is *teresate,* from the verb *tereo* which means to keep, to guard, to observe, to pay attention to, to attend to carefully. Therefore, it means more than 'to obey'. After all, it is possible to obey rules for fear of punishment. *Tereo* implies obeying what God says because we value His commands[2]. They are important to us because we love Him[3].

Although we are saved by God's grace through faith in Jesus' work at Calvary and not by our obedience[4], our obedience brings God's blessings. Indeed, keeping God's laws "brings great reward" (Psalm 19v11)[5]. Disobedience, on the other hand, has negative consequences and brings God's discipline and a withdrawal of His blessings[6]. God cannot bless our disobedience because He cannot bless sin. He loves His children too much to let them continue in their disobedience. As in Jonah's case (Week 22),

---

[1] www.scripture4all.org/OnlineInterlinear/Greek_Index.htm

[2] Psalm 119v97-98 (NIV): *Oh, how I love your law! I meditate on it all day long. Your commands make me wiser than my enemies, for they are ever with me.*

[3] See John 14v15 above. Also Romans 13v10 (NLT): *Love fulfils the requirements of God's law.* Therefore, obedience is the fruit of our love for God. The more we love Him, the more we will want to obey Him.

[4] Ephesians 2v8-9 (NKJV): *For by grace you have been saved through faith, and that not of yourselves; it is the gift of God, not of works, lest anyone should boast.*

[5] Also, James 1v25 (NLT): *But if you look carefully into the perfect law that sets you free, and if you do what it says and don't forget what you heard, then God will bless you for doing it.*

[6] Hebrews 12v10 (NIV): *Our fathers disciplined us for a little while as they thought best; but God disciplines us for our good, that we may share in His holiness.*

He will allow troubles to come our way to stop us in our track until we turn to Him in repentance[7].

In choosing to respond to God's kindness by obeying Him, we not only prove our love for Him, we also receive His blessings. Our obedience to what God tells us to do may put us in difficult situations, but we can be sure our obedience will bear good fruit and bring eternal rewards (Weeks 29 and 33).

In early 2011, the 'Arab Spring' swept through Libya, but the rest of the world knew little about what was happening inside the country. This is a story of God's call to His daughter in Canada to intercede regarding this situation. Knowing that her prayer had been answered is a real blessing, although some may doubt that the answer has made a real difference to the people of Libya. One thing is sure, however; her obedience will bring eternal rewards.

God Answered My Prayer for Libya

In February 2011 I watched events in the Middle East unfold over several weeks and stayed glued to the TV to learn all that I could. The Lord used what I saw to really teach me and to open my eyes to human suffering particularly in Libya. Some news was trickling out of Libya about the massive anti-government protests and the government's brutal crackdown. However, the world could not really hear much about what had been happening in the country because the Libyan government had been maintaining tight control over media and communication. Foreign journalists had been practically barred and local reporters faced intimidation and threats from the regime of Muanmar Gaddhafi who had governed the North African country since 1969. I cried out to God for the poor Libyans who were so cut off from the rest of the world, unheard by foreign journalists and risking their lives to get even the grainiest Youtube or Facebook footage out to the world, the only way they could.

For several days and nights I was on my knees praying for Libya. On 21 February, I cried out, "LORD... PLEASE... MAKE A WAY![8] Find a way to get reliable foreign journalists into Libya so that they can report to the rest of the world and enable the Libyans to be heard. Let the truth be revealed and documented for the leaders of the nations of the world to finally get a clear picture of what is happening in this country." It seemed an impossible thing to happen, but the Lord really put Libya on my heart.

---

[7] Repentance is not simply a cessation from sin. It is a change of heart and mind that produces godly sorrow and a change of ways, a '180-degree turn'. It is more than an act. It is an attitude that moves one to desire to obey God at all costs.

[8] Isaiah 43v19 (NIV): *See, I am doing a new thing! Now it springs up; do you not perceive it? I am making a way in the desert and streams in the wasteland.*

Approximately six hours later, breaking news appeared on CNN that one of their journalists, Ben Wedeman, managed to cross into Eastern Libya from Egypt and was reporting by phone from an undisclosed location inside Libya just after 6 PM, Eastern Time (USA and Canada). He was the first western television journalist to enter Libya during this crisis. The ONLY foreign journalist to have entered the country at this time was actually IN Eastern Libya to report on his findings!

I couldn't believe it! This was the breakthrough needed! Because of his step of bravery, Wedeman was able to show the world that opposition ("rebel") forces appeared to be in firm control of much of the eastern region of Libya.

I knew then that it was only a matter of time before more foreign journalists would begin to take that brave step forward. Was it illegal? Yes and no, given that what's legal and illegal in that country depends on whose side you are on, and the opposing side was proving to be the majority.

That one journalist, the first one and CNN at that, spoke of how, when he and his companions reached the border, they were immediately greeted with warmth and welcome by the citizens now patrolling the border. (The former officials had abandoned their posts.) When he and those with him in the van pulled into Benghazi, they felt like the first American soldiers in their jeeps coming in to liberate France in World War II. That was how they were received. Since then, more foreign journalists have defied the ban as well.

Desperate to be heard, the people were ecstatic that the world was finally going to really hear their voice. Being heard more and more can make all the difference for how events can unfold....

I thanked God profusely for answering my prayer, the prayer of one intercessor praying for a nation.

- Jeannie (Vancouver, British Columbia, Canada)
March 2011

The next story is my recollection of an assignment the Lord gave me some years ago.

An Assignment

My family and I were living in Grange-over-Sands and were due to move to Cockermouth (in North Cumbria) in a year's time when the Lord directed us to attend a church in Kendal (in South Cumbria) in 2002. Sometime after we started going there, the Lord impressed on me the story of Joshua. Joshua had become a special Bible character to me since 2001 when I had a vision (a picture in my mind) reminiscent of the Bible character, followed by a message from two people on separate occasions that the Lord had called me "to be a Joshua". I was told that the Lord would reveal to me what that meant.

When I was reminded of that prophecy, I saw a vision of myself walking around the walls of the church in Kendal. I then phoned my sister about the vision. As it turned out, she too was reading about Joshua and remembered the prophetic word spoken to me in 2001. I took this as confirmation that indeed, the 'Jericho walk'[9] was an assignment from the Lord for me in this particular church. The Jews under the leadership of Joshua marched around the walls of Jericho once every day for six days. Since I could not go to Kendal every day, I did the 'six days' within a few weeks. Each time, I would walk for about five minutes around the church on a weekday.

When I finished my 'sixth day', I asked the Lord to reveal to me when He wanted me to do the 'seventh day' for which I would have to walk around the church seven times[10]. A few days later, I was flipping the pages of my Bible when I happened to open it in Joshua chapter 3. I was drawn to verse 5, "Consecrate yourselves for tomorrow the Lord will do amazing things among you" (NIV). That word 'tomorrow' seemed to jump out of the page so I took this to mean that I was to do that seventh walk the following day. I called my sister, but before I could share my prayer request, she interrupted me to say that the Lord wanted me to read Joshua chapter 3! To me, that was confirmation to do the walk the next day. I consecrated myself to the Lord with prayer and arranged to meet my prayer partner Liz in the church prayer room at 11 AM. I had hoped she would be praying for me as I did my walk, though I didn't tell her about my assignment.

The next day (a weekday) came but before I left home, I called an intercessor-friend to ask for his prayer. Our conversation took longer than I anticipated so I dashed out of the house. Because it would take me thirty minutes to walk to the bus stop, I realised I would miss my bus to Kendal and my 11 AM appointment. I repented for not keeping an eye on the time and asked the Lord to help me catch my bus. Just then, an empty taxi stopped beside me. Praise God the driver agreed to drive me the short distance to the bus stop, so I managed to catch my bus.

As I got off the bus in Kendal, doubt overcame me and I began to wonder if I was being presumptuous. I cried out to the Lord, "If You really want me to do this, Lord, You will have to give me a sign!" A second later I heard in my spirit, "Number seven!"

---

[9] The story of Joshua and the walls of Jericho is found in Joshua chapter 6.

[10] Joshua 6v4b (ESV): *On the seventh day you shall march around the city seven times, and the priests shall blow the trumpets.*

I answered, "Number seven? Alright, Lord. If anyone mentions anything to me about number seven, I will take that to mean You really want me to do this!"

I arrived at the church and waited in the empty prayer room for Liz. Several minutes passed, and then an hour, but still no sign of her. Finally, Liz arrived soon after another lady, Denise, who I wasn't expecting, walked in. The three of us got talking, though my mind was on my assignment the whole time. Several minutes later, Liz excitedly spoke about doing the scripture reading in a church service for the first time. I asked her what scripture she was going to read, to which she replied, "It's about Naaman dipping himself in the Jordan River SEVEN times!"[11] I couldn't contain my tears when I heard this! Responding to their quizzical looks, I explained that I was just overwhelmed by the fact that the Lord would give me such a confirmation. I then told them about my assignment. They soon sent me off to do my 'Jericho walk' around the church, promising to pray for me as I did the walk. (The Lord must have sent Denise so that together with Liz, they could agree in prayer for me.[12])

It took a while to do seven walks around the church and at one point I wondered what the vicar (who probably could see the church grounds from the vicarage some distance away) would think if he saw me. But I really didn't care! God had confirmed my assignment in amazing ways and nothing was going to stop me from accomplishing it!

At the end of the walk, I did as I was instructed. I recited Psalm 24v7-10[13] before I opened the church door and walked in. I then prayed and declared what I believed the Lord told me to say as I stood facing the altar. After this, I joined the two ladies in the prayer room and together we thanked the Lord and committed the outcome to Him, the King of glory.

The military strategy given by God to Joshua was something any military commander would find bizarre and absurd. But when Joshua and the people obeyed, they were rewarded with victory – the fall of Jericho. It has been years since I left the church in Kendal. To be honest, I don't really know what major difference my obedience has made (although there have been many changes that have happened to the church and to the town since). Perhaps I will have to wait until I get to heaven

---

[11] In 2 Kings 5v1-14

[12] Matthew 18v19 (ESV): *Again I say to you, if two of you agree on earth about anything they ask, it will be done for them by My Father in heaven.*

[13] Psalm 24v7-10 (NIV): *Lift up your heads, O you gates; be lifted up, you ancient doors, that the King of glory may come in. Who is this King of glory? The Lord strong and mighty, the Lord mighty in battle. Lift up your heads, O you gates; lift them up, you ancient doors that the King of glory may come in. Who is He, this King of glory? The Lord Almighty – He is the King of glory.*

to find out. Sometimes the Lord just wants us to leave the results of our obedience to Him! For now, I am blessed by the knowledge that my obedience is precious to the Lord, and that He certainly blesses obedience to His word.

- Haide (Lancaster, England)
October 2011

Father God, help me to love You enough to treasure Your commands and to love being obedient with all my heart! Grant me the grace to soar like an eagle and receive revelations of what You want me to do. Send me confirmations I need that I may be bold and confident of Your partnership with me. Grant me the grace to act on what You have revealed to me and help me to commit to You the results of my obedience. Forgive me for those times I have disobeyed You. Thank You that You have not given up on me! I love You Lord!

Week 24: True Grit

Therefore, since we are surrounded by such a huge crowd of witnesses to the life of faith, let us strip off every weight that slows us down, especially the sin that so easily trips us up. And let us run with endurance the race God has set before us. We do this by keeping our eyes on Jesus, the champion who initiates and perfects our faith. Because of the joy awaiting Him, He endured the cross, disregarding its shame. Now He is seated in the place of honour beside God's throne. Think of all the hostility He endured from sinful people; then you won't become weary and give up. (Hebrews 12v1-3, NLT)

It is easy to start a race, but more difficult to finish it. An athlete in a long distance race may feel like dropping out, but if he wants to make it to the finish line and get the prize, he has to overcome distractions, weariness and discouragement with endurance, perseverance, true grit! The same is true in the marathon of life. Hebrews 10v36 (ESV) tells us, "For you have need of endurance, so that when you have done the will of God you may receive what is promised".

How can we overcome weariness and endure the race to the end?

1. Remember the great crowd of witnesses who have gone before you.

There will be times when doubt tries to overtake your faith and you feel like giving up and abandoning God's call on your life. Whenever doubt comes, remember the saints who have gone before you (like those in the 'Hall of Fame' in Hebrews 11). They are cheering you on! If they endured to the end, so can you! God will give you the grace[1] He gave them because He shows no favouritism[2].

2. Strip off every weight that slows you down.

An athlete will shed off any excess weight before a race and any extra clothing just before he runs. God may tell you to give up something that may not be bad in itself, but may be an extra weight that is impeding or distracting you. Sin definitely has to be stripped off or it will trip you up. Some people who say they "received Jesus Christ as Saviour" but never really repented of their sin (there was no real desire to strip it

---

[1] Hebrews 4v16 (NLT): *So let us come boldly to the throne of our gracious God. There we will receive His mercy, and we will find grace to help us when we need it most.*

[2] Acts 10v34 (NIV): *Then Peter began to speak: I now realise how true it is that God does not show favouritism.*

off) may find at the end of their lives that they not only lost the race, they never even made it to heaven's door[3]!

3. Keep your eyes on Jesus!

Your obedience to the Lord is important, but if you think focusing on not giving up and on obeying to the end will help you endure, then you are setting yourself up for disappointment. Focusing on your own obedience or efforts may remind you of past failures and when weariness sets in, such reminders may lead you to conclude that as you are a failure anyway, why bother persevering[4]? Or if you find yourself doing better than others, you may be tempted to think it is because of your own efforts and perseverance, only to discover at the end of the race that you have been disqualified from getting your reward because of your arrogance[5].

The scripture in Hebrews 12 tells us to focus on Jesus, not on our efforts or obedience. He is the One who gave us His faith ("initiator") and the One who is helping us to live out that faith to the fullest ("perfecter"). 2 Corinthians 10v5 (NASB) declares that we must "take every thought captive to the obedience of Christ". The word in the original Greek text for captive here is *aichmalotizo* which means 'to capture one's mind' or 'to captivate'. Captivated by what? By the *hupakoe* or "obedience" of Christ! Christ obeyed the Father and endured to the end the shame and the excruciating pain of slow death on a cross (Week 40). Although He could have called thousands of angels to save Him from this cruelty[6], He chose to give Himself up because He kept the vision of His Bride, the assembly of the saved, ever before Him. He fulfilled His purpose to be your sin-sacrifice because He saw you and remembered that the only way for Him to save you from hell's fire and to enjoy your company for all eternity is for Him to endure to the end. How can you not be captivated by such love?

We must be obedient, but we are not to keep our focus on our obedience, but on Jesus' obedience which showed His great love for us. As we allow ourselves to be captivated

---

3   Matthew 7v21-23 (NIV): *Not everyone who says to Me, 'Lord, Lord,' will enter the kingdom of heaven, but only he who does the will of My Father who is in heaven. Many will say to Me on that day, 'Lord, Lord, did we not prophesy in Your name, and in Your name drive out demons and perform many miracles?' Then I will tell them plainly, 'I never knew you. Away from Me, you evildoers!'*

4   Proverbs 23v7 (NKJV): *For as he thinks in his heart, so is he.* A person acts out his own perception of himself. If you think you are no good and a failure, you will fail! If you are a Christian, remind yourself who you really are in Jesus. See Appendix 2.

5   James 4v6 (NASB): *God is opposed to the proud, but gives grace to the humble.*

6   Matthew 26v53-54 (CEV): *"Don't you know that I [Jesus] could ask My Father, and right away He would send Me more than twelve armies of angels? But then, how could the words of the Scriptures come true, which say that this must happen?"*

by this, we receive a greater revelation of His love. This causes us to fall more in love with Him such that He becomes our very goal, our "magnificent obsession". Now that produces true grit!

Below is a story of one called by God to minister to seamen coming to the UK from different nations. It is a ministry that is often met with indifference, resistance or rejection, which can easily cause anyone to lose focus and give up. It is a ministry that requires true grit! But our storyteller perseveres for love of Jesus. One of the lessons he learned that helped him to endure is that.....

Often Things are Not What They Seem

In my experience as Port Chaplain to seamen, I have discovered that a person's real response to the Bible may not actually be what it seems. So often over the years, God surprised me!

About a year after the breakup of the Soviet Union, when there were no longer restrictions about owning a Bible, I visited a ship from Russia and met with a group of seamen in the officer's mess room. Among them was Viktor, the Second Officer. As he eagerly accepted a Bible and other Christian books in Russian, he said he thought he recognised me. Gradually we remembered that he had been the Political Officer on board a Russian ship I visited ten years before. (As Political Officer, it was his job to stop people like me from distributing Bibles to the Russian seamen.) He confided to me that by the time we met, he already regretted having to report to authorities in Moscow, among other things, any interest on the ship in Christianity. He probably also had me secretly photographed like other Port Chaplains who were in contact with Russian seamen.

Every Russian seaman on board was afraid of Viktor, as one word from him could send them home. They could not have known, any more than I did, that he actually wanted for himself one of the Bibles he suspected I had given to some of his men! Meeting him again after the fall of the Soviet Union, he exploded with laughter when I explained how I distributed Bibles to some of his crew. I revealed to Viktor that when I saw seamen, usually in pairs, leaving a Russian ship and walking towards the dock-gate, I would offer them a lift into town in my car. After small talk about their families, they would usually accept my invitation to a café for coffee. Eventually I would offer them each a small Bible in Russian, which after just a little hesitation they would usually accept. They would hide away the forbidden book they had taken out of curiosity; no doubt, some would have thought of selling it. I would drive them around the local historical sites of Southampton and, after some time, we would become friendlier with each other. Before returning them to their ship, I would ask if they knew of others on their ship who would like a Bible or Christian book for their children. Only with their agreement did I ever take it any farther, as I knew they were taking a risk.

Later before the 3 PM tea-break, I would go to the head of the gangway to tell the watchman that I had been invited to the ship by friends I had met earlier. The watchman would use the internal phone to call the Political Officer who would call my new friends from their cabins. Their bear hugs which lifted me clear of the deck were always convincing enough, but before being given permission to go to their cabin, the Political Officer would ask what was in my large plastic bin liner. Peeping inside, all he could see were woollen hats, which were always popular with seamen who work outside on the deck. Sometimes in a jovial manner I would pop a hat on his head. Then in the privacy of the cabin, as I quietly shared a little of what the Bible teaches about the way of salvation, other crew members, carefully chosen by my new friends, would come to the cabin for their copies of the Bible which were hidden at the bottom of the bag.

I believe that just as God had given me a way years ago to get the Bible into the hands of Russian seamen, He was also creating a hunger for the Word of God in Viktor's heart. When I saw him again ten years later, he took me to his cabin where he was particularly happy to receive Christian books suitable for each of his children. Then I asked how he could teach his children if he did not know the Lord himself. Although I did not meet Viktor again, I believe God opened his heart and mind, as I taught him from His Word.

Viktor reminds me of a Turkish seaman I met some years ago. I remember that all eyes turned to me when I walked into the crew's mess room full of Turkish seamen one day. I felt awkward when each man refused to accept a leaflet with Bible teaching or a portion of the Bible. I was about to leave when one man asked if I could give him a lift, as the container terminal was some distance from the town. We made our way in single file down the long gangway. A strong wind threatened to sweep us into the water as we walked along the narrow path between the quayside and the straddle cranes. Not a word was spoken until I drove along the dock road. Then at a quiet area out of sight of the ship, he frightened me for a moment when with a loud voice he bellowed, "Stop car!" Just when I thought I had wasted my time going to that ship, the man confessed that he did not really want to go to town and that all he wanted was a Bible in Turkish! I then took him to my large store of Christian literature in several languages where he picked out a small Turkish Bible. He informed me he had recently moved from a previous vessel where crew members who were Muslims caught him reading his Bible and threw it into the sea. Scars on his leg showed where they had attacked him. He added that he had already come to love the Lord Jesus and nothing could take that from him.

After a while, I dropped him near his ship, but not before making an arrangement. Container ships work to a schedule, so on the given date every few weeks when the ship was in Southampton, I would visit his ship. Like the rest of the crew, my new friend would refuse Christian literature I offered. Then I would make my way back to my car alone and wait. Eventually he would join me to go to my literature store and to enjoy a few minutes of precious fellowship and prayer before returning to his ship.

- David Thomson (Troon, Scotland)
March 2011

Father God, help me never to give up living for You. Help me never to give up doing what You have called me to do. Help me not to give in to the devil's distractions and discouragements, but to put my focus on how much Jesus loves me. Thank You for this promise in Philippians 1v6 (NLT): "And I am certain that God, who began the good work within you, will continue His work until it is finally finished on the day when Christ Jesus returns." Thank You that You will never give up on me! Lord Jesus, help me to endure to the end and finish for You. Amen.

Week 25: Training for the Race

All athletes are disciplined in their training. They do it to win a prize that will fade away, but we do it for an eternal prize. So I run with purpose in every step. I am not just shadowboxing. I discipline my body like an athlete, training it to do what it should. (1 Corinthians 9v25-27, NLT)

The apostle Paul, who penned the letters to the Corinthians, doubtless alluded to the Corinthian Games (Week 21) in the scripture above, but his illustrations are applicable to all athletic events in ancient Greece, including the Olympiad.

The *kotinos* (olive crown or wreath) for an Olympic victor came with great honour[1] which he would receive throughout Greece, especially in his home town. As the victor entered his town, there would be great celebration. He would be showered with flowers and praises. Sculptors would create statues of him and poets would sing odes about his victory. He would be cited as an example to young people. He would be sought for his counsel. A victor knew that the Olympic honour carried with it great moral responsibility since he was expected throughout his life to be worthy of the honour bestowed on him.

For the prize of high honour that went with the *kotinos*, the ancient Olympic athletes trained very hard. They would spend years of intense physical training and preparation. Today's athletes do the same. They train for years to develop speed, agility, strength and endurance. They also need to have discipline in following the rigours of training, exercise and diet.

1 Timothy 4v7-8 (NIV) says, "Have nothing to do with godless myths and old wives' tales; rather, train yourself to be godly. For physical training is of some value, but godliness has value for all things, holding promise for both the present life and the life to come". Physical training is good, but its benefits are only enjoyed in this life, whereas spiritual training is profitable for our life now as well as prepares us for eternity.

The Greek word for 'train' in 1 Timothy 4v7-8 is *gymnaze*, from which we get the word gymnasium. Training for godliness is similar to physical training in a gymnasium in that it also requires discipline, in this case, spiritual discipline which involves reading, studying and meditating on the Scriptures, prayer and fellowship (Week 49).

---

[1] The olive crown or wreath was said to be "for men who do not compete for possessions, but for honour".

Spiritual discipline has another aspect. Proverbs 22v6a (ESV) says, "Train up a child in the way he should go..." The word in the original Hebrew text for train here is *chanak* which originally meant 'to narrow down' or 'to constrict as by throttling'. It eventually came to mean 'to train to be disciplined such that the trainee chooses the narrow way of obedience'[2]. This is how our Father in heaven trains us: He lets us see that obedience to His word and His will is the <u>only</u> way to live life on earth because He is not only training us to fulfil our earthly calling, He is also training us now for the bigger job He will give us on the other side of eternity. No, we will not be spending eternity on clouds playing the harp. We will have important jobs to do for the King of Kings![3]

A very important part of our training comes in the form of trials and temptations[4]. In fact, we cannot be trained without them. This is why God allows these to come our way. Our Lord is honoured when God's children endure and persevere to the end. And He is worthy of all the praise, honour and glory!

Here are two stories about two women who, in their role as mothers, are being trained by trials, one as she is challenged as a new mother caring for her baby, and the other as the mother of two handicapped children, one of whom needed liver transplant.

Consider It All Joy...

I've always struggled to understand why the Bible tells us that we have to "consider it all joy" when we fall into various trials (James 1v2). In my experience, trials don't

---

[2] Matthew 7v14 (NIV): *But small is the gate and <u>narrow</u> the road that leads to* [eternal] *life, and only a few find it.*

[3] These verses may give us a clue as to what we may be doing for God on the other side of eternity: Genesis 1v28 (ESV): *And God said to them, "Be fruitful and multiply and fill the earth and subdue it, and <u>have dominion</u> over the fish of the sea and over the birds of the heavens and over every living thing that moves on the earth."* Revelation 5v10 (ESV): *... and you have made them a kingdom and priests to our God; and they shall <u>reign on the earth</u>.* Revelation 22v5b (ESV): *.... and they will <u>reign forever and ever.</u>* Revelation 21 speaks of the heavenly Jerusalem that will come down from heaven one day and Jesus reigning on earth with His people. God is training us to reign with Him!

[4] In the original Greek New Testament books, the same word, *peirazo*, is used for trial, test, and temptation. In English we use 'test' or 'trial' when *peirazo* refers to hardships or difficult situations allowed by God. By God's grace we learn to rely on Him when faced with these. We use 'temptation' when *peirazo* refers to inner struggles with sin. It does not come from God (James 1v13-14), but from our own carnal desires which the devil takes advantage of. We can either choose to fall or stand against the temptation with the help of the Holy Spirit. God allows trials and temptations to reveal to us our character weakness and His power to transform.

equal joy. They equal anxiety, stress and worry. That was until I gave birth to my baby daughter.

Since becoming a mum, I've been overwhelmed by the love that wells up inside me for her. I find myself gazing at her when she's sleeping and laughing at her cute giggles, even when changing her dirty nappy at two o'clock in the morning! Sometimes I could cry I love her so much.

Alongside this overwhelming love I have for my daughter, I've also been overwhelmed by the responsibility I have as a mother to provide for her needs and to give her the opportunity to grow up and mature into a young woman of God. Everyday I'm faced with these challenges of how best to look after her and I'm constantly leaning on God and asking Him for wisdom.

One such challenge has been trying to get her to settle down to sleep at bedtime. For the first few months of my daughter's life, she has had her night time feed and quickly dropped off to sleep. My husband or I would then put her in her cot and have the evening to ourselves. But over the last month or so, every time we've put her into her cot, she has started waking up. We would then pick her up and rock her back to sleep only for her to wake up yet again as soon as we put her back in her cot. Some nights it would take us four or five tries before she would eventually stay asleep. It was then occurring to me that Mairi, my daughter, was going to have to learn to fall asleep on her own. Even at four months old, she was going to have to start growing up!

Leaving Mairi to cry herself to sleep was one of the hardest things I've had to do since becoming a mum. My heart would break as I heard her wail and all I wanted to do was run into her room, pick her up and cuddle her. I had to go to God and ask Him for the strength to be able to allow her to learn this important skill. When I did this, God reminded me of James 1 verses 2 to 4 (NKJV), "My brethren, count it all joy when you fall into various trials, knowing that the testing of your faith produces patience. But let patience have its perfect work, that you may be perfect and complete, lacking nothing". Not only was this situation a trial for me hearing my baby cry, but it was also a trial for Mairi being left on her own to cry herself to sleep. However, in leaving her for a short period of time she would then learn to fall asleep on her own, allowing her to begin to grow up and become more independent.

Once I received the revelation that putting Mairi down for a sleep was an opportunity for her to mature, I actually started looking forward to and getting excited about nap times and bedtime. I considered it a joy that Mairi would get the opportunity to begin to grow up!

Now, I understand that not all the trials we go through in life are as small as the one I've illustrated here. God allows us to go through much more challenging situations such as the loss of a job, divorce or the death of a loved one. It's often difficult to find "joy" in these tough situations. It may even feel as if God has left us when we are going through these difficult times. But God promises that He will "never leave us nor forsake us"[5]. Mairi may have felt all alone as I left her to cry herself to sleep, but I was actually just at the other side of her bedroom door ready to go in and reassure her when I felt it was getting too much for her.

God is our Father, and His love for us is even more perfect and complete than my love for Mairi or any other parent's love for their child. As I learned how to deal with Mairi's 'sleeping trial', I was reminded that in all the trials we face, God is with us. As we trust in Him and remember that He hasn't left us or forsaken us, then we can grow stronger in our faith[6], giving us a deeper and closer relationship with our loving Father.

- Heather (Lancaster, England)
June 2011

The next is a touching story of a mother's struggle and fight to see that her son got the best medical attention that would prolong his life. What is noteworthy is that Ave chose not to be bitter, but to be thankful for those years she could spend with her son. She ran this particular race and won!

What about her son? Was he able to fulfil God's purpose for his life after only sixteen years in this world? Ave could only trust God that He made the right decision regarding her son's time on earth. Vaughn is not really in her past, but in her future. When she gets reunited with him, they will never be separated again. God is good!

My Special Son Vaughn

I was born in Jamaica and accepted Jesus as my Saviour and Lord at a young age. I married my high school boyfriend and had two sons who were both special children. My oldest, Dwight, was diagnosed with myopathy at two, and my younger son Vaughn had a liver disorder. The marriage lasted for five years and I was left with a two and a half-year old and an eleven-month old to care for.

Vaughn was a very smart and talented child who was gifted in poetry and drawing (he could draw in three dimensions as early as three), but his body did not keep up

---

[5] Hebrews 13v5 (NKJV):*"I will never leave you nor forsake you."*
[6] That is, we grow in our understanding of how to use the faith of Jesus that God has already given us (Week 8). It is about learning to focus on the fact that Jesus is faithful and full of faith!

with his advanced intellect. His malfunctioning liver led to the build-up of bilirubin in the blood and thin and poorly formed bones. Although he could talk at eleven months old, he was unable to sit up by himself. The doctors thought that he would not live beyond his second birthday.

The only way for Vaughn to realise a normal, longer life was to have a liver transplant. This could not be done in Jamaica because the hospitals were not equipped for this procedure. A Jamaican parent who started the Liver Association of Jamaica told me that her son successfully underwent liver transplant at the Children's Hospital in Pittsburgh, USA. To my dismay, the price was US$250,000! There was no way I could afford that with my salary as a lecturer. I recall talking to God and telling Him that He owns ALL the resources of this world. I then gave the matter of Vaughn's life-saving surgery to Him.

I sought advice from friends and relatives who pointed me to possible sources of financial help for Vaughn, but most of these channels ended up in a dead end. I wrote several letters, but although the recipients were sympathetic, I was told they could not provide me with financial assistance. Then one of the organisations I had approached decided to assist me due to a default situation that arose. It took six months, however, before a sum of $165,000 was sent to the hospital in the USA for Vaughn's surgery. Another hurdle came when I was told the full amount of $250,000 had to be deposited as I did not have health insurance to cover the difference. I tried to raise funds, but another three months passed and Vaughn's health deteriorated further.

As I was looking for another hospital, I was informed that the hospital in Pittsburgh had placed Vaughn on the active transplant list. In less than one month, I was in a plane bound for Pittsburgh with Vaughn who was now four years old (but physically looked like a two year-old). We had to stay near the hospital because the donor liver had to be transplanted within six hours of removal from the donor. We only had enough funds to pay for one month's accommodation at an inn in Pittsburgh, but we ended up waiting for the donor liver and staying in Pittsburgh longer than we had anticipated. Praise God someone in a church in Pittsburgh offered us reduced price accommodation so our funds lasted longer.

Finally after eight months of arriving in the US, Vaughn was called into surgery. The surgery lasted over ten hours with a 50-50 chance of Vaughn coming out alive. I called friends from all over the world and they joined me in prayer. The surgery went very well and Vaughn's recovery was remarkable. He was discharged two weeks later. As an outpatient, Vaughn and I qualified to stay at the Ronald MacDonald house. Two months after the surgery, Vaughn was given a scholarship to attend the Rehabilitation Institute of Pittsburgh where he had special physiotherapy to loosen his muscles. (He had never walked before.) Six weeks into the physiotherapy, another miracle took place – Vaughn took his first step at five years old! What joy!

We finally returned home to Jamaica a year and two months since we left. Many were shocked at Vaughn's remarkable recovery. He was indeed a living testimony of God's power, love and favour! Vaughn attended regular school at six years old and became a computer expert, writing programmes in Java script at twelve years old.

Vaughn lived a few more years and died just after his sixteenth birthday. He packed a lifetime into those sixteen years on earth. I thank God for loaning me Vaughn and giving me a longer time to enjoy my son who left me not only a legacy of beautiful memories, but also his own poems and art.

My oldest son Dwight is now twenty-five years old and uses a motorised scooter to get around. He graduated from the University of the West Indies three years ago with a BSc in Mathematics and Computer Science.

- Ave (Kingston, Jamaica)
September 2011

2 Corinthians 4v17 (NLT) says: "For our present troubles are small and won't last very long. Yet they produce for us a glory that vastly outweighs them and will last forever!"

Thank You my Father that You are aware of the trials and temptations I go through and that they have been screened by You before they hit me[7]. Please give me Your perspective on the difficulties that challenge me – that my troubles are small and won't last very long compared to the eternal glory I will bask in when I meet You face to face. Thank You for this promise: "The temptations [and trials][8] in your life are no different from what others experience. And God is faithful. He will not allow the temptation [or trial] to be more than you can stand. When you are tempted [and tried], He will show you a way out so that you can endure" (1 Corinthians 10v13, NLT). I only need to call on You and I know You will help me to stand strong, for You are faithful to Your promises! In Jesus' name, I praise You!

---

[7] We see this principle in the book of Job chapter 1 where God tells satan what he could and could not do as regards the testing of Job. Job's faithfulness to God proved to satan that his accusation was wrong. Job possessed true devotion to God for who God is and not for what he could get from Him. Do not let the trials and temptations you face rob you of your love and devotion to God. Hang in there! More about Job in Week 52.

[8] The word in the original Greek text has the root *peirazo*, hence, temptations or trials.

Week 26: What We Are Really Up Against

For we are not wrestling with flesh and blood [contending only with physical opponents], but against the despotisms, against the powers, against [the master spirits who are] the world rulers of this present darkness, against the spirit forces of wickedness in the heavenly (supernatural) sphere.
(Ephesians 6v12, AMP)

In the races we have to run for God, we are not contending with and battling against other runners, but against evil spirits who want to sidetrack or prevent God's people from succeeding in their assignments and fulfilling their God-given purpose. Satan, through his demons, will do what he can to stop us, but Jesus promised that He would empower us to do His will. This is what He said before He ascended to heaven: "And these signs will accompany those who believe: in My name they will cast out demons; they will speak in new tongues; they will pick up serpents with their hands; and if they drink any deadly poison, it will not hurt them; they will lay their hands on the sick, and they will recover" (Mark 16v17-18, ESV). What an amazing promise!

Many Christians find it difficult to believe this promise because their Bibles contain a footnote saying that verses 9 to 20 of chapter 16 of the Gospel of Mark are "absent from the most reliable early manuscripts" and that these were later on appended to the original (implying that these may not be divinely-inspired). If so, it is strange for Mark to end his Gospel in verse 8 with the women "afraid" and with no confirmation of the angel's news about Jesus' resurrection. [1]

Although the earliest existing manuscripts of the Greek New Testament from the fourth to fifth centuries (Codex Alexandrinus, Codex Sinaiticus and Codex Vaticanus) do not contain Mark 16v9-20 (plus a few other passages in the New Testament), there is evidence that the passage did exist in the original text of Mark's Gospel because reference to it had been made in the writings of Iranaeus (second century), Hippolytus (third century) and Lucian of Antioch (third century). This would indicate that the passage was not appended, but was actually deleted from the original. It had been suggested that this was done due to the influence of Gnosticism, which was already

---

[1] The women went to anoint Jesus' body with spices, but encountered the angel who told them the news. Mark 16v8 (ESV): *And they went out and fled from the tomb, for trembling and astonishment had seized them, and they said nothing to anyone, for they were afraid.*

causing trouble when John the apostle was still alive[2]. The Gnostics were considered heretics by the early Church fathers because they did not believe in the deity and resurrection of Christ. Many of them claimed that Jesus was merely a man who had attained divinity through *gnosis*.

To determine the authenticity of the Greek text of Mark 16v9-20 (i.e., that the passage was not appended to the original), mathematician and Bible scholar Ivan Panin[3] studied the 'numerical design' of the passage based on the 'heptadic' (sevenfold) structure of the Bible[4]. Panin discovered that the Greek text of Mark 16v9-20 has several heptadic features. Here are ten: the passage has 175 (7X25) words and 98 (7X14) different words; it has 553 (7X79) letters of which 294 (7X42) are vowels and 259 (7X37) are consonants; the conclusion (v19-20), like many other parts, is heptadic (7X5 words); the total numerical ('gematrical') value[5] from vs. 9-20 is 103,656 (7X14,808); the Greek word for "deadly", not found elsewhere in the New Testament, has a numerical value of 581 (7X83) and is preceded in the vocabulary list by 42 (7X6) words, and in the passage by 126 (7X18) words. Try writing a passage

---

2   Gnosticism (Greek *gnosis*, 'knowledge') is a loose religious and philosophical movement that began when the Christian Church was in its infancy. It teaches that the "unknowable" God created lesser divinities, including an evil god who made the universe (matter therefore is evil). This evil god prevents the souls of mortals from ascending to God, keeping them imprisoned in their physical bodies. Deliverance from matter is attainable only through special knowledge revealed by special Gnostic teachers. Gnosticism believes that Jesus was the divine Redeemer who first revealed this knowledge, but it rejects the Incarnation (that God became man), thereby denying the atoning value of Jesus' death on the cross. (If He is not God, He could not have atoned for us and we cannot be saved from our sins. But Jesus, the living Word of God, is God – John 1v1!) In early Christian literature, Simon Magus (Simon the Sorcerer of Acts 8) is regarded as the arch-heretic who fathered Gnosticism. Gnosticism flourished in the 1st and 2nd centuries and Alexandria, the source of Codex Alexandrinus, was its headquarters. The 2003 novel *The Da Vinci Code* was based on Gnostic literature.

3   Ivan Panin was born in Russia in 1855 and moved to the US where he became a Christian. In 1890, he discovered the presence of mathematical designs underlying both the Hebrew text of the Old Testament and the Greek text of the New Testament. He spent 50 years exploring the mathematical structure of the Scriptures and wrote over 43,000 pages of analysis. He went to be with the Lord in 1942.

4   The recurrence of the number 7 is found throughout the Bible: the Sabbath on the 7th day, the 7 years of plenty and the 7 years of famine in Genesis 41, the 7 priests and 7 trumpets in Joshua 6, the 7 churches, 7 lamp stands, 7 seals, 7 trumpets, 7 bowls in the Book of Revelation, etc. Ivan Panin noted that 7 also occurs in the way Scriptures were written and he believed that this intricate numerical design testifies to a supernatural origin. Some have attempted to show that such numerics can be found in other writings. However, these fall very short of the heptadic structure of the Bible. Panin's work was not flawless, but there is enough evidence in his and others' work to convince us that the heptadic structure of the Bible does exist.

5   Greek letters, like Hebrew letters, have numerical values.

in which the number of words, letters, vowels and consonants are all divisible by 7. Incorporate six other heptadic features. You would need at least 282,475,249 (or 7^{10}) unaided attempts to come out with a passage with only 10 heptadic features. Panin found 75 in Mark 16v9-20! No human mind could have written a text with such an intricate mathematical design, and at a time when there were no computers!

Therefore, Mark 16v9-20 must have been meticulously planned and designed by no other than God Himself. In that case, the passage must have been deleted from and not added to the original Gospel of Mark, believed to be the first Gospel to be written[6]. Since it may have been the first written account of the life of Jesus, the Gnostics would have been very interested in its contents.

What bothers some Christians is Mark's reference to handling venomous snakes and drinking deadly poison. Paul's experience in Acts 28v1-6[7] illustrates the former. There is no exact Bible illustration for the latter[8], but there are stories about missionaries not getting ill even after being given poisonous food or drink. Metaphorically, picking up snakes may refer to our authority over demons, and being unharmed by poison, to the protection from evil the Lord promises (Week 11). In any case, we can believe that God had given us supernatural gifts[9] (Appendix 3) and power against the supernatural forces sent by the devil to stop us from accomplishing our God-given assignments.

Here is a story of believers in Zambia who believed Jesus' promise in Mark 16. If you face a similar situation and the Lord tells you to confront the problem, what will you do? Will you run from it, or will you believe Jesus' promise and act on it?

The Night Peter Was Set Free

When I was at university in my home country of Zambia, I was part of a Christian student group that met weekly for praise and worship in a university hall. Most students who attended these meetings were mainly from the Pentecostal churches. The number of attendees grew as students began to hear about the goodness of the Lord and the good things people were experiencing in these meetings.

---

[6] Mark's Gospel is generally accepted as the first Gospel to be written ('Markan Priority'), sometime between 68 and 73 AD. The earliest New Testament writing, however, is believed to be Paul's letter to the Thessalonians, written in the early 50s AD, some 20 years after Christ.

[7] Acts 28v5 (NIV): *But Paul shook the snake off into the fire and suffered no ill effects.*

[8] The closest Bible stories perhaps are the "healing" of the water in 2 Kings 2v19-22 and of the pot of soup in 2 Kings 4v38-41, both through the prophet Elisha.

[9] Regarding "new tongues": The gift of tongues (6th footnote, Week 15) had proven to be a powerful aid especially in evangelism. The speaker supernaturally speaks in a human language he does not understand and another person who understands the language hears it and gets convicted by the Holy Spirit, as on Pentecost Day in Acts 2.

A friend of mine, whom I shall call Ben, invited someone whom he was concerned about because each time he met him, this person's face showed that something was not right. My friend could sense the darkness inside this man who looked worried, unhappy and quite unloved. So because of the love that we have from our Lord and which we are commanded to extend to others, my friend Ben decided to invite this man, whom I shall call Peter, to our midweek meetings. Peter welcomed the invitation and said he would come. On one particular night Peter did come, but when he arrived in the hall, we had already started singing, worshipping and praising the Lord. He sat down and listened and observed what was happening as people sang, praised, worshipped and danced to the Lord. It was obvious that the people were enjoying the presence of the Lord, something which could be felt by everyone in the room. Quite a number of people got touched and blessed even before the word of God was preached.

After listening and watching for some time, Peter quickly stood up, headed for the door and left the hall. Ben got concerned over the way Peter stood and left, so he decided to follow him. He followed him all the way to Peter's hostel and then to his room. When Peter discovered that Ben had followed him, he got angry and violent, threatening to injure Ben with the knives and spears which he drew out from under his mattress! It was then that God revealed to Ben that he was in a spiritual battle and that Peter's angry response was due to the evil spirits that were holding him captive[10]. He also revealed to Ben that this battle could only be won by prayer. Ben immediately started to pray, calling upon the name of Jesus. However, each time Ben mentioned the name of Jesus, Peter got more and more angry.

Before I relate what happened next, I'd like to tell you more about Peter. Sometime before this, Peter had stayed with his uncle and aunt during a long holiday. He soon discovered that while his uncle was on a night shift at work, a man would visit his aunt in her bedroom. This disturbed Peter so he informed his uncle about it. One night after midnight, the uncle unexpectedly came home from his night shift work and found his wife with a man in his bedroom. This resulted in a fierce fight and Peter's aunt ran away. Peter's uncle was overpowered by the man and suffered terrible beatings. By this time Peter was awakened and decided to help his uncle fight the intruder. Peter, a very strong young man, and his uncle beat the intruder so badly that he dropped to the floor unconscious. Seeing the man was not regaining consciousness, Peter quickly left and hid in the bushes when the police came. The man was pronounced dead on arrival at the hospital and the police started to look for Peter. A few months later, he was discovered, charged with murder and found guilty. After some time in prison, he won his appeal and was released on the grounds that Peter only wanted to help his uncle, who was being battered by the intruder, and never really intended to kill him.

---

[10] In Mark 5, Jesus heals a mentally-disturbed man who was held captive by a "legion" of demons. A Roman legion had around 5000 soldiers.

Despite his release, Peter was never the same again. He was clearly tormented by the incident and would often be heard talking loudly to himself. After some time, he felt better and started attending university. However, the evil spirits had already taken hold of his life.

Going back to the night Peter came to our meeting, Ben realised he could not handle the situation on his own and so he left Peter's room and came to the room where other Christian brothers and I were gathered. He requested our friend Andrew to accompany him to Peter's room so that together they could pray for Peter's deliverance and minister to him. Upon hearing this, Andrew got excited because he had been involved in deliverance ministry before. He got so excited that he forgot to pray and commit everything into the hand of the Lord before leaving. He left with Ben and both went to Peter's room and when they got there, they found Peter lying on his bed. They began to pray. Meanwhile, the other students and I interceded where we were and prayed for Peter to be set free from his demonic captivity.

After midnight Andrew came back panting as if he had been chased by a lion. When we asked what had happened, he narrated that each time he and Ben said "in the name of Jesus" in Peter's room, Peter became more violent and things got worse. He also said that as they continued to pray to Jesus and commanded the evil spirits in Peter to go, he drew out a short spear from under his mattress and threatened to kill them. As they prayed, he advanced towards them ready to strike, and Andrew dashed out of the room leaving Ben behind!

But Ben remained and cried to God for protection. With all the faith he could muster, Ben then started declaring that God is the Almighty, great in power and the great Protector of all His children who believe and trust in Him. He said, "God, in Your word You promised, 'I will never forsake or leave you' and 'I will be with you forever and ever'[11]. God, if I am really Your child, protect me from being killed or injured by these demons because my trust is not in anything else but in You alone." Looking directly at Peter, Ben then said, "In the name of Jesus, I rebuke these evil spirits in Peter and command them in the mighty name of Jesus to depart from Peter and set him free!"

Immediately the spear and the knife just dropped from Peter's hand! From Peter's mouth Ben heard these words, "OK, we are leaving!" Shortly afterwards, Peter's countenance changed. The evil spirits had left him. Peter had been set free![12] By this time, it was three in the morning.

---

[11] Hebrews 13v5b (ESV): *"I will never leave you nor forsake you."* Also Matthew 28v20b (ESV): *"And behold, I am with you always, to the end of the age."*

[12] There are many incidences in the Gospels and Acts of deliverance from demons. For example, Luke 11v14 (NIV): *Jesus was driving out a demon that was mute. When the demon left, the man who had been mute spoke, and the crowd was amazed.*

After Peter's deliverance, he began to associate with other Christians and learned how to pray (something he thought he would never do in his lifetime) and joined a church. Set free by the Lord, he was able to freely testify to the truth of God's word that says, "Where the Spirit of God is, there is liberty"[13] – liberty to worship Him, to sing to Him and to tell others about His love.

Peter's story is a story of victory in the name of Jesus, the One who forgives confessed sins and delivers us from all the things that bind us, just as He delivered Peter from the bondage of evil spirits. To God be all the glory forever and ever!

- Samson (Kitwe, Zambia)
Sent from Carnforth, Lancashire, England
June 2011

Mighty God, I believe Jesus lives in me and that He is greater and mightier than the devil. I believe Your Spirit empowers me to overcome him and to do what You want me to do. I believe that supernatural signs will accompany me as Jesus promised. Make me bold when You want me to use Your supernatural gifts[14], but protect me from presumptuousness. Help me to be submitted and obedient to You and grant me wisdom in using these gifts for Your name's sake. Amen.

---

[13] 2 Corinthians 3v17 (NASB): *Now the Lord is the Spirit, and where the Spirit of the Lord is, there is liberty.*

[14] Appendix 3 briefly discusses the supernatural gifts of the Holy Spirit.

Week 27: Demonic Resistance, Angelic Assistance

Are not all angels ministering spirits sent to serve those
who will inherit salvation? (Hebrews 1v14, NIV)

Berit of Week 21 is one who will take the opportunity God gives her to bring people into the Kingdom, as her English friend Betty would testify. The two met through Girl Guides/Scouts many years ago. When Betty went to Norway, Berit's native land, Berit took her to churches there. Berit's efforts paid off. Although she did not understand Norwegian, Betty gave her life to Jesus! Perhaps it is because of such enthusiasm for God and His work that God one day sent an angel to assist Berit in her ministry to the orphans. Berit naturally took the opportunity to tell a friend about her amazing experience.

There are evil spirits led by satan who are working to stop us from completing our assignments and fulfilling our God-given calling (Week 26), but there are also angels, "ministering spirits", whom God sends to aide us, as Berit would testify.

Angels are mentioned several times in both the Old and New Testaments. They were created by God[1], like we were, but of a separate order, as spirit beings who are able to appear in physical form[2]. They have amazing powers and abilities, but these nevertheless are limited in comparison to those of the omnipotent and omniscient God.

God created myriads of angels, one of whom was a cherub[3] called "Lucifer". Like other cherubim, "Lucifer" was involved in the worship of God in heaven and probably led the angelic host in singing praises to God. He was probably the highest-ranked angel and the most beautiful (Ezekiel 28v11-17[4]). But "Lucifer" rebelled against God.

---

[1] Psalm 148v2 (NIV): *Praise Him, all His angels; praise Him, all His heavenly hosts.* Verse 5: *Let them praise the name of the Lord, for He commanded and they were <u>created.</u>*

[2] This is why Hebrews 13v2 (NLT) advises us: *Don't forget to show hospitality to strangers, for some who have done this have entertained angels without realising it!*

[3] Ezekiel 28v14 (NIV): *You were anointed as a guardian cherub, for so I ordained you.*

[4] Theologians believe that Ezekiel 28v11-17 refers to the devil, the power behind the "King of Tyre". He was the cherub "full of wisdom and perfect in beauty" (v11) until "wickedness was found" in him and he was expelled in disgrace (v15-16).

137

Some suggest that God may have told him about His plan to create a new order of beings called "man" who would be made "a little lower than God"[5] and would be equal to the angels[6], and in fact would be ministered to and served by angels (Hebrews 1v14). "Lucifer" must have been so troubled by this and saw man as a challenger to his esteemed position. From then on he planned to destroy the human race, choosing arrogance[7] and rebelliousness over submission. The cherub led one-third of the angelic host[8] in a rebellion against God Almighty[9], which was squashed. "Lucifer" (now called the devil or satan[10]) and his fallen angels (demons[11]) were thrown out of heaven[12].

The name/title "Lucifer" was derived from the Latin *lucis-fero,* 'light-bearer'. "Lucifer" first appeared in Isaiah 14v12 in the Latin version of the Bible (Vulgate) and then in the King James Bible[13]. Originally, the name was given to the planet Venus, the brightest star that continues to shine as the dawn breaks (hence, "son of the morning/dawn"). For this reason, instead of "Lucifer", other versions of the Bible use "star of the morning" (NASB), "daystar" (AMP) and "morning star" (NIV). None of these titles, unfortunately, convey the full meaning of the original Hebrew word in the Isaiah 14 passage that was translated into "Lucifer" (and daystar, morning star, etc.). The Hebrew word is *heylel,* which can mean 'shining one', especially one that shines with wisdom and intellect (this week's 4th footnote). However, *heylel* can also mean 'one who raves or boasts foolishly'! Because of the cherub's foolish boasting, as recorded in Isaiah 14 (this week's 7th footnote), 'the shining one who boasts' may

---

[5]   Psalm 8v5 (NASB): *Yet You have made him a little lower than God, and You crown him with glory and majesty!* The Hebrew for God in this verse, as in Genesis 1v1, is *Elohim,* a plural term for the triune Godhead, hence "God" in this rendition of Psalm 8v5.

[6]   Luke 20v36 (AMP): *For they cannot die again, but they are angel-like and equal to angels.* Jesus here is talking about the state of believers in the future after His return.

[7]   Isaiah 14v13-14 (NKJV): *For you have said in your heart: "I will ascend into heaven, I will exalt my throne above the stars of God* [the angelic host]; .... *I will ascend above the heights of the clouds; I will be like the Most High".*

[8]   Revelation 12v4 (NLT): *His tail* [of satan, the dragon] *swept away one-third of the stars* [angels] *in the sky, and he threw them* [they were expelled with him] *to the earth.*

[9]   Rebellion against God is refusal to do God's will and to submit to God's authority. Ultimately, this refusal is what makes a person "evil" like satan.

[10] From Greek *diábolos* and Hebrew *Ha-Satan* = 'the accuser' or 'the adversary'.

[11] Greek *daimonion* = 'the divine power', a spirit that is inferior to God. In Hebrew, the word is *sa`iyr* which means 'a male goat or buck' and is associated with the worship of the male goat (e.g., Baphomet).

[12] Revelation 12v7-9 (NLT): *Then there was war in heaven.* [The angel] *Michael and his angels fought against the dragon* [the devil] *and his angels. And the dragon lost the battle, and he and his angels were forced out of heaven.*

[13] Isaiah 14v12 (KJV): *How you are fallen from heaven, O Lucifer, son of the morning!*

be a better translation for it conveys the fuller meaning of *heylel*. After all, Jesus, the "light of the world"[14] is the real "bright Morning Star"[15] and "Daystar"[16]!

One could say that the title "Lucifer" tells half of the story of this fallen cherub. He was created to be resplendent in beauty, intellect and wisdom, then he became arrogant and rebellious. His story is a warning to us: If the light in us, the light of the glory of God[17], is darkened by arrogance and rebelliousness against God[18], it deteriorates into a foolish and dark vision of self-glorification.

Heylel took with him a third of the angelic host. However, two-thirds stayed with God and they are for us! Although our all-powerful God can act independently without them, He has chosen to partner with them (and us) to accomplish His will. In the Bible we read about angels acting as God's messengers[19] (e.g., they announced Jesus' birth to the shepherds in Luke 2). Angels were also sent to help God's people who were in need or in trouble, like Peter who was released from prison by an angel in Acts 12.

God hears the prayers of His people and may send angels to aid us for the sake of His Kingdom and His purpose. Most of the time we do not see them with our natural eyes, but often they have helped us without us even realising they were there. One day we will discover how many times we have been protected from accidents or untimely death through angelic intervention!

There may be demonic resistance, but angels are watching over you! Here is Berit's angel story.

The Airport Angel in Indiana

In the summer of 2010 I went to the US and received gifts for the children of the orphanage in the village of Ilula, Kilolo District in Tanzania. It is run by the Ilula

---

[14] John 8v12 (ESV): *Again Jesus spoke to them, saying, "I Am the light of the world. Whoever follows Me will not walk in darkness, but will have the light of life."*

[15] Revelation 22v16 (NIV): *I, Jesus, have sent My angel to give you this testimony for the churches. I Am the Root and the Offspring of David, and the bright Morning Star.* As a creation of the triune Godhead, *Heylel* was a "son" of the bright Morning Star.

[16] "Daystar" appears in 2 Peter 1v19 KJV, but not in capital letters, unfortunately.

[17] Since all people were made in God's image (Genesis 1v27, NLT: *So God created human beings in His own image.*), we were all born with this light, but sin darkens it.

[18] Arrogance in that one places self on the throne of one's life and not God, and rebelliousness in that one refuses to submit to God. 1Samuel 15v23 (NIV) says: *For rebellion is like the sin of divination* [or witchcraft = desire to take control], *and arrogance like the evil of idolatry* [arrogance = worship of self, hence idolatry].

[19] Both the Hebrew word for angel (*mal`ak*) and the Greek word (*angelos*) mean 'messenger'.

Orphan Program, of which I am the coordinator (Week 21). I planned to stop by the Netherlands on my way back to Tanzania to visit my friend Pejita who, like me, is in her sixties. I was at the airport in Indiana in the US to board a flight to the Netherlands and, as usual, my luggage became an issue. I hadn't anticipated this problem because it was not too heavy this time. Besides, I had visited the travel agent in Vincennes (Indiana) the day before to ask how many bags I could take. I was told I was allowed two bags and so I packed two bags.

However, the lady behind the airport counter did not agree! I explained to her that the travel agent told me I was allowed two bags. I added that one of them was full of gifts for orphan children in Tanzania. She insisted that my plane ticket only allowed me one bag and that I must pay for the other one. This was completely unexpected and I was not prepared to pay the extra fee.

There were no raised voices that would have annoyed anyone around us. In fact, there was no one waiting behind me. Suddenly, I noticed a lady standing about ten feet away from me. I wondered where she came from and if she was in the queue. Why was she standing on one side and not behind me? She did not look at me, she said nothing, and with her arms folded in front of her, she held on to something.... Was it her passport? My attention went back to the lady behind the counter. I asked again if I could send the second suitcase through, and again I was told that if I did not pay for it, I would have to leave all the gifts for the orphans behind in Indiana. I thought about all the happy, small faces in the orphanage who would be asking me if they could each have a gift!

My heart sank and I swallowed to avoid crying. To my amazement, the lady standing to the side of me jumped up to the counter and said, "May I pay for the suitcase for her?" She quickly handed over her credit card. The lady behind the counter took it, slid it through the card machine and handed it back to her. With my mouth open I asked, "Was that for me? ..... Who are you?" "I am nobody!" she replied and winked her eye at me. I turned to the person behind the counter, still with my mouth open – then back to the other lady who had quickly disappeared through the airport door. As the door closed behind her, I turned again to the person at the counter and asked, "Do you know that lady?" She replied, "I have never seen her before!"

I was stunned! It all happened within a few seconds. The airport lady handed me a receipt for $55 for the extra suitcase and for the rest of the day I felt strangely perplexed... Where did this woman come from? She appeared from nowhere, disappeared into nowhere and she wasn't in line for a boarding pass to fly!

Excited over this encounter, I told my friend Pejita about this amazing experience at the US airport. She listened looking at me with a sense of "Are you sure you have had enough sleep lately?" We have been friends for four decades and Pejita is not a Christian, but the story about "my angel" impressed her, I could tell! During my one week stay at her house, she repeatedly asked me to tell the story about "the American Airport Angel" in Indiana to our not-believing Dutch friends!!

You see, I believe that when small things in life are put together by God's hand, we can see the whole picture! God's interest not only in the orphan children in Tanzania, but also in Pejita may have caused the Airport Angel to appear so that I could trigger an interest in her and share God with her. It all works together – and in the end we shall all understand it!

So, do you doubt there are angels among us? I think even Pejita is not so sure any more ….

- Berit Skaare (Ilula, Kilolo District, Tanzania)
Ilula Orphan Program
www.ilulaorphanprogram.org
May 2011

Thank You Father that if I need it, You will send an angel to supernaturally protect, assist or encourage me. I realise You do not always deliver Your children supernaturally from danger or supply our needs through angels or by Your direct intervention. I know that You are more concerned about my character than my comfort so there are times when You decide not to deliver me from, but take me through difficult times, using these to conform me to the character of Christ. Thank You for this promise: "He Who lives in you is greater (mightier) than he who is in the world" (1 John 4v4b, AMP). Thank You, Jesus, for living in me!

Week 28: Straighten Your Priorities

David had served God's purpose in his own generation. (Act 13v36, NIV)

We have training to go through, assignments to complete, demonic resistance to pray against, angelic intervention to be grateful for, a race to finish and a calling to fulfil. Even so, our focus must not be on any of these. If an athlete wants to win, he has to focus on his race since he has to be the first to get to the finish line. He has to be aware of how the other runners are doing so he can do better. The race we are talking about is different in that we do not compete against and compare ourselves with other runners, but we do run to win, and to win is to finish our course before we leave this earth.

In the marathon of life and in the assignment sprints we need to run, we should not focus on other runners (what and how well they are doing), nor on the spectators (those we have been called to minister and witness to). There is really no point in focusing on being transformed into Christ-likeness or even on fulfilling our unique calling (Week 18) since these are mainly the work of the Holy Spirit, and all He wants is our cooperation. Rather, we have got to focus on Jesus (Week 24). In the sense of Him being the object of our love and the longing of our soul, He becomes our very goal, as a thirsty deer pants for water[1]. We run to Him, after Him and for Him!

The foregoing implies the need to have our priorities sorted out. Some people make their careers their main priority and when they become successful in their careers, they conclude they have succeeded in life because they have earned fame, honour or the respect of others. But is this true success? Some, for the sake of financial security, make the acquisition of worldly wealth their main priority in life, but because one cannot serve both God and "mammon", they may end up choosing mammon over God[2]. How will they feel when they finally face God at the end of life's road?

Some, for reason of worry over perceived lack, make the acquisition of resources their main priority, especially in today's current economic climate. But did not God

---

[1]   Psalm 42v1-2a (NKJV): *As the deer pants for the water brooks, so pants my soul for You, O God. My soul thirsts for God, for the living God.*

[2]   Matthew 6v24 (NKJV): *No one can serve two masters; for either he will hate the one and love the other, or else he will be loyal to the one and despise the other. You cannot serve God and mammon.* "Mammon" is a Biblical term, probably Aramaic in origin, which refers to material wealth or possessions, and especially, to one's attitude towards these; e.g., people define themselves in terms of what they own and they view success in financial and material terms.

promise He would provide for all our needs?[3] There is no need to be anxious and to make our wants or needs our main priority. This is not an excuse for inactivity, but a reason to be expectant of God's provisions.

Some choose their relationship with a person as their priority over their relationship with God. This is idolatry because anyone (or anything) that takes God's rightful first-place in our lives becomes our god. Do you have an idol?

Some Christians, even those who are mature in their faith, make their ministries their main priority. This may lead to big, popular and well-funded ministries, but sadly, the very thing they build for God takes God's place.

We naturally give priority to whatever we focus on and what we focus on exerts power over us! Although the honour, relationships, resources and ministries that we now have may all be blessings from above, they will eventually control us if we give them first place in our life. While we are here on earth, we have to straighten our priorities and put our relationship with God above all. The paradox is when we do, we will never feel controlled, manipulated or taken advantage of, but will feel free[4] to live life to the fullest![5]

Let your relationship with Jesus be your main priority and let the Apostle Paul's cry be the cry of your heart, "I want to know Christ!"[6] This is the only priority that can guarantee true success, and true success is this: when your Creator can say that you have served His purpose in your own generation.

Below is the story of a post-graduate student who got his priorities jumbled up and learned to straighten them out.

Doing a PhD for God

While I was working for a non-government organization in a far-flung province in the Philippines, I got word that my application to do Masters in Applied Sociology

---

[3]   Philippians 4v19 (CEB): *My God will meet your every need out of His riches in the glory that is found in Christ Jesus.* We can choose to see the current economic situation either as a crisis, or as an opportunity for us to use the faith Jesus gave us to the fullest by believing what God promised.

[4]   2 Corinthians 3v17 (NLT): *For the Lord is the Spirit, and wherever the Spirit of the Lord is, there is freedom.*

[5]   John 10v10 (NCV): *A thief comes to steal and kill and destroy, but I* [Jesus] *came to give life – life in all its fullness.*

[6]   Philippians 3v10a (NCV): *I want to know Christ and the power that raised Him from the dead.* In Week 5 we learned that 'to know' God means to have intimate knowledge of Him.

at the National University of Singapore (NUS) was accepted, and with a scholarship to boot. I quickly packed my stuff and flew to Singapore in 2005 telling God, "You know that I've been busy working for You all this time: leading the youth ministry in our local church in the Philippines, being part of the leadership and even playing the keyboard for You. This time, I want my stay in Singapore to be all for myself. I will be no busier than a good and faithful Sunday attendee." That was my first thought because I was exhausted by ministry work back home and I also anticipated that the postgraduate work at NUS would be pretty tough.

True enough, the first semester was demanding – with four postgraduate level modules. Every week, I had to finish reading books and hundreds of pages of photocopied materials, so as I had expected, a lot of time was devoted to my studies. At that time I was attending Hope Church here in Singapore and though I had some levels of involvement, my heart was still focused on school work. After all, I thought it was the reason why I was in Singapore.

The first semester rounded up and I thought I would get wonderful grades. On 24 December (while on vacation in Manila), I went online to check the results and I was devastated by what I saw. My grades were below what I was expecting. I had to monitor my performance as I was under an intensive scholarship scheme. The competitive spirit within me was shocked. A couple of minutes after my state of shock, I realised that I could pray and did so. God's response was loud, clear, and blunt: "But I did not send you to Singapore to study!" It was then that I spoke to God, repented and resolved to give my life back to His purposes.

At that time, my leaders in Hope Church were already seeing the potential that I had in the ministry. When I came back from Christmas vacation in Manila, they sent me to a cell leadership course called "Nehemiah Class". In my heart I became convinced that my lifestyle in Singapore needed to be aligned with God's intentions. One day I was in an intense prayer meeting with others at Hope when God gave me a moving revelation: since we could not go to China to do missionary work, He was sending Chinese students to us in Singapore. The international students in Singapore are admittedly brilliant and have the potential to take on influential positions once they go back to their respective countries. If they had God in their hearts, that would make an impact on their societies.

On that same day, a Filipino PhD student I met here in Singapore came with a Filipina, a new Master's student in Economics. She, too, was a Christian who received the same revelation prior to her arrival in Singapore. Can you imagine God devising a plan that involves bringing together at a certain time three different individuals who do not know one another and through their meeting discover that they have been destined for a specific purpose? Though I didn't have the intention to become a cell leader at that time, I realised that God was gradually planting the desire in my heart to lead a group of postgraduate students. Weeks later, we had a staunchly atheistic Chinese PhD student attending our group who was there because he was interested in one of our sisters, the Filipina Master's student. Consistently every week, he received the word of God even though he didn't want to accept the Lord. One Missions Sunday, he voluntarily answered the altar call! Our group was in tears for this was a transformation that only God could do. When asked why he finally said yes to God, he answered that he felt a big urge in his heart that he couldn't say no to.

It's amazing that after one semester of trying to get myself as far from ministry as possible, I saw tremendous breakthroughs left and right when I chose to obey God! Eventually, we became the pioneer members of the first cell group in our church that targeted postgraduate students and young professionals.

My desire to serve God in Singapore became the reason why I decided to stay at NUS, this time as a PhD student. Initially, I was hesitant because I had the option and ambition to go to a British university (as my performance in the Master's improved), but God assured me that He would be in control as long as I just followed Him. He assured me that He would be the one to fight the battle for my future as long as I allowed Him to lead my life. By the time I finished my Master's in December 2006, my over-all academic performance literally leapt from okay to outstanding, and amazingly, God blessed me with a prestigious scholarship grant for PhD from the Asia Research Institute.

Having experienced God's grace, I wholeheartedly decided to serve God as a PhD student by leading my cell group (we saw another Chinese and a Korean turn from atheism to Christ!), playing the keyboard in the music team, overseeing a musical presentation for our congregation's anniversary, shepherding lives, and being involved in many other exciting things in the church. I did these on top of my PhD workload. How did I balance it all?

God taught me that it's not about balance because trying to balance things with already full hands signifies two things. First, we are depending on human effort; and second, God is just one of the many compartments in our 24/7 lifestyle. It's not really about balancing, but a desire to put God first and expecting Him to battle it out for you. This is not a proposition to just put aside our books, stare at the teacher and pray for God to reveal to her the high mark we deserve because we are serving God. No. I learned to plan my schedule well so that I was able to finish all my tasks on time. In following this plan, I always sought God's presence so that my work wouldn't be laborious but enjoyable.

God never failed to provide the grace and efficiency that I needed to accomplish my projects excellently. When I placed the most excellent God at the centre of my life, I acquired the desire and ability to do my best for Him. Mediocrity in any area of our lives – studies, ministry, relationships, family – does not glorify God. As The Message Bible (TM) says, "So here's what I want you to do, God helping you: Take your everyday, ordinary life – your sleeping, eating, going-to-work, and walking-around life – and place it before God as an offering. Embracing what God does for you is the best thing you can do for Him. Don't become so well-adjusted to your culture that you fit into it without even thinking. Instead, fix your attention on God. You'll be changed from the inside out" (Romans 12v1-2).

My experience as a postgraduate student taught me that when we honour God with everything in our lives – studies, ministry, relationships, family – we can expect Him to give us the grace that we need to carry on. Why? So that people may realise that it's not about us, but about God.

I am someone whom God continues to transform and use so that His Name may shine forth in this dark world. He placed me as a PhD student where I was, not simply to enable me to obtain a PhD and then enter the real world afterwards, but because He wanted me to glorify His name in an environment where the very identity of God is challenged in ideological terms.

It is possible that you are where you are because God wants you there to shine forth for Him. Each one of us has only one life to live; we either make good use of it for God, or we don't.

- Jayeel Cornelio (Göttingen, Germany)
Sent from Singapore
May 2011

God Almighty, when I finally leave this world, I pray it will be said of me, especially by You, that I have served Your purpose in my own generation. I know I cannot do it without Your Holy Spirit enabling me to set my priorities right. Please help me to give my relationship with Jesus utmost priority each day that comes despite my busy schedule. I offer to Him everything I need to do, even the mundane, 'non-spiritual' things. I know I can depend on the Holy Spirit to empower me to do my best for Jesus. May my everyday life bring Him honour![7] Amen.

---

[7] 1 Samuel 2v30 (NCV): *I will honour those who honour Me.*

Week 29: Run to Receive the Prize

Do you not know that in a race all the runners run, but only one gets the prize? Run in such a way as to get the prize. Everyone who competes in the games goes into strict training. They do it to get a crown that will not last; but we do it to get a crown that will last forever. (1 Corinthians 9v24-25, NIV)

Some Christians seem to be satisfied with just being 'saved'. They are not really interested in discovering what God wants them to do because they do not want to run races for God. When they get to heaven, instead of hearing God's precious, "Well done, My good and faithful servant!" (Matthew 25v21), they will likely hear Him say, "Well?"

God wants His children to do something for Him here on earth as His partners. Although we are not saved by our good works[1], they will bring us rewards (Week 33). God blesses those who are obedient and may reward them materially here on earth, as He did Abraham. But better than material rewards are rewards that will last throughout eternity, which is a very long time compared to our time on earth.

If we are only aiming for rewards on earth (material rewards and/or the approval or recognition of others), then we will get something like the olive crown or wreath (*kotinos*[2]) that an ancient Olympic victor got (Week 25), a crown that will soon fade and wither. All those (not just one!) who run their races for God and win (finish the race) will receive an eternal reward, an incorruptible crown reserved in heaven for them.

In Revelation 4v19-11, John describes a vision of the 24 elders in God's throne room in heaven who fall down before Jesus and lay their crowns at His feet. Would you like to have a crown that you can lay at Jesus' feet?

Here is a story of one intercessor who would have missed her earthly blessing and eternal reward had she persisted in saying no because of her wrong assumption that God is not interested in the secular music industry[3].

---

[1] Ephesians 2v8-9 (ESV): *For by grace you have been saved through faith. And this is not your own doing; it is the gift of God, not a result of works, so that no one may boast.*

[2] The *kotinos* was made of wild olive leaves from a tree considered sacred and that grew near the temple of Zeus at Olympia.

[3] John 3v16 (NLT): *For God loved the <u>world</u> so much that He gave His one and only Son...*

Susan's Reluctant Intercessor

In April 2009, something remarkable was featured on CNN news: a Youtube video showing a contestant auditioning for Britain's Got Talent, a video that rapidly became viral in the world-wide-web in a matter of days and is now considered one of the most inspirational videos of our time[4]. The video was heart-breaking in the way Susan Boyle was ridiculed and mocked by the audience because of her age and looks, and heart-warming in the way she melted the hearts of the same people with the sound of her beautiful voice. It was a very gripping story and the triumph that night of the woman who, at the age of forty-seven, wanted to be a "professional singer" both challenged and inspired many around the world to 'follow their dream'.

I googled that particular video and as I watched and listened to Susan sing 'I Dreamed a Dream', I received a revelation from the Lord, an impression that the woman needed prayer. And so this intercessor, who cared little for talent shows and the secular music and entertainment industry, started praying for Susan Boyle! During the semi-finals of Britain's Got Talent, I watched the show for the very first time and prayed that Susan would get through to the finals, which she did.

On the night of the finals, Susan looked tired and anxious. The international media attention as well as the negative news about her brush with the paparazzi days before must have made the intensity of the competition unbearable for Susan. As I watched her perform, it was as if I could feel the anxiety she was feeling, so much so that I grumbled, "Lord, I don't think I really want to carry this burden for a secular singer. I will pray for her only until this is over." Then I went upstairs to my bedroom asking, "How should I pray regarding this final competition?" The Lord dropped in my spirit three prayer points: (1) that Susan would not win first place, (2) that she would instead come second, and (3) that she would not lose to another singer, but to a non-singing act. I asked why and the answer I got (which I didn't understand) was this: "It's not good for her to win!" This came to me through 'a still small voice' that I heard not with my ears, but with my spirit and I prayed for those three specific points.

After all the telephone votes were tallied, the results of the finals were announced later that night: the dance group Diversity won, and Susan came second!

With a sense of relief I exclaimed, "Praise God it's over!" I didn't have to pray for Susan any longer. My job was done! I went to bed feeling I had accomplished something. However, I could sense that the Holy Spirit was not happy. "Something is wrong!", I heard Him say in that still small voice. I knew He was referring to Susan

---

[4]   www.youtube.com/watch?v=wnmbJzH93NU

and that He wanted me to continue interceding for her, but I ignored it.[5] Surely, the Lord would rather have me pray for nations, the state of the economy and more important people like government leaders, concerns outside my own that I've been praying for before Susan Boyle got my attention! I conveniently concluded that the message was just in my imagination.

Morning came and as usual, my husband turned on the radio for the news. One news item was about Susan. Apparently, Susan had suffered a nervous breakdown after the finals and was taken to a hospital in London called The Priory. I was in a stupor when I heard this. This was what the Lord referred to when He stated something was wrong, but I hadn't listened because I was not willing to commit myself to intercede for a person in the secular music and entertainment industry. I thought it was all too insignificant in the plans and purposes of Almighty God!

I repented, asking the Lord to forgive me for my disobedience and my lack of compassion for this woman, Susan Boyle. For as long as He wanted me to, I said I would pray for Susan. I began to think that perhaps God had actually chosen this woman who doesn't fit the celebrity mould to impact the secular music industry "for such a time as this"[6]. This led me to look for more information about the singer.

I found out that Susan was the last of nine children born to poor parents. Her mother was already forty-five when she conceived Susan and was advised to terminate the pregnancy. Being a devout Catholic, the mother refused. During her birth, Susan suffered oxygen deprivation which may have led to learning difficulties and Asperger's syndrome. She became an object of bullying by classmates and teens in her neighbourhood. For years she competed in talent shows in an attempt to achieve a professional singing career, but failed. She never held a proper job, but cared for her elderly parents until the death of her father (a miner and war veteran) in the 1990s and more recently, the death of her mother at ninety-one in 2007, something that so traumatised Susan that she suffered panic attacks afterwards. I also learned that her mother prayed a lot for her unmarried daughter. Her prayers for Susan must have touched God's heart!

---

[5] 1 Timothy 2v1-3 (NLT): *I urge you, first of all, to pray for all people. Ask God to help them; intercede on their behalf, and give thanks for them. Pray this way for kings and all who are in authority so that we can live peaceful and quiet lives marked by godliness and dignity. This is good and pleases God our Saviour.* The word for 'authority' here in the original Greek text is *huperoche* which can also mean elevation or pre-eminence; i.e., "Pray for people who are in influential positions".

[6] This phrase appears in the Book of Esther, chapter 4 verse 14.

My search for information eventually brought me to a blogging site, a Susan Boyle fansite. At this point I must backtrack a little and tell you what happened in March 2009, a month before Susan's viral video was first posted. I had a strong impression that I needed to call the person who had been my prophetic mentor. Just as I thought, he had a message for me: "The Lord will soon direct you to post on the Internet. What you post will affect and influence many". Naturally, I had big ideas about this, like my own website, but an Internet-savvy Christian guy advised me, "Try blogging!" It was after I had blogged for the very first time on that blogging site that this seemingly preposterous idea came to me – the Lord had directed me to a Susan Boyle fansite and this was what the prophecy was about!

I was amazed when people began to respond to my posts, apparently touched and affected especially by the prayers I posted for Susan and the music industry. I was also pleasantly surprised to meet on the site other Christians from different countries who said they were also praying for Susan. With the ones I became close to, we formed a prayer circle to pray for Susan and the music industry. Then in June 2009, prophetic words were released to the Body of Christ saying that God would be moving in the "mountain of music and media" and would be raising up an "army of intercessors" to pray for the entertainment industry! The prophetic words encouraged and emboldened us and we began to post prophetic prayers for Susan and her first CD, 'I Dreamed a Dream', which contained secular and Christian songs.

To our astonishment and delight, 'I Dreamed a Dream' (released November 2009) sold millions of copies, broke chart records, gained multi-platinum status in several countries and became the world's biggest selling album of 2009. Her second CD, 'The Gift' (November 2010) also topped the charts in the US and UK and broke records as a Christmas album[7].

Such achievements in the space of only a year (2009-2010) by an artist who came on the scene at forty-seven years of age are quite impressive, and they undoubtedly attracted the attention of the music industry. As to how Susan is truly influencing the moguls of the secular entertainment business is something my prayer group is not privy to. However, one only needs to read some comments on Youtube to appreciate the impact of her music on so many.

Until today, I come across Internet posts that describe the effect of Susan's voice, like this one: "Susan's voice is healing, yet can break your heart as you connect personally with each song." I've read stories about the calming effect of her songs

---

[7] In November 2011, Susan made UK music history again by becoming the first female artist to have three consecutive albums debut at No.1 in the UK album chart in less than two years with her third album, 'Someone to Watch Over Me'.

on children and adults with mental health problems. I've read posts from people who had contemplated suicide, such as this one: "Today I considered killing myself. I see no light at the end of this darkness. This song (Susan's 'Who I Was Born to Be') made me cry like I haven't in a long time, and for the first time I feel like perhaps there is a future for me. Thank you, Susan Boyle!" Reading these comments led me to conclude that God has anointed her voice for purposes that actually go beyond impacting the music industry.

It appears that God wants to move in and through secular music and had chosen an unlikely person by the name of Susan Boyle to fulfil His purpose for such a time as this. As an intercessor, I have learned not to question the Lord although I may not understand His plans, His strategies or His choices. I started out as a reluctant intercessor for Susan, but through obedience I was rewarded with the joy of seeing my prayers answered, and with the blessing of partnering with God and with other intercessors to bring about His plans and purposes on earth. The reward for my intercession goes beyond music charts and statistics. Much greater is the joy of knowing that I am praying for someone who, even through secular music, is touching hearts, healing souls and saving lives[8].

- Y.A.L. (blogger from Lancashire, England)
September 2011 (updated November 2014)

My Father in heaven, help me to be so sensitive to Your Spirit that I will not miss anything You say to me, and not be unwilling to do what You tell me to do because of my biases and presuppositions. I expect there will be times that You will ask me to do things that don't make sense to me, so please give me discernment so I can know deep in my knower that it is You. At the end of my time here on earth, I would like to earn a crown that I can lay at Jesus' feet. For love of Jesus, enable me to earn a crown! Amen.

---

[8] In 2010 Boyle's autobiography, *The Woman I was Born to Be,* was published and was the subject of a musical in 2012 which received rave reviews from the public and theatre critics. Recently, Boyle did a concert tour of several cities in the UK (2013) and the US (2014) and performed to sell-out audiences.

Week 30: Run for Love of God

Love the Lord your God with all your heart and with all your soul and
with all your mind and with all your strength. (Mark 12v30, NIV)

To straighten our priorities and give God first place in our lives (Week 28) is to love the Lord our God with all our heart, soul, mind and strength. The Greek verb for love in the verse above is *agapao*[1]. How do we know if we *agapao* our Lord?

With all our heart: Jesus gave Himself as our atonement[2] sacrifice so that we can be 'at-ONE-ment' with Him. We therefore consider ourselves married and bound to Jesus. We love nothing and no one more than Him, so much so that we are willing and ready to give up anything or anyone when He says so. We love to obey Him simply because we love Him[3].

With all our soul: The Greek word for soul above is *psuche* which can also mean 'life'. We are willing and ready to give up life's comfort rather than dishonour God. We are willing to obey Him at all costs. Our life is completely surrendered to Him, everything we are and have. We devote our life wholly to His service, even die for Him if necessary. This is how the Bible describes those who love Jesus: "They did not love their lives so much that they were afraid to die" (Revelation 12v11b, NLT).

With all our mind or intellect: We choose to fix our mind on God, rejecting thoughts that do not glorify Him and setting aside what we want in favour of what He asks us to do. We love His word and let it guide our decisions. Our intellect is willingly and completely surrendered to Jesus. We understand His truths and accept His counsel because His Spirit lives in us and "we have the mind of Christ"[4].

With all our strength: We hold fast to Him as the object of our love and we labour for His glory, offering all we do to Him. With all our strength, we do good works to serve His purpose and to expand His Kingdom on earth.

---

[1] From the noun *agápē*, the voluntary, committed, unmerited, sacrificial, unconditional love that God has for us and what we are to give to our fellowmen. Although God certainly merits our love, the term is also used for man's reciprocal love for God.

[2] Atonement in the Christian sense can be simply defined as the reconciliation between God and man through the sacrificial death of Jesus Christ as "the Lamb of God who takes away the sin of the world" (John 1v29, NKJV).

[3] Romans 13v10b (NIV): *Love is the fulfilment of the law.* See Weeks 23 and 24.

[4] 1 Corinthians 2v16 (NLT): *But we understand these things, for we have the mind of Christ.*

So, do you honestly *agapao* the Lord?

John recorded a conversation between Peter and the resurrected Jesus in John 21 in which Jesus asks Peter, "Do you love Me?" three times, apparently for the three times Peter denied he knew Jesus[5]. Unfortunately, the English translation fails to capture the intensity of the occasion and its deeper meaning. On the first and second times, probably because Jesus remembered how Peter claimed that he loved Jesus more than the other disciples did, that he would never abandon Him and would even die for Him[6], Jesus actually asked Peter, "Peter, do you *agapao* Me?" Peter's answer on both times was, "Yes, Lord. You know I *phileo* You." Peter had been humbled by his denial of Jesus so he could not claim he had actually *agapao* Him. Instead, he answered that he had *phileo* (had brotherly affection for) Jesus. Peter was being honest. His experience had taught him that loving Jesus should involve the will (as in *agapao*), more than the emotion (as in *phileo*).

On the third time, Jesus came down to Peter's level: "Peter, do you *phileo* Me?" Peter's answer was, "You know that I *phileo* You." Then Jesus repeated Peter's new assignment to look after His disciples because He was about to leave them for heaven. He also prophesied that Peter one day would die as a martyr[7]. Indeed, Peter would come not just to *phileo*, but to a*gapao* his Lord to the extent of dying for Him through crucifixion in an upside-down cross[8].

At this time you may just *phileo* Jesus, but as you come to know Him more intimately, you cannot help but to *agapao* Him back!

In the story below, we find another aspect of *agápē* love for our Lord. It is a story of an intercessor who, through her failure, came to a better understanding of what it means to run her race for love of Jesus, her Friend.

---

[5] Peter's denial of Jesus is recorded in Matthew 26v69-75, Mark 14v66-72, Luke 22v55-62 and John 18v16-18, 25-27.

[6] As in John 13v37, Matthew 26v33, Mark 14v29.

[7] John 21v18-19 (NLT): *"I tell you the truth, when you were young, you were able to do as you liked; you dressed yourself and went wherever you wanted to go. But when you are old, you will stretch out your hands* [the early Christians understood this as prophecy of crucifixion], *and others will dress you and take you where you don't want to go." Jesus said this to let him* [Peter] *know by what kind of death he would glorify God. Then Jesus told him, "Follow Me."*

[8] Tradition says that in the time of Nero, Peter was crucified upside down on an inverted cross because he considered himself unworthy to be crucified in the same way Jesus was crucified.

Confession of an Intercessor

I was washing the dishes one Sunday when this message invaded my thoughts: *"A powerful earthquake will hit in a few days – this week!"* I dismissed this thinking it was just me; that maybe the thought came to me because I had not heard of any earthquake news for some time.

Two days later, on 22 February 2011, my attention was arrested by news on TV about an earthquake that struck Christchurch in New Zealand. I heaved a sigh of relief when I learned that it was of 6.3 magnitude. "That's not really powerful", I thought to myself. However, when I saw the pictures of the devastation and heard about the many people feared trapped under collapsed buildings, I realised that the earthquake had been, in fact, quite powerful.

In September 2010, a 7.1 earthquake struck northwest of Christchurch. Even though the February 2011 earthquake was weaker, it did more damage than the September one apparently because the February earthquake was much shallower (5 km as opposed to 10 km deep) and the epicentre was much closer to Christchurch, a city that sits on the sedimentary soil of the Canterbury Plains. This type of soil is most susceptible to liquefaction such that when the earthquake hit, liquefaction caused the ground beneath the city to quiver like jelly. The resulting destruction was harrowing. The pictures of traumatised people walking about dazed and in intense grief were particularly upsetting to me. I realised then that the message that Sunday was a warning from the Lord and a call to intercede, but I ignored it.

At least, I could say that my failure in 2004 to pray over the warning I received through a dream on New Year's Day about the opening of "floodgates on earth" was excusable in that the experience was quite new to me. During that year, devastating floods hit India, Bangladesh, Haiti, the Dominican Republic and China. These were climaxed by the Indian Ocean tsunami, one of the deadliest natural disasters in recorded history and which affected fourteen countries. Only after 230,000 people were swept to their death on 26 December did I realise that the January dream was a call for prayer for the nations, the very first one I received from the Lord. After 2004, other warning messages/calls for intercession came to me, but I failed to respond with prayer to most of them. After each failure, I thought I finally understood and had learned my lesson. Not so. I could not watch and listen to the news coming from Christchurch without crying. How could I have failed again as an intercessor?

A day after the Christchurch earthquake, when I clicked the reply button to an email, I saw the word 'busy' on my computer screen even before I typed anything! "How did that get there?", I wondered. As I thought about this later that night, it dawned on me that the reason I ignored the warning about the earthquake (and most likely the earlier ones as well) was that I was too busy to realise the Lord was talking to me. I was too busy to pray.

I was overcome with remorse when the Lord told me the reason He shared with me the warnings was because I am His "friend". I remembered He said this of Abraham. When I checked my Bible concordance for "friend", I was referred to the story in Genesis 18 in which God told Abraham about the judgment coming on Sodom and Gomorrah. As God's friend, Abraham was not only made privy to God's plan, but was also given the privilege to appeal to God's nature and promise of protection for the "righteous" in these twin cities (Psalm 91 and Week 11). These famous words came back to me, words that explain why we need to intercede: "Because without God, we cannot; and without us, God will not". We can see this principle in one of the saddest verses in the Bible – Ezekiel 22v30-31[9]. Although God can do everything by Himself, He had chosen from the time of creation to work on earth with humans as His partners, not independently of us[10].

As I flipped through the pages of my Bible, the page fell on Psalm 18. I glanced at the opening line, "I love You, O Lord" and remembered studying this intriguing verse years ago because of the song 'El Shaddai'. "I love You, O Lord" in the original Hebrew is *Erkamka Adonai*[11]. *Erkamka* is a verb form of the word *racham* which appears many times in the Bible. *Racham* is usually translated as compassion and tender mercy, but here in Psalm 18, it is translated as 'love'. However, "I love You, O Lord" does not reflect the absurdity of what David said in Hebrew in this psalm because *racham* implies that the one doing the action is showing or giving

---

[9] Ezekiel 22v30-31 (NIV): *I looked for a man among them who would build up the wall and stand before Me in the gap on behalf of the land so that I would not have to destroy it, but I found none. So I will pour out my wrath on them and consume them with My fiery anger, bringing down on their own heads all they have done, declares the Sovereign Lord.* An intercessor is like a 'watchman on the wall' who keeps watch. Because God loves to be merciful, He looks for such a person who would stand in the gap in the 'wall or hedge of protection' around a person or people through prayer. He looks for a *mashal* (see next footnote) who would give Him the right to intervene.

[10] Psalm 8v6-8 (NIV) says: *You* [God] *made him* [man] *<u>ruler</u> over the works of Your hands; You put everything under his feet: all flocks and herds, and the beasts of the field, the birds of the air, and the fish of the sea, all that swim the paths of the seas.* The Hebrew word for ruler in this verse is *mashal* which means 'one who has dominion as a manager or steward'. God had made man His manager and steward on earth and hence, His partner.

[11] This expression (as *Erkamka-na Adonai*, with the added *na* as an aid in singing) appears in the refrain of the song 'El Shaddai' composed by Michael Card and John Thompson and sang by Amy Grant. *Adonai* means Lord.

compassion or tender mercy to the one receiving it (e.g., Isaiah 49v15[12]). When David sang *Erkamka Adonai*, he was in effect declaring, "I love You, Lord, so much I want to be as a mother to You, carrying Your burden and wiping away Your tears"! How absurd is that?[13]

But is it really absurd to say, *Erkamka Adonai?* I was reminded that in the account of Matthew and Mark's Gospels, Jesus said to His closest disciples (His best friends), "My soul is overwhelmed with sorrow to the point of death. Stay here and keep watch with Me" (Matthew 26v38 and Mark 14v34, NIV). I was also reminded of Paul's obsession – "I want to know Christ and the power of His resurrection and the fellowship of sharing in His sufferings" (Philippians 3v10, NIV). All these dropped a bombshell of revelation into my spirit. Each time the Lord gave me those calls for intercession, He wanted me to respond, "*Erkamka Adonai!* Let me watch with You. Tell me what is troubling You today and let me share in Your pain. Let me wipe away Your tears. I am Your friend!"

Yet, I was too busy to pray, even too busy to feel His pain for the lost who need to repent, and His concern for the protection of His people, those who are considered "righteous" because they belong to the Lord Jesus. "Without God, we cannot; and without us, God will not."

Abraham's prayer for Lot and his family were answered, but the unrepentant, like Lot's wife, were destroyed with Sodom and Gomorrah (Genesis 19v1-29). I would never know on this side of eternity what would have happened had I not failed to intercede during those times the Lord called on me. All I know is that I have failed because the truth is, I regarded God's call to intercede as a duty, rather than a privilege that He gives to a friend to share in the pain Jesus' feels for the lost, and to partner with Him in bringing about the Father's will and purpose on earth. It's no wonder I did not feel the urgency and passion to pray about those things that were revealed to me. A sense of duty does not really generate passion. Love does. *Erkamka Adonai!*

There is a song entitled 'I Am a Friend of God' written by Israel Houghton that goes like this, "I am a friend of God. I am a friend of God. I am a friend of God; He calls me friend."

---

[12] Isaiah 49v15 (NKJV): *Can a woman forget her nursing child, and not have compassion* ['racham'] *on the son of her womb? Surely they may forget, yet I* [the Lord] *will not forget you.* 'Racham' is from 'rechem' = 'womb', hence, the 'mother' connotation.

[13] David adds "my strength" right after *Erkamka Adonai*, perhaps to show that the recipient of his deep love (*racham* implies deep emotion) is greater than him.

Are you Jesus' friend? Are you willing to share with Him His burden and pain for the lost and the nations of the world? He calls you "friend".

I sensed in my spirit that the world will experience more shaking in the coming days, and that Jesus is looking for friends who will join Him passionately in His ministry of intercession. Jesus, I am Your friend!

- An intercessor[14] from Lancaster, England
March 2011

The February Christchurch earthquake turned out to be the first most notable earthquake of 2011. This story was submitted before a magnitude 8.9 to 9 earthquake hit Japan on 11 March 2011, so strong it triggered a devastating tsunami and caused a nuclear power plant meltdown. It was the most powerful earthquake in 2011 and in Japan in 140 years, as well as the fifth most powerful earthquake in the world since 1900. Here is an update (given in May) from the intercessor:

On March 9 I saw a playing card from a pack of cheese strings on our table. It had a representation of islands which I recognised to be Japan. The islands were in black and this impression came to me: "Japan is mourning its dead". I remembered the many Japanese people who committed suicide the year before[15]. I prayed that God Almighty would bring hope to that nation.

I was awakened early in the morning of March 11[16] and I saw a 'vision' (mental picture) of a wall with two holes and water forcing itself through these holes. The wall collapsed because of the pressure of the water. Then in my spirit I heard someone say to me, "If there were more holes, the water would not have destroyed the wall". I understood the wall in the vision to represent fortification/protection, and the water, the destructive force against nations. The nations of the world are heading towards

---

[14] The intercessor here chooses to remain anonymous or 'hidden' because intercession is a hidden ministry. An intercessor gets before God in his/her 'prayer closet' to pray for others, asking God to meet their needs for salvation, healing, deliverance, protection, etc., according to His word. To intercede is to plead on another's behalf. Hebrew 7v25 says that Jesus "makes intercession" for us. This can mean that Jesus pleads with the Father on our behalf and reminds Him that He had already paid the penalty for our sins. This can also mean that Jesus, together with the Father and the Holy Spirit, because They are one, are making intercession for us in that They plead with us, on Their behalf, to repent of sin and rebelliousness and be restored to God and His plan for our lives (e.g., Revelation 3v20 says that Jesus knocks at the door of our heart and pleads with us to open it for Him). Perhaps it means both.

[15] Japan has one of the world's highest suicide rates, especially in men between 20-44 years old. There is a long history of honourable suicide in this country.

[16] The earthquake hit at 5:46 AM London time, Friday, 11 March 2011.

destruction because of sin. The holes that act as 'release valves' are made by our prayers which protect the nations from self-destruction. I believe the vision was God's call for His people to PRAY FOR THE NATIONS[17]. But why the water, wall and holes symbolism[18]?

Later I heard the news in the radio about the Japanese earthquake and the tsunami warnings for the Pacific Rim nations. I then emailed my Internet prayer partners. Praise God He answered our prayer for protection for these nations against the tsunami! (They were not badly affected.) In Japan itself, 15,000 people died, but I believe God is answering my prayer for hope for that nation. Many Christian ministries are reporting that exceptional opportunities have opened for them to share the gospel message as they offer practical help to the victims of the earthquake and tsunami, and people are responding.

Dear Father, help me to agapao You back. Help me to feel Jesus' love and pain for the nations and for the lost and suffering. Give me a passion to partner with Him in His ministry of intercession. Erkamka Adonai! Jesus, I am Your friend!

---

[17] Psalm 2v8 (NIV): *Ask of Me, and I will make the nations your inheritance, the ends of the earth, your possession.* The original Hebrew word for 'ask' here is *sha'al* = to enquire; i.e., enquire of the Lord what and how to pray regarding the nations.

[18] *Holes:* Valves are located at the base of floodgates to regulate flow and to dissipate energy. *Water:* The earthquake triggered powerful tsunami waves up to 40.5 metres high. *Wall:* Several tsunami walls along coastal areas of Japan were breached. They were thought to be high enough! The tsunami caused more deaths than the actual earthquake. The Pacific Rim nations were alerted about the approaching tsunami wave.

Week 31: Run for the Sake of Covenant and Community

"Love the Lord your God with all your heart and with all your
soul and with all your strength and with all your mind; and,
love your neighbour as yourself." (Luke 10v27, NIV)

The above is a similar summation of the Ten Commandments Jesus gave in Mark 12v30 (Week 30), but this was the response of an expert in Jewish law who wanted to test Jesus. When he asked Jesus, "Who is my neighbour?", Jesus told him the parable of the Good Samaritan[1]. The conversation continued with Jesus asking, "Which of these three [men] do you think was a neighbour to the man who fell into the hands of robbers?" The expert in the law replied, "The one who had mercy on him". Then Jesus exhorted him, "Go and do likewise"[2]. In effect, Jesus' answer to "Who is my neighbour?" was "Anyone you meet or hear about, especially one who needs help".

In the original Greek text of the verse above, the verb for love is *agapao* from the noun *agápē* (Week 30). However, to more fully understand the implications of Jesus' words, we need to look into the Hebrew context. (After all, Jesus and the expert were Jewish!) This is necessary because most of us have been influenced greatly by the Greek mindset of individualism. Many Christians today think of the gospel of Jesus on an individual or personal level: Jesus died for *my* sins; *I am* forgiven; *I* have received salvation; *I* have a great inheritance; God loves *me*. Although these are all true and the individual is indeed important to God, community is equally important to Him because, as He said in Genesis 2v18, "It's not good for man to be alone." We were not designed to live alone; we were meant to be in community. This is reflected in this recurrent theme throughout the Bible: "I will be your God and you will be *My people*" (in Exodus 6v7, Jeremiah 11v4, Ezekiel 36v28, 2 Corinthians 6v16, Revelation 21v3, etc.). Although God made His covenant with specific individuals we read about

---

[1]   Briefly, the parable (simple story that illustrates a moral or spiritual lesson) is about a man who had been attacked by robbers and had been left half dead. A Jewish priest came by and saw him, but the priest passed by the other side of the road. Next, a Levite (temple assistant) did the same thing. Then a Samaritan travelled down the road, saw the injured man and helped him (Luke 10v30-35). The Samaritans of Samaria descended from Israelites who stayed in the land during the exile of the people of the Northern Kingdom by the Assyrians during the Assyrian captivity. (There was a time when Israel was divided into Israel in the north and Judah in the south.) These Israelites intermarried with other ethnic groups settled there by the Assyrian conquerors. The Samaritans were therefore looked down upon by the Jews (from the word Judah) as half-breeds and not true Israelites.

[2]   Luke 10v36-37, NIV.

in the Bible (especially Noah, Abraham and David), it was always about a community of people and not just the individual.

God still interacts with His people on the basis of covenant, a contract or binding agreement between Him and us as a community of believers. This is why we need to understand the Jewish concept of love which has both covenantal and communal connotations – *chesed*. We find this word in how YHWH[3] describes Himself in Exodus 34v6-7 (ESV): "merciful and gracious, slow to anger, and abounding in *steadfast love* [*chesed*] and faithfulness, keeping *steadfast love* [*chesed*] for thousands, forgiving iniquity and transgression and sin, but who will by no means clear the guilty". *Chesed* is translated in English Bibles in various ways (love, steadfast love, loyalty, loving kindness, compassion, mercy, grace, etc.), but there is really no English (and Greek?[4]) word for it. Perhaps the following is the easiest way to explain *chesed*.

It begins with God showing His undeserved favour or grace (Hebrew *hen*) to a person solely because of His *ahava*[5]. When a person accepts this kindness, a covenant bond is formed between him and God and the chain of *chesed* begins. God has now obligated Himself to show *chesed* to him because of this bond. Since both parties to a covenant are expected to maintain *chesed* towards each other, the person is now constrained to reciprocate by showing *chesed* to God[6] through his love, loyalty and obedience. The recipient of *chesed* is also expected to show *chesed* to others[7]. This is where community (hence, our 'neighbour') comes in because God invented *chesed* so that He can have a big family, which is what community is in essence. *Chesed* therefore precludes the individualistic and "What's in it for me?" mentality.

Although it is the basis of the Ten Commandments[8], *chesed* is not just an Old Testament principle for it is at the heart of Christianity. Jesus started the Good News. Like *chesed*, the Good News is not individualistic but relational, proactive and dynamic. The one who hears about God's *hen* in the Person of Jesus and receives it because of another's testimony enters the bond of *chesed* and passes it on to Jesus by

---

[3] This tetragrammaton (meaning '4 letters') is short for the holy name of God, the original pronunciation of which is not known and traditionally regarded to mean "I Am Who I Am". Its short form is "I Am" (Exodus 3v14). "Yahweh" and "Jehovah" are vocalisations of the tetragrammaton. See 8th footnote of Week 16 and Appendix 1.

[4] The Septuagint (the ancient Greek translation of the Old Testament) uses the word *eleos* (compassion, mercy or pity) for *chesed*.

[5] The Hebrew word used for *agápē* is usually *ahava*. Its root word is *hav* which means 'to give', so *ahava* is more concerned about giving than receiving, like *agápē*.

[6] 1 John 4v19 (KJV) reflects this reciprocity: *We love Him because He first loved us.*

[7] Micah 6v8 (NIV): *He has showed you, O man, what is good. And what does the Lord require of you? To act justly and to love mercy* ['chesed'] *and to walk humbly with your God.*

[8] It can be said that all of God's commands in the Bible are characterised by *chesed*.

making Him the Lord and focus of his life, and to others in obedience to what Jesus commanded – to "love our neighbours" and to "make disciples of all nations"[9].

If you are not living in this dynamic of *chesed*, then you are not fulfilling your God-given purpose. If you are not living in obedience to God, you are rejecting His *chesed* and the blessings of being in covenant with Him. Therefore, run your race for the sake of *chesed*. Pass it on!

The following stories from Ron are very good illustrations of *chesed*.

A Changed Life

I was on my way to Rwanda and Zaire in my capacity as Managing Director of a Christian relief and development agency. The year was 1994 and I was following the mass murder of an estimated 850,000 persons in the small east African nation of Rwanda. Tribal war had broken out between the Tutsis and Hutus. Most of the dead were Tutsis and most of those who perpetrated the violence were Hutus. It was a situation that shocked the world at large.

During the genocide, an estimated two million people had fled from Rwanda into Zaire, mainly centred on Goma and then Bukavu. During the first month alone after the influx, approximately 50,000 refugees died due to a lack of food, clean water and medical aid.

The agency I worked for was based in Bukavu and we were there to assist larger humanitarian agencies such as Care International and Save the Children. We had a team of ten volunteers, some working for a month and some working longer shifts. My role was to write a paper report on the effectiveness of our operation.

The agency had been able to purchase three old Soviet army trucks which we airlifted into Zaire. Our main responsibility was delivering food and transporting refugees and medical aid to the various refugee camps. It was a seven-days-a-week operation which was not only very tiring, but quite dangerous, particularly at night time.

My first full day in Bakavu was spent in one of the largest refugee camps. I had never been in such a camp before and the thought filled me with some trepidation. It was a day that was to change my life forever!

---

[9]   Matthew 28v19-20 (NIV): *Therefore go and make disciples of all nations, baptising them in the name of the Father and of the Son and of the Holy Spirit, and teaching them to obey everything I have commanded you. And surely I am with you always, to the very end of the age.*

My driver for the day, who was a volunteer on our team, was a newly qualified lady doctor who briefed the refugees when they arrived. Everyone had to first register and was then given two poles and a large piece of UN blue sheeting. This was to represent their new home! The refugees were fed only once every two days. Although there was plenty of food available, the authorities did not want them to make a permanent home in Zaire and therefore restricted the food distribution. The scene was terrible with thousands of desperately poor, tired, frightened and hungry people, most of whom had walked day upon day to find shelter and food. Many families had been separated and many lives lost on the long journey from Rwanda.

As we were driving up the long track to the entrance of the camp, there were seemingly hundreds of people, particularly young children who looked extremely weary and tired, making their way to register. Knowing we had bags of crisps and tins of sardines on board, I asked the doctor to stop the jeep we were driving in. That was a big mistake, for suddenly, we were engulfed by about two hundred children begging for food. Imagine the situation, breaking crisps into little pieces in order to give every child something! It was heart-breaking and already my emotions had been shaken to the core.

Once through the entrance to the camp, we stepped out of the jeep and were immediately surrounded by a large group of people who probably thought we looked like people with some authority. A dear old lady dressed in a very thin and torn clothing that barely covered her and who, we later discovered, was 84 years of age, stood before us. She grabbed hold of my T-shirt, shook me and explained that it had taken her two weeks to get to the camp. On the journey, she had lost her husband, her children and grandchildren and the only thing she had left in the world was the dress she was wearing. She continued to shake me and to ask what was I going to do about it. For the first time in my life, I was really frightened and lost for words. I was hot one minute and then freezing cold the next and my emotions were all over the place. Fortunately, the lady doctor rescued me and we went on our way through the camp.

We had only been in the camp less than one hour when we saw a man in the distance waving towards us. As we got a little nearer to him, we realised he was stark naked. He sat down in this awful mess and tried to cover himself with a dirty old blanket. The lady doctor examined him and said he needed treatment straight away because he had dysentery. With the help of other refugees, we carried the man to a medical tent situated about a quarter of a mile away. Although there was a long queue of people waiting to be treated, we asked a Dutch-speaking doctor if he would quickly look at the man we had brought to him. He took one look at him and said he could not help him; he was too far gone. One hour later, the man died. We were instructed to take the man to a huge pit that contained the bodies of over five hundred people. With all the care we could muster, we gently placed the man down.

At this point I could not contain myself any longer. All I wanted to do was to go home, or go anywhere from this place. All around me were desperate people who needed help, my help, and it seemed I had nothing to offer. I was cold, although it was a sizzling hot day and my emotions were all over the place. As I stood there looking at all these make-shift tents through tear-filled eyes, I cried out to God, "Why God? Why me?" Almost instantly, there beside me was a dear Christian African brother who put his arm across my shoulder and said, "I have a message for you!"

The message: "You are here to experience My love for people, to know how high and how wide, how deep and how long, is My love for you and mankind. For I have touched your heart today and not just your emotions. For it is time for you to take new steps in your ministry and these steps will come out of really knowing the depth of My love for people. For I want you to realise it is not sacrifices that I desire, but a heart in love with Me and My people. Love the Lord your God with all your heart and your neighbour as yourself."

That message and my new experience changed my life, and my ministry was never the same again.

- Ron (Lancaster, England)
Sent from Malaga, Spain
March 2011

My First Visit to the Underground Church in China

We travelled by car throughout the night to reach our destination, "a village somewhere" in China. Our driver suddenly pulled up and told us the rest of the journey (approximately two and a half hours) would be covered by foot as the road, or rather track, to the village was no longer accessible by car. It was still dark and by this time I was feeling somewhat weary, but nevertheless excited at the prospect of my first meeting with my Chinese Christian brothers and sisters.

Dawn was breaking as we neared the village and to my amazement, a crowd of people, which turned out to be the total population, were there shouting, waving and urging us on the last few steps. We were greeted with great enthusiasm and the joy of the Lord was so much in evidence. Later, we established that we were the very first Christian westerners to visit their village. It was a 'first' for everyone concerned.

Following some breakfast (I know not what I ate!), I spent some time with the leader of the village. I asked him about the total population of the village. He replied, "One hundred eighty-four adults plus children". I then asked how many of the adults were Christians, and he said, "Why, one hundred eighty-four of course!" I thought he had

163

misunderstood my question, so I asked him the question again, and again I received the same answer. I was amazed. No wonder the whole village had turned up to greet us so enthusiastically on our arrival! Could this ever happen in my western world?

By western standards this was unheard of so I had to find out what method/s had been used to evangelise a whole village. The leader shared with me how those who were Christians had simply loved and served their neighbours and as a result, one by one, those who did not know the Lord asked those who did why they were being so kind, why they wanted to help them, and why they were always so joyful! This then led to the gospel being preached and conversions being made. Amazing! We were told of the many miracles that God had done and that there were no needy people amongst them. They wanted to know *my* news, but it seemed to pale to insignificance in the light of theirs!

During the two whole days we were in the village, twenty-four hours were spent in teaching God's word, and guess what? The whole village attended because they were hungry and thirsty for the word! Every time we sat down for a rest, even at meal times, we were urged to continue. I wondered if we would ever get any sleep at all whilst we were amongst these people.

At that time there were few Bibles in the village and those who were fortunate to have one would share with those who did not, so that everyone would at some time during the week feast on the word. For me, it was just another experience of the power of God at work amongst His people.

By western cultural standards, my new Chinese brothers and sisters were extremely poor. They had few material possessions, but in those two days amongst these beautiful people, I saw and experienced a richness of life that could only have been of God – a life I longed for.

With tears rolling down our faces, we kissed, hugged and said our goodbyes and set off walking again. As I turned to wave to my new friends, there they all were, shouting, waving and urging US ON. What an experience!

- Ron (Lancaster, England)
Sent from Malaga, Spain
March 2011

One line of the song 'Pass it On' ('It Only Takes a Spark') composed by Kurt Kaiser (1969) goes like this: "That's how it is with God's love, once you've experienced it, you want to sing its fresh-like spring, you want to pass it on!"

Father God in heaven, rid me of selfishness, self-centredness and self-consciousness which hinder me from reaching out to my neighbour. I want You to delight in me, so by Your grace help me to practise chesed to any person You send to me. Please help me to seize the opportunities You give me to tell others about Jesus and to demonstrate His love. Grant me a greater revelation of Your love that I may run with it and pass it on to others. In Jesus' name, amen.[10]

---

[10] There are many websites where one can get more information about *chesed* (or *hesed*), e.g., www. bible-researcher.com/chesed.htm, preceptaustin.org/lovingkindness-definition_of_hesed.htm, and even Wikipedia!

Week 32: Have You Failed?

For though a righteous man falls seven times, he rises again.
(Proverbs 24v16, NIV)

In the marathon of life, have you allowed sin to trip you up? Perhaps you lived outside *chesed* (Week 31) and had been disobedient, refusing to run the sprint God told you to do, like Jonah who flatly refused to accomplish the Nineveh assignment God gave him for a specific time (Week 22). Or perhaps you have been obedient and faithful, but you feel demoralised because your work has not shown the results you want to see. For whatever reason, you feel you have failed.

The Bible reveals that many great men of God experienced failure at some point, men like Abraham, Moses, Elijah, David and Peter. God's amazing grace, however, took them from where they were and brought them to where He wanted them to be. They learned how to handle their failure such that they finished the race victorious in God. Late in life, Paul declared, "I have fought the good fight, I have finished the race, and I have remained faithful" (2 Timothy 4v7, NLT). How many times you fail is not as important as this: at the end of your life on earth, will you be able to honestly say like Paul that you have finished the race?

Like the great men of God who tripped, we must acknowledge and repent of sin where sin was involved[1], learn valuable lessons from the failure, put it behind us and move on, not allowing the fear of failing again to stop us from taking risks for Jesus. Although there may be consequences to live with and heart and character weaknesses to work through with the Holy Spirit, we can recover from our failures and overcome them to fulfil God's purpose for our lives. These stumbling blocks can become our stepping stones! God can use even our failures to teach us, grow us, transform us into the character of Jesus, and bring us closer to the fulfilment of our purpose (more in Week 48).

If Jesus is your Saviour and Lord, then you are righteous in God's sight[2]. You may have failed, but Jesus will not humiliate you or even ask you to promise Him you will try your very best not to fail again. He will not overlook your faults or just tell you to do better next time, but He will ask you to evaluate your love for Him, as He asked Peter: "Do you *agapao* Me?" (Week 30). He knows your heart and when He senses

---

[1] 1 John 1v9 (NIV): *If we confess our sins, He is faithful and just and will forgive us our sins and purify us from all unrighteousness.*

[2] 2 Corinthians 5v21 (NIV): *God made Him [Jesus] who had no sin to be sin for us, so that in Him we might become the righteousness of God.*

your repentance and your desire to be reconciled to Him and His purpose for your life, He will reaffirm you and empower you to get up and get on with the marathon race of life. Our God is the God of the second chances!

With regards to those who, after comparing themselves with others, come to the conclusion that they are successes, watch out! Your ministry may appear successful because you attract large crowds, receive lots of financial support and publish lots of bestsellers. Just as the apparent absence of positive results is not a proof of failure[3], the presence of visible results is not a proof of success in God's eyes! If your motives are wrong and you have manipulated people for your own purpose, God's test of fire (Week 33) will show your work's true worth.

No doubt about it, there will be many surprises when we get to heaven. For one, those Christians who were perceived as failures on earth may well be afforded the great honour we did not expect them to receive!

Below is a story about two couples, one of whom persevered in praying for the storyteller, not knowing if their prayers were bearing fruit and if their intercession had been a 'success'. The other couple, Canadian missionaries to the Philippines, were judged to have failed in their ministry. Praise God He is the real judge!

Our Labours and Prayers Do Bear Fruit

A few years ago, Arthur, a very good friend of mine whom I've known since our university days in the Philippines in the late sixties and early seventies, called me from his home in Lancaster, England with a most incredible story. He and his family were invited to dinner by an elderly couple, Keith and Molly, who live in the neighbouring town of Morecambe and whom they met in one of the local churches in Lancaster. During the conversation after dinner, Arthur happened to mention that he went to university in Mindanao in Southern Philippines. At the mention of Mindanao, Keith and Molly recollected that their good friends Rev. and Mrs. Earl Howard (a missionary couple from Canada) had spent time in that part of the Philippines. Keith and Molly also remembered the album containing photos from the Philippines that were put together by the Howards and given to them as a keepsake.

Keith found the album and Arthur and his family were soon peering through the old photographs taken in the 1970s of students the Howards met in Mindanao State University. As it turned out, it was the same university Arthur attended. Arthur recognised some of the students in the photographs, particularly one young girl.

---

3   A good example is the prophet Isaiah. God sent him to preach and prophesy to a people who would not listen to him (Isaiah 6). In people's eyes, he was a failure, but not in God's eyes.

The captions under the two photographs of this girl confirmed his guess – they were photos of me!

Earl and Isolde Howard ministered at the university where I went and it was through them that I came to know Jesus as my personal Saviour and Lord. Although I grew up going to Sunday school and church services in a denominational church, I didn't really know Christ in a personal way. I would regularly read the Bible just as a force of habit, to get some inspiration or to feel good. One day, a friend saw me reading my Bible and asked me some really hard questions. One of the things she asked was if I had the assurance of going to heaven when I die. I remember telling her I was not really sure, but I hoped that by doing good deeds I would gain favour in God's sight.

From that conversation, I got interested in knowing more about being a follower of Christ. I started going to Bible studies conducted by Earl and Isolde among university students. I soon came to realise that I was a sinner in need of redemption through Jesus Christ, and that salvation is by God's grace and not because of good deeds (Ephesians 2v8-9)[4]. In August of 1969, I accepted Jesus into my life and since then I received the assurance that it's because of Him that I have everlasting life (John 3v16)[5].

One note about the Howards' ministry at that university in Southern Philippines is worth telling. They were actually sent to share the gospel to the Muslim community where the university was located. (The Muslims in the Philippines are concentrated in the island of Mindanao.) By living within the university area, the Howards were able to reach out to the students, especially those who had no nearby church to go to, and many of them came to know the Lord, including myself. However, despite more than a decade of ministering, they were able to convert only one Muslim to Christ. It was because a Muslim who would convert to Christianity would end up being persecuted and disowned by his or her family. When the Howards returned to Canada and were evaluated by their sending mission, their missionary work was deemed "unsuccessful or a failure". Eventually, the Howards resigned from this Mission.

It is now forty years since the Howards did their missionary work in Mindanao and amazingly, many of those they led to the Lord have actually been successful in sharing the gospel with Muslims! Through them, the succeeding generations have also been able to bring the good news of salvation to Muslims who are now following

---

[4]   Ephesians 2v8-9 (NKJV): *For by grace you have been saved through faith, and that not of yourselves; it is the gift of God, not of works, lest anyone should boast.*
[5]   John 3v16 (NKJV): *For God so loved the world that He gave His only begotten Son, that whoever believes in Him should not perish but have everlasting life.*

the Lord Jesus Christ. The seeds that the Howards sowed have grown and multiplied through God's amazing work!

Now, back to Keith and Molly's role in the story. Apparently, Earl and Isolde would assign couples they knew were 'prayer warriors' to pray for new Christians they were discipling. I was assigned to Keith and Molly! It blew me away that a couple I didn't even know and have not even met had been faithfully praying for me for so many decades in a faraway country. To think that they would meet a person who is personally close to me was indeed incredible. My friend then proceeded to 'update' Keith and Molly about me and what had happened since the time they started praying for me.

I consider this meeting between Keith and Molly and Arthur a divine arrangement. What an encouragement it has been for me to know that I had a Christian couple praying for me all those years. It must have been an encouragement also to Keith and Molly to know that the person whom they have never met but have supported in prayer for so many years have kept the faith sown by the faithful ministry of the Howards. And I'm sure this has been an encouragement for my friend, Arthur, as well.

I share this with my family and friends as a way of inspiring them to "pray without ceasing" (1 Thessalonians 5v17, NKJV), that is, to persevere in prayer. As Ephesians 6v18 (NIV) says, "And pray in the Spirit on all occasions with all kinds of prayers and requests. With this in mind, be alert and always keep on praying for all the saints". First Peter 3v12[6] assures us that our God is attentive to our prayers.

If you had been serving the Lord and you think you are a failure, I hope that what I have shared regarding the Howards' ministry will lift you out of despondency. If you had been praying for someone for years not knowing if your prayers are bearing fruit, I hope that the story of Keith and Molly's faithful ministry of praying for me will encourage you to keep on keeping on! Your labour for the Lord will certainly bear fruit!

- Alcestis (Bing) Llobrera (Butuan City, Philippines)
Sent from Massachusetts, USA
June 2011

Romans 8v28 (NASB) declares: "And we know that God causes <u>all things</u> to work together for good to those who love God, to those who are called according to His purpose".

---

[6] 1 Peter 3v12 (NIV): *For the eyes of the Lord are on the righteous and His ears are attentive to their prayer, but the face of the Lord is against those who do evil.*

Mighty God and everlasting Father, I recognise that You are the only true Judge who can give right judgments. Forgive me for judging other people's work or ministry as failures. I realise I myself could have judged Jesus' ministry a failure just because His followers abandoned Him at the most trying time! Forgive me for the times I dared not take the risk of doing something for You because of the fear of failure. Thank You for the blood of Jesus that washes away all my sins! Thank You that you can cause even my failures to work together for my good and for Your glory. Help me to step out in the faith that Jesus gave me and to fulfil my God-given purpose. "Thanks be to God! He gives us the victory through our Lord Jesus Christ" (1 Corinthians 15v57b, NIV).

Week 33: The Test of Fire

For no one can lay any foundation other than the one we already have – Jesus Christ. Anyone who builds on that foundation may use a variety of materials – gold, silver, jewels, wood, hay, or straw. But on the judgment day, fire will reveal what kind of work each builder has done. The fire will show if a person's work has any value. If the work survives, that builder will receive a reward. But if the work is burned up, the builder will suffer great loss. The builder will be saved, but like someone barely escaping through a wall of flame. (1 Corinthians 3v11-15, NLT)

At the ancient Olympic Games, there was only one winner per event and he was crowned with *kotinos* (Week 25). In the first modern Olympics in Athens in 1896, first-places winners received silver medals, and the second-places, bronze medals. In the 1904 Games at St. Louis, Missouri, USA, gold, silver and bronze medals were awarded for the first time to first-, second- and third-places winners, respectively.

The medals of the 2012 London Olympiad were the biggest (85mm diameter, 8-10mm thick) and heaviest (412g for gold and silver, 357g for bronze) summer Olympic medals ever made. The gold medals were actually 925 parts per thousand Sterling silver discs plated with 6 grams of gold (as per minimum requirement; the last solid gold medals were awarded in 1912 in Sweden). Each medal, which took ten hours to process, depicted Nike, the winged Greek goddess of victory (Victoria in Roman mythology) who was believed to fly over battlefields to reward victors with fame and glory.

God may not be handing out medals, but His athletes who fulfil their call may expect to receive not only everlasting life and the joy of eternally beholding Him, but also treasure in heaven[1] (Matthew 6v20, 19v21), crowns (Revelation 2v10, 3v11), honour from the Father (John 12v26), authority over cities (Luke 19v17, 19) and over nations (Revelation 2v26-27) in the age to come when Jesus comes back to earth and we will rule in close partnership with Him. God will be so pleased to reward His people with these and with fame and glory because these rewards will be a public testimony of the victors' love for Jesus, that He is their real 'goal', not rewards or treasures. These eternal rewards will certainly surpass the glory and honour of a finely-crafted Olympic gold medal!

---

[1] Part of the treasure may well be gold, pure and solid, not gold-plated! John in Revelation 21 describes the heavenly Jerusalem as one made with the purest of gold and precious stones. But these are just 'construction materials'! They are nothing compared to the beauty, splendour and glory of the Triune God that we will behold!

Paul issues a warning in the scripture in 1 Corinthians regarding the fire that will test what a "builder" uses to build on an existing "foundation". The foundation is Jesus and the builder is the believer, the work being his good deeds and completed assignments. Just as there is a coming judgment day for unbelievers[2], there is also a coming judgment day for believers, a day when believers will each give to the Lord an account of what they did with their lives[3]. On this day, our services to God will be assessed and evaluated.

2 Corinthians 5v10 (NIV) says, "For we must all appear before the judgment seat of Christ, that each one may receive what is due to him for the things done while in the body, whether good or bad". For Christians, this is not about judgment of our sins (which have been dealt with by Jesus at the cross), but of our works. It is for the purpose of establishing whether or not we will receive rewards for the works we have done with what God gave us – our gifts, talents, money, time, possessions and resources. Although we will not be judged for our sins, our sins can of course affect the 'quality' of what we are building on the foundation, which is Jesus. We may think we are adding gold, silver and precious stones, but may actually be piling up wood, hay and straw, things that will not stand the test of God's fire. This will mean the loss of eternal rewards. Even for believers, therefore, the bad things we do as well as our lack of service to God have eternal consequences!

The Lord declares: "I the Lord search the heart and examine the mind, to reward a man according to his conduct, according to what his deeds deserve" (Jeremiah 17v10, NIV). The things we do for God while on earth will go through a test of fire, to test the quality of each believer's work. Did we do our work well, with our whole heart and mind? What motivated us? Was it to get people's recognition or approval? Was it merely for material gain? Was it to gain influence and authority over others? Was it for our own glory and fame and not the Lord's? It is not just the work we do for God that is important; it is also our motive for doing it.

---

[2] Revelation 20v11-15 (NIV): *Then I saw a great white throne and Him who was seated on it... And I saw the dead, great and small, standing before the throne, and books were opened. Another book was opened, which is the book of life. The dead were judged according to what they had done as recorded in the books. The sea gave up the dead that were in it, and death and Hades gave up the dead that were in them, and each person was judged according to what he had done. Then death and Hades were thrown into the lake of fire. The lake of fire is the second death. If anyone's name was not found written in the book of life, he was thrown into the lake of fire.* The "second death" is eternal punishment in the lake of fire. The "book of life" contains the names of all believers.

[3] Romans 14v10b (NLT): *Remember, we will <u>all</u> stand before the judgment seat of God.* And v12: *Yes, <u>each of us</u> will give a personal account to God.*

Is it not a sobering thought that something we did for the Lord may not pass the test of fire on the day of God's judgment and we may lose rewards that should have been eternally ours?

In the following story, the Christian's motive was undoubtedly questioned by the object of her kindness, but her desire to be obedient to God ultimately paid off. May her kindness pass the test of fire!

My Neighbour Miss Wood

Miss Wood was a lady out of her time. She exuded a prim gentility seldom seen since the 1930s. Her social standing had taken a nose dive when she had to relinquish, due to financial necessity, the ownership of her large Victorian house to a local property landlord. She had however retained the life-long use of one of the proposed flats and henceforth lived in resentment of her fellow tenants. New arrivals were subjected to a barrage of spiteful comments, withheld mail and constant complaints. These lasted until a new tenant arrived and the cycle would start all over again. There was nothing personal in Miss Wood's tirades; she just didn't like change.

I lived in the new block which had been built much later than the main house and my efforts at tending the shared garden drew accusations of interfering and attempting to "take over the place"! Miss Wood liked to dominate her once domain in spirit, if not in ownership.

Change for Miss Wood started on a day I was out shopping. While choosing some flowers, a familiar voice spoke into my thoughts: "And get some for Miss Wood!"

"What Lord?" I retorted out loud, "You are joking?"

"No, get some for Miss Wood," He replied.

On the journey home I questioned the sanity of such an action and contemplated with horror its reception. I was not disappointed. In response to my knock, the door opened a minuscule and one eye met mine. "Yes, what do you want?"

Her tone of voice was coloured with suspicion. In reply I said, "I thought you would like some flowers." This brought a sneering, "Why?"

"No reason," I replied, "just thought you might like some."

Her thin bony hand reached out and grabbed them, but further conversation ended with the sharp closing of her door. I muttered words such as "Ungrateful old bag! What does she think I'm going to do? Poison her with flowers?"

"Lord, what is going on here?!"

My next encounter with Miss Wood was occasioned at the sight of her staggering up our long hill laden with shopping. "Stop and pick her up!", came the command. I sighed and slowed to a halt.

"Would you like a lift Miss Wood?" I inquired.

"Well, I don't know that I do," she replied haughtily.

I made the observation that she had a lot of shopping and it was a hot day, and there was another car waiting to pass. Huffing, she condescended and piled in. At once she began complaining about John, our handyman.

"Put in a positive for every negative," whispered my Counsellor.

When she stopped to draw breath, I interjected with, "Miss Wood, John thinks the world of you. He is always in your flat fixing things." John was my childhood friend and I resented her condemnation of his kindness.

"Well yes," she acquiesced, "but he's a busybody and a gossip."

I defended him. "Oh no Miss Wood, you're wrong! I have known John all my life and he is none of those things." She replied by hauling herself and her shopping from the car and slammed the door.

This pattern of encounters continued in a similar vein, for some two years. The *pièce de résistance* came just before Christmas 1991. I had planned to spend the day with a close friend. Looking forward to this exclusive company, I heard the now familiar voice, "Invite Miss Wood."

"That, Lord, is a step too far!"

Surprisingly, she was quite charming and delighted in my mother's pink and grey bathroom, exclaiming, "O, Hollywood!"

Henceforth, there was a subtle change in Miss Wood. I detected a softening in her manner and she was less hostile to the other tenants. When I called, she welcomed me in and even offered me tea!

One day I happened to mention that my mother was a dressmaker by trade. She admitted she too had been a tailoress. With this admission came another – Miss Wood had been in love with a married man and rather than break-up his marriage, she had given him up, but he had remained forever the love of her life. She graciously offered me her scissors as a gift. For a tailoress, no higher compliment could be offered. I humbly accepted.

Several months passed and Miss Wood began to look frail and she confided that she had been diagnosed with breast cancer. I was not to worry. "After all, at seventy-nine you have to die of something, my dear."

I visited her in the hospice a few days before she died, and you would have thought it was a different woman, and indeed it was. Miss Wood's physical frame was wasted, but her spirit radiated a peace and calm that could only have had its source in heaven.

- Gill Linder (Cockermouth, Cumbria, England)

March 2011

"Search me, O God, and know my heart; test me and know my anxious thoughts. See if there is any offensive way in me, and lead me in the way everlasting" (Psalm 139v23-24, NIV). Reveal to me any wrong motive and purify my heart. Refiner's fire, burn away any dross[4] in my character so that I will be building on the foundation of Jesus only 'things' that will pass the test of fire. May I receive rewards when the Day of Judgment comes so that I can lay them at the feet of my Saviour. For He is worthy of all the honour and glory! Amen.

---

[4] Malachi 3v3 (NLT): *He will sit like a refiner of silver, burning away the dross.*

Week 34: Wait for the Lord

*But they who wait for the Lord shall renew their strength; they
shall mount up with wings like eagles; they shall run and not be
weary; they shall walk and not faint. (Isaiah 40v31, ESV)*

Running a race is an intense activity that can easily zap one's strength to the point of weariness. It is more energy-demanding than soaring and walking, so as we end this section on God's athletes, let us do a little study of God's promise in the verse above.

In Week 19, we learned that human beings are first and foremost called *to be* in relationship with God, and only secondly called *to do* good works for Him. Although Jesus promised He would never leave us nor forsake us[1], it is easy for us to be caught up in the busyness of doing things for God that we forget that *we need* to spend time with Him and that *He wants* to spend time with us. The secret of Jesus' effective ministry and overcoming life was that He made it a point to spend time with His Father, to begin each day in communion with Him. If Jesus needed such time, surely it is the same for us?

Some versions of the Bible use the preposition "on" or "upon" instead of "for" in the verse above. One can say that we must first wait *for* the Lord and when He comes, then we wait *on* or *upon* Him, as a waiter waits on a customer for instructions. What we wait for is His 'manifest presence'. It may come in a dramatic way (like the way the Holy Spirit came to the waiting disciples on Pentecost in Acts 2, as the sound of a strong wind and as "tongues of fire" resting on each person in the room), or usually, as a "still small voice"[2]. However His manifest presence comes, you will learn to recognise it as you get to know Him more. We also wait for His answer to our prayer, His solution to our problem. This may take longer than we expect. So whether it is *for*, *on* or *upon*, what is more important is the word *wait*. How should we wait?

In the original Hebrew text, the word for 'wait' above is *qavah* which means to wait, to hope[3], to expect, and interestingly, to bind together as in a rope. From this last one, it can be said that *qavah* may also mean 'to intertwine'. Shirley of Week 3 and 11 shared with me her insight regarding this: since arms intertwine in an embrace, the verse above can be paraphrased as, "They who stay in an embrace with the Lord shall renew their strength".

---

[1] Hebrews 13v5 (NIV): *Never will I leave you; never will I forsake you.*

[2] In 1 Kings 19, God made His manifest presence known to the prophet Elijah as "a still small voice" or "a gentle whisper".

[3] Hence, some Bible versions, like the NIV, say, *"They that <u>hope</u> in the Lord..."*

176

Ecclesiastes 4v12 says that a cord (or rope) of three strands is not easily broken[4]. What "three strands" do we "bind together as in a rope" as we wait in hope for or on or upon the Lord so that we can stay in an embrace with Him?

1) Promise: With eagle eyes we need to look beyond any problem and see God's promise of protection, provision, guidance, peace, favour, joy, etc. We need to get fresh revelation of His promises in His written word so that we can regain our strength to do what He tells us to do and to face life's challenges. Reminding ourselves that He is faithful to His promises helps us to trust His ability and willingness to accomplish His purpose for our lives.

2) Prayer: Praying is simply talking to God (Week 6) especially about His promises. Doing this in solitude and allowing Him to speak to us especially through His written word deepens our intimacy with Him. Spiritual eagles, athletes and pilgrims cannot go on without this vital communication link. Prayer also gives God the right to intervene on behalf of His children on earth as well as to partner with them in the divine work of redemption (Week 30).

3) Praise: Praising God in spite of our circumstances is a sign that we are using the faith that Jesus gave us (Week 8), without which it is impossible to please God[5]. Praising God also returns to us the joy of the Lord, and the joy of the Lord is our strength![6] It is God's joy to help His children to soar like eagles with revelation, to run the race and win, and to walk the path of life all the way to eternity. In this we find the strength to persevere and endure[7]. We may find ourselves in the middle of Pharaoh's army and the Red Sea, but believing God's promises, keeping in communion with Him through prayer and praising Him in faith before the answer comes is the attitude we must adopt as we "wait". God may not be early, but He is never late. He is always on time!

In the Hebrew text, the word for 'renew' in the verse is *chalaph* which means to renew, to substitute, to change or exchange for something better. According to Shirley from Texas, "Those who stay in an embrace with the Lord exchange their weakness

---

[4] Ecclesiastes 4v12 (NLT): *A person standing alone can be attacked and defeated, but two can stand back-to-back and conquer. Three are even better, for a triple-braided cord is not easily broken.*

[5] Hebrews 11v6 (NIV): *And without faith it is impossible to please God, because anyone who comes to Him must believe that He exists and that He rewards those who earnestly seek Him.*

[6] Nehemiah 8v10b (ESV): *... for the joy of the Lord is your strength.*

[7] Colossians 1v11-12 (NLT): *We also pray that you will be strengthened with all His glorious power so you will have all the endurance and patience you need. May you be filled with joy, always thanking the Father. He has enabled you to share in the inheritance that belongs to His people, who live in the light.*

for His very strength and Life Force". His strength or Life Force enables them to soar like eagles and get revelation, to run like athletes without getting weary, and to walk like pilgrims without fainting. Tell yourself: "I can do everything through Him who gives me strength!"[8]

"Wait" – that was what the Lord told Joyce, our next storyteller. He revealed to her what she had to do regarding her husband's problem, but she had to wait for the right time, His time.

My Husband Became an Alcoholic

In the second year of my short marriage, I discovered my husband had developed a drinking problem. Mike was the sweetest, smartest, most fun and loving man in the world, but even though he did not drink every day, true to the definition of an alcoholic, once he took one drink, he could not stop. This man with the sweet countenance would get so drunk his dark brown eyes would glare at me as if he could kill me. In fact, he did beat me – once – on my face and head, to the point that I was unrecognisable for a couple of weeks. I knew I was dealing with demon spirits, even though at the time I didn't understand how someone "born again" could have that kind of demonic influence.

In the church I had grown up in[9], I had been taught that all this was hogwash, but I knew I needed divine empowerment and went looking for the baptism of the Holy Spirit, despite having been told it was "from the devil". I got counsel on the subject and one night after Mike left to go get more liquor before the store closed, I knelt by my bed and asked the Father to baptise me with the Holy Spirit. I received the Holy Spirit by faith after I asked, remembering that Jesus had said, "You fathers – if your children ask for a fish, do you give them a snake instead? Or if they ask for an egg, do you give them a scorpion? Of course not! So if you sinful people know how to give good gifts to your children, how much more will your heavenly Father give the Holy Spirit to those who ask Him" (Luke 11v11-13, NLT).

In the days ahead, when Mike would get drunk and start looking at me with hate-filled eyes, I'd go to the garage and stutter in fear, "Sa Sa Sa Satan, I bi bi bi bind you in Mike in the na na na name of Jesus!" When I would re-enter the house, he would have passed out, giving me peace for the night.

---

[8] Philippians 4v13, NIV
[9] The storyteller had grown up in a traditional denominational church and then later began attending a charismatic church.

To make a long story short, I prayed for four years of my five and a half-year marriage for Mike's deliverance, during which God did a work in ME. He purified ME and He spoke to ME. One day in exasperation, I yelled, "God, WHY did you give me Mike?" That's when He replied so clearly, "Because I made woman for man, not man for woman[10], and Mike and Johnny need what you have to offer!" (Johnny is my stepson from Mike's first marriage. He was three when I got him.) Jesus didn't like His assignment either! The cross wasn't fun, but thank God His love for the Father and for us was His motivation to endure.

During a time of intercession for Mike at a church altar on a Sunday morning, the Lord told me He was going to deliver him…. "by my hand"…. and even gave me the prayer of deliverance I was to pray. I got all excited until I heard, "Only thing is, you have to wait till he wants it." Then I was depressed again. I could see another fifty years going by! However, it was only three months!

One night Mike said, "I'm so tired of this bondage. Will you pray for me to be free?" The room got supernaturally still. As he sat in his recliner and I sat on the arm of it, I didn't deviate one syllable from the prayer God had given me. I bound the three demon spirits the Lord had told me to bind (that had "attached" themselves to him when he was a little boy). I commanded them to leave him and never come back, and then, as instructed, I placed my hand on his forehead and quietly said, "Mike, in the name of Jesus, receive the Holy Ghost." With that, I heard a man's voice softly praying in tongues!!! I KNEW instantly he was different.

I was in charge of the vacation Bible school for the little church near my house where Mike and I attended, and my now-delivered, Spirit-filled husband was helping me with it. The night before his accident, he asked me to ride to the church with him so that he could hang a very large street sign he had made, advertising the Bible school. While he was getting ready, Mike stopped shaving and said to me, "Contrary to some of your friends' opinions, I have always known Jesus as Saviour. I just didn't know God very well and was bound by alcohol. But when I met you, you made me want to know God, and I want to tell you that if the purpose for your having been born was to bring me to God, your life has been worth it!"

I was in shock! My husband had a difficult time expressing what was in his heart, so what he said to me was indeed miraculous. I shared it with an evangelist friend of mine who said, "That wasn't your husband talking. That was your heavenly Father saying, 'Well done, daughter!'"

---

[10] 1 Corinthians 11v8-9 (NASB): *For man does not originate from woman, but woman from man; for indeed man was not created for the woman's sake, but woman for the man's sake.*

Sadly, six months after his deliverance from alcohol, my husband died from a motorcycle accident.

Some friends of mine were upset with God for giving me only six months with my transformed husband Mike. I told them that although I would have loved having him longer, I am grateful that what the devil meant for evil (Mike's and my destruction), God turned into victory before He took him home. I had my delivered and Spirit-filled husband for six whole months before his fatal motorcycle accident!

I heard someone say recently that "no suffering for the present time is worthy to be compared with the glory that shall be revealed to us"[11]. That's one of the things the Lord made clear to me while I was in this situation. Because of my endurance and persistence, Mike is in heaven. So, yes, in light of the eternal rewards, the price was nothing.

Scripture says we are pilgrims and we look to the eternal rewards that are waiting for us. After years of grief, I'm now happy that God used me as an instrument of deliverance for my precious husband. While there is no marriage in heaven[12], there is LOVE. The love of God, placed in our hearts by the Holy Spirit while we are here on earth, is eternal. Therefore, in heaven, it remains in our hearts for our loved ones and in their hearts toward us. I only had five and a half years on earth with Mike, but I will have an eternity with him!

- Joyce (Houston, Texas, USA)
April 2011

Romans 8v24-25 (NASB): "For in hope we have been saved, but hope that is seen is not hope; for who hopes for what he already sees? But if we hope for what we do not see, with perseverance we wait eagerly for it."

Psalm 37v7 (NASB): "Rest in the Lord and wait patiently for Him."

Loving and faithful God, thank You that You know the best way and the best time to answer my prayer and fulfil Your promises to me. Keep me in an embrace with You as I wait with patience, perseverance, hope and eager expectation. Help me to rest in You while I wait, reminding myself of Your precious promises and Your ability and

---

[11] Romans 8v18 (NASB): *For I consider that the sufferings of this present time are not worthy to be compared with the glory that is to be revealed to us.*

[12] Matthew 22v29-30 (NLT): *Jesus replied, "Your mistake is that you don't know the Scriptures, and you don't know the power of God. For when the dead rise, they will neither marry nor be given in marriage. In this respect they will be like the angels in heaven.*

willingness to keep them. Help me to remain in continual communion with You and to praise You before the answer to my prayer comes. When waiting gets difficult and I grow impatient and anxious, renew my soul's strength and refresh me as I soak in Your presence[13]. With You, I can soar above my problems like an eagle, run like an athlete without getting weary, and walk this long road of life like a pilgrim without fainting. Thank You Jesus!

"Scripture says we are pilgrims and we look to the eternal rewards that are waiting for us." These words of Joyce from Houston introduce us to the last section of this devotional – stories of pilgrims who are walking the road of life en route to their eternal destination.

---

[13] Acts 3v19-20 (ESV): *Repent therefore, and turn back, that your sins may be blotted out, that times of refreshing may come from the presence of the Lord.*

Section 3

Walking like Pilgrims on Earth

(Week 35 to Week 52)

Week 35: All Roads Lead to Rome, But Not to God

Jesus answered, "I am the way and the truth and the life. No-one comes to the Father except through Me". (John 14v6, NIV)

Whether you believe it or not, you are a pilgrim on earth and you are just passing through. The road you are on matters a lot for it will either lead you to God or to eternal destruction.

In the days of the Roman Empire, Rome was "the capital of the world" and practically every road in the Empire led to it, either directly or by being linked to major roads that radiated from the city like the spokes of a wheel. This system improved trade and moved troops more efficiently. This is the etymology of the expression, "All roads lead to Rome". The sentence has come to mean "different methods will produce the same result", "there are different ways of doing something", or "different paths can take us to the same goal".

Many have applied the expression to "religion" in that they believe that the religion an individual practices does not matter, for all religions lead to God anyway. But what is religion? Even a cursory study of the world's main religions causes one to conclude that religion defines the things that a person must do in order to put him in right standing with God (or gods). In this sense, Christianity is not really a religion because it is not about man trying to do the right things to be accepted by God, but rather, about God reaching out to man and offering him the free gift of salvation through the atoning sacrifice of God's Son, Jesus Christ[1]. It was God who took the initiative to bridge the gap between Himself and mankind, and all a man must do is to receive the gift. The things he does for God after this are expressions of his love and gratitude for the standing he now has with God that he never worked for, as well as the result of the transforming work of the Holy Spirit in his life.

In its early days, Christianity was called "the Way"[2]. This most likely comes from what Jesus said about Himself in the verse above from John's Gospel, that He is the way to the Father who is none other than Almighty God. Jesus therefore claimed that there is only ONE road that leads to God, and that is through Him, through Christianity. Although Christians are often accused of dogmatism and "narrow-mindedness", the

---

[1] Ephesians 2v8-9 (NLT): *God saved you by His grace when you believed. And you can't take credit for this; it is a gift from God. Salvation is not a reward for the good things we have done, so none of us can boast about it.*

[2] This phrase is used in Acts 19v9 and v23, NIV.

assertion that there is only one way to God was made by Jesus Himself, and to be a real Christian is to believe what He said.

The Jews who heard Jesus' claim would have understood exactly what Jesus was alluding to when He said those words in John 14. They would have remembered the Tabernacle that Moses had built and that their ancestors had carried during their sojourning in the desert before they entered the Promised Land[3]. They would have recalled that the Tabernacle had represented God's dwelling place on earth and that the first entrance which led to the outer court of the Tabernacle was traditionally called "the Way"; the second entrance which led to the Holy Place was called "the Truth"; and the last entrance that led to the innermost sanctuary or the Holy of Holies, the place of God's presence, was called "the Life". In claiming that He is the only way to God, the ultimate revelation of truth about God, and the only source of eternal life, Jesus was in effect claiming that He is God[4].

Today, in your sojourning as a pilgrim on earth, you can know (*yada*, Week 5) Jesus as *Immanuel*[5], "God with us", who tabernacles or lives with and in His people through His Holy Spirit. You may claim that you know Him because you call yourself a Christian. However, if your religious beliefs do not line up with Jesus' claims and teachings as recorded in the Bible, then you are on the wrong road, pilgrim! There is only one road that leads to God. Are you on this one? Please get on the right road while you still have the choice!

---

[3] The Tabernacle which God told Moses to construct (Exodus 35-40) was a mobile tent with various portable furniture. It represented the dwelling place of God on earth among His people. God gave very specific instructions regarding its construction to teach man that he can only approach God on God's terms. The tent had 2 parts: the innermost Holy of Holies and the Holy Place. All the furniture here were made of gold (symbolic of divinity and kingship). The tent was surrounded by an outer court with its bronze altar for burning sacrifices, and bronze basin for washing (bronze = judgment of sin) before entry to the Holy Place where the golden lampstand (the menorah), the table of showbread and the altar of incense were located. Inside the Holy of Holies was the golden Ark of the Covenant. The sockets upon which the golden boards of the Tabernacle stood were made of silver (silver = redemption). The Tabernacle and its furniture had prophetic symbolisms and served as object lessons that were meant to teach the Jews about the nature and ministry of the Messiah who would come.

[4] John 14v9b-10 (NIV): *Anyone who has seen Me has seen the Father. How can you say, 'Show us the Father'? Don't you believe that I* [Jesus] *am in the Father, and that the Father is in Me? The words I say to you are not just my own. Rather, it is the Father, living in Me, who is doing His work.*

[5] Isaiah 7v14 (NKJV): *Therefore the Lord Himself will give you a sign: Behold, the virgin shall conceive and bear a Son, and shall call His name Immanuel.*

Here is a story of one lady who discovered that she was not on the right road. Once she got on it, she also discovered that she could enjoy living life free from bondage.

<u>Christine's Story</u>

When I was twenty-two, I got pregnant with my second child. Blood tests indicated probable spina bifida and I was advised to abort my unborn baby, but I didn't want to. Upset over the news, I wondered if there was indeed a God and if I could appeal to Him for help. Whilst I was anxiously waiting for the results of the amniocentesis, a couple of people from a church came to our house. They seemed to know God and had answers to my questions.

Although the amniocentesis proved negative for spina bifida, I persisted in my search for God and so I continued to welcome the couple to our home. One day my husband, Alan, came home unexpectedly and found me studying scriptures with this couple. I persuaded him to join us. Soon afterwards we attended their services. Encouraged by the birth of a beautiful, perfectly normal baby girl, we stayed with the group for six years.

To become part of their church, we had to give up celebrating Christmas, a tradition in our family. This disturbed my father who was brought up as an Anglican. He asked my mother's relative and her husband to talk to Alan and me. My father wanted this couple, who are born-again Christians, to counsel us about the truth. We were adamant we knew the truth, but we said we were happy to go and see them. And so one day, we met with them just to prove our point.

After David and Doreen questioned us about what we had learned from the church we had been attending, they gently but firmly declared to us that we did not in fact know the truth about God. They spoke to us about salvation being a free gift made possible by the crucifixion and resurrection of Jesus. As I listened to this heart-warming story, I could not stop crying. On the drive home, Alan and I reflected on what we had heard and we felt something lift from our spirits.

After this, we threw away all of the literature which we received from the church that we thought represented the Jesus of the Bible and informed the group that we did not want to continue studying the scriptures with them. Having realised that we were deceived for six years, I did not feel the desire to attend any church. When Alan decided to check out our town's Brethren Church which David suggested, I refused to go with him, saying I did not want to be deceived again. On Sundays, Alan would ask me to accompany him to church and each time I would say no. I told him that because I pray and believe in God, I was 'okay' and didn't need to go to church. Coming home one night from church, Alan confessed, "Something happened to me. I got born-again!" Nevertheless, this news did not persuade me to go to church with him.

After a while, Alan asked me to prepare a meal every evening of the week for a visiting evangelist who was coming to town for 'Mission Kendal'. So, for one week, this man joined us for dinner. On one of these evenings I inquired, "How can one know if one is a Christian or not?" After giving me a short explanation, he then added, "If you have to ask this question, you can't be a Christian! You don't have that assurance of salvation!"

This shocking revelation led me to accept the little booklet this evangelist gave me, *Journey into Life*[6], which I had read before but hadn't taken much notice of. I read through the booklet again, this time pondering on what I was reading. Sometime later, as I was ironing, I recalled what I had read and tears began to fall. I stopped my chore, fell to my knees, prayed the prayer of salvation printed in the booklet, and accepted Jesus as my Saviour and Lord. I was ecstatic! I could feel warmth coming from my head into my heart. Bursting with joy, I began to sing 'Amazing Grace' – the little that I knew of it!

I was thirty when I got saved, but I remained captive to a smoking habit which began when I was just fifteen. Thinking that I must first get myself right, this habit prevented me from joining a church even after I got saved. However, when I heard about a church in Lancaster, a small city south of our town, I asked my husband to check it out. He came back with a report that the church wouldn't suit me because it was a "happy-clappy" one!

I went and visited it anyway, met the pastor and perceived him to be a man of God. I believed he had something I wanted for myself, so I continued to go. Sometime later, the pastor told me I needed to be baptised. I explained to him that I had been christened as a child and had been born-again. Weren't these enough? Our conversation led me to read about baptism by immersion. What I read brought not only conviction of my need to be baptised, but also of my need to be delivered of my bad habit. Yet, no matter how hard I tried, I could not stop smoking!

One Sunday, as I was smoking in a pub, I audibly heard these words that seemed to come from above, "I do not want you to smoke!" I knew that it was God! I threw away my cigarette and did not light up another one that night.

The following morning, having achieved some victory over the habit overnight, I thought it would be okay to smoke. I lit up a cigarette, but was surprised to discover

---

[6] *Journey into Life* by Norman Warren was published by Kingsway Books in 2005.

I could not smoke it. The Lord just wouldn't let me! This went on for a few days – I would try to smoke, but could not. Finally, I told myself I would never smoke again. I discovered to my amazement that I was delivered of my addiction without going through withdrawal symptoms!

Shortly after this, Alan and I were baptised. At first he agreed to be baptised with me because of my fear of being immersed in water. Then the Lord told him his reason should be that he really wanted to be baptised, not because of me. Fully convinced that this was what we definitely wanted to do, Alan and I went down the water of baptism together, as husband and wife and as children of Almighty Father God.

Saved at thirty and baptised and delivered from a twenty-one-year smoking habit at thirty-six, I can say that my life is a testimony of God's amazing grace!

- Christine (Kendal, Cumbria, England)
March 2011

In the Holy of Holies (or Most Holy Place) of the Tabernacle of Moses (and later on, of the Temple of Solomon) was a wooden box inlaid with gold – the Ark of the Covenant (see this week's 3rd footnote). Tradition says that between the golden pair of cherubim on the cover of this box (called the "Mercy Seat") was a mysterious glow, the only source of light inside the room and which was referred to as the *shekinah*, the visible symbol of God's presence in His dwelling or resting place[7]. This golden box then became the main symbol of God's presence among the Israelites as they journeyed to and fought for the Promised Land. Many years later after they had settled in the Promised Land, the Ark of the Covenant was captured by the Philistines (1 Samuel 4). The Israelites became very troubled because the symbol of God's presence was no longer with them.

This shows that the Promised Land, the promised dwelling or resting place for God's children, is actually none other than God Himself. He is our "Promised Land"! Man was created to dwell in this "Eternal Home"[8]. Away from this home, man would feel like a restless and troubled wanderer. Jesus is the only 'road' to this "Promised Land". My prayer is that everyone who reads this book and is not yet a Christian would

---

[7] *Shekinah* is derived from the verb *shakan*, as in Exodus 40v35, NKJV: *And Moses was not able to enter the tabernacle of meeting, because the cloud* (God's cloud that led the way for the Israelites when they left Egypt) *rested* ['shakan'] *above it, and the glory of the Lord filled the tabernacle*. 'Mishkan', the word for tabernacle, is from the same root and is used in the Bible to mean dwelling-place.

[8] And God created man to be His dwelling or resting place, the *shekinah* of His Spirit. This is why the Bible says that the believer is "the light of the world" (Matthew 5v14).

answer God's call to take this road. If you made the decision before but have wandered off, my prayer is that this book would encourage you to get back on this road.

Pilgrim, Jesus is calling you home!

Softly and tenderly Jesus is calling,
Calling for you and for me.
See, on the portals He's waiting and watching,
Watching for you and for me.

Why should we tarry when Jesus is pleading,
Pleading for you and for me?
Why should we linger and heed not His mercies,
Mercies for you and for me?

Time is now fleeting, the moments are passing,
Passing from you and from me;
Shadows are gathering, deathbeds are coming,
Coming for you and for me.

Oh, for the wonderful love He has promised,
Promised for you and for me!
Though we have sinned, He has mercy and pardon,
Pardon for you and for me.

Come home, come home,
You who are weary, come home.
Earnestly, tenderly, Jesus is calling,
Calling, O sinner, come home!

('Softly and Tenderly' by Will Thompson, 1880)

Week 36: The Road Less Travelled

Enter through the narrow gate, for wide is the gate and broad is the road that leads to destruction, and many enter through it. But small is the gate and narrow the road that leads to life, and only a few find it.
(Matthew 7v13-14, NIV)

Pilgrim, your final destination depends on which road you are on. You know you are on the right road if you have entered through the right gate.

In the Scripture above, Jesus talks about gates and roads. Jesus' Jewish hearers would have pictured in their minds the gates and roads of their cities which were surrounded by walls and everyone entered through gates. A public road to a city would have been 16 cubits[1] wide and would have a wide gate. In contrast, a private way would have been 4 cubits wide and would have a narrow gate. More people would have entered through the broader gate and walked along the broader public road.

In last week's reading, there was a reference to the Tabernacle of Moses and its three entrances: the Way, the Truth and the Life. These are also known traditionally by their other names. The one that led to the Holy of Holies (the gate called the Life) was also called "the Veil"; the one that led to the Holy Place (the Truth) was also called "the Door"; and the outermost entrance that led to the Outer Court (the Way) was also called "the Gate".

Jesus said about Himself, "I am the gate; whoever enters through Me will be saved."[2] Saved from what? From eternal separation from God which is basically what 'hell' is[3]. Jesus' declaration in Matthew 7 above essentially means the same thing as, "I am the way.... No one comes to the Father except through Me" (John 14v6). The gate that leads to eternity in the presence of God our Father (eternal or everlasting life[4]) is narrow because there is no other way through it except by receiving Jesus as Saviour and Lord.

---

[1] A cubit is a unit of linear measure, from the elbow to the tip of the longest finger of a grown man. It is commonly converted to 45.7 centimetres or 18 inches.

[2] John 10v9, NIV

[3] Hell is a real place, as well as a spiritual condition.

[4] The believer in Christ already has eternal life or "life": *Whoever has the Son has life* (1 John 5v12, NIV). When he dies and leaves earth, he gets to enjoy it in a greater measure in heaven.

The gate and the road that lead to eternal death and hell are both wide because there is a wide spectrum of reasons why people are on their way there[5], from the most obvious (e.g., heinous crimes like genocide and terrorism) to the not so obvious reasons such as the seemingly harmless assessment of oneself as being "deserving of heaven" because one is "good-enough". Such a statement reflects one's ignorance of God's passing grade which is 100%![6]

Regarding the seemingly harmless side of the spectrum, C.S. Lewis[7] once said, "The safest road to hell is the gradual one – the gentle slope, soft underfoot, without sudden turnings, without milestones, without signposts". Hell is a place of eternal pain, misery, agony and loneliness, so why would anyone want to go there? Yet, many people end up there because they reject the narrow gate!

On the other hand, no one will experience any need, pain, misery and boredom in heaven once they get there after their time on earth, not one who enters the narrow road through the narrow gate. In Week 25, we learned that God trains us *to choose the narrow way of obedience*. It is only through our obedience, our co-operation with the transforming work of the Holy Spirit, that we become more Christ-like as we walk the narrow road on our way to heaven. One day, we will be awesomely transformed as we behold God in all His glory[8]!

Our next storyteller was not only on her way to hell, she was practically in hell! But the light of Jesus shone through the darkness she was in. She entered the narrow gate and is now on a journey on the narrow road. She is finding the journey "wonderful, challenging and sometimes painful, but also transforming and purposeful".

His Light Invaded My Darkness

One day I walked into a conference room and heard the speaker talk about a particular psychological condition called misogyny, the hatred and mistrust of women. She

---

[5] A person without God is spiritually dead and becomes eternally dead and separated from God when he physically dies and goes to hell.

[6] James 2v10 (NLT): *For the person who keeps all of the laws* [God's commandments] *except one is as guilty as a person who has broken all of God's laws.* We all have broken at least one of God's laws, so no one is "good-enough".

[7] Clive Staples Lewis, better known as C.S. Lewis (1898 –1963), was a novelist, academic, poet, literary critic, essayist, theologian and Christian apologist from Belfast, Ireland. His faith profoundly affected both his fiction (e.g., *The Chronicles of Narnia, Space Trilogy* and *The Screwtape Letters*) and non-fiction work (e.g., *Mere Christianity* and *The Problem of Pain*).

[8] 1 John 3v2 (NLT): *Dear friends, we are already God's children, but He has not yet shown us what we will be like when Christ appears. But we do know that we will be like Him, for we will see Him as He really is.* (More about the transformation in Week 51.)

explained that misogynists are terrified of being abandoned so they develop a system of domination and intimidation mainly directed at their spouse or partner, devaluing their opinions and destroying their self-confidence through verbal, emotional or physical abuse. The goal of the misogynist is to maintain control over another at all costs. I was stunned as I listened to the speaker. She was describing my father!

As children we look to our parents for guidance, safety, refuge and life. Unfortunately, Dad couldn't give these to me. Dad was a damaged child who carried a lot of pain and, like many misogynists, had grown into adulthood with this philosophy: "Someone has to pay for my pain". His mother was killed in an accident when he was six and no one told him about it for quite some time. At such a young age, the trauma and feeling of abandonment must have been severe. Dad once told me that I look like his mum. I grew up feeling I was responsible for all the problems in the family.

Mum and Dad hardly knew each other when they got married. They had three children, all girls (I'm the middle child). Mum did love me, but caring for three girls with only a year's gap in between and with very little money must have been difficult, especially because of the verbal, emotional, and occasionally, physical abuse by Dad. I had often wondered if Mum was the real problem because of Dad's treatment and disrespect of her. Mum was a very out-going, creative and positive person, but Dad controlled her, wore her down and broke her spirit. Despite this, she stayed with him. Where could she go at that time with three children and no money?

Looking back, I realise that my parents were not able to connect emotionally. I remember when I was little there were occasions when Dad read stories to me, but he didn't seem to take delight in spending that time with me. It was the only time we ever spent together. I don't remember him ever saying one positive thing to me, only destructive and endless criticisms. I grew up in a constant state of anxiety and fear! Because of this and the feeling that I could not trust Dad or my mother to be there for me, I developed severe panic attacks from around the age of six as well as difficulty sleeping. During these times I would be overwhelmed by a sense of abandonment, which to a child dependent on another to survive, means death. By age twelve I began to have suicidal thoughts, seeing the homes in my neighbourhood as endless rows of meaningless boxes and wondering if there was really any point in living.

I often did very well at school, but have no recollection of any affirmation from my parents. By the time I was sixteen, I hated my parents and grew up in rebellion over Dad's anger, rage, criticism and resentment. When I was seventeen, I left for a holiday in France although I was not well. I just wanted to get away from a place called 'home' which for me was a place of misery rather than a safe place of refuge and loving protection. When I returned, I was very ill with glandular fever. My immune system took a battering and since then I have been susceptible to illnesses.

When I was eighteen, I was desperate to get away from everything I knew so I went to college in Manchester. Desperate to be loved and lacking self-worth, I became promiscuous and had lots of boyfriends. I was emotionally and psychologically messed up and I got involved with drugs and a boyfriend who was a big drug dealer in Manchester. My search for significance led me to seek spiritual guidance and spiritual experiences, so I joined a Hindu ashram for a while. However, this did not prevent my life from spiralling downwards.

Towards the end of my third year at college, I was gripped with a severe and extreme form of anxiety. I cannot really explain what happened to me, but I believe it was demonic. I remember being paralysed with fear for many months. I could not sleep and could not swallow so I lived off tomato soup. Later I was told I looked like a walking dead! I felt no one in the entire universe cared for me. Eventually, in desperation, I went to the doctor's surgery, not believing they could help. Because of how I looked, I didn't have to wait and I was seen straight away by a female doctor. She put me on very strong sedatives and asked me if I would like to meet some Christians. (She was a Christian herself.) I said yes, but at that time it was meaningless to me. The doctor then gave me an address to visit if I chose to, which amazingly was only a few houses away from where I was living.

Because I was desperate and didn't feel I could live much longer, I called on the address. It was the home of Gill and Steve and their two young children. I remember sitting in their kitchen thinking I couldn't relate to this Christian family and it seemed to me this really was the end. It felt like I was being strangled when I was with them. Looking back, I realise there was a clash of worlds, of darkness versus light. But I continued to visit them because I could tell that they cared for me. I will never forget the words Gill spoke: "If ever you need us, day or night, we are here for you." It changed everything... I was not utterly alone!

At some point I made a personal decision. I bumped into a girl from the ashram I had visited. She heard that I met some Christians and she asked me, "Have you made a decision what to do?" I answered that I wanted to be with the Christians! I never went back to the ashram and moved house to live with some Christians who, like Steve and Gill, were members of a Christian organisation called The Navigators[9]. With my housemates I learned about the value that God placed on my life[10] and the

---

[9] www.navigators.org or www.navigators.co.uk

[10] That God values your life is reflected in the scriptures such as Genesis 1v27 (NLT): *So God created human beings in His own image. In the image of God He created them; male and female He created them.* Also Psalm 8v4 (NLT): *What are mere mortals that You should think about them, human beings that You should care for them?*

price Jesus paid for me[11] to live in His freedom and grace[12]. God's light invaded my darkness and I asked Jesus into my heart!

As a Christian I want to become the person God desires me to be. I decided to look at those areas of my life which I felt were hindering that maturing and healing process. I was greatly helped by the prayers and love of many gifted people, but especially by the teaching ministry of Valerie Acuff and her late husband Walt through their Skills for Living teaching programmes. These were designed to help people identify and deal with issues that hinder personal development and healthy relationships – issues such as identity, connecting, boundaries and personal authority[13]. As I grew in my relationship with Jesus, I experienced the power and faithfulness of God's promises to bring wholeness and freedom. One of the scriptures which has come to mean much to me is Psalm 103, especially in the Amplified version.

For many years I couldn't go back home to my parents without fear, knowing the emotional battering and stress I would most likely encounter. Now I can go without any problem. In his later years, Dad has mellowed and now respects and appreciates Mum – an answer to prayer! I hope that someday I will see God's answer to my prayer for my parents, siblings and their families to come to know the Lord. Being artistic, I also pray that the Lord will use me to bring healing and restoration to others using imagery and colour. I know He has given me a real ability to connect with people, especially those who are on the fringes of society. I believe God is taking me on to complete recovery from the effects of the exhaustion and stress of the past.

Sadly, my experience of marital life as a child was one of misery and pain. This coloured my view of marriage as I grew up. By protecting my heart from being hurt, I was unable to receive love. But the Lord has healed my heart with His love and I would now love to share my heart with a life partner.

My journey so far has been wonderful, challenging and sometimes painful, but also transforming and purposeful. Jesus has brought me from a place of isolation to a place of intimacy. He excels in turning things around![14] One thing I have learned is that there is much in relation to God and ourselves we have yet to experience and

---

[11] 1 Peter 3v18 (NIV): *For Christ died for sins once for all, the righteous for the unrighteous, to bring you to God.*

[12] Galatians 5v1a (NASB): *It was for freedom that Christ set us free...*

[13] See www.skills.org/AboutUs.htm

[14] Romans 8v28 (NASB): *And we know that God causes all things to work together for good to those who love God, to those who are called according to His purpose.*

discover[15]. As a good friend of mine always says, "You don't know what you don't know!".... Until we see Him!

- Helen (Lancaster, England)
August 2011

Pilgrim, do you have a painful past like Helen? What is more important than where you came from is where you are heading! Please enter the narrow gate now if you have not yet chosen to do this.

"Bless (affectionately, gratefully praise) the Lord, O my soul; and all that is [deepest] within me, bless His holy name!" (Psalm 103v1, AMP). I bless Your Holy Name O Lord for You saw me with the throng travelling the wide road to eternal destruction, called my name and gave me a revelation of Your love and grace. Because of You, I have entered the narrow gate and now I have salvation through Jesus Christ. You redeemed my life and "beautify, dignify and crown me with loving-kindness and tender mercy"[16]. Thank You for Your grace that enables me to fulfil my purpose and to walk this narrow road of obedience to You. My past may not be something anyone could be proud of, but because of Jesus I have a future I can look forward to, an amazing eternity with You! Bless the Lord O my soul, and all that is within me, bless His holy name!

---

[15] Ephesians 3v20 (AMP): *Now to Him Who, by (in consequence of) the [action of His] power that is at work within us, is able to [carry out His purpose and] do superabundantly, far over and above all that we [dare] ask or think [infinitely beyond our highest prayers, desires, thoughts, hopes, or dreams]...*

[16] Psalm 103v4 (AMP): *Who redeems your life from the pit and corruption, who beautifies, dignifies, and crowns you with loving-kindness and tender mercy...*

Week 37: Strangers and Pilgrims on the Road

[They] confessed that they were strangers and pilgrims on the earth.
(Hebrews 11v13b, NKJV)

We are just passing through this planet on our way to our final destination, either through the narrow road to an eternity with God (eternal life[1] and heaven) or through the broad road to everlasting suffering in hell (Week 36). Hell is unimaginably hideous, but the road to it is full of attractions and many are fooled into taking that route, so God pleads with us, "Choose life!"[2]

In a sense, we have to "choose life" over and over again in that although our eternal destination is determined by our decision to receive Jesus as our Saviour and Lord[3], we have to choose again and again whether to fall for satan's temptation (but suffer the consequence and grieve God), or to obey Jesus as Lord (and feel His approval and delight and have peace and joy). God loves us unconditionally and He never stops loving us. But although He loves the sinner, He hates the sin and cannot therefore give unconditional approval because he cannot bless sin. As long as we are on the journey, we have to choose time and again to truly live for God.

God's Holy Spirit is our companion on our journey and to help us make the right choice, He frequently reminds Christians of *who we are and whose we are*. He reminds us that we are children of God[4]. We are not our own, we have been bought by the precious blood of Jesus[5]. Like Jesus, we do not belong to this world[6] which will

---

[1] 'Everlasting life' is a more accurate term because only God has 'eternal life' in the sense that only He does not have a beginning and end.

[2] Deuteronomy 30v19 (NLT): *"Today I have given you the choice between life and death, between blessings and curses. Now I call on heaven and earth to witness the choice you make. Oh, that you would choose life, so that you and your descendants might live!*

[3] 1 John 5v11-13 (NLT): *And this is what God has testified: He has given us eternal life, and this life is in His Son. Whoever has the Son has life; whoever does not have God's Son does not have life. I have written this to you who believe in the name of the Son of God, so that you may know you have eternal life.*

[4] Galatians 3v26 (NLT): *For you are all children of God through faith in Christ Jesus.*

[5] 1 Corinthians 6v19-20 (NIV): *Do you not know that your bodies are temples of the Holy Spirit, who is in you, whom you have received from God? You are not your own; you were bought at a price. Therefore honour God with your bodies.*

[6] John 17v14 (NIV): *I [Jesus] have given them Your word and the world has hated them, for they are not of the world any more than I am of the world.*

197

pass away so we should not be too attached to it[7]. The Holy Spirit also reminds us that we are strangers and pilgrims[8] on earth, as Hebrews 11v13 says. We are citizens of heaven who speak on Jesus' behalf as His "ambassadors" on earth[9]. We represent heaven and Jesus to those on earth who must perceive something different about us if we are truly 'aliens' on this planet.

The fact that we are strangers and pilgrims is emphasised by Peter: "Dearly beloved, I beseech you as strangers and pilgrims, abstain from fleshly lusts, which war against the soul" (1 Peter 2v11, KJV). The word in the original Greek text for pilgrim here is *parepidemos*, someone from a foreign land who comes to a place to reside with the locals or natives[10]. It would be tragic if, as Christ's ambassadors, we set our hearts on what the 'locals' or 'natives' of earth set their hearts on and forget our real home. Our spirits crave for God and our heavenly home and so we "set our hearts on pilgrimage"[11]. The attractions of earth diminish as we value the fact that we are heading for our glorious home where God is.

As you journey on the road to your glorious home, your identity will constantly be challenged. Whatever your background, your past failures, people's opinions of you, your self-doubts and the temptations and trials you face, remember that your true identity is in Christ and that you are not of this world. Act out who you truly are[12]. Choose life each time!

Here is a story of a lady who had a bad start in life and poor self-image because of her father's view of her. But she found Jesus who gave her a new identity (her real one!) and with that, she reached out to her father with the love God gave her so that he too could be on the road to heaven.

God Gave Me Love for My Father

My birth in 1934 wasn't a great cause for celebration. I shocked my parents and the doctors when I was born with severe spina bifida. The spinal cord from my back was the size of an adult's clenched fist protruding through a hole where a vertebra was

---

[7] 1 Corinthians 7v31 (NLT): *Those who use the things of the world should not become attached to them. For this world as we know it will soon pass away.*
[8] 'Pilgrim' is from Latin *peregrinum* which means foreigner or stranger.
[9] 2 Corinthians 5v20 (NLT): *So we are Christ's ambassadors; God is making His appeal through us. We speak for Christ when we plead, "Come back to God!"*
[10] *Parepidemos* means 'foreigner' or 'sojourner in a strange place'.
[11] Psalm 84v5 (NIV): *Blessed are those whose strength is in You, whose hearts are set on pilgrimage.*
[12] Proverbs 23v7a (NKJV): *For as he thinks in his heart, so is he.* Appendix 2 gives a list of Bible verses about our identity in God.

missing. The doctors decided to "leave it to nature", meaning I would be nursed on my tummy till such time as nature took its course and the mass would rupture and that would be that. Well, the cord didn't rupture and day by day it began to go back through the hole. God obviously had a plan for my life though it took a very long time for me to realise this.

When the doctors realised I was going to live, they told my mother not to expect too much because I would probably be "retarded" and might not be able to walk. But she was a physiotherapist and spent ages massaging my legs to strengthen them and I did finally walk.

My father was ashamed of me. As I grew up, the word "imbecile" would ring in my ears. I didn't know what it meant, but it didn't sound nice the way he said it and the way he looked at me. I didn't do well at school so my mother would conveniently lose my reports before my father got home. Stumbling through school greatly lacking confidence, I felt it was my fault that I was stupid.

(Many years later, when I was already married and had children, I decided to prove to myself and others that I wasn't really so stupid. I started a day course for mature students and surprised myself by getting five O levels! I believe this showed that my inability to learn as a child wasn't because I was "retarded", but because I became what I was repeatedly told – "stupid". How important it is to praise and encourage a child, something my father said was bad for a child!)

I used to freeze in fear each night when my father came home from work. My three brothers and I would often get a whack on the head and we wouldn't know what for. My father would ask, "What have you done wrong?" If we couldn't think of anything, he would get really angry, so we made things up. There was a cane that was frequently used. This, though, wasn't nearly as bad as the psychological punishment, which left deeper scars.

One day when I was five or six, my father was late from work. My eyes lit up with hope as I blurted out to my mother, "Oh Mummy! Perhaps he's got run over!" I'll never forget her face as she said, "Rosemary! Don't ever say a thing like that again!" I thought she'd be pleased if he wasn't around anymore because he was cruel to her too.

Through no fault of mine (I was too frightened to be naughty), I was often sent to my bedroom without dinner. There I would talk to God, hoping He cared. At school I'd met Christians and I wanted to become one, but was too shy to ask them how. I remember often praying, "Please God, make me a Christian." Years later, He answered that prayer!

When I was thirty-two and married, my mother died of cancer. This sent me spiralling into depression. She was a wonderful person and I wouldn't have survived without her. I never got the chance to talk to her about life after death. I had struggled with this as I didn't really know where she stood with God although she did attend a church. It was years later I heard in my heart, "Your mother is with Me, Rosemary!" I knew this was God speaking and after that, I never doubted that I'd see my mother again.

My father remarried fairly quickly. Up to this point I never thought of praying for him to become a Christian perhaps because, subconsciously, I thought that if he was in heaven, it wouldn't be heaven for me! One night I had a dream. I was entering heaven and there sitting on a stone was my mother. She jumped up in delight and said, "Rosemary!" Then she looked over my shoulder and asked, "Where's your father?" "Oh, don't worry! He's not coming!" I answered. She looked at me with reproach saying, "Rosemary!" I realised then that I had chosen to condemn my father by not speaking to him about Jesus and by not praying for him. Because the dead can't go back to earth, I knew it was too late for me to tell him. I was filled with an awful despair! The dream was so real that when I woke up, I thought that God had made an exception and sent me back to earth to talk to my father. God then did an operation on my heart. For the first time, I felt a real love for my father instead of fear. More than anything, I wanted him to be with us in heaven!

I stumbled downstairs to write to him about my dream and my desire for him to be in heaven with us more than anything. I added that I was sending him a Bible. The tears were pouring down my face when my husband, Christopher, came in and asked, "Whatever's the matter?" Between sobs I said that my mother had done everything to deserve my love. My father had done nothing, but I loved him as much as I had loved my mother. It was like a miracle!

My father's reply to my letter tore me to shreds: "You've obviously eaten cheese at night and had a stupid dream. I don't want to ever hear about your sadistic religion again!" But God had changed my heart and I started praying for him, and so did my husband and children. My father was sixty-three at the time and for the next twenty-five years I tried to talk to him, but he went wild each time. I didn't know how I was going to reach him and wondered if someone else would.

When he was eighty-eight, I got a phone call from my stepmother to say he'd had a stroke and was unconscious. I went over the next day to Harrogate where they were living. To my surprise, he was sitting up in bed when I arrived. He tried to speak, but there were no words. He'd been struck dumb! I felt God say, "There you are. Now you can tell him!"

I sat down beside him, held his hand and the Holy Spirit began to give me the words to say: "Father, I want you to listen very carefully. You and I know it won't be long before you'll be standing before the gates of heaven. God will be there and He'll say one of two things, either, 'Denis! How lovely to see you! Come on in!', or, 'Denis? I don't know you!'[13] And the gates will close and you'll be left outside."

A tear started to trickle down his face. I then went on to remind him that he'd done things which I knew he wasn't proud of. More tears. I explained how Jesus died to take the punishment that he deserved[14]. I talked about the white robe of righteousness[15] we put on when we ask to be forgiven and for Jesus to come into our lives. Then when we stand before God, He will welcome us in because we acknowledge the price that Jesus paid so that we could be forgiven of our wrongdoing[16]. I told him what he needed to do – to tell Jesus that he was sorry[17] and to ask Him to come and live in his life[18]. I said, "I can't do this for you; only you can[19]. I'm going now, but Jesus isn't. He's here with you and I'm going to pray for you before I go." I asked God to take the darkness away and enable my father to give his heart to Jesus. Then I left, amazed at the way God had struck him dumb so I could talk to him.

The following day my stepsister, who lived in Harrogate, phoned me: "Whatever have you been saying to your father? He's got his speech back and he's going round the hospital ward saying, 'Listen! I've got a place in heaven!'" I was thrilled to hear this! The next day he had a massive stroke and died.

I know the gates of heaven were open wide for my father and that God greeted him with, "Denis! How wonderful to see you! Come on in!" Talk about the eleventh hour! Isn't God amazing?

- Rosemary (Lancaster, England)
August 2011

---

[13] Luke 13v27 (NIV): *"But He will reply, 'I don't know you or where you come from. Away from Me, all you evildoers!'..."*

[14] Romans 4v25 (NLT): *He was handed over to die because of our sins, and He was raised to life to make us right with God.*

[15] Isaiah 61v10 (NIV): *For He has clothed me with garments of salvation and arrayed me in a robe of His righteousness...*

[16] Hebrews 8v12 (NIV): *For I will forgive their wickedness and will remember their sins no more.*

[17] Luke 18v13b (NIV): *"God, have mercy on me, a sinner."*

[18] Revelation 3v20 (NIV): *"Here I [Jesus] am! I stand at the door and knock. If anyone hears My voice and opens the door, I will come in and eat with him, and he with Me."* Fellowship meals in the Bible were a celebration of man's union with God.

[19] John 3v16 (NIV): *For God so loved the world that He gave His one and only Son, that <u>whoever</u> believes in Him shall not perish but have eternal life.* Everyone who has a cognitive understanding of sin must decide for or against Jesus. There is no neutral ground.

Dear Father in heaven, I confess that I belong to Jesus who redeemed me from the devil by His precious blood. I confess that I am Your child, a citizen of heaven and a stranger and pilgrim on earth. By the power of the Holy Spirit who lives in me, help me to set my mind on things above and not on earthly things[20]. Help me to hold on loosely to material possessions and worldly honour. Help me to always remember who I really am and to live each day for You as I walk the narrow road. Thank You that by Your grace I will someday reach heaven and see Your glorious face. Someday my pilgrimage will be over and I will be home with You. Thank You, Jesus!

---

[20] Colossians 3v2 (NIV): *Set your minds on things above, not on earthly things.*

Week 38: Danger – Roadside Ditches!

And remember that the heavenly Father to whom you pray has no favourites.
He will judge or reward you according to what you do. So you must live
in reverent fear of Him during your time as "foreigners in the land."
(1 Peter 1v17, NLT)

The road on which Christians journey is not only narrow, it is also flanked by ditches on either side. One ditch is called *libertinism,* which is the belief that since God loves us unconditionally and since Jesus died to set us free[1], God requires nothing of us and Christianity is all about our love relationship with Him, not about rules or codes of conduct. This ditch is also called *antinomianism (anti* = against, *nomia* = law) or *lawlessness.* An extreme form of libertinism was practised by a heretical group within the early Church called the Nicolaitans[2], who taught that freedom in Christ gave Christians the licence to compromise with the pagan society. They believed that an ungodly lifestyle, sexual immorality and idolatry could be practised without affecting one's standing in Christ. Their understanding of the liberty we have in Jesus, however, was fallacious because, according to the Greek lexicon of the New Testament, the original Greek word for liberty in 2 Corinthians 3v17 (1st footnote below) is *eleutheria,* "the liberty to live as we should, not as we please".

Are you living as you should, or as a Nicolaitan? You may not believe in the Nicolaitan doctrine, but you are already in the ditch of libertinism if you think that you can continue to live in sin because God understands, loves you unconditionally and forgives you anyway. You are being presumptuous of God's love and mercy![3] If you do not get out of this ditch but persist in living contrary to God's word while professing the name of Jesus and placing a claim upon His mercy and grace, you risk falling deeper into this ditch and ultimately turning away from God. Danger!

Legalism is the ditch on the other side of the road. In contrast, it emphasises rules above our love relationship with God. In religious terms, legalism focuses on the letter or text of God's law to the exclusion of the intent or spirit of the law, concentrating on strict adherence and ignoring compassion and even common sense. In its extreme form, legalism believes that salvation can be earned through good works. If this is

---

[1] 2 Corinthians 3v17 (NKJV): *Now the Lord is the Spirit; and where the Spirit of the Lord is, there is <u>liberty</u>.*
[2] In Revelation 2v6 (NIV), Jesus says: *You hate the practices of the Nicolaitans which I also hate.*
[3] Psalm 19v13 (ESV): *Keep back Your servant also from presumptuous sins; let them not have dominion over me!*

right, then there is no need for God's grace, salvation is not a gift but a payment for work done, and a person can boast about having earned it. The Bible clearly teaches us that this is not so![4]

You may not believe in legalism and may know that God gave the Ten Commandments not to save man through it, but to inform man about the nature and character of God, to define and identify sin[5], as well as to reveal to us that we are all guilty before God and can never be righteous by our own efforts[6]. You may accept that we cannot be saved by observing God's law, but only by God's grace through faith in Jesus. However, you are already in this ditch if you unwittingly use God's law as a system of merit by basing your own or someone else's standing in God on how well you think a person is living the Christian life and obeying God. Like a judgmental Pharisee[7], you criticise other Christians for being "less spiritual". You may end up imposing your opinions on others. If you do not get out of this ditch, you risk falling deeper into it and into arrogance and rebelliousness – and be opposed by God Himself![8]

To protect us from falling into the roadside ditches, there are 'restraining fences' on both sides of the narrow road to eternity. The restraining fence that protects us from legalism is called "The Love of God". Knowing intimately the love of God helps us to see that God cannot love us less when we have failed to measure up, nor can He ever love us more when we have done well. He already loves all His children "to the max"

---

[4] Ephesians 2v8-9 (NIV): *For it is by grace you have been saved, through faith – and this not from yourselves, it is the gift of God – not by works, so that no one can boast.* Even the Old Testament never taught that salvation could be achieved by keeping God's laws. The animal sacrifice the Jew had to present to the priest every time a commandment was broken emphasised the atoning aspect of the sacrifice and pointed to the atoning sacrifice God Himself would give in the person of Jesus, the Lamb of God.

[5] Anything man does that is contrary to the nature or the character of God is sin: *Sin is the transgression of the law* (1John 3v4, KJV). Sin is also failing to do what we ought to do: *It is sin to know what you ought to do and then not do it* (James 4v17, NLT).

[6] Romans 3v19-20 (NLT): ... *its* [God's law] *purpose is to keep people from having excuses, and to show that the entire world is guilty before God. For no one can ever be made right with God by doing what the law commands. The law simply shows us how sinful we are.* Also James 2v10 (NLT): *For the person who keeps all of the laws except one is as guilty as a person who has broken all of God's laws.* God's passing grade is 100%! We all fall short of this, even those who judge others, so we all fail. This is why we need salvation through Jesus, the God-Man who took the test for us and passed it!

[7] The *Pharisees* ("the separated ones"), also known as *Chasidim* ("loyal to God"), were members of a Jewish religious sect noted for their strict observance of Jewish rites and ceremonies. Those who were the most bitter opponents of Jesus were preoccupied with the minute details and not the weightier matters of the law.

[8] James 4v6b (ESV): *God opposes the proud, but gives grace to the humble.*

even though we do not deserve it! Knowing God's love intimately also helps us to unconditionally love others and to live in humility, thereby protecting us from being self-righteous, sanctimonious and judgmental like the Pharisees who resisted Jesus.

The restraining fence that protects us from libertinism is called "The Wrath of God". It reminds us to keep our reverential fear of the Lord. Proverbs 1v7 (ESV) declares, "The fear of the Lord is the beginning of knowledge". The word in the original Hebrew text for knowledge here is *da'ath* whose root word is *yada*. Remember that *yada* means 'to know intimately' (Week 5). The holy fear of God leads us pilgrims to greater intimacy with Him. It keeps us from sinning against Him[9] and presuming on His love and grace.

These 'restraining fences' are reminders of the mercy and justice of God, His kindness and severity[10], and that Jesus is Saviour as well as Judge, the Lamb and the Lion. Aim to understand these fences better for they will protect you from deceptions and strong delusions. They are both aspects of God's character, like the two sides of a coin. When you emphasise one at the expense of the other, you are in a ditch and misrepresenting God. Get out of the ditch! Do not be obstinate but run back to Jesus! Obstinacy may lead you to deliberately and wilfully renounce Him, to fall into a state of unbelief and become an apostate[11].

Here is a story of one who fell into both ditches, but mainly into libertinism because of the lack of the fear of the Lord. May this story warn us to "walk circumspectly"[12] along the narrow road and move us to stay close to God.

Blood in the Wardrobe

My younger sister, Rosalie (my very first 'convert'), married Andy[13], a man my family hardly knew. They got married without our knowledge and at a time when my family

---

[9] Proverbs 8v13 (NIV): *To fear the Lord is to hate evil.* Also Proverbs 16v6 (NIV): *Through the fear of the Lord evil is avoided.*

[10] Romans 11v22a (NLT): *Notice how God is both kind and severe. He is severe toward those who disobeyed, but kind to you if you continue to trust in His kindness.*

[11] Hebrews 6v4-6 (NLT): *For it is impossible to bring back to repentance those who were once enlightened – those who have experienced the good things of heaven and shared in the Holy Spirit, who have tasted the goodness of the word of God and the power of the age to come – and who then turn away from God.* Salvation is not just a state; it is a Person because Jesus is Salvation! (*Yeshua*, Jesus in Hebrew, means 'Yahweh, the I Am, is salvation'.) If a person who claims to be a Christian renounces Jesus, he renounces salvation and has become an apostate. Most likely, his faith was never genuine.

[12] Ephesians 5v15 (NKJV): *See then that you walk circumspectly, not as fools but as wise.*

[13] To protect the identities of the people in this story, fictitious names were used.

were still enjoying the benefits of wealth obtained from the sale of our mother's land which she had inherited in a beautiful and popular island. Sometime after the marriage, Rosalie persuaded Andy to quit his job (for he was always travelling) since they were receiving an income from Rosalie's share of the money which had been invested in a company, the same one the rest of the family heavily invested in. Rosalie also encouraged Andy to train to become a pastor in response to prophetic words regarding Andy's call to the ministry.

Then disaster struck. After several months, it was discovered that the company we invested in was nothing but a Ponzi scheme. (This was years before the largest financial fraud in US history, the Ponzi scheme of NASDAQ's former non-executive chairman, Bernard Madoff, was exposed.) The CEO went to jail, but my family couldn't recover the money. We took it as a lesson to be learned. After all, we hadn't honoured God by asking Him what He wanted us to do with the money that He gave us[14]. Rosalie and Andy's standard of living was particularly affected because both didn't have jobs and were depending on the investment's income.

Sometime later, another tragedy struck. Rosalie lost her baby in her eighth month of pregnancy. The entanglement of the umbilical cord around the neck (cutting the baby's blood supply) led to stillbirth. It was Rosalie's first and last pregnancy. Her self-esteem plummeted because of her inability to bear children. The trauma probably also led Rosalie to think that Andy was the only person she had left to live for. Rosalie and Andy then fell out with their pastor, left their church and started a church in their area. Upon my request, they also looked after my condominium flat (which my parents had given me) and its rental income and the tithe.

In the summer of 2010, I visited my native land and stayed with Rosalie and Andy. It had been six years since I had last seen them. I went to their church and soon observed that Rosalie practically ran the church. She organised meals after the service for the members, many of whom were poor. She would buy Christmas presents and school materials for the children of the congregation. (In that country, schools don't provide school supplies.) She organised the worship songs and music group practices. The couple would regularly meet with the teens of the church to exhort them to practise sexual purity. They were reprimanded for missing church and for going out with members of the opposite sex, especially if they belonged to another congregation. I felt that this was bordering on legalism.

It was during my stay in Rosalie and Andy's house that I had a dream one night. In the dream I was in one of the bedrooms. I noticed a wardrobe with some blood stains

---

[14] Proverbs 3v9 (NLT): *Honour the Lord with your wealth and with the best part of everything you produce* [or earn].

on its door. I opened the wardrobe and found that it was empty, except for the paper lining the bottom of the wardrobe. It was soaked in fresh blood, as if the wardrobe had been bleeding!

In the morning I told Andy and Rosalie about the dream. (The Lord gives me prophetic dreams and I felt this one was definitely from Him.) Andy said it could be about the land on which the houses in their estate were built; it used to be a cemetery. He implied that it was an issue that had already been dealt with through prayer. However, I was not convinced because the blood was fresh, though I had no clue what the dream meant. The interpretation came to me on my return to England.

The wardrobe stood for something hidden: a sin that was bleeding life[15] out of a person. The opening of the wardrobe signified that the secret sin was about to be exposed. The paper symbolised a contract made, something that got stained with guilt. In the dream I was in Rosalie and Andy's house, so I concluded that the 'paper' had something to do with them, a secret they were keeping. It was sometime later when the secret was finally uncovered.

My family discovered that Andy was already married when he met Rosalie. His first marriage was a farce since it had been arranged only to help Andy obtain a visa for the USA, but he never went there. Rosalie told us they got married, but she never consulted my father (who was a retired lawyer) about the legal consequences. The blood-stained paper would pertain to Andy and Rosalie's 'marriage contract', as well as to other contracts they entered into as a couple, such as the moral contract with their congregation and with the Christian leaders who oversaw them. Andy broke these contracts by having an extra-marital affair which led to a pregnancy and subsequent miscarriage or abortion (we don't know which one). Rosalie did not tell the Christian leaders who oversaw them about this and about their questionable marriage. They also entered into contracts with my mother and with me to look after our finances. These became blood-stained because they used the money without our knowledge or approval to fund a lifestyle they could not afford.

The empty wardrobe also symbolised an empty heart. I believe Andy loved God, but his heart had been emptied of intimacy with Him. His spiritual sensitivity to God bled away because he didn't fear God enough to turn away from his sins. No wonder this led to behaviour unexpected of a pastor. Andy and Rosalie were hiding something, but I also believe that they wanted to be free of the burden of guilt.

---

[15] Blood is symbolic of life.

The blood on the bottom or the 'floor' of the wardrobe also symbolised the blood of Christ. What do you do to a floor? You tread on it! Preaching the truth while living a lie is like treading or trampling on the precious blood of Jesus.

I lost a lot of money, but I was partly to blame because I was careless with God's blessing by not keeping track of my income and how it was being managed. Although I had forgiven them, it was difficult for me to have magnanimous thoughts because of the uncovering of more incidents involving Andy and money. This reminds me of what the Bible says: "The love of money is the root of all kinds of evil. And some people, craving money, have wandered from the true faith and pierced themselves with many sorrows" (1 Timothy 6v10, NLT).

Andy was removed by his bishop from his post as pastor. The couple moved away and Rosalie now works to support the family. Andy justified his unfaithfulness by blaming Rosalie's inability to have children. He wanted to leave her for his mistress, but my sister insists on staying with him for fear that he might become homeless and kill himself. Some pastors, including their former bishop, have warned Rosalie that Andy is destroying her, but she rejects their advice. She believes God sent her to "save" Andy and his siblings, and therefore feels she has to stay with him. She also cites her "covenant" with Andy which she believes she has to keep.

My sister feared losing Andy and so had allowed herself to be manipulated by him. As for Andy, perhaps the fact that he had gotten away with the lie about their marriage for such a long time caused him to forget about the holy fear of the Lord, and one bad thing just led to another.

God disciplines those whom He loves[16]. It was because of His love that He waited for repentance, but when it didn't come, His love necessitated the exposure of what was hidden[17]. The Bible tells us, "Do not be deceived: God cannot be mocked. A man reaps what he sows" (Galatians 6v7, NIV).

God is good and merciful and therefore, I prayed for and believed that there would be a happy ending to this story. Recently, Rosalie and Andy were reconciled to me and the rest of the family. They are now helping an elderly pastor in his difficult

---

[16] Hebrews 12v6 (NLT): *For the Lord disciplines those He loves, and He punishes each one He accepts as His child.*

[17] Romans 2v4 (NLT): *Don't you see how wonderfully kind, tolerant, and patient God is with you? Does this mean nothing to you? Can't you see that His kindness is intended to turn you from your sin?*

ministry to barely-reached people groups. Their love for God and for each other had been strengthened by the experience. Indeed, God is sooooo good!

- Corazon (Manchester, England)
September 2011 (updated August 2013)

Almighty and merciful God, thank You for Your promise that if I confess my sins, You will forgive me and cleanse me[18]. Protect me from deliberately sinning against You, from acting unlovingly like a legalistic Pharisee towards others, and from becoming a Nicolaitan by forgetting the holy fear of God. Help me to abhor sin the way You do! Grant me a greater revelation of Your holy love and of Your holy wrath that I may keep to the narrow road and not fall into the ditches. Grant me Your grace to abide in You. In Jesus' name I ask, amen.

---

[18] 1 John 1v9 (ESV): *If we confess our sins, He is faithful and just to forgive us our sins and to cleanse us from all unrighteousness.* God is faithful in that He will forgive us as He says, and just in that He accepts that Jesus already paid for our sins with His blood.

Week 39: The Road Called Amazing Grace

For the grace of God has appeared, bringing salvation for all people, training us to renounce ungodliness and worldly passions, and to live self-controlled, upright, and godly lives in the present age, waiting for our blessed hope, the appearing of the glory of our great God and Saviour Jesus Christ.
(Titus 2v11-13, ESV)

People, even Christians, have a natural tendency towards either legalism or libertinism (Week 38). Several parts of the New Testament were written to clarify the purpose of the Mosaic Law[1] and to address the issue of legalism such as Acts 15, the book of Galatians and Romans 7. Parts of the New Testament were also written against libertinism and the misuse of our freedom in Christ, such as Galatians 5, Romans 6 and 8, and the verses in Titus chapter 2 above. These passages also help us to gain a proper understanding and a greater appreciation of God's grace.

What is the 'grace of God'? In the Old Testament, these two Hebrew words are often translated into English as 'grace': *hen* and *chesed* (Week 31). *Hen* is goodwill, loving-kindness and undeserved favour. *Chesed* is favour, mercy, loving-kindness, graciousness, steadfast love, faithfulness, etc. All these words can be used to define the grace of God. In the New Testament, however, God's grace (Greek *charis*) means a lot more than these words put together because *charis* points to Jesus, the ultimate manifestation of God's grace. The New Testament tells us that grace came through and found its realisation in Jesus Christ[2]. It tells us that we are saved by the grace of Jesus[3], and that we are strengthened by His grace[4].

This strengthening or empowering aspect of God's *charis* is strongly implied by Jesus' words to Paul: "My grace is sufficient for you, for My power is made perfect

---

[1] The Mosaic Law comprises of all the laws given by God to the Israelites through Moses. It includes the Ten Commandments or Moral Law which gave guidance as to what is right and wrong (Exodus 20v1-17). It also includes the Social Law which governed the social, political and economic life of Israel (Exodus 21v1-23v13). Lastly, the Mosaic Law also includes the Ceremonial Law which guided Israel in her worship and fellowship with God, including the priesthood and the Tabernacle/Temple sacrifices (Exodus 25-31, Leviticus).

[2] John 1v17 (NIV): *For the law was given through Moses; grace and truth came through Jesus Christ.*

[3] In Titus 2 above and other scriptures like Acts 15v11 (NIV): *No! We believe it is through the grace of our Lord Jesus that we are saved, just as they are.*

[4] 2 Timothy 2v1 (NIV): *You then, my son, be strong in the grace that is in Christ Jesus.*

in weakness" (2 Corinthians 12v9, NIV). When we recognise that we are weak and cannot do anything by our own strength, we can tap into this grace that <u>empowers us</u>.

The verse in Titus 2 tells us that *charis* also <u>trains us</u>[5] to renounce ungodliness, resist temptations and live godly lives. The empowering and training side of *charis* is reflected in Hebrews 12v28 (NKJV): "Therefore, since we are receiving a kingdom which cannot be shaken, let us *have* grace (*charis*), by which we may serve God acceptably with reverence and godly fear". The word in the original Greek text for 'have' here is *ekho* which means 'to lay or take hold of' and 'to cling or hold fast to'. God exhorts us to *ekho* His *charis*! If we think that it is okay for us to fall into the ditches by the narrow road and wallow in the mud there because God's grace forgives us and wipes us clean, we are making a mockery of God's grace and deceiving ourselves. God's grace trains and empowers us not to fall, and if we take hold of and hold fast to it, we will not fall!

We have limited God's grace to its steadfast love, favour and forgiveness aspects and this is why we have misunderstood the saying: "We are not under law but under grace"[6]. Child of God, we have been set free from the Mosaic Law so that we can be under a higher law which calls us to a higher standard of morality than that demanded by the Mosaic Law[7]. We have been called to be under the Law of the Spirit which is the Law of Grace[8], and this law tells us that we can stay on the narrow road and live the Christian life of godliness, holiness, obedience and service to God because God's *charis* does not only train us, it also empowers us to be overcomers[9]!

God's *charis* trains and empowers us to live out our new identity in Jesus. It trains and empowers us to be the humble, obedient, wise, generous, loving, faithful, persevering, joyful and gracious Christ-like individuals that God envisioned us to be. It empowers us to move in Christ's anointing to "heal the sick, raise the dead and cast out demons"[10].

---

[5] Some versions of the Bible use the verb 'teach' in place of 'train'. The original Greek word is *paideuo*, which means to teach and also to train.

[6] Romans 6v14 (NIV): *For sin shall no longer be your master, because you are not under the law, but under grace.*

[7] Jesus speaks about this higher standard in Matthew 5, e.g., v27-28 (NLT): *"You have heard the commandment that says, 'You must not commit adultery.' But I say, anyone who even looks at a woman with lust has already committed adultery with her in his heart.*

[8] Romans 8v2 (ESV): *For the law of the Spirit of life has set you free in Christ Jesus from the law of sin and death.*

[9] Romans 12v21 (ESV): *Do not be overcome by evil, but overcome evil with good.*

[10] Matthew 10v8 (NIV): *Heal those who are ill, raise the dead, cleanse those who have leprosy, drive out demons. Freely you have received; freely give.*

Therefore, God's grace empowers us to transcend the labels that mar our true identities in Christ, labels we wear either because of our background or our past failures. Consider Matthew, the writer of the first Gospel that appears in the Bible. He was a Jew who collected taxes from his own people for the hated Romans and was therefore regarded by the Jews as an outcast and a reject. He must have burst into worship as he wrote the first chapter of his Gospel which contained the genealogy of Jesus, having been reminded that some of Jesus' ancestors were people who had bad reputations like himself: Judah was the mastermind behind the idea to sell his brother Joseph into slavery; Rahab was a Canaanite who was known as a prostitute or a harlot; Ruth was another foreigner who came from the child-sacrificing Moabites, a people who descended from Moab, the child of the incestuous union between intoxicated Lot and his daughter; Bathsheba was the wife of Uriah when she first slept with King David; and David was an adulterer and murderer. Jesus came from people who, like Matthew, needed God's grace, people who would have been rejected and disqualified by God to be the Messiah's ancestors on the basis of their background or failures. God's grace came to them and it still comes in the person of the Spirit of Grace to those who are messed-up and rejected, to train and to empower them to be the people they are meant to be in Christ Jesus. God's grace is truly amazing!

Below is a story from a lady in the Philippines who encountered the grace of God and discovered that in spite of her background and failures, she is.....

Not a Reject

I grew up in Quezon City in the Philippines. I helped my parents look after three younger siblings, a boy and two girls, since I was the eldest child in the family, as I was led to believe. When I found out that I was not the real child of my parents, I rebelled against them although they were kind to me. I suppose my anger against my biological parents for giving me up for adoption translated into anger and resentment against my adopted parents, especially when they split up. I took their separation as a sign that they didn't really love me. Deeply hurt by the rejection I felt from both my real and adopted parents, I searched for love and acceptance elsewhere. I looked for unconditional love, but I ended up with the wrong kind of people who only accepted those who conformed to what the others in the group were doing[11]. I thought I was having the time of my life!

I attended a good college but I often skipped classes to hang out with my friends. I joined a sorority group and got into the habit of smoking and drinking, as well as taking cough syrups with narcotics to get high. I collected boyfriends and even had relationships with lesbians. I knew I was destroying my life and future, but I

---

[11] 1 Corinthians 15v33 (NIV): *Do not be misled: Bad company corrupts good character.*

didn't really care because I felt unwanted and useless[12]. My feeling of rejection led to self-rejection.

Sometime later, my family and I moved to another part of the city. One day I heard music and singing coming from our neighbours' house and something stirred inside me. Perhaps this was when God started to move in my life. One day, the neighbours who lived in the "noisy house", a couple with two children, knocked on our door and invited me to join the people gathered in their house. I found out that they were "born-again Christians". I joined their fellowship and received Christ into my life in 1987. The following year, they helped my boyfriend and me to get married. My new husband and I had to find somewhere to live and we moved to the town of Parañaque, away from the fellowship. Three children came one after the other, but I felt there was something lacking in my life for I had no joy and peace. This was not surprising because I didn't have fellowship with other Christians[13] and I neglected fellowship with God and His word.

Since I was the breadwinner of my family at this time, I thought I deserved some kind of outlet. I started smoking and drinking again and got into another relationship with a lesbian who introduced me to 'shabu', an amphetamine derivative. My life spiralled downwards again. Looking back, I believe that at this time I didn't really understand God's unconditional love. I knew the things I was doing were wrong, but instead of running to Him, I ran farther away from Him, thinking that He had the right to reject me.

One day a Christian friend invited me to her church. By this time I was sick and tired of the way my life had been going so I accepted her invitation and began to attend church again. Then I joined the music group as a back-up singer and I found myself enjoying this. I began to draw nearer to God.

Haunted by the mess of my past, I prayed the prayer of salvation and received Jesus as my Saviour and Lord several times because I did not have the assurance that I had been truly saved. This was because I could not count myself worthy of salvation. Gradually, however, I realised that God really loves and accepts me and that He considers me worthy to receive salvation simply because He truly loves me! I began to change my perception of myself and to love myself. I used to think of myself as inconsequential and unimportant. After all, I believed I was a reject. Now I know I am important to God and that He values me and takes pleasure in me!

---

[12] It appears that a child can feel unwanted and unloved even while in the womb.

[13] Hebrews 10v24 (NLT): *And let us not neglect our meeting together, as some people do, but encourage one another, especially now that the day of His* [Jesus'] *return is drawing near.*

The Lord also helped me to forgive my parents. He set me free from the feeling of rejection and self-rejection and from my vices and bad habits. I can say God really changed me from the inside out!

Today, my whole family worships with me in church, including my husband. Our eldest child is now working and the other two children are still in school. Although both my husband and I are jobless at this time, we know the Lord owns all the wealth in the world and will continue to supply all our needs as He had done in the past. He never leaves and forsakes His children! I lead worship in church as a singer and sometimes I also share the word of God in front of the congregation. The Lord is using me mightily for His glory, something I never dreamt would happen. Praise God for His amazing grace!

- Dolly Antonio (Montalban, Rizal, Philippines)
September 2011

Thank You Father God for Your amazing grace! Please help the reader "not to receive it in vain"[14], but to embrace the training and the empowering by Your Holy Spirit to live the Christian life of obedience and holiness. Empower him/her to be an overcomer and to serve You with faithfulness and passion. For the reader who has low self-esteem and feels rejected and disqualified because of the past, please pour out Your grace so that this person may know Your unconditional love and Your power to transform. Use him/her mightily to move in the anointing of our Lord Jesus to proclaim the Good News, to heal the sick, to raise the dead and to cast out demons according to Your will. In Jesus' name, amen!

If you have received Jesus as your Saviour and Lord, then you now have a new identity because of God's amazing grace. Do you know who you are in Christ Jesus? Check out Appendix 2 for some things the Bible says about this new identity.

---

[14] 2 Corinthians 6v1 (NKJV): *We then, as workers together with Him also plead with you not to receive the grace of God in vain.*

Week 40: Dead Man Walking along the Narrow Road

I am crucified with Christ: nevertheless I live; yet not I, but Christ liveth in me: and the life which I now live in the flesh I live by the faith of the Son of God, who loved me, and gave Himself for me. (Galatians 2v20, KJV)

Crucifixion (from Latin *cruciare* = to torture and torment) was probably invented by the Persians and introduced by Alexander the Great to the people of Egypt and Carthage. The Romans borrowed the idea from the Carthaginians and perfected it as a form of torture and capital punishment of rebellious slaves, revolutionaries, foreigners and the vilest of criminals. Their version was designed to maximise suffering and pain during a slow death. It was probably the most cruel and disgraceful form of execution ever conceived by man. It was intended not only as a punishment, but also as a warning to others.

The Persian version was quite simple. The guilty man was either tied to a tree or impaled on a vertical post. The Romans used a true cross consisting of the upright post (stipes) and a horizontal crossbar (*patibulum*). The condemned man usually carried the *patibulum* from the scourging site to the crucifixion site where the stipes were permanently located. There the man would be given a drink, made of wine mixed with myrrh, which would deaden the pain[1].

The man's wrists would be nailed to the *patibulum*. The nails would damage the median nerves of the wrist, causing intense bolts of pain in both arms. After hoisting the man onto the stipes, his feet would then be nailed to the stipes[2]. In his bent and twisted position on the cross, breathing would be shallow and exhalation would be difficult. The condemned man would have to push up on his nailed feet against the foot rest to exhale. This would cause more unbearable pain. The wounds on his scourged back would rub against the rough wooden stipes, adding to the pain and extreme discomfort. Muscle cramps and contractions due to fatigue would further hinder respiration. Each attempt to respire would become more and more agonising and death due to asphyxia would result in three hours to four days, depending on his health and the severity of the scourging. To hasten death, the Roman soldiers would break the legs of the condemned man. This would prevent the man from lifting himself up to exhale and death would come quicker, within minutes. Asphyxia and hypovolemic shock were usually the main causes of death of the crucified, but dehydration, congestive heart failure and others were contributing factors. To make

---

[1] The Gospel accounts tell us Jesus refused this drink.
[2] The Romans preferred nailing to tying with ropes.

sure the person was dead, a Roman guard would pierce the heart through the right side of the chest, inflicting a fatal wound.

In the case of Jesus, the Roman soldiers did not have to break His legs because He was already dead when they examined Him and before a spear was thrust through His chest[3]. He may have died of cardiac rupture (literally, of a broken heart) or cardio-respiratory failure after enduring six hours[4] of intense, excruciating[5] pain on the cross. He was no vile criminal and was aware of the agony of crucifixion, but Jesus gave Himself up to die on a cross to redeem us from the devil and hell and to set us free from the law of sin and death. Given these details, what is your response to all that Jesus suffered for you?

American preacher, pastor and author A.W. Tozer (1897-1963) once said, "Among the plastic saints of our times, *Jesus has to do all the dying,* and all we want to hear is another sermon about Him dying." What did he mean by this? Consider the verse in Galatians 2 above, as well as the following passages, just four of the many relevant ones in the Bible:

1) "He personally carried our sins in His body on the cross so that we can be dead to sin and live for what is right" (1 Peter 2v24, NLT).

2) "We know that our old sinful selves were crucified with Christ so that sin might lose its power in our lives. We are no longer slaves to sin. For when we died with Christ we were set free from the power of sin. And since we died with Christ, we know we will also live with Him. We are sure of this because Christ was raised from the dead, and He will never die again. Death no longer has any power over Him. When He died, He died once to break the power of sin. But now that He lives, He lives for the glory of God. So you also should consider yourselves to be dead to the power of sin and alive to God through Christ Jesus" (Romans 6v6-11, NLT).

3) "But I will never brag about anything except the cross of our Lord Jesus Christ. Because of His cross, the world is dead as far as I am concerned, and I am dead as far as the world is concerned" (Galatians 6v14, CEV).

4) "So, my dear brothers and sisters, this is the point: You died to the power of the law when you died with Christ. And now you are united with the One who was raised

---

[3]   John tells us (John 19v36) that this fulfilled the Old Testament prophecy that none of Messiah's bones would be broken (Psalm 34v20).

[4]   Mark 15 tells us that Jesus was crucified on the "third hour" (9 am) and died on the "ninth hour" (3 pm). The Last Adam died for man whose symbolic number is 6.

[5]   'Excruciating' is from the Latin *excruciatus* = 'out of the cross'.

from the dead. As a result, we can produce a harvest of good deeds for God… Now we can serve God, not in the old way of obeying the letter of the law, but in the new way of living in the Spirit" (Romans 7v4 and 6, NLT).

Are you getting it, child of God? God expects us to live out our new identity in Christ: dead to sin and self and living for Him by the faith that He gave us (Week 8). So let us respond to temptations as a dead man would! Let us hold fast to God's grace that empowers us to walk along the narrow road in this new identity (Week 39 and Appendix 2).

Here is a challenging story of a man who had a 'road to Damascus experience'[6] which turned his life around and led him to finally answer God's call to die to his old selfish nature, to offer his life to Jesus' service and to go where the Lord told him to go, as Paul, the apostle to the Gentiles, did.

Here Am I, Lord!

Growing up as a child, my faith in God was so real! I trusted His word and believed what He said. I was moved by the incredible faith that caused ordinary men to stand victorious for truth against opposition. My heart stirred while reading stories of God's power displayed through the lives of His children who submitted to His will and purpose. As a boy, I even envisioned being in David's shoes and knew with every fibre of my being that I could face any giant that stood against me as long as God was by my side!

Sadly, this gradually faded with time as I began to view God and everything else through the faulty lens of circumstance. What happened around me subtly became more real than who God was and who I was in Him. My faith in God took a gradual shift back to self. With the reins of control back in my hand, my pursuits and desires became more about gratifying my flesh than pleasing God. I became like the ones described in Isaiah 29v13 (NIV), "These people… honour Me with their lips, but their hearts are far from Me…" The way I was living was in essence saying, "I don't need God. I am doing OK on my own". I was good at including God when it suited me. He was in the backseat of the car and when direction was not clear, I would get His input. All the while I went to church, but even that was about me and what I could get, rather than what I could offer to God and His Church. Instead of answering God's call to die to self and live wholly devoted to Him by faith, I was headed down an all too common but dangerous path of independence.

---

[6] Paul was on his way to Damascus when Jesus appeared to him (Acts 9). It was an experience that would forever change his life.

All this changed in a moment when a friend and I embarked on a long-awaited trip from Cyprus to Egypt and Israel. Little did I know what awaited me five hours out in the sea. An unexpected storm, the worst seen in twenty years, reared its ugly head. Even the crew of the ship struggled to stay alive as this massive cruise ship was pummelled by fifty-foot waves. As I was hearing the sound of terror in people's screams and was being tossed like a rag doll amongst other passengers, I was thinking of two things. Firstly, I was not ready to face God! My heart was not in a right place with Him and the face of death made that very clear. As my life flashed before my eyes, what I was seeing did not comfort me. Secondly, I desperately wanted to find a phone to call home just to say a final goodbye to my family.

By some miracle, the ship got turned around and made it back safely to the port in Cyprus. Upon setting my feet on land, I was hit with the blunt revelation that although death would have ushered me into the presence of God (even if by a sliver), I would not hear God say with a smile, "Well done, My good and faithful servant!" This reality hit me so hard that all the noise around me was silenced with the seriousness of this truth. I was fully aware at that moment that my life had been all about me. I was going through the motions of what appeared good and even religious, but I was not doing anything for Christ that carried weight or eternal significance.

My heart literally felt like it was bursting inside of me. Conviction over my grave sin brought me to my knees and set me on a journey of restoring the simple yet profound faith of my childhood. It was that journey to know God more intimately that my true life began! I realised that love for self really does lead to all other sins as we read in 2 Timothy 3v2-5[7]. Living life for myself enslaved me to anxiety, fear and insecurity. Living life for Christ freed me from bondage and set me on a path of purpose where fulfilment is discovered in dying to self. The reality of Matthew 16v24-25[8] rings so true. It is a dead end track when we pursue life on our terms. Only by giving up our life to Christ do we gain real life – abundant and eternal!

As my relationship with God took on more depth, an amazing thing happened. His burden for others and His vision for the nations took root as well. I began to feel His heartbeat for the lost. I cared less about my standard of living and more about others living. On my first mission trip to the Philippines, I saw the people through God's eyes.

---

[7] 2 Timothy 3v2-5 (NIV): *People will be lovers of themselves, lovers of money, boastful, proud, abusive, disobedient to their parents, ungrateful, unholy, without love, unforgiving, slanderous, without self-control, brutal, not lovers of the good, treacherous, rash, conceited, lovers of pleasure rather than lovers of God – having a form of godliness but denying its power.*

[8] Matthew 16v24-25 (NLT): *Then Jesus said to His disciples, "If any of you wants to be My follower, you must turn from your selfish ways, take up your cross, and follow Me. If you try to hang on to your life, you will lose it. But if you give up your life for My sake, you will save it."*

It came to the point where all I wanted was God and I never felt more alive! Letting go of my grasp on the 'things' of the world released me to fall into the loving and secure arms of my heavenly Father. Each day I found myself anticipating more of God and making myself available to Him in ways that forced me to trust in Him and His goodness. It was these daily steps that prepared me for living a life 'by faith', the kind lived out by men and women of the Bible. My future was in good hands and the sky was the limit!

One day I heard the same question Isaiah heard, "Whom shall I send. And who will go for us?" (Isaiah 6v8, NIV). Isaiah's response stirred in my spirit: "Here am I, Lord. Send me." Wow! As God revealed to me His burden for the world and His desperate search and call for His children to capture His heart, I humbly came and responded as Isaiah did, saying "Lord, here I am. Send me!" After a few years of Bible college and mission trips back and forth to the Philippines, I accepted God's call to long term missions.

For years I was on the front lines as a single man, then God blessed me with a great wife who shared my heart for the lost and the thrill of adventure. Without even stepping foot in the Philippines before, she moved with me to Siargao, a small island in the south that shared nothing in common with life in Canada. With very little savings to work with and no clear set of plans revealed by the Lord, we moved into a ten-foot square nipa hut[9]. Many people in Canada struggled with our decision to step out in faith without 'all our ducks in a row'. Even family repeatedly asked us what plan B was. My firm response, "The same as plan A – trust God"! This was a difficult concept for people to wrap their minds around. Each step of faith was met with God's provision in one way or another.

The call to start the ministry of Hope for the Island (HOPE) in Siargao was one that required seeking God at every turn. Our faith continued to strengthen as God confirmed we were right where He wanted us to be. We had an incredible peace that we were in God's will despite the fact that our first year was faced with challenges that should have had us packing for home. Without going into the graphic details, we faced for the first time true hunger, tropical diseases, spiritual attacks, physical threat, and even physical paralysis. All the while we knew God was by our side and we had joy! Each trial was an opportunity to grow and respond in faith. God had, in His own way, allowed all of these things to happen to prepare us for starting the ministry of HOPE. We were more aware of the needs around us because we lived and breathed them. Although we were foreigners, we were able to identify with the islanders. God was breaking us in a good way – breaking away the things in our lives that needed to

---

[9] The nipa hut is a native house built by the indigenous people of the Philippines before the Spaniards arrived, but is still built today in rural areas. It is constructed of bamboo poles tied together. The roof of the house is made of the leaves of the nipa tree, a type of palm tree.

fall off so that God could have His way in and through us. I can honestly say it was the worst year of our lives, but at the same time, the best year!

As a young couple, God led us to start HOPE by faith. We felt like David with only a few small stones and a sling facing so many things that were well beyond us. But just like David, we pressed forward in faith against all odds because God had our backs. Even though HOPE had small beginnings, it was birthed with big faith! With a vision to love God, love one another and extend His love to the world around us, HOPE has grown beyond what we could have envisioned. Countless lives have been impacted by the hope and love of Christ!

It is amazing what God can do when we give Him first place in our lives. The exploits of faith that we read in the Word and through the lives of men and women who went before us will not just be read like fiction. It will be our story as well!

> - Derek Van Ryckeghem (Winnipeg, Canada)
> www.hopefortheisland.org
> Sent from Siargao Island,
> Surigao del Norte, Philippines
> April 2011

Paul in his letter to the Colossians chapter 3 verses 5 to 8 (ESV) admonishes us, "Put to death therefore what is earthly in you: sexual immorality, impurity, passion, evil desire, and covetousness, which is idolatry. On account of these the wrath of God is coming. In these you too once walked, when you were living in them. But now you must put them all away: anger, wrath, malice, slander, and obscene talk from your mouth."

Dear heavenly Father, thank You again for Jesus, Your "gift too wonderful for words"[10]! Thank You, Jesus, once more for not refusing the pain and the scorn of the cross so that I could have forgiveness for my sins and an amazing future and eternity. Grant me Your grace to die to self. Empower me by Your Holy Spirit to daily choose to die to selfishness, die to covetousness, die to the desire to impress, die to the fear of man, die to ungodly fear, die to worry, die to insecurity and inferiority, die to sexual sins and evil desires, die to judgmentalism[11], die to libertinism and legalism, and die to all that is contrary to Your holy nature. Help me to count myself as crucified with You and grant me the power to live by Your faith as I walk daily on the narrow road on my way to glory. These I pray in Your precious name, amen.

---

[10] 2 Corinthians 9v15 (NLT): *Thank God for this gift too wonderful for words!*

[11] Judgmentalism is the eagerness to find fault with others while ignoring one's own faults. Matthew 7v1-2 (NIV) says: *Do not judge, or you too will be judged. For in the same way as you judge others, you will be judged, and with the measure you use, it will be measured to you.*

Week 41: Via Dolorosa, the Road of Suffering

If you refuse to take up your cross and follow Me, you are not worthy
of being Mine. If you cling to your life, you will lose it; but if you give
up your life for Me, you will find it. (Matthew 10v38-39, NLT)

The *Via Dolorosa* (Latin for way of grief or suffering) is a winding six hundred-metre stretch of road within the old city of Jerusalem which is believed to be the route Jesus took when carrying His cross to the site of His crucifixion. It starts from the place where Jesus was tried and convicted by Pontius Pilate (Fortress Antonio on the eastern side or the Muslim quarter) and ends in the place of crucifixion, Golgotha or Calvary (now the site of the Church of the Holy Sepulchre), on the western side of the old city (the Christian quarter). The road had been a place of pilgrimage since Constantine legalised Christianity in the fourth century.

For Jesus, *Via Dolorosa* was a walk of intense physical suffering because of the Roman scourging he had received, perhaps the worst and most feared kind of flogging ever administered to a man. It was not a form of execution, but of torture. However, it was so horrific and brutal that it proved fatal to many.

The purpose of Roman scourging was to humiliate and to punish slaves and non-Roman citizens as well as to weaken a man condemned to die by crucifixion so that death would come quicker[1]. The victim would be stripped to the waist and tied to a post. A torturer to his left and another to his right would each lash a *flagellum* at him. The *flagellum* had three or more straps of leather to which were attached metal balls and sharp fragments of bronze and bone. As the strands struck the prisoner, the sharp objects would lacerate the skin, flesh and blood vessels. Whole pieces of skin and flesh could be torn apart, exposing the ribs, spine and even the bowels. The victim would have deep lacerations on his back, stomach, buttocks, chest, legs and arms. Because Jesus was scourged by Roman soldiers and not by Jews, He would have received more than forty lashes[2], but they did not stop with the scourging.

The soldiers mocked Jesus and parodied His Kingship by putting a scarlet robe on Him and placing on His head a crown of thorns (which may have been shaped like a

---

[1] Jesus died on the cross sooner than Pilate expected most probably because of the severity of the scourging He received. Mark 15v44 (NIV) tells us: *Pilate was surprised to hear that He was already dead.*

[2] Deuteronomy 25v2-3 limited to 40 the number of lashes Jews could give a prisoner, but they would do only 39 in case they miscounted. Out of spite for the Jews, the Romans would do more than 40 with their more deadly *flagellum* because they were not limited by Roman law.

cap). Most likely, this was made of the Arabian thorn plant which has spikes of one to one and a half inches long. This crown was violently pushed down Jesus' head[3] and then He was repeatedly struck on the head with a staff, the mock sceptre which they put in His hand. The thorns would have torn the flesh on Jesus' head and damaged the nerves on the scalp resulting in trigeminal neuralgia (a stabbing and electric-shock type of pain in the face), one of the most intense and painful conditions known to man. The soldiers heaped insults and spat at Him. Congealed blood and swelling would have marred His face beyond recognition[4]. Then Jesus carried His cross (the *patibulum* would have weighed between 40 to 55 kg[5]) on the way to Calvary. He would have continued to bleed profusely as He walked. He would have been intensely thirsty because of the loss of blood and body fluids[6]. He was so weak that He fell under the weight of the *patibulum*. Simon of Cyrene was forced to carry it part of the way to Golgotha because the Romans did not want Jesus to die before the actual crucifixion[7].

Jesus, who could have called on angels to fight for Him, gave Himself up not just to be crucified, but also to be brutally scourged because He knew that His wounds and His blood would bring healing to our spirit, soul and body[8].

Knowing the gory details of Jesus' scourging and crucifixion gives us no reason to gloss over the intensity of the suffering He went through voluntarily for our sake. It

---

[3] The Greek word used to describe the action of putting or setting the thorny crown on Jesus' head in John 19v2 and Matthew 27v29 was *epitithemi* which implies a violent action.

[4] The Gospels do not tell us what the beaten Jesus looked like, but Isaiah gave this prophecy 600 years before the Messiah came: *His appearance was so disfigured beyond that of any man and His form marred beyond human likeness...* (Isaiah 52v14, NIV).

[5] Various references give different weights.

[6] Jesus lost more blood during the scourging than the crucifixion. Little blood would be lost during crucifixion since no major blood vessel would be damaged.

[7] There are several Old Testament prophecies regarding the passion of the Messiah and these were fulfilled during the crucifixion of Jesus. It was God's will for His crucifixion to happen because it was the only way for Him to save us.

[8] Isaiah 53v5 (NLT): *But He was pierced for our rebellion, crushed for our sins. He was beaten so we could be whole. He was whipped so we could be healed.* The atoning sacrifice of Jesus would bring healing to believers, first to our spirits through justification, then to our souls through sanctification, and finally to our physical bodies when we receive new imperishable bodies. The last will happen when Jesus comes again (Week 51). Until then, illness and death, which came to all creation as a result of Adam's fall, will continue to be experienced by mankind, including the believers. God is not obligated to heal them all, although He does heal as He pleases. Many believe that as the second coming of Christ approaches and the Holy Spirit is poured out as in Acts 2, the manifestation of spiritual gifts, including the gifts of healing and the gift of the working of miracles, will increase and we will see more healings and miracles.

should give us a greater appreciation of what He has done to save us from the eternal agony of suffering in hell because of our sins. It helps us to fall more in love with Him. The loving response He expects is no less than that we carry our cross and follow Him along the *Via Dolorosa*.

The cross is a symbol of death. When Jesus asked all His disciples to carry the cross and follow Him[9], He was asking us to consider ourselves as dead to self and sin (Week 40), to be totally committed to Him and to share in His suffering[10]. This means that we are willing to be broken by the things which break His heart, and to act in obedience to His call. It means that we commit ourselves to run our God-given races. It means that we engage with the culture in which we live and present the message of the gospel through our words and actions.

Are we prepared to face the consequences? We will be vilified for our convictions. We will be persecuted. We will suffer[11]. We may even have to lay down our lives for the sake of Christ and His Church. As the time of Jesus' second coming approaches, persecution will increase in intensity, as the Bible warns us (e.g. Luke 21, 2 Timothy 3). The words of Jesus in Matthew 10 above tell us that if we refuse to carry our cross and follow Jesus, then we are not worthy of being called Christians. We will only be making a mockery of His Kingship over our lives. But if we say yes, He will give us the grace (Week 39) to carry the cross and to follow Him. We will then live life in all its fullness!

Below is another story from Rosemary of Week 37. It is about how her broken leg was amazingly healed and about a revelation she received regarding sharing in Jesus' suffering and what that would entail for her.

Rosemary's Car Crash

One dark night, my children, Tim (twelve) and Richard (thirteen), and I were coming back from Norwich along a country road. Unknown to us, a sugar beet lorry had stalled in the road ahead of us, doing a three-point turn with headlights in the hedge. Because the lorry was the same colour as the road, we did not see it until it was too

---

[9] Mark 8v34 (NLT): *Then, calling the crowd to join His disciples, He said, "If any of you wants to be My follower, you must turn from your selfish ways, take up your cross, and follow Me".*

[10] 1 Peter 4v12-13 (NLT): *Dear friends, don't be surprised at the fiery trials you are going through, as if something strange were happening to you. Instead, be very glad – for these trials make you partners with Christ in His suffering, so that you will have the wonderful joy of seeing His glory when it is revealed to all the world.*

[11] Philippians 1v29 (NLT): *For you have been given not only the privilege of trusting in Christ but also the privilege of suffering for Him.*

late. As we went crashing into the lorry, I remember thinking, "Here we come, Lord!" Then there was utter silence.

When I realised I was still alive, I looked for my boys. Tim had gone straight through the windscreen and just his legs were in the car. Richard had slid down under the seat in front and was very still. I thought they were both dead and knew this was more than I could handle, so I just gave this to God saying, "I know You'll help me to carry this Lord because it's too much for me!" Peace swept over me because I knew He would. Then I heard Tim shout. He was alive! The firemen arrived to cut us out of the wreckage. We were laid on the grass verge though they couldn't move Richard far as he had neck injuries, but he was okay. Tim's first words were, "Mum, are you alright?" I answered, "Yes Tim. We're going to be alright." "Mum," he said, "let's pray!" As I prayed, there were policemen, firemen and ambulance crew milling around, but I didn't care. When I stopped, Tim protested, "Don't stop Mum!" "Okay, but you pray too", I said, meaning for him to join me in his heart. But before I had the chance to pray again, Tim had started a beautiful prayer, thanking God for all the kind people who were helping us and that He was there for us. For me, it was as though a beautiful light shone around us, transforming that ugly scene. I felt as though we were being surrounded in a beautiful blanket of God's love. Tim went unconscious after this.

My husband, Christopher, was called by the police to tell him that we had an accident. When he asked how bad it was, they replied they weren't allowed to say, so the poor man had to drive for half an hour not knowing what he would find. Before he left, he had rung our vicar who was about to go to a church meeting. I gathered that a lot of the meeting was taken up with them praying for us, especially for the children, that the children's minds would be healed of the trauma and that they wouldn't be able to remember the crash. And they don't remember a thing about it!

Tim had a broken leg, thirty-seven stitches in his face and subsequent plastic surgery. Praise God he has no visible scars on his face today. Richard suffered painful neck injuries. They were both in hospital for two weeks. My injuries were more serious. I was in hospital for two months and on traction as my knee had been crushed.

One day a vicar came to visit the patient in the bed next to mine. He asked me what had happened and I narrated the story to him. He then spoke about a young man who had come to see him on the night of the accident and had told him how he'd stopped to help at the scene. He was very emotional when he informed the vicar how Tim and I had prayed. I requested the vicar to give me the young man's address so I could thank him for helping. Asking God to hold the pen as I wrote, I thanked the young man for stopping to help and went on to say that I felt it wasn't a coincidence that he was there as God has a lovely plan for our lives. I quickly posted it before I could change my mind.

Two days later, there was a rustle beside me and there stood this young man clutching a bunch of grapes! He introduced himself and confessed that he'd been plucking up courage for two weeks to come and see me and then my letter had come. "You're right when you say it wasn't a coincidence," he agreed. Then he went on to tell me how his life was a struggle. He decided that if there was a God, he needed to find Him. He added that he'd been to various churches, but hadn't found God. He gave up the search thinking God didn't exist anyway. He was late home from work on the day of the accident, having gone out to pay a parking fine. He decided to take a short cut home which he normally didn't take and came across the accident. He helped to get Tim out of the car. Then, as Tim and I prayed, tears rolled down his face because he had realised that there was a God. "Can you tell me how I can find Him too?" he asked. So I talked to him about a loving God, prayed for him and put him in touch with a lively church in Norwich.

On another day, whilst the curtains were around me, I had what I can only call a vision. It was as though I was transported to another place. I found myself outside a garden and inside the garden, Jesus was walking. I knew somehow that it was a place of suffering, but I also knew that to walk in the garden with Jesus and to share in His suffering was one of the most privileged places to be in. I began to plead with Him to allow me to come into the garden, to walk with Him and to share in His suffering. He looked at me with a look that meant, "You don't know what you're asking!" I went on pleading, with tears streaming down my face. Finally, He looked at me again and, with what I felt was almost reluctance, He said, "Alright." I then cried tears of joy! I soon became aware of the hospital again.

I thought, "What was all that about?" I put two and two together and made five. Because of the talk from the medical staff of me being crippled, I felt that this was the suffering I was to share and I was so happy to do that. If anyone wanted to pray for me, I would fend them off! I lived with pain and dragged my leg around, but never minded as I felt that in some way I was sharing in Christ's suffering. I finally left the hospital, but my leg was bent as that was the best that they could do. I was advised to come back for major surgery when I couldn't stand the pain any more.

Two years later, I was at a meeting in Lowestoft with my family. In the middle of the meeting God spoke to me very clearly, "Rosemary, you're not doing Me a favour by carrying that bad leg around. I want to heal you tonight!" What about that! Well, there and then the pain left my leg and I felt as though I was floating! Later in the service, people were invited to stand if they wanted healing, so although I felt I'd already been healed, I stood. Afterwards my children said delightedly, "Mum, see what you can do! Hop! Skip!" And off I went hopping and skipping down the road! Praise God, I was healed!

The next day, I had the mums and toddlers group at my house. One of the mums who'd been to the Lowestoft meeting asked me about my leg. I answered that I had no pain in the leg and could run up and down the stairs and get on my bike. She was more interested in knowing whether my leg was straight, because that was something she could see. I had to admit that I hadn't dared to look down at it in case it was still crooked, making me doubt my healing. But with persuasion I rolled my trousers up and put my feet together. I was more shocked than anyone. My legs were straight! Now that was a miracle!

I was forty-two when I was healed and since then I've climbed Helvellyn, cycled round France for two weeks with the family and done loads of other stuff. Gratitude to God would flood me every time I put a foot out of bed and felt my miracle of healing. I'm now seventy-seven and I've had two knee replacements in latter years, but these have been due to wear and tear and nothing to do with the accident.

Because I didn't understand the vision God had given me in the hospital, I shelved it. As time went on, I began to realise that it wasn't physical suffering He meant, but the pretty severe persecution I was suffering as a Christian in the village we were living in at that time. I resented this badly. When the Lord reminded me that He too was rejected and persecuted, I repented in tears. Now I can "count it all joy" when I run into various trials[12]. I'm free! Hallelujah!

- Rosemary (Lancaster, England)
September 2011

The narrow road Christian pilgrims walk on is the *Via Dolorosa* because Jesus calls us to be His faithful witnesses.[13] Peter says: "Since Christ suffered physical pain, you must arm yourselves with the same attitude He had, and be ready to suffer too" (1 Peter 4v1, NLT). Peter wrote these words to mentally prepare his contemporary readers for the intense persecution that was coming under the Roman emperor Nero. The Bible warns us of a coming intense persecution before Jesus' second coming. God wants us to be prepared for this! Jesus says in Matthew 24v9-11 (NKJV): "Then they will deliver you up to tribulation and kill you, and you will be hated by all nations

---

[12] James 1v2-4 (NKJ): *My brethren, count it all joy when you fall into various trials, knowing that the testing of your faith produces patience. But let patience have its perfect work, that you may be perfect and complete, lacking nothing.* (See Week 25.)

[13] A moving song entitled 'Via Dolorosa' was composed by Billy Sprague and Niles Borop. There are several Youtube sites on the Internet that feature this song.

for My name's sake. And then many will be *offended*, will betray one another, and will hate one another. Then many false prophets will rise up and deceive many. And because lawlessness will abound, the *love* of many will grow cold."

The first italicised word, *offended*, is *skandalizo* in the original Greek text. It means to put a stumbling block or impediment on someone's way, to entice to sin, or to offend. It is from the noun *skandalon* which means 'a thing that offends', but it literally refers to the trigger of a trap, or the object that holds the bait, or the snare or the bait itself[14]. The second italicised word, *love*, is *agápē* (Week 30), the kind of love that God imparts to believers. Jesus' warning is therefore to Christians! Persecution and suffering will be used by satan to get us offended at God and at each other. The offence, satan's bait, can cause our love for Jesus and for fellow believers to grow cold and consequently, for us to renounce Jesus, if we allow it to.

Jesus, my Saviour and Lord, I give my life to You. Together with Paul I declare: "I want to know Christ and the power that raised Him from the dead. I want to share in His sufferings and become like Him in His death" (Philippians 3v10, NCV). Give me the grace to be faithful to You at all costs, whether or not You will deliver me from suffering and persecution[15]. Protect my love for You and for other Christians from getting cold! For Your name's sake, amen.

---

[14] It is for this reason that John Bevere calls offence "the bait of satan" in his book, *The Bait of Satan*, first published in 1994 by Charisma House.

[15] John Foxe's *Book of Martyrs* (first published in English in 1563 as *Actes and Monuments*) contains true stories of men, women and children who gave their lives for the sake of Christ in the face of cruel persecution.

Week 42: The Road of Transformation

Do not be conformed to this world, but be transformed by
the renewal of your mind. (Romans 12v2, ESV)

Jesus invites us to share in His sufferings (Week 41), but He is not a cosmic kill-joy who wants us to suffer for suffering's sake! When we are serious about our calling 'to be and to do' (Week 19), we will inevitably suffer, but the joy we will possess when Jesus' glory is revealed to the world[1] and when we receive our eternal rewards (Week 33) will far outweigh any suffering we will ever bear. He endured the scourging and the cross to make sure of this!

We share in Jesus' sufferings through the trials that come our way, not as consequences of our sinful actions, but for doing something that is right in God's eyes, or simply because we are Christians[2]. These trials train us for our unique purpose in life (Week 25). They also have a purifying effect[3] as the Holy Spirit uses them to progressively transform[4] us into Christ-likeness (Week 18).

Christ-likeness is holiness. God is transforming us into holiness because He is holy. He is also committed to doing this because it is His desire for ALL believers to walk in the power and authority Jesus demonstrated in the Gospels. The more conformed we are to the character of Jesus, the more we will manifest His glory, power and authority. God gave us spiritual gifts (Appendix 3) so that we can manifest His glory, power and authority through the works He wants us to do before Jesus returns. Perhaps it is for our own good that God has not yet allowed us to see the fulfilment

---

[1]   1 Peter 4v12-13 (NLT): *Dear friends, don't be surprised at the fiery trials you are going through, as if something strange were happening to you. Instead, be very glad – for these trials make you partners with Christ in His suffering, so that you will have the wonderful joy of seeing His glory when it is revealed to all the world.*

[2]   1 Peter 4v14-16 (NIV): *If you are insulted because of the name of Christ, you are blessed, for the Spirit of glory and of God rests on you. If you suffer, it should not be as a murderer or thief or any other kind of criminal, or even as a meddler. However, if you suffer as a Christian, do not be ashamed, but praise God that you bear that name.*

[3]   1 Peter 1v7 (NLT): *These trials will show that your faith is genuine. It is being tested as fire tests and purifies gold--though your faith is far more precious than mere gold.* God tests His children to purify them and to prepare them for heaven. He judges the rest, who do not accept Christ's sacrifice, to mete out just punishment for their sins.

[4]   The original Greek word for 'transform' in Romans 12v2 above is *metamorphoo* = to metamorphose, to change into another form, to transfigure, i.e., into "a new creation". *Therefore, if anyone is in Christ, he is a new creation...* (2 Corinthians 5v17, ESV).

of John 14v12[5] and Mark 16v17-18 (Week 26) in a way the Church has been longing for because power and authority can be dangerous if mishandled. They can corrupt us unless Jesus' character has been forged in us to the degree that our motives have been sufficiently purified and we can be trusted with the 'anointing' (Week 13, 3rd footnote)[6]. God is therefore transforming His children so that our character will be able to carry the anointing for the "greater works" Jesus prophesied.

Transformation or sanctification is mainly the work of the Holy Spirit, but He needs our co-operation. If we truly love the Lord, then we will desire to grow into Christ-likeness and this can only happen by submitting to the "refiner's fire" of the Holy Spirit[7]. The original Greek word for 'fiery trials' in the verse in this week's 1st footnote is *purosis* which refers to fire used to refine metals. *Purosis* also pertains to calamities or trials that test our character. How do we submit to God's *purosis*? By not getting offended at God because of the testing that happens to us (Week 41), by asking for His grace and wisdom to respond to these the way He wants us to, by having an eternal perspective on our sufferings, and therefore, by choosing to be joyful in spite of these because we have reason to be[8].

Romans 12v2 above tells us that transformation necessitates the renewal of the mind. This is because spiritual battles begin in the mind! This was probably the reason why Jesus was crucified on Golgotha or Calvary[9], which both mean 'place of the skull'. There is a battle between our old carnal mind inside our skull and the new "mind of

---

[5] John 14v12 (NLT): *I tell you the truth, anyone who believes in Me will do the same works I have done, and even greater works, because I am going to be with the Father.* By "greater works", Jesus most likely meant that the miracles and other works His followers would do would have a greater impact on mankind than His own. This is because the things Jesus did on earth were limited to Israel and seen only by thousands. The works the early Church did were witnessed by more people of different nations. With advances in travel and communication, surely the Church of the present can have more extensive impact on millions of people all over the world!

[6] In Acts 8 we read about power-hungry Simon the Sorcerer who offered Peter and John money to possess the gifts of the Spirit. He is regarded as the arch-heretic who fathered Gnosticism (see 2nd footnote, Week 26). He may have been an apostate.

[7] Malachi 3v2b-3a (NIV): *He will be like a refiner's fire or a launderer's soap. He will sit as a refiner and purifier of silver; He will purify the Levites and refine them like gold and silver.* Jewish priests came only from the tribe of Levi, but all believers in Jesus are now members of God's 'holy priesthood', as 1 Peter 2v5 says. We all need to be purified!

[8] Romans 8v18 (ESV): *For I consider that the sufferings of this present time are not worth comparing with the glory that is to be revealed to us.*

[9] *Golgotha* is Aramaic. The English name *Calvary* is from the Latin *Calvariae.*

Christ"[10] that is given to all of God's children, and this new mind can overcome the old by God's grace. How do we *take hold of* (*ekho*) God's grace (Week 39) in this battle for mind domination?

Let us remember what the word of God says about our true identity, that we now belong to Jesus, not to ourselves, that we have been crucified with Him, and are dead to sin (Appendix 2). Let us guard our mind against the garbage that satan wants us to see and hear[11]. Since we empower what we focus on, let us "set our mind" not on satan's temptations, but on "things above"[12], especially on the love of Jesus for us (as proven by His extreme obedience at the cross) so that we can again get captivated by His love, rather than by satan's temptations (Week 24). Let us refuse to be passive regarding our thoughts (a passive mind is attractive to the enemy because he wants to exercise mind control), but actively think about what is pure and good and wholesome[13]. Let us speak the word of God to our situations to counteract every lie the enemy throws at us, for our mouth has the power of death and life[14].

The more we let God's word saturate our thoughts, the more this translates into our words and actions and then into new habits. By the empowerment of God's grace, we can "put off" old habits and "put on" these new ones[15]. These prove that as we walk along the narrow road, our character is effectively getting transformed.

Below is the story of the transformation that happened to Elisabeth of Sweden and how God "restored" and "prospered" her soul. God can also do it for you!

---

[10] 1 Corinthians 2v14 (NLT): *But people who aren't spiritual can't receive these truths from God's Spirit. It all sounds foolish to them and they can't understand it, for only those who are spiritual can understand what the Spirit means....(v16b) But we understand these things, for we have the mind of Christ.*

[11] Remember the principle: garbage in, garbage out! It is little wonder why satan wants to control the entertainment industry (Week 29).

[12] Colossians 3v2-3 (ESV): *Set your minds on things that are above, not on things that are on earth. For you have died, and your life is hidden with Christ in God.*

[13] Philippians 4v8 (NIV): *Finally, brothers, whatever is true*, whatever is noble, whatever is right, whatever is pure, whatever is lovely, whatever is admirable – if anything is excellent or praiseworthy – think about such things. *What is truer than God's word?*

[14] Proverbs 18v21 (ESV): *Death and life are in the power of the tongue...*

[15] Ephesians 4v22-24 (NIV): *You were taught, with regard to your former way of life, to put off your old self, which is being corrupted by its deceitful desires; to be made new in the attitude of your minds; and to put on the new self, created to be like God in true righteousness and holiness.*

He Restores My Soul

In Psalm 23v3 we read that God "restores our soul"[16]. This means that He heals our mind, will and emotions. The third letter of John verse 2[17] says it in another way: He wants to "prosper" (to cause to grow strong, to succeed, to flourish) our soul. Do you believe that God cares so much about you that He wants to restore or heal and prosper your soul? I am a living testimony of the truth that He does!

My story began in autumn 2003 when I studied at the university in Örebro, Sweden. God put a longing in my heart to go abroad to do my placement as I wanted to improve my English. I thought it was too late to apply for placement abroad, but when I went to the placement co-ordinator at the university, I was told that it wasn't. I applied and was accepted to do my placement in the city of Lancaster in the Lancashire area of England during the spring term of 2004. I flew over to lodge with a girl who was at university and not long after I arrived in the UK, God brought me to Christians Alive Church. This was an answer to prayer as my sister and I had been praying that I would find a church in Lancaster during my placement there.

Unfortunately, my placement in Lancaster didn't meet my expectations. I discovered I had more problems with English than I thought I would have. But God spoke to me about moving to England after I finished my degree. In fact, He even prepared me for this move before I went to Lancaster for my placement. He did this by giving me Isaiah 54, especially verses 2-3 (NIV): "Enlarge the place of your tent, stretch your tent curtains wide, do not hold back; lengthen your cords, strengthen your stakes. For you will spread out to the right and to the left..." Amazingly, the same scripture was later brought to my attention by the pastor of the church at Christians Alive! I would say that God commanded me to move to Lancaster even though I didn't want to go back because of my disappointment with my placement. I still remember how tears fell from my eyes when I felt God's calling to go back to England. However, I surrendered to His will and said to Him, "If this is what You want me to do, I'll do it!"

So I did. After finishing my degree, I went back to Lancaster in February 2005. It didn't take long before I got a job and God got busy doing things in my life!

The Bible says that the way of the godly is directed by the Lord[18]. That was exactly what I experienced during my second time in England, and the most amazing part

---

[16] The Hebrew word for soul here is *nephesh* which can mean soul, life or person.

[17] 3 John v2 (NASB): *Beloved, I pray that in all respects you may prosper and be in good health, just as your soul prospers.* The Greek word for soul here is *psuche* which means soul or life.

[18] Psalm 37v23 (AMP): *The steps of a [good] man are directed and established by the Lord when He delights in his way [and He busies Himself with his every step].*

was about what God did in and for me. I didn't know anyone when I first went to Lancaster, but God knew exactly which church He needed to put me in and why He needed to put me there. I went back to Christians Alive Church where I experienced in a greater measure the love of God because the people in the church were so lovely and became my friends. God also used this church to heal me and to "restore my soul". Although it took longer than I thought, God answered my prayers and prospered my soul!

A lot of years ago, I asked God to heal me of things in my soul-life that might be a problem in a future marriage mainly because I had seen so many couples struggle in their marriages with problems that had to do with wounds in the soul. Before I came to the UK I had a problem with men – in trusting them and in believing that there were good men in the world. This had to do with the bullying I suffered, mainly from boys, when I was at school. In the church at Lancaster, I met wonderful men who treated their wives and other women in a good way. My broken picture of men was healed! This was helped tremendously by the character of the pastor, the father figure at Christians Alive. Through him, God showed me what a father can be like. Not that I had an abusive dad. No, he has always been very kind. But through the pastor, my picture of my heavenly Father "prospered" – it grew and flourished!

Another problem I struggled with was my emotional ups and downs. I remember one time when the pastor said to me that he couldn't understand why my mood changed so suddenly and described it as one moment I was happy and the next second I was really sad. I said I didn't understand why either, but after a while God revealed to me the reason: I did not understand that I was loved for who I was. God used the church at Christians Alive to heal me of this. It came through the leaders trusting me enough to give me the responsibility (some would probably say I shouldn't have had) to lead a pioneering work in the city, the management of a newly-opened Christian debt counselling centre in Lancaster, a branch of a national Christian charity in the UK. Why would anyone doubt my ability to do this? Well, as a foreigner who wasn't really good in English, I didn't feel comfortable to speak to people. Nevertheless, I had to talk to clients as part of my job. I also had to give talks about the ministry in front of a lot of people, like in church services. I still remember that when I talked in front of the congregation at Christians Alive, the church held their breath and tried to help me because I was so nervous. And all the time I felt their love. There were times when I felt like giving up in this pioneering work and if God hadn't put people around me to cherish me, guide me and encourage me on, I would have thrown in the towel!

The last thing I would like to tell you about has to do with another kind of emotional healing that happened to me. I used to cry a lot! One day a man came to me to tell me that my crying wasn't healthy or helpful. I didn't like what he said back then, but when I came back to Sweden, God showed me that he was right! As I was reading a secular book, the Holy Spirit showed me that I had used crying when I was a little girl to get attention. Unfortunately, this habit didn't disappear when I became an adult. When the Holy Spirit revealed this to me, I confessed it before the Lord as sin. I hardly ever cry nowadays, at least not for the wrong reason.

Through my step of obedience to go back to Lancaster, God healed me inside. When I moved back to Sweden, friends and relations told me that I was a totally different person, which I also realised. If God did it for me, I'm sure He wants to do it for you, too! He is so good. He wants to restore and prosper your soul!

- Elisabeth (Bromölla, Sweden)
June 2011

Dear Father, I confess that there have been many thoughts I had dwelt on that did not line up with what Your word says. Forgive me for those times when I allowed the enemy of my soul to hijack my thoughts. Help me to take hold of Your grace so that the mind of Christ that You have given me will be victorious over the carnal mind I still struggle with. Give me a desire for Your word as well as the discipline to read and study it and to allow it to dominate my thoughts, so that my mind can be renewed and my character transformed. Do Your work in my life, Holy Spirit. Transform me into the person My Father envisioned me to be, that I may bring glory to my Lord and Saviour. For Christ's sake, amen.

Week 43: The Road to Freedom

So if the Son sets you free, you will be free indeed.
(John 8v36, ESV)

The verb 'to set free' and the adjective 'free' in the verse above in the original Greek text come from the word *eleutheria,* "the freedom to live as we should, and not as we please" (Week 38). True freedom, *eleutheria,* is therefore found in our obedience to God and in fulfilling our God-given purpose. *Eleutheria* is freedom from our old, sinful self so that we can live out our new and true identity in Jesus Christ (Appendix 2).

Eleutheria is "slavery" to righteousness[1]. Its opposite is slavery to sin[2]. We are either a slave of one or the other[3]. Slavery to righteousness is liberating for the gracious God is the Master. Slavery to sin is slavery to satan which leads to evil actions, fear, insecurity, a disturbed mind, and to other dreadful consequences. When a person becomes a Christian, he is justified[4] by faith in Jesus and is loosed from the bondage of sin. He has now become a slave to righteousness, a child of God and therefore righteous in God's eyes[5]. It is a new identity that he, through the empowerment of the Holy Spirit, must choose to live out daily by counting himself dead to sin and to self. He occasionally falls into sin, but he listens to the conviction of the Holy Spirit, confesses and repents of his sin and is restored to intimacy with God. As the Christian matures in his new identity and as he becomes more intimate with Jesus through prayer and the study of His word, he takes sin more seriously. Sin loses its enticement[6].

A Christian who gives in to temptation each time gradually weakens his conscience. He becomes enslaved to sin and sinning becomes his lifestyle. The Bible says that such a person is "like a dog that returns to its vomit, or a washed pig that returns to

---

[1] Romans 6v18 (NIV): *You have been set free from sin and have become slaves to righteousness.*

[2] John 8v34 (ESV): *Jesus answered them, "Truly, truly, I say to you, everyone who practices sin is a slave to sin".*

[3] 2 Peter2v19b (NIV): *People are slaves to whatever has mastered them.*

[4] The term 'justified' was used as a legal term by a court of law to declare that the accused had not broken the law. This is different from being pardoned. A pardoned man was guilty of an offence, but had been released. However, a man who is 'justified' is declared innocent of any wrong-doing. Those who believe in Jesus are considered 'justified' because Jesus took our sins upon Himself.

[5] 2 Corinthians 5v21 (ESV): *For our sake He* [God the Father] *made Him* [Jesus] *to be sin who knew no sin, so that in Him* [Jesus] *we might become the righteousness of God.*

[6] Psalm 119v9, 11 (NIV): *How can a young person stay on the path of purity? By living according to Your word.... I have hidden Your word in my heart that I might not sin against You.*

the mud"[7]. God has to judge (discipline) the unrepentant and He may do so by handing him over to the master the person chooses to be a slave to, the devil. God is just, so He must judge, but He is also merciful even in His judgments in that He metes them out to redeem and to set free[8].

John 8v36 above was spoken by Jesus before the events of Holy Week. He knew that His death and eventual resurrection would indeed set many free. Although we are set free from satan's kingdom as soon as we receive Jesus as our Saviour and Lord, *eleutheria* is something that has to be worked out in our lives, just as a person who is set free from imprisonment has to learn to live as a free man. This is especially true because of 'demonic strongholds'[9]. Demonic strongholds are pretensions that claim to be true and meritorious when in fact, they are lies and mere "imaginations". They start as ideas, arguments or deceptions that contradict God's word and which then gain a strong influence over individuals and even over communities and nations. They grow into false beliefs, ungodly ideologies, fears, addictions and ungodly behaviour and habits. Demonic strongholds are therefore mindsets[10] promoted by satan.

Here are some examples of demonic strongholds: all religions that reject or distort the word of the God of the Bible, the idea of racial supremacy, "I can never succeed because I'm not clever enough", "Once a junkie, always a junkie", "I am a reject", "There's nothing wrong with sex between consenting adults", "God is love so He has nothing against homosexual relationships".

Are you held captive by a demonic stronghold? Do you need to be set free from unhealthy and paralysing fear, from insecurity and from feelings of inferiority? Do you need to be set free from the desire or need to control and manipulate? Do you need to be rid of bad habits and behaviour? Do you want to be free from addiction to drugs, alcohol, sex, gambling, shopping, etc.?

The first step to *eleutheria* is to recognise your captivity and confess it. Then receive God's gift to you, eternal life through faith in Jesus (if you have not done this yet).

---

[7] 2 Peter 2v22, NLT

[8] 1 Corinthians 5v5 (NLT): *Then you must throw this man out and hand him over to Satan so that his sinful nature will be destroyed and he himself will be saved on the day the Lord returns.* The judgment of God may be to shorten a man's life in order to save him from getting deeper into sin, from apostasy and from eternal damnation.

[9] 2 Corinthians 10v3-5 (KJV): *For though we walk in the flesh, we do not war after the flesh: (For the weapons of our warfare are not carnal, but mighty through God to the pulling down of strongholds;) casting down imaginations, and every high thing that exalteth itself against the knowledge of God, and bringing into captivity every thought to the obedience of Christ...*

[10] A mindset is a habitual mental attitude or disposition that determines how a person interprets and responds to situations. It can be good or evil.

Ask Him to deliver you from your captivity. Determine to get to know Jesus more and more. Let your mind be captivated by His love for you and let Him be the focus of your thoughts. Abide in Him and His word. He will complete what He began in your life as He had promised[11], if you will allow Him to. Receive His empowering grace whenever the battle for your *eleutheria* rages. Like the man in our next story, do not give up but persevere, especially in prayer. The Son is setting you free from your demonic strongholds and old self. You will be free indeed!

The Long Road to Recovery

At seventeen years old I was a supermarket manager with a great career ahead of me. One afternoon I came home feeling somewhat fed up after a bad day at work. Leaning out of the window, I could hear my flat mates having a great time and I simply craved what they had. I knew they were on LSD so I started using this drug. I soon lost my job as I could not get the drug out of my system and I began 'tripping' every week.

It was in this state that I met Angie. Recognising that she was addicted to barbiturates, I decided to rescue her. As a very compassionate man, I wanted to save people and I thought I could help Angie all by myself! After all, as the eldest of six children, I looked after my brothers and sisters. I managed to get Angie away from her boyfriend who was giving her drugs and got her into hospital. Later on, she became my girlfriend and we went away together – 'saved', or so I thought. However, after a few days we had a massive argument. Angie walked out and headed back to her old city and boyfriend. By the time I found her, she had taken an overdose and tragically died.

Desperately disappointed by my failure to help Angie, I allowed my life to go down the drain. Even though I had various relationships, got married and had two beautiful children, I could not hold my life together. Alcohol and drugs became my masters. Despite trying hard along the way to stem the destructive tide and rescue myself, my marriage and family life collapsed. For some time I had my daughter Mick with me, but when I could no longer cope because of my addiction, she had to go and live with her mum. I slowly lost practically everything, including my self-respect.

In an attempt to save me, my sister Gill came and asked me to go back with her to Aberdeen. Thinking that leaving Oldham would give me the opportunity to come off drugs, I went with her. However, I had to return to Oldham to attend a court hearing for possessing drugs. I told the court about my history and received a lenient sentence of two years' probation, community service and a large fine. I did my community service and then returned to Aberdeen and had my probation transferred.

---

[11] Philippians 1v6 (ESV): *And I am sure of this, that He who began a good work in you will bring it to completion at the day of Jesus Christ.*

Three months later I was still drug-free so Mick came to live with me and Gill in her council flat. I got a job and was fairly settled, but because I allowed myself to be influenced by the drinking culture, I ended up substituting one addiction for another. Soon my friends' and my drunken behaviour led to our eviction from the flat and we became homeless. For Mick's sake we went to join our family who by this time had moved to Morecambe. I eventually got a flat for Mick and myself and found a cleaning job at a pub. However, the drinking problem did not go away.

In Morecambe I met a lady called Di who was also a single parent with a daughter. We set up home together in Morecambe and then moved to Preston. Mick, who was sixteen at this time, was not happy with this and left school and home. I think I blamed Di for this and I started to drink too much again. Di and I parted company and I went back to Morecambe to live with my brother Phil while Mick lived with a family in Morecambe. I continued to drink and started taking heroin and amphetamines as well. My life spiralled out of control. To help me to stop taking heroin, my doctor put me on methadone, a synthetic drug used as a substitute for heroin, but legal and less harmful and which somehow allows an addict to lead a life that is closer to normal. However, the weaning on to methadone created in me a new habit, a new addiction.

Eventually, in 1992, I went to a rehab in Sheffield and stayed there for three months. Here I learned that with support I could live a clean and effective life. I met some good people and started to go to church again. Unfortunately, I left this program early and went back to live with my brother. I relapsed and soon became very ill from using a combination of drugs and alcohol. I was given another chance to do a 'detox' at the Castle unit of Ridge Lea Hospital in Lancaster. This was in spring of 1994. This time my life really began to change. There was something different about this detox and it was to become my last one in hospital.

This time was indeed different. It was the worst time in my life, but it was also the best because during this detox I felt some definite changes in my outlook. I was forty years old and knew that this was my last chance. I began to seek God, read my Bible and asked my family to pray for me. It is hard to explain, but when I read about the journey of Jesus to the cross, I felt I was going through a similar journey and I knew that after my time in hospital, I would recover and dedicate my life to God.

After I came out of hospital, I went to live in a flat in Morecambe and tried my hardest to live without drinking or taking drugs and then discovered that the hardest part of recovery is not the detox, but living a good life and continuing to recover. I could not do that on my own. I realised something had to change. In June 1994, I went to a small Christian fellowship in the west end of Morecambe, repented of my past, asked Jesus to be my Saviour and Lord and asked the Holy Spirit to dwell in me.

Although I was still on methadone, I continued to learn about my new life in Jesus. With prayer and fellowship I was able to start reducing the drug. It was a slow process but I had a lot of support. Part of my recovery involved helping at a workshop for people with mental health problems. For the two years I was doing this, I had support from some wonderful people who helped me a lot to stay away from drugs and to learn a different way of life. There was always someone there for me, either at church, at the workshop or in my family. Without their support, I don't think I would have made it this far!

I moved to Lancaster in 1998 and went to college to do horticulture. I also started going to a new church, Christians Alive, and began to work harder at my recovery. After I finished horticulture, I felt God's call to minister to the down-and-out and so I volunteered to help at a homeless centre to gain practical experience of working with people.

In 2002, I was at last free from methadone. It was a long road to recovery and freedom from alcohol and addictive drugs, but God never gave up on me! "He reached down from on high and took hold of me; He drew me out of deep waters. He rescued me from my powerful enemy, from my foes, who were too strong for me" (2 Samuel 22v17-18, NIV). Finally, I have something real to offer to society!

Since 2003 I have been working at the Homeless Centre in Lancaster and I'm now involved in Christian ministry with the Prison Fellowship[12] and The Olive Branch[13]. More recently, I joined the Lancaster Street Pastors[14], engaging people where they hang out, be it on the streets or in pubs. I serve my community with other Christians who share the same desire to see others rescued from alcohol and drugs using the Higher Power available – the power that rescued me and set me free, the power of the Lord Jesus Christ now living in my life!

> - Grahame (Lancaster, England)
> May 2011

"It was for freedom [*eleutheria*] that Christ set us free; therefore keep standing firm and do not be subject again to a yoke of slavery" (Galatians 5v1, NASB).

Lord Jesus, You suffered so much so that I may gain my freedom – freedom from slavery to satan and sin, freedom to overcome my weaknesses, freedom from fear and worry, freedom from insecurity and feelings of inferiority, freedom from the desire

---

[12] www.prisonfellowship.org.uk
[13] www.the-olivebranch.org.uk (See Week 17)
[14] www.streetpastors.co.uk

to control and manipulate, freedom to serve You by serving others, and freedom to be all that I can be according to the Father's will and purpose. I can never thank You enough, Lord! I praise You because the road I'm walking on is a road to freedom. Protect me from receiving Your grace and then wasting it by not allowing it to train and to empower me to keep standing firm against sin and to live for You each day[15]. Thank You that Your grace is sufficient for me, for Your power shows its strength when I know I am weak on my own[16]. Blessed be Your holy name!

---

[15] 2 Corinthians 6v1 (GNT): *In our work together with God, then, we beg you who have received God's grace not to let it be wasted.* See prayer and 14th footnote, Week 39.

[16] 2 Corinthians 12v9 (GNT): *My grace is all you need, for My power is greatest when you are weak.*

Week 44: The Road Called Meaningful Life

Fear God and keep His commandments, for this is the whole duty of man.
(Ecclesiastes 12v13, ESV)

The book of Ecclesiastes in the Old Testament is a compilation of sayings of "the Teacher" (or Preacher), a "son of King David"[1]. The name of the teacher is not given, but there are many parts in the book which indicate that Solomon may have been the teacher, the *Qoheleth*. He succeeded David as king of Israel.

As a young king, Solomon started well. God was so pleased with his request for wisdom to rule Israel, rather than for riches, honour and influence, that He gave Solomon wisdom and all of these. Unfortunately, Solomon married many wives, many of them from heathen nations, most likely for diplomatic reasons. This was in disobedience to God's command. The consequence that God warned about for such disobedience happened.[2] Solomon's wives seduced him into tolerating idolatry. He gave in to their demands for temples to their own gods. (The bickering of 700 wives and 300 concubines probably got too much to bear!) Solomon went farther than this by worshipping these demons. Despite God's many blessings, Solomon chose to ignore his covenant relationship with God and *chesed* (Week 31). As judgment for his unfaithfulness (his 'divided heart'), God told him that his kingdom would be divided after his son succeeded him as king. True enough, ten tribes rebelled against Rehoboam, Solomon's son, to form the northern Kingdom of Israel with Samaria as capital (see 1st footnote, Week 31), leaving the two tribes of Judah and Benjamin to form the southern Kingdom of Judah, with Jerusalem as capital, under the kings of David's (and Solomon's) lineage.[3]

---

[1] Ecclesiastes 1v1 (NIV): *The words of the Teacher, son of David, king of Jerusalem...*The original Hebrew word for teacher/preacher here is *qoheleth* = speaker in an assembly. The Septuagint (Greek translation of the Old Testament) uses the word *ekklesiastes* for *qoheleth*. *Ekklesia* referred to citizen assemblies in Greece. The Septuagint uses *ekklesia* for the Hebrew *qahal* to describe Israel gathered as a religious assembly. The word *ekklesia* with reference to the Christian Church is first seen in Acts 5v11.

[2] Deuteronomy 7v3-4 (ESV): *You shall not intermarry with them, giving your daughters to their sons or taking their daughters for your sons, for they would turn away your sons from following Me, to serve other gods.* See also Exodus 34v14-16 and Joshua 23v12-13. The events in the life of Solomon mentioned above are recorded in 1 Kings chapter 11.

[3] Solomon's covenant unfaithfulness had far-reaching consequences. The ten tribes made a covenant with David (2 Samuel 5v3), but they rebelled against Rehoboam. Idolatry continued to plague both Israel and Judah such that years later, God judged them with expulsion from their land. Many of the inhabitants of the Kingdom of Israel were exiled by Assyrian invaders beginning 740 BC, and never returned (hence, "the ten lost tribes of Israel"). Many in the Kingdom of Judah were carried off into captivity in Babylon by Nebuchadnezzar beginning 587 BC. They returned 70 years later, as prophesied by Jeremiah, under Zerubbabel and Ezra. The term 'Jew' comes from the name 'Judah'.

Ecclesiastes was written mostly from the perspective of a man who grappled with the meaning of life. The ageing Solomon probably penned the book to share his philosophical and theological reflections on his experiences with younger readers. He started off with the wisdom of God, then abandoned it and relied on his own wisdom. He had all the material possessions he wanted, but he allowed his possessions to possess him, rather than placing his reliance on God. He sought pleasure, satisfaction and enjoyment through sex, entertainment and building projects, but neglected intimacy with God, only to realise that he had been "chasing the wind"[4]. The *Qoheleth* in Ecclesiastes declares that life not centred on God, that is, life "under the sun"[5], is *hebel* (Hebrew for vapour or breath), which is translated into English as meaningless[6], vanity, purposeless, emptiness, futility, etc. He concludes that nothing in life can have true meaning and satisfaction if God is not in it, and that for life to be meaningful, one needs to recognise God's gifts and enjoy them without neglecting the holy, reverential fear of the Lord. Because Jesus is God's greatest gift to mankind and because it is only by His grace that we can live in the holy fear of God and serve Him wholeheartedly (not with a divided heart), we can add this to what the Teacher says: *the key to living a meaningful, purposeful and significant life is to live not "under the sun", but 'under the Son'!*

What is life 'under the Son'? It is wholehearted devotion to God (*chesed*). It is a life of total surrender to Jesus, every aspect of it turned over to Him – possessions, work, pleasure, relationships, etc. It is doing all that we do for Him, knowing that these have eternal consequences (Week 33). Since it is living in the reverential fear of God, then it is walking in obedience and submission to the Holy Spirit. It is trusting Him with all of our heart to direct our path even when things are not going well[7]. Life 'under the Son' is looking at trials, tribulations, difficulties and sufferings with an eternal perspective. This perspective helps us to view positively the things that are beyond our control as situations God is using to "stir our nest" and to transform us into mature spiritual eagles (Week 10), as our next storyteller testifies. To live life 'under the Son' is the "whole duty of man" and this life is never meaningless and futile!

---

[4] Ecclesiastes 2v10-11 (NLT): *Anything I wanted, I would take. I denied myself no pleasure. I even found great pleasure in hard work, a reward for all my labours. But as I looked at everything I had worked so hard to accomplish, it was all so meaningless – like chasing the wind.*

[5] This phrase appears several times in Ecclesiastes in the NIV, ESV, KJV and others.

[6] Ecclesiastes 1v2 (NIV): *"Meaningless! Meaningless!" says the Teacher. "Utterly meaningless! Everything is meaningless."*

[7] Proverbs 3v5-6 (NIV): *Trust in the Lord with all your heart and lean not on your own understanding; in all your ways submit to Him, and He will make your paths straight.*

He Stirred My Nest

I was born in Taiwan into a family familiar with Christianity. As a result of a family tragedy thirty years ago, someone from the hospital shared Christ with my grandma who then became the first Christian in my family. I still clearly remember the time Grandma's church would come to our house every week to worship and pray before their church building was built. The loud sounds they made seemed to penetrate through our roof, and my brother and I would go somewhere quieter until they finished the service.

Although I grew up in this kind of Christian environment, I had no interest in Christianity. I was a straight-A student who did great in school. In the eyes of my teachers, I was a model student. Though I acted humble and friendly on the outside, I knew I was very proud on the inside. My thoughts were very logical and self-centred. I didn't believe in any kind of religion because I didn't think God was necessary in my life. The actions of some Christians disappointed me very much, leading me to conclude that religious beliefs were purely superficial and that there was no such thing as real faith.

The turning point took place after I graduated from university. At that time my mum was diagnosed with breast cancer. During the long period of waiting for her diagnosis report, not only was my whole family extremely anxious, I was also struggling with a heavy workload. Suddenly, I fell into deep depression. My pride was shattered and my mind was completely taken over by negative thoughts.

One day, two of my Christian relatives came to my house to visit my mum. They brought two Bibles and led us to read some verses, sing some gospel songs and finally led us to a prayer. Strangely, I started to feel a warm spring flowing through my body and I experienced perfect peace in my heart. At that very moment I began to think – maybe the Christian faith is something real and reliable, not just a superficial religion.

Thanks to God, my mum's medical report indicated 'carcinoma in situ' and the operation she had afterwards went very well. During the time of my mum's recovery, I began to deeply ponder the meaning of life. I wasn't able to find a perfect answer, but I was sure of one thing: that life is fragile and full of uncertainties so I should hold on tight to the present. In the end, I quit my job and flew to my dream city, Cambridge in south England, to start a new life.

During the first month of my stay in Cambridge, I faced culture shock and tried as many new things as possible, like most international students do. My friends invited me to pubs or night clubs almost every night. Though I am not the partying type, I joined them because I considered these invitations as great opportunities to practise

English and to make friends. However, I soon found the conversations we had in pubs and night clubs very shallow and I began to feel sick every time I saw terribly drunk people on the streets. Then one day, an idea suddenly came to my mind – what about going to church to have a look? So I asked my host mother if there were churches nearby and she suggested that I join the International Café especially held for international students at St. Barnabas Church every Thursday night. In addition, a Japanese friend invited me to do Visa Course with her (a kind of Alpha Course for international non-Christian students). [8]

After I started participating in these, God really began working in my heart. I became very open to everything about Jesus and the Bible. The friends I met at Visa Course came from different countries and backgrounds. They were really kind to me. They helped me understand different aspects of the Bible as well as clarified some things I found puzzling. Their kindness and great joy motivated my interest in Jesus and I felt a desire to know more! As a result, Lisa, my Chinese friend from Beijing, started a small Bible study group for me and my Japanese friend. We met once every week to read the book of John together.

By digging into the Bible, I found several answers to the meaning of life and became more and more aware of my sinful nature. I realised that I unconsciously committed a lot of sins on a daily basis and I was ashamed of myself. Yet, I fully understood the love of Jesus and was often deeply touched by God's words. One afternoon, when I read John 8v12[9], I was very moved. I received Jesus into my life and asked God to turn my darkness into light.

One Sunday morning, my pastor in Cambridge announced the date of the annual baptism ceremony. Without hesitation, I walked up to him and told him I would like to be on the baptism list. Soon after my baptism, while I was preparing for my return back to Taiwan, a friend from International Christian Fellowship asked me if I would be willing to stay in England for another year to serve international students! It was something totally beyond my plan. Although I was quite excited about this offer, I felt very diffident and unsure if I would succeed in this short-term mission. To make things worse, my parents reacted angrily and commanded me to return home as soon as possible and didn't want to communicate with me for nearly half a month. Feeling deeply hurt and disappointed and not knowing what to do, I spoke to the Lord and asked for His guidance every night. The Lord is such a gentle father and I often felt

---

[8] See 7th footnote, Week 15 for information about the Alpha Course. For information about the Visa Course, see www.friendsinternationalguildford.org.uk/visa.html

[9] John 8v12 (NIV): *When Jesus spoke again to the people, He said, "I am the light of the world. Whoever follows Me will never walk in darkness, but will have the light of life."*

that He listened to me quietly, comforting my depressed heart and giving me courage to speak to my parents again.

The Holy Spirit must have somehow worked in my parents' hearts because they dramatically changed their attitude and decided to support my decision in the end. So I took a five-hour train ride from Cambridge to Lancaster in northwest England for an interview with a Friends International staff worker and their regional director. Everything went perfectly well during and after the interview. I had enough time to rush back to Taiwan for my volunteer visa and even found a nice Christian family to stay with in Lancaster! I realised that God had everything prepared for me and that He just wanted me to learn to trust Him with all my heart. So in September 2007, I became a Reach volunteer with Friends International[10].

As a Reach volunteer, my task was to befriend international students and share the gospel with them. Since I had no experience with similar student volunteer work before and because Lancaster was a brand new place for me, I had felt nervous and had quite a lot of challenges in the first term. However, God never abandoned me. I learned a lot from my supervisor, Elspeth, and Christian friends helped me overcome my difficulties. Sooner than expected, I built up a good friendship with international students, started meeting them regularly and invited them to church with me.

Everything was going well on track when I received terrible news from home right before Christmas. My dad was diagnosed with stage two colorectal cancer and was scheduled to have surgery in a few weeks. Upon hearing this, I felt myself falling apart, heading down into depression again. Friends and churches from different places started praying for my family, asking the Lord to do miraculous healing on my dad. The night before my dad's surgery, God softened his heart and he decided to commit his life to the Lord! Even though my dad went through six months of chemotherapy after the operation, my heart was completely filled with peace and thankfulness in seeing his stubbornness gradually disappearing. With the Lord's blessing, I was also able to complete my Reach year in Lancaster and to grow in Christ through all sorts of training, serving and even difficulties.

Deuteronomy 32v11 (NIV) says, "...like an eagle that stirs up its nest and hovers over its young, that spreads its wings to catch them and carries them on its pinions...."[11] I understand that God is like the mother eagle who must teach her eaglets to fly. Everyone who accepts Him is meant to serve Him in different ways. He didn't want me to stay in my comfortable nest forever, so He stirred my nest and allowed me to

---

[10] www.friendsinternational.org.uk
[11] See Week 10.

go through difficulties so that I could grow into a mature eagle that can soar high in the sky and live a meaningful life.

- Daria Tsai (Kaohsiung City, Taiwan)
May 2011

Blaise Pascal, the 17th century French philosopher and mathematician, once wrote: "There is a God-shaped vacuum in the heart of every man which cannot be filled by any created thing, but only by God, the Creator, made known through Jesus"[12].

Thank You my Father for giving me Jesus. Because of Him, my life is meaningful! There are those in my family and among my friends who have not found Him yet and are trying to fill the hole in their soul with possessions, money, entertainment, sex, work, human approval, religion and others things "under the sun". Grant me the confidence to tell them about Jesus that they too may learn of Your wonderful gift. Prepare their hearts, O God, to accept this gift of eternal life in Jesus, a meaningful and purposeful life under the Son. In His name I pray, amen!

---

[12] The quote is taken from Pascal's *Pensées* ("Thoughts"), a collection of notes which he wrote in defence of Christianity. The book was first published in French in 1669.

Week 45: The Road of Abundance

I have come that they may have life, and that they may
have it more abundantly. (John 10v10b, NKJV)

A Christian pilgrim's life 'under the Son' is meaningful (Week 44) because the road he walks on is a road of abundance, as the words of Jesus above indicate. The word for abundant here in the original Greek is *perissos* which also means extraordinary and superior. Jesus came so that we may *ekho* (to have, to take hold of, to cling fast to) extraordinary, superior and abundant life! The original Greek word for life in this verse is *zoe* which speaks of more than physical life (Greek *psuche[1]*). *Zoe* is life as God intended it to be – life in its absolute fullness, life that is abundant, meaningful and significant[2]. *Zoe* is everlasting or eternal life which can only be experienced by those who receive Jesus as their Saviour and Lord[3]. It is not only for the 'sweet by and by', but also for the present. God desires all people to enjoy *zoe* now and forever!

Why is *zoe* 'under the Son' meaningful and abundant? It is because the Christian is "blessed with *every* spiritual blessing"![4] We have considered many of these spiritual blessings in the previous weeks. In Ephesians 1v3-14 (NLT), Paul names some of them: God chose us and adopted us into His family; He brought us to Himself through Jesus; He poured out His grace on us; He purchased our freedom with Jesus' blood; He forgave our sins; He showered us with His kindness; He gave us His Holy Spirit. These are present-day realities which we can draw on at any time, spiritual blessings that are eternal and inexhaustible, not material and temporal. Every spiritual blessing we need has already been provided. We are eternally rich!

Ephesians 1v12 (NCV) says, "We were chosen so that we would bring praise to God's glory". Based on this, we can say that another specific blessing is that we can now experience the most satisfying and profound human experience possible: worshipping God in a way that gives Him praise, glory and pleasure. God created us to worship

---

[1] *Psuche* means soul or life and implies physical or carnal life. John 12v25 (NIV) reflects the difference between *psuche* and *zoe*: *Anyone who loves their life* ['psuche'] *will lose it, while anyone who hates their life* ['psuche'] *in this world will keep it for eternal life* ['zoe'].

[2] Jesus in effect says in John 10v10: "I have come that they may have abundant life, and have it more abundantly!"

[3] John 5v24 (ESV): *Truly, truly, I say to you, whoever hears My word and believes Him who sent Me has eternal life* ['zoe'].

[4] Ephesians 1v3 (NLT): *All praise to God, the Father of our Lord Jesus Christ, who has blessed us with every spiritual blessing in the heavenly realms because we are united with Christ.*

Him[5]. However, unless He accepts our worship, we will not find the experience as it should be. This is illustrated in the story of Cain and his younger brother Abel, the sons of Adam and Eve. Genesis chapter 4 tells us that both men brought offerings to God as a sign of worship. Cain, the tiller of the soil, brought "*some* of the fruits of the soil" (v3, NIV), whereas Abel, the keeper of flocks, brought "*fat portions* from some of the *firstborn* of his flock" (v4). God "looked with favour" (v4) on Abel's offering, but not on Cain's because Abel worshipped with the right heart and attitude.[6]

Of course we should offer God our very best, not our 'leftovers', but we can never worship Him favourably (with the right heart and attitude) unless we do so "in the beauty of holiness"[7]. Jesus made this possible because when we receive Him as Saviour and Lord, He imputes His righteousness on us[8]. As righteous people in God's eyes, we can now worship Him not only with passion, but also "in the beauty of holiness". Even if our worship cannot compare with the perfection of the angelic choir, God looks upon our offering with favour and we will therefore feel His pleasure. This makes life truly meaningful and abundant!

Ephesians 1v11 (NASB) reads: "In Him (Jesus) also we have obtained an inheritance". Verse 14 says that the Holy Spirit, who lives in every believer, is the guarantee that we will receive all of this inheritance. Part of that inheritance we can now enjoy is *shalom*[9] (the

---

[5] Isaiah 43v7 (NLT): *Bring all who claim Me as their God, for I have made them for My glory. It was I who created them.* To worship God means to give Him proper recognition of His greatness and worth by giving Him the glory, praise, honour, and service which He deserves. Worship is a response to who He is and what He does. Because we were created to worship, man will always be looking to worship someone, even self, or something if he refuses to worship God.

[6] Unlike Cain's, Abel's offering was generous, thoughtful and his best. He chose firstborn animals as a sign of his recognition that God was the source of his possessions and that He owns everything.

[7] Psalm 96v9 (AMP): *O worship the Lord in the beauty of holiness; tremble before and reverently fear Him, all the earth.*

[8] For all who would receive Jesus as Saviour and Lord, a 'divine exchange' had been made possible on the cross: our sins for Jesus' righteousness. Jesus was credited with our sins, and His righteousness was credited to or 'imputed' on us. We are reckoned to be righteous and on this basis, we are 'justified' or declared to be righteous by God (4th footnote, Week 43). Experientially, we are not righteous or holy like Jesus (who never sinned at all), but God legally considers us righteous because of the imputation of Christ's righteousness on us through the divine exchange. This means therefore that all our sins, past, present and future, have already been washed away by the blood of Jesus and we have the assurance of life in heaven (Week 4). However, this does not give us licence to sin because sin brings God's discipline and the possible loss of rewards (Week 33). Confession and repentance are therefore necessary (Week 38). Apostasy, the renunciation of faith in Jesus, is a renunciation of this divine exchange and *zoe*.

[9] As in Isaiah 26v3 (ESV): *You keep him in perfect peace* ['shalom'] *whose mind is stayed on You, because he trusts in You.*

Hebrew word in the Old Testament), or *eirene*[10] (the equivalent Greek word in the New Testament). These words are often translated into English as 'peace', but they actually mean much more for they also mean wholeness, completeness, welfare, security, well-being, harmony, tranquillity, rest, contentment, fulfilment, blessedness, prosperity[11]. *Shalom/eirene* therefore is abundant life! The Old Testament points to the fact that one can only find true *shalom* in a covenant relationship with God, and therefore, in God's word or *logos,* for one in covenant with God cannot neglect His written *logos* (Week 8). *Eirene* in the New Testament practically means the same thing as *shalom*, but it takes on a new dimension in that *eirene* is *shalom* that comes to a person in a covenant relationship with God through Jesus, the living Word or *Logos* of God (Week 8). Therefore, one cannot have *shalom/eirene* without daily laying down his *psuche* (this week's 1st footnote) and honouring his covenant with God by surrendering to and abiding in Jesus the Christ, *Yeshua ha Mashiach.* When you abide in Him[12], you will have *shalom/eirene* despite your circumstances because Jesus is *Sar Shalom*, the Prince of Peace![13]

In the following weeks we will look into more of these spiritual blessings. Meanwhile, meditate on the names/titles of God in Appendix 1. These reflect His blessings because they speak not only of who He is, but also of what He does for us and why *zoe* in Christ is truly meaningful and abundant! May the next story of a lady who discovered that Jesus had laid before her a "road of abundance" be a blessing of encouragement to you.

Shannon's Story

Honestly speaking, my life had been watched over by God since the day I was born in the year 1983. As a baby only forty days old, I was sent to a paediatrics centre after catching a terrible flu. While staying at the centre, I was infected with salmonella which eventually found its way into my brain. My parents sent me to a local emergency centre where shortly afterwards, I was diagnosed with severe meningitis. The paediatricians at the hospital had to exercise first aid resuscitation on me whenever I went into severe spasm. Each time they did, an imminent death notice was issued to my parents, asking them to prepare for the worst. My grandma

---

[10] As in Romans 1v7 (NIV): *Grace and peace* ['eirene'] *to you from God our Father and from the Lord Jesus Christ.*

[11] It is prosperity in mind, body and spirit as implied in 3 John v2 (AMP): *Beloved, I pray that you may prosper in every way and [that your body] may keep well, even as [I know] your soul keeps well and prospers.*

[12] 1 John 2v28 (ESV): *And now, little children, abide in Him, so that when He appears we may have confidence and not shrink from Him in shame at His coming.* To "abide in Christ" is to remain in fellowship with Him.

[13] Isaiah 9v6 (ESV): *For to us a Child is born, to us a Son is given; and the government shall be upon His shoulder, and His name shall be called Wonderful Counsellor, Mighty God, Everlasting Father, Prince of Peace* ['Sar Shalom'].

Tsai, who was already a Christian then, desperately prayed for me in the hospital every night. She and her entire church group prayed by my bedside and asked God for a miracle. Amazingly, after two months in the hospital, my condition stabilised and I miraculously recovered without any trauma or functional damage to my brain. God heard and answered my grandma's prayers. Even before I came to know Him, He sent an angel to pray for me and eventually, saved me!

As a Taiwanese kid, I was very blessed to have experiences other Taiwanese kids never had. When I was five, my family moved to and lived in the United States for three years. Those years contained some of my best life memories. From my experiences in the US, I developed a strong passion for English and English literature. As a kid attending school in the States, I began building my love for reading and writing English stories. Thanks to my parents, when my family moved back to Taiwan, we brought back tons of English books. These books varied in themes and writing styles and reading them became my biggest hobby. After reading each one, I loved to create my own stories.

As a youngster in school, my overall grades were not satisfactory at all. Yet, English was always my secret weapon for success! I do believe that God knew that I was not an all-round strong learner like most of my other classmates, and He took care of it. When the time came for me to apply for university, I realised that I was not only unique in not being required to take entrance examinations, I was also, perhaps unlike most Taiwanese students, very clear on what I wanted to major in – English. Thus, I spent four wonderful years studying English and English literature in university.

After university, I applied for and got accepted into an English post-graduate program. Considering my passion for English literature, I thought that it would be another great experience. However, my post-graduate studies were tough and I had a very rough time completing my master's thesis. I would never have imagined that studying what I loved the most could make me suffer so much. This thought tormented me greatly and I hit rock bottom. Suddenly, my passion in life was smashed and it felt like I was left with nothing to live for. I started seriously doubting my commitment to English literature as well as doubting my own abilities. I started shutting myself off from the world, as I found that the words and judgment from my teachers and family only brought more despair and misery instead of the real comfort that I so badly needed. Even though I still completed my degree, I knew that something inside me had been forever changed by the trauma I experienced and I feared that I may never reclaim that same passion I used to feel for English literature.

Even when I felt lost in my broken self, God still looked after me. Before my graduation, God already had a great job opportunity prepared for me. For my first attempt at job hunting, I was able to successfully get a job that related to my love for literature and that allowed me to utilise my English skills. He miraculously provided jobs for my sister and me at the same institute in Taipei, so we were able to keep each other company when starting a new life in the new city. For this, I am truly grateful, for God understood how much I needed the support of my family. Above all, God led me to Taipei Glory Church, a local church that is not far from where we live.[14] After attending this church every week for only a few months, I started to feel the change and growth in me. I was very much aware that God was leading me back to Him.

In the past I had attended church regularly, but I knew, and I believe God knew as well, that my heart was not truly passionate for Him. I could not really feel the presence of God with me outside of church. I used to consider attending church simply as a routine or stipulation I had to follow and Christianity was not a part of my daily life. Sometimes, I even felt embarrassed by my religion, especially when I had to pray in front of others. Attending Taipei Glory Church changed my life dramatically. I started to restore intimate connections with God and the Church. For the first time in my life, I truly considered my church as my family. God started healing me from deep within. He guided me to boldly face all my past and present problems, whether comprehensible or incomprehensible. He placed me in a wonderful church group and surrounded me with His healing love through the loving care of my fellow group members. They made me feel at home even when in fact, I was in a city far away from home. I learned to build a strong relationship with God through the Holy Spirit and I started becoming a devoted believer for the first time in my life!

The most inspiring lesson God taught me at Taipei Glory Church was the lesson of faith. In the past, I used to have very little faith and self-confidence. The only times I felt strong and powerful in God were after attending church or special Christian sessions and conferences. Nevertheless, this feeling of strong faith usually faded quickly and eventually vanished when I returned to my everyday life outside of church. Especially after my traumatic experience in post-graduate school, it became extremely difficult for me to believe in God when I could not see the road ahead. However, God understood my difficulty and in a Christian healing conference a month ago, He miraculously healed me of my trauma and doubts. He not only restored my faith in Him, He also made me see that He is undoubtedly the one and only true God, and that His intention was to heal me of my weaknesses, for the road He has laid before me is a road of abundance. Shortly after the healing conference, God once again proved His trustworthiness when He answered my long-term prayer – to serve Him in the choir and glorify Him through worship. Thanks to the Lord, this experience turned out to be so much more than I had expected!

Looking back on my past and also reflecting on my future, I realise how blessed I am to have God alongside me, guiding me every step of the way. Even when I could

---

[14] www.glorychurch.org.tw

not see the path, He was always there for me. I believe God is leading me back onto the right path – the path He has for my life – which is a meaningful life destined for Him. Through His careful guidance, I have been healed and redefined as a new-born being in His eyes. Though of course there will be lots of obstacles and struggles along the way, with God's amazing power invested within me, I truly believe that I can accomplish anything through Him.

God saved me from early death as a baby, healed me of my traumatic experience in post-graduate school and blessed me with a job that allows me to use my passion and skills in English. Amazing as these are, they cannot compare with the blessing of a greater passion He has given me – a passion for Him!

- Shannon Lee (Taipei, Taiwan)
July 2011

Shalom (abundant life) is the climax of the priestly benediction which God commanded Aaron and his sons to pray over His people as they blessed them[15]. For you, this is the priestly blessing of Jesus, our High Priest forever[16]. May you know in experience God's *shalom/eirene*, and that your life in Jesus is eternal, meaningful and abundant.

---

[15] Aaron, from the tribe of Levi and Moses' elder brother, was the first High Priest of Israel. His sons and subsequent male descendants, "sons of Aaron", were all priests, with the eldest son or any worthy son of the current High Priest inheriting the position. The High Priest represented God to the people, and the people to God. It was only the High Priest who could go once a year, only on the Day of Atonement (*Yom Kippur*), into God's throne room, the Holy of Holies, in the Tabernacle of Moses and subsequently, the Temple in Jerusalem. (See Week 35.)

[16] Hebrews 6v19-20 (NIV): *We have this hope as an anchor for the soul, firm and secure. It enters the inner sanctuary* [the Holy of Holies or Most Holy Place] *behind the curtain, where our forerunner, Jesus, has entered on our behalf. He has become a high priest forever, in the order of Melchizedek.* Jesus is the ultimate High Priest who entered God's throne room not with the blood of animals, but with His own blood as atonement for our sins. He is different from the previous High Priests in that He was born into the tribe of Judah (the tribe of the Davidic kings), not of Levi. Melchizedek (which means 'king of righteousness' according to Hebrews 7v2) was the King of Salem (Salem = Peace) in Genesis 14 who blessed Abraham. Genesis 14v18 tells us that he was "priest of *El Elyon*" (God Most High). Melchizedek was therefore a king-priest. Jesus' priesthood is of the "order of Melchizedek" in this sense. The writer of Hebrews shows us that Christ's priesthood is superior to the old Levitical order and therefore, to the priesthood of Aaron (Hebrews 7v1-10). Because Jesus' sacrifice was perfect, He only needed to present the sacrifice of His own blood once and for all people who would believe, not like the Aaronic priests who had to present to God the blood of animals every year. God showed His acceptance of and pleasure for Jesus' sacrifice when He tore from top to bottom the thick curtain of the Holy of Holies on the day Jesus was crucified (Matthew 27v51). The tearing symbolised that God was opening access to Him to all people who would come through *Yeshua ha Mashiach*. Access to meaningful, abundant and eternal life is available through Him!

Week 45: The Road of Abundance

And may –

The Lord bless you and keep you;
The Lord make His face to shine upon you and be gracious to you;
The Lord lift up His countenance upon you
and give you peace ['shalom'].
(Numbers 6v24-26, ESV)

Week 46: The Supernatural Road

God also testified to it by signs, wonders and various miracles, and gifts of the Holy Spirit distributed according to His will. (Hebrews 2v4, NIV)

In the days of the early Church, as described in the book of Acts, God testified to the validity of the gospel message of salvation through faith in Jesus (the "it" in the verse above) by signs, wonders and miracles. There are still many people today whom God wants to reach with the gospel and this is why we can expect the supernatural (signs, wonders and miracles) to naturally accompany us (Week 26) as we go about doing what God wants us to do.

In 1 Corinthians 12, Paul talks about "spiritual gifts" which show that the Holy Spirit is operating supernaturally through an individual. (These are listed and briefly explained in Appendix 3.) Paul adds that it is the Holy Spirit who determines what spiritual gift or gifts each believer should have[1]. These gifts are supernatural signs which are meant to point people to Jesus, the One the Holy Spirit seeks to glorify[2]. They are also intended to build up the Church[3], the community of believers, and are not to be used for selfish motives. Simon the Sorcerer (2nd footnote, Week 26) wanted spiritual gifts so that he could show-off, whereas the Holy Spirit's purpose is to show-off no one but Jesus. Simon's wrong motive apparently led him to accept satan's counterfeit gifts instead.

Wrong motives and wrong heart attitudes can indeed cause us to fall into satan's trap. This warning becomes more and more important as Jesus' second coming approaches. Many believe that Joel 2v28-29[4], which was partially fulfilled on Pentecost Day (Acts 2), will be completely fulfilled just before Jesus' return and that God will pour out His Spirit, not just for people to have prophetic dreams and visions, but also for God's servants to move in signs, wonders and miracles to reveal to the world the glory of the

---

[1] 1 Corinthians 12v11 (NIV): *All these are the work of one and the same Spirit, and He distributes them to each one, just as He determines.* This means that the Holy Spirit has a spiritual gift or gifts for YOU! One can pray for certain gifts, but it is God who makes the decision.

[2] John 16v14 (ESV): *He [the Holy Spirit] will glorify Me, for He will take what is Mine and declare it to you.*

[3] 1 Corinthians 14v12 (ESV): *So with yourselves, since you are eager for manifestations of the Spirit, strive to excel in building up the church.*

[4] Joel 2v28-29 (ESV): *And it shall come to pass afterward, that I will pour out My Spirit on all flesh; your sons and your daughters shall prophesy, your old men shall dream dreams, and your young men shall see visions. Even on the male and female servants in those days I will pour out My Spirit.*

Lord in order to bring many people into the Kingdom of God. The Bible warns that there will also be an increase of signs, wonders and miracles that are from the devil, the great deceiver[5]. Those who do not believe in Jesus are more likely to fall prey to these counterfeit supernatural manifestations[6]. However, even the most mature Christian needs to ask the Holy Spirit for discernment because if one thinks he can never be deceived, he is already deceived. We stand strong only by the grace of God!

Stories are included in the Bible not to entertain us, but to encourage, warn and teach us (as with the stories in this devotional). Let us look at two stories from which we can draw lessons regarding our walk on the supernatural road.

The first is the story of Ananias and Sapphira in Acts 5. Many of the believers in the young Church were selling properties and voluntarily giving the money to the apostles to be used for the Lord's work. Ananias and his wife Sapphira sold a piece of property and presented the money to Peter. Although they had the right to hold back some of the money, they lied to Peter (and the Holy Spirit) by pretending that they were giving the whole amount. They did this in order to appear generous and spiritual. This was during a very important and critical period in the history of the Church, the beginning of the Church age. So that new believers would not think that they could sin and get away with it, God's discipline on the couple was prompt and decisive – they were struck dead there and then![7] Child of God, we are approaching another important and critical period in the history of the Church, the end of the current Church age which will culminate in the return of our Lord (Week 51). Let us

---

[5] Matthew 24v24 (NLT): *For false messiahs and false prophets will rise up and perform great signs and wonders so as to deceive, if possible, even God's chosen ones.*

[6] These signs and wonders will deceive people into thinking they are acts of God when it fact they are of the devil. This is the reason why *"a time is coming when people will no longer listen to sound and wholesome teaching. They will follow their own desires and will look for teachers who will tell them whatever their itching ears want to hear. They will reject the truth and chase after myths"* (2 Timothy 4v3-4, NLT).

[7] This incident shows that God can choose to punish people with immediate physical death in order to guard the integrity, purity and unity of the Church, the 'Bride of Christ'. This can happen even to those who are believers and yet deliberately sin and remain unrepentant. This serves as a warning for Christians to take seriously the consequences of deliberate (carefully weighed, studied, intentional) sinning. *God cannot be mocked* (Galatians 6v7, NIV)! 1 Corinthians 5v5 (NIV) says, *Hand this man* [the immoral Christian in the preceding verses] *over to satan for the destruction of the flesh, so that his spirit may be saved on the day of the Lord.* The untimely death of a Christian who deliberately sins or continues in a lifestyle of sin actually shows God's mercy in that God takes the action either to prevent the person from committing a sin that will cause more damage to him and to the Church, or to prevent him from going down the path of apostasy and then be eternally lost. See also 8th footnote of Week 43.

use His spiritual gifts in the reverential fear of God to glorify Him and not ourselves, and certainly not for selfish gain.

The other story is that of the Roman centurion in Matthew 8. He came to Jesus for the sake of his servant who was very ill, but he suggested to Jesus that there was no need for Him to physically go to where his servant was because he believed that the servant would be healed by just a word from Jesus. He explained to Jesus that as a centurion, he was a man under authority and with authority over other soldiers who would obey him when he gave them orders. The centurion understood that just as he had authority over his soldiers because he himself submitted to the authority above him, Jesus had authority over demons, illnesses and diseases because He submitted to the Father. Jesus commended him for his "great faith" and told him to return to his servant who would be healed as he believed. And it was so. Child of God, remember this principle especially in the use of the spiritual gifts God gives you: you have no authority against the devil and his demons if you yourself are not submitted to authority. So stay submitted to Jesus and to all people who have legitimate civil or religious authority over you[8].

The following stories testify that the road we walk on is indeed a supernatural one. May these stories encourage and prepare you to receive the spiritual gifts God wants to give you, and to move in signs, wonders and miracles according to His directions.

An Angelic Visitation

This reminiscence of mine is one of first hand, but without being present at the event nor even immediately after the event. The couple in question, Lee and Margaret Brown, had married late in life after having raised their families from earlier marriages. Both Lee and Margaret were tender-hearted toward the Lord's work in their personal lives.

By the time Margaret and Lee married (they were both grandparents), each had their share of elder-illnesses, although both were doing mostly well at the time of this event. They had relocated to a sleepy coastal town on the Atlantic shore of Florida. While there, they were privileged to become charter members of a new Presbyterian church.

---

[8]   1 Peter 2v13-15 (NIV): *Submit yourselves for the Lord's sake to every human authority: whether to the emperor, as the supreme authority, or to governors, who are sent by him to punish those who do wrong and to commend those who do right. For it is God's will that by doing good you should silence the ignorant talk of foolish people.* The emperor at the time Peter wrote this letter was the brutal Nero who had many Christians murdered. Does this mean that Christians should obey evil authorities or Christian leaders who are not doing God's will? To submit does not necessarily mean to obey, but it does mean to respect and to honour. Our obedience to any person, human institution or law should never violate our obedience to God and His law. Acts 5v29 (NIV) says, *We must obey God rather than human beings!*

The congregation remained small although they were able to build an attractive brick church along a busy business route. Within the congregation, everyone knew everyone else, and when visitors came to services, the visitors were appropriately noticed and acknowledged.

For many months the Browns had been unable to attend church during a period of cancer treatment for Lee. God had prevailed on Lee's behalf and this particular Sunday was their first back to worship service in many months. That Sunday morning, they were warmly welcomed back by their friends in a spirit of love and rejoicing for Lee's return to health.

As the Browns exited carefully down the church's front steps, a handsome, well-dressed man was coming UP the steps and greeted them. "Lee, it is so good to see you back again!", remarked the man and the customary "Thank you" left the couple's lips automatically, but also with perplexity. They stopped and looked at each other, each asking the other the same question: "Do *you* know him?", referencing the visitor who had now entered the church's small foyer. Neither of the Browns had recognised this gentleman, yet the visitor had even addressed Mr. Brown by his first name, Lee.

Margaret was never one to slight someone by not fully acknowledging a kind word such as this gentleman had given. Leaving Lee anchored to the railing, she quickly returned back into the foyer, but the visitor was nowhere in sight. With only a few classrooms, restrooms and office, it didn't take more than a couple minutes to make her rounds looking for him. Each of the regular members still present was asked the same: Had they seen the nice looking stranger? And she related to them his wardrobe and appearance details. The answers were all in agreement: "No, had not seen a soul come back in, much less a visitor of that description."

Years prior to their marriage, Mrs. Brown had been a part of a faith-filled ladies' Bible study group in Alabama where she had been able to share the benefits of a more mature walk with the Lord. The idea of miracles had already entered her daily walk with Him, and this particular experience at church that Sunday in Florida fit a certain category of events.

Returning to Lee, Margaret filled him in on her search, and that no one had seen anyone at all enter the church. Looking Lee squarely in the eye, Margaret realised what the conclusion meant in her walk of faith. They had experienced an encounter with an angel of the Lord that day!

Where they had been perplexed only ten minutes before, the Browns were now wide-eyed with wonder over that realisation. A perfectly ordinary Sunday had been transformed by an encounter which took less than a minute!

Having wondered prior to their return to church if Lee's health and healing would stabilise and remain, their conclusion now was "Yes!". It certainly would be as the Lord Himself had sent a greeting to commemorate the event!

This encounter was related to me a few months later when Margaret and I were getting caught up on family news. I, too, had been a part of that ladies' home Bible study group in Alabama, and knew that Margaret would not spread any stories or misconceptions regarding the event.

Since then, I have never doubted that the Browns had an encounter with an angel of the Lord, and have never doubted that the same attention or visitation could happen to any other Christian believer. God is faithful, and extends His care toward us daily. It is up to us to be in the place where He wants us to be – in the case of the Browns, their return to Sunday worship at their first opportunity to praise and thank the Lord for Lee's recuperation – and for us believers, to remain *alert* to God working in our lives. That day, it was the Browns' delight to be honoured with this angelic visitation. Reflecting upon that event is certainly a call to me as well to maintain such an alertness in my own life.

- Gayle Haffner (Davison, Michigan, USA)
April 2011

My Friend was Shot

Yes she was! Or was she?

In the mid-seventies, my friend Lorri, who was a Jehovah's Witness for fifteen years, found the Jesus of the Bible after a gentleman began witnessing to her. He later became her husband and they embarked on a new life together. Through the subsequent years, the ministry they formed was to be used by the Lord to lead hundreds and hundreds of people out of the various cult groups that claim to be "Christian" to freedom in a saving relationship with Jesus Christ. I was one of those people she 'de-programmed' after my exposure to one of these groups. Lorri had become a close personal friend and told me this account.

Lorri and Keith had travelled to a Christian conference in Phoenix, Arizona. In between speakers, Lorri went out to their R.V. (recreational vehicle, a camper van or caravan) in the parking lot to retrieve some of her ministry pamphlets for an evangelist they had met at the meeting. Just before she left to get them, Keith called out to her, "Let me keep your purse while you go out." He soon followed this with, "I don't know why I said that!" She replied, "I don't know either, but here it is," and tossed it to him after taking out her keys. The purse had all their credit cards, money, I.D. etc.

Lorri reached the R.V.'s living room and entered it, but didn't close the door behind her. Just then a man got in and pointing a gun at her, demanded money. At that moment the most incredible wave of fear washed over her. My friend believes that if you have enough of the Word of God "in your gizzard", it rises up when you need it. The first thing that came to her mind was, "God has not given us a spirit of fear" (2 Timothy 1v7, NKJV), and "Perfect love casts out fear" (1 John 4v18, NKJV). Then she calmed down and said, "Young man, if you need money, I will gladly give you money. You don't have to live a life like this." Standing resolute, she added, "Jesus changed my life. He can change your life too. You don't have to steal money from me. I will gladly give it to you in the name of Jesus because Jesus loves you and everything I have belongs to Jesus."

Apparently unaffected by this, the man proceeded to search the van, all the while holding the gun on her and insisting repeatedly that she give him money. All this time, Lorri was perfectly calm (although she confided she got shaky later when it was all over); she just felt the peace of the Lord. She kept on witnessing to him, "Jesus can change your life. I don't care what kind of trouble you're in. Jesus is the answer. He loves you and I love you and want to tell you about Jesus."

When he realised there was no money, the man backed down the stairs to a waiting car and said, "I'm sorry lady. I didn't really want to hurt you!" He then pulled the trigger and left. After the incredible BANG of the gun and the smell of gun powder, Lorri just kept saying, "Jesus, Jesus, Jesus!" because she thought, "If I'm going to die, I'll die with the name of Jesus on my lips!"

The men were gone, the R.V. was quiet and after about twenty Jesus-es, Lorri noticed she still wasn't dead! She slowly surveyed the damage, but there didn't appear to be any. "Oh," she thought, "he used a blank!", and ran inside the building to find her husband and to call the police.

The blank theory worked okay until the police found the bullet all mushroomed up in a corner of the van. Even though he had shot her at point blank range with a REAL bullet, Lorri was not harmed! However, when she changed into her night clothes that evening, she found a number of bullet holes in the BACK of the skirt of her dress even though he shot her facing her!

That night when Lorri's mother thanked the Lord for saving her daughter, the Lord revealed to her in prayer that the man who shot her was a messenger of the enemy[9], sent to destroy Lorri and Keith's ministry as it was just beginning. In the subsequent thirty-five years, thousands of souls have been set free from cults through the efforts

---

[9]   Satan, the devil, is the believer's enemy.

of their ministry, as God saw fit. They have taught, preached, fostered and promoted the gospel of Christ through all forms of media including radio, television and the printed word[10].

Lorri's story appeared in their local newspaper in Nelson, British Columbia. There's a photo of her holding the dress up with her fingers through the bullet holes, a testimony of the fact that our God is an awesome God. He is mighty to save!

- Linda Greenfield (Ontario, Canada)
February 2011

In the book of Acts, people were added to the Church because of the preaching of the apostles with a demonstration of "signs, wonders and miracles". Acts 5v12, 14-16 (ESV) says: "Now many signs and wonders were regularly done among the people by the hands of the apostles…. And more than ever believers were added to the Lord, multitudes of both men and women, so that they even carried out the sick into the streets and laid them on cots and mats, that as Peter came by at least his shadow might fall on some of them. The people also gathered from the towns around Jerusalem, bringing the sick and those afflicted with unclean spirits, and they were all healed."

In his first letter to the Corinthian church of his day, the apostle Paul wrote: "My message and my preaching were not with wise and persuasive words, but with a demonstration of the Spirit's power, so that your faith might not rest on human wisdom, but on God's power" (1 Corinthians 2v4-5, NIV).

There are still many people, even people you know, who need to hear the good news about Jesus. God does not want anyone of them to go to hell and perish. He wants them to come to His Kingdom![11] Do you want God to use you to reach them? Remember His promise in Mark 16 (Week 26).

Almighty God, give Your servant, the reader, great boldness in preaching Your word. Stretch out Your hand with healing power! May miraculous signs and wonders be done by Your servant through the name of Jesus to set free those who are still held captive by satan[12]. May Your power and authority be demonstrated in Your servant's life as he/she walks on the supernatural road for Jesus' glory. Amen!

---

[10]   Visit mmoutreachinc.com for more information.

[11]   2 Peter 3v9 (NASB): *The Lord is not slow about His promise, as some count slowness, but is patient toward you, not wishing for any to perish but for all to come to repentance.*

[12]   Acts 4v29-30 (NLT): *And now, O Lord, hear their threats, and give us, Your servants, great boldness in preaching Your word. Stretch out Your hand with healing power; may miraculous signs and wonders be done through the name of Your holy servant Jesus.*

Week 47: The Road of Breakthroughs

The breaker goes up before them. They break out, pass through the gate and
go out by it. So their king goes on before them, and the Lord at their head.
(Micah 2v13, NASB)

Although we cannot see them with our natural eyes, the reality is that satan and his cohorts are at war with believers and God does not want us to be like sitting ducks. As part of our spiritual blessings, we have been given spiritual weapons (for both defensive and offensive spiritual warfare)[1] that are able to demolish demonic strongholds (Week 43). The effectiveness of these weapons and that of our spiritual gifts (Appendix 3) is guaranteed by these incredible promises given by Jesus to His followers – Acts 1v8 and Luke 10v19.

Acts 1v8 (NIV) declares, "But you will receive *power* when the Holy Spirit comes on you; and you will be My witnesses in Jerusalem, and in all Judea and Samaria, and to the ends of the earth". The Greek word for power here is *dunamis*, from which we get the word dynamite. *Dunamis* is a manifestation of the Holy Spirit working through a believer, as demonstrated by the acts of the apostles in the book of Acts. Paul says in 1 Corinthians 2v4-5 (NIV): "My message and my preaching were not with wise and persuasive words, but with a demonstration of the Spirit's power (*dunamis*), so that your faith might not rest on men's wisdom, but on God's power (*dunamis*)". Just like Jesus and the first believers, Christians today are to use God's *dunamis* to bring His Kingdom to people who are held captive by the enemy. Because *dunamis* is related to anointing (see 3rd footnote of Week 13), its manifestation differs from believer to believer, and this is determined by the Holy Spirit.

Jesus in Luke 10v19 (NIV) says, "I have given you *authority* to trample on snakes and scorpions and to overcome all the power (*dunamis*) of the enemy". The Greek word for authority here is *exousia*. This same word also appears in John 1v12 where it is translated as 'right' in the NIV: "Yet to all who received Him, to those who believed in His name, He gave the right (*exousia*) to become children of God." Your *exousia* is your delegated right and authority given by Jesus to represent the *dunamis* of God (the ultimate source of *dunamis* and *exousia*) whose will must be obeyed. *Exousia* exercises the right to command and *dunamis* enforces that command, hence why demons obeyed when Jesus and the apostles commanded them to leave. Jesus passed on His *exousia* to us to continue His ministry on earth and the Holy Spirit still empowers believers today. To advance God's Kingdom, we have the privilege and responsibility to use this God-given *dunamis* and *exousia* according to His will.

---

[1] These weapons are discussed in Appendix 4.

The believer may be directed by God to move in His *dunamis* in a spiritual battle by using his spiritual weapons and spiritual gifts (like the gift of healing or the working of miracles). But in all spiritual battles, he is expected to use his God-given *exousia*. Satan, who has *dunamis* but was not given *exousia* on earth, coveted man's *exousia* (dominion right[2]) that was given to humanity at creation. Adam handed this over to satan when he succumbed to his temptation. Jesus regained it for every human being who would believe in Him by buying it back with His own precious blood! He says in Luke 4v18-19 (NLT): "The Spirit of the Lord is upon Me, for He has anointed Me to bring Good News to the poor. He has sent Me to proclaim that captives will be released, that the blind will see, that the oppressed will be set free, and that the time of the Lord's favour has come". Just as the Father sent Jesus and just as the Holy Spirit anointed Him to do the Father's will on earth, *you have been sent and anointed to will God's will on earth as He is willing it in heaven* by using your delegated *exousia* against the demonic forces that are trying to destroy your faith and resolve. This means that you choose to resist the enemy's words and to believe in God's *rhema* word which can be a confirmed prophetic word given to you (Week 14), or a relevant scripture from the Bible that God had highlighted to you. It means that you speak those words over the discouraging or tempting situation and that despite your circumstances, you choose to believe in God's faithfulness and refuse to get into a pity-party. You also remember who God is (Appendix 1) and who you are in Jesus (Appendix 2), you persevere in prayer, and you stay submitted to His authority and other legitimate authority over you[3]. If you step out of being under authority (8th footnote, Week 46), you are like a sitting duck!

The verse in Micah above is 'messianic'; i.e., it speaks about the Messiah who would come. Jesus, the Messiah, is the Breaker, King and Lord. He is the Way Maker who makes the impossible possible! If you are a Christian, you are now His representative on earth. He calls you to use His *dunamis* and especially His *exousia* to break open the way for God's will to be done and for God's Kingdom to come into your situation as well as into other people's lives or circumstances. Take the baton and use it for His glory. You will discover for yourself that the road you walk on is a road of breakthroughs!

Here is a story from a former post-graduate student in Lancaster who now has an experiential knowledge of Jesus as the Way Maker. A prophetic word was spoken over her. She could not foresee how it would come about, especially because of a string of disappointments. But she reminded herself of who God is and chose to see a 'closed door' as divine intervention. Then the breakthrough in the battle for her future came.

---

[2] Psalm 8v6 (NKJV): *You have made him* [man] *to have dominion over the works of Your hands.*
[3] So that the enemy has no ammunition against us, we need to keep away from sin, and quickly confess and repent of any sin committed.

Jesus, the Way Maker

One night in a prayer line at church, a pastor prophesied to me and told me that the Lord had plans to bless me financially in a big way. He said he was seeing that I was about to get lots of money. Of course for a moment I was confused, since I was looking for a job with no avail. I had gone to interviews after interviews and although they went well, I still was not selected for the jobs that I applied for. So I wondered where all this money was going to come from. Even if I did get a job, I would not be able to get a decent salary because of my lack of work experience. Anyway, as fast as I began to doubt, I immediately remembered who God was and is.

While I was applying for jobs, I was also applying to local and international universities and for a scholarship to do my Master's degree. However, I preferred a local university over a foreign one because I had hoped to work and bring in extra cash while studying part-time. I knew balancing the two commitments would be difficult, but I wanted to earn the money to purchase a car.

I prayed and asked God for the wisdom to make the right decisions throughout the entire process. I also asked Him for His will to be done. But I didn't hear God's answer and I continued to struggle with the decision of whether to go away and study full time or stay in my country and study part-time, provided that I got a job. Going to England for my Master's degree looked appealing because I would finish in one year as compared with the two and a half years of study in my local university. However, if I got a scholarship, it would not allow me to work to secure the finances to buy my car. Additionally, I would be away from my family, friends and ministry – something I had never done before. Separation from family and friends bothered me a lot since I was a big 'family person' and I had now started to grow in ministry.

Eventually, the Lord began orchestrating events that would assure me later on that "God causes all things to work together for good to those who love God, to those who are called according to His purpose" (Romans 8v28, NASB). Not only did God close the doors to a job, He also closed the door at my local university[4]. This was by far the most surprising and disappointing event because I didn't consider for one moment that the university where I had previously earned my Bachelor's degree – the same university where I did excellently, having gained a first class degree – would reject my application! This was very unnatural and it was then that I knew that this must be God's intervention. With that rejection from my local university and no job, I knew that my only hope was to go abroad and study full time.

---

[4]   Revelation 3v7b (NLT): *What He opens, no one can close; and what He closes, no one can open.*

262

One afternoon I received a call which informed me that I had been awarded the full scholarship I had applied for to study at any university of my choice. The scholarship would include a plane ticket to and from England, payment of tuition fees, a book allowance, a clothing allowance, a laptop computer allowance and monthly payments to cover accommodation, food and other necessities over the course of one year. I was elated!

The entire process from applying to universities in England (I was accepted to all and opted to go to Lancaster University) to obtaining my student visa went smoothly. Before I knew it, I was saying my goodbyes to my family at the airport. With tear-filled eyes but strength in my soul, I walked humbly but confidently to the plane. Not knowing what lay beyond, I whispered as the plane began to lift off, "Jesus, it's You and I from here on now!"

God wanted me to depend on Him completely. He wanted to build my faith. He wanted to work on the inside of me. He separated me to take me to a higher place with Him like He did with all the great men of God in the Bible – Noah, Abraham, Moses and others.

In that year I grew spiritually, and although there were times I fell, I didn't stay down. I learned to love people more. I learned to be joyful and content. I learned to exercise my faith. I was involved in ministries that I wasn't involved in back at home and God used me in a mightier way to touch people's lives. I made lots of friends from around the world and I even found a best friend. To this day, even though we are physically apart, she continues to be a blessing in my life. I even got to travel and see my family within that year which lessened the pain of not seeing them at all. I also discovered an amazing technological tool, 'skype', which I did not know existed before and which allowed me to talk to and see my family and friends back home in real time without any cost for an unlimited period of time. God just continued to work things out for me!

The pastor's prophecy was made reality. The money he saw was in the form of the scholarship I received that was worth close to $200,000 in my currency. But God didn't stop there. With the scholarship came a guaranteed job upon my return to my country. I am now employed with the government and I am earning a decent salary – much more than I would have had I been successful in my previous job applications! I also now have a Master's Degree from a university that holds more recognition and credibility than my local university. I am back at my local church and I'm stronger in my ministry than before I left. What's more, I also managed to save a lot of money in England from my scholarship allowances and was able to purchase my car without having to work!

Indeed, God knows the plans He has for His children. When I thought He didn't hear or care, He was actually working behind the scenes to give me the desires of my heart. I can testify to the truth of what Ephesians 3v20 says (NKJV): "He is able to do exceedingly abundantly above all that we ask or think, according to the power[5] that works in us". Bless the Lord oh my soul and all that is within me, bless His holy name!

- Samantha Glasgow (Trinidad and Tobago)
April 2011

Dear God, help me to see every crisis as an opportunity for the Divine Breaker to show up and break a way through for me, and every disappointment as a divine appointment with Him to help me break out of situations or habits that hinder me from fulfilling my assignments. Guide me as I exercise the dunamis and exousia You have granted me as Your child to break the strongholds that imprison people. Use me to preach the Good News, to heal the sick and to raise the dead according to Your way, time and purpose. For Jesus' sake, amen!

---

[5] The original Greek word for power here is *dunamis*. This is the NIV rendition of this verse: *Now to Him who is able to do immeasurably more than all we ask or imagine, according to His power that is at work within us...* God's power can work in and through you more than you can ever imagine!

Week 48: The Romans 8v28 Road

And we know that God causes everything to work together
for the good of those who love God and are called according
to His purpose for them. (Romans 8v28, NLT)

One of the most popular stories in the Bible is the victory of Israel in the conquest of Jericho under the leadership of Joshua in Joshua chapter six. Even those who have never read the Bible most likely have heard about the incredible story of the fall of Jericho after Israel followed a seemingly ridiculous strategy given by God. The victory no doubt was a miracle and could only be attributed to God's presence in the midst of His people.

Then comes chapter seven, an altogether different story, a story of Israel's unexpected and humiliating defeat at the next battle for a much smaller city named Ai. Joshua asked the Lord why He had let them down, and the Lord's answer was, "Israel has sinned; they have violated my covenant, which I commanded them to keep. They have taken some of the devoted things; they have stolen, they have lied, they have put them with their own possessions. That is why the Israelites cannot stand against their enemies" (Joshua 7v11-12a, NIV). God had classified Jericho (the first city in the Promised Land that He gave to Israel) and everything in it as *cherem*, to be devoted to God[1]. Despite Joshua's warning to the people not to take any *cherem* lest trouble comes to Israel, one man named Achan hid a Babylonian robe, pieces of silver and a golden wedge. Achan's sin brought trouble not only to himself and his family, but also to the whole community of Israel. To purge the community of the sin, Achan and his family were stoned to death and burned[2] in the valley that was since called the *Valley of Achor* (valley of trouble).

The stories of the incredible victory in Jericho and that of the defeat in Ai and the judgment of Achan illustrate the privilege and responsibility of God's people

---

[1]   The whole city was *cherem,* something to be given over to God. This meant that every living thing in Jericho was to be destroyed, and the articles of gold, silver and bronze were to be consecrated and put in the Lord's treasury (Joshua 6v19, 21). This was God's judgment on the wickedness of the people of Jericho. Rahab (Week 39), a resident of Jericho, helped the Israelites and was thus spared with her family (Joshua chapter 2).

[2]   This may seem harsh, as was God's judgment on Jericho and on Ananias and Sapphira (Week 46), but God is the judge, not us! How can one claim to be more just than God?

concerning His holy presence among them[3]. His presence ensures victory over the *dunamis* of the enemy, but also demands that the whole community of people who bear His name live in holiness and purity. (Therefore, as Christians, our covenant is not just with Jesus, but with His Church as well.) In the case of the defeat in Ai, only Achan actually sinned, but the whole community of Israel was judged (hence, the defeat) because Israel was considered one body, unified by God's presence and by His covenant with them. Just as the state of health of one member of the human body can affect the whole, one member's sin affected the whole congregation[4]. After the sin was purged, victory came to Israel when she went against Ai the second time (Joshua chapter 8).

The Valley of Achor was a place of trouble, shame and sorrow. But then comes God's promise in Hosea 2v14-15 (NIV): "Therefore I am now going to allure her; I will lead her into the wilderness and speak tenderly to her. There I will give her back her vineyards, and will make the Valley of Achor a door of hope." God tells Israel that He would lead her to the wilderness where she would be tried and tested[5]. But in her trouble, trial and affliction, she would listen to God speaking hope to her, and she would turn to Him. The intimate relationship would be restored, and Israel would be fruitful again (the metaphor of the vineyards).

So it is with the Church collectively, and with Christians, individually. Our sins get us into trouble and God must discipline us with trials and adversities (the 'wilderness') because as people who bear Christ's name, we must grow into Christ-likeness. In some cases, the sin is not our own, but God allows us to go through the wilderness in order to make us more Christ-like so that we can handle the blessings and the greater anointing for a new assignment (the fruitfulness) that will later come. Trials and adversities have a sanctifying effect. Suffering and pain force us to look to God and to be sensitive to what He is saying to us regarding changes that He wants to happen in our lives. We must therefore have an eternal perspective on trials and adversities,

---

[3] Leviticus 11v44 (NIV): *I am the Lord your God; consecrate yourselves and be holy, because I am holy.* As God's children, our privilege and responsibility go together. Our privilege – to receive everlasting life, to be identified with God, to bear His presence, to receive spiritual gifts and eternal inheritance, and to be trusted with His *dunamis* and *exousia* – comes with our responsibility: to consecrate or dedicate and devote ourselves to Him.

[4] Galatians 5v9 (NIV): *A little yeast works through the whole batch of dough.*

[5] Jesus was led by the Holy Spirit to the wilderness to be tried and tested for 40 days to prepare Him for His ministry (Matthew 4v1-11), as Israel was tried and tested in the wilderness for 40 years before entering the Promised Land (Joshua 5v6). The prophecy in Hosea may ultimately point to a coming time of great trouble for Israel ("the time of Jacob's trouble" in Jeremiah 30v7, KJV) before the second coming of the Messiah.

for as Paul says, "Our present troubles are small and won't last very long. Yet they produce for us a glory that vastly outweighs them and will last forever!"[6]

This brings us to the promise in Romans 8v28. God can turn our crises into opportunities and our pain into our gain. Whatever troubling situation we are facing, we can rest in Him like an eagle in a storm (Week 11). All of life's experiences can be turned around by God for our good and for His glory, even the times when we messed up, the times when we were rejected, hurt, abused, humiliated, betrayed[7]. For the child of God who is consecrated to Him, none of life's experiences are wasted, for every trial in the end becomes a triumph, and every test a testimony of God's Romans 8v28 faithfulness. His grace is turning your Valley of Achor into a door of hope because He makes everything beautiful in His time[8]!

Our next story is a testimony of how God turned a heart-breaking situation into rejoicing. He is so good!

He Causes All Things to Work for Good

For ten years, my husband and I had put our hearts into serving the Lord in ministries at our local church that we felt He had gifted us for and called us to. My husband's ministry was teaching God's Word to adults and mine was teaching God's Word to children.

The pastor of this church for twenty-two years retired two years ago and was replaced by a younger pastor from another city about three hours away. This new pastor systematically began to "get rid of" (his own words) the leaders of ministries within the church that had served under the former pastor and to replace them with hand-picked friends. My husband and I were among the very first to be told we could no longer teach or hold leadership positions. Since God gives each of us gifts to use for service, we knew we could not just be pew warmers. We therefore withdrew our membership and left the church. Exactly one year after he got rid of my husband and I, the new pastor fired the church secretary of twenty years, called the assistant pastor in and basically gave him no choice but to resign. The pastor knew it was the same date and he told other staff that he was showing everyone who was boss.

Many wrote and signed petitions and others wrote personal letters, all of which were sent to the bishop to ask for the removal of this new pastor. Even though

---

[6]   2 Corinthians 4v17, NLT.

[7]   Isaiah 65v10 (NLT): *The plain of Sharon will again be filled with flocks for My people who have searched for Me, and the valley of Achor will be a place to pasture herds.*

[8]   Ecclesiastes 3v11 (ESV): *He has made everything beautiful in its time.*

the membership went quickly from over 600 members to under 200, the petition apparently was of no avail as the new pastor's father had a high position in the denomination and was friends with the bishop.

We were devastated to have to leave our church family and see so many that we loved leaving as well. Some went to other churches and some were so burnt and hurt they went nowhere. Everyone was in shock and grieving. My husband and I did not feel called to serve in another church in the community. How would God cause this situation to work for our good? I wondered. Little could I have imagined how quickly He would show me as we started to pray for His direction and guidance!

We began to feel led to start a non-denominational ministry of teaching and missions from our home. We applied for and got tax exempt status. We are both retired and God has seen to it that our needs are met so we need no salaries. All donations we receive go to missions. We now hold weekly adult Bible studies in our home and I am working on a curriculum and hope to start the children's ministry up this coming fall. We do not have a large home but so far it has been more than sufficient for storage of donations and Bible study materials. We have a good size basement to use for the children's ministry.

In just six months God has opened so many doors and we have been amazed at how He is working out Romans 8v28! We are now serving and using our gifts in the community instead of just in one church as before. The ministry has expanded to include many volunteers from the community. Through donations, the ministry is now sponsoring seven African orphans. Individual members are sponsoring five more and four members are paying the salaries of employees in an orphanage in Africa. We were able to hold a dinner benefit through working with different denominations and this raised $21,000 for this orphanage. Through a community day event we were asked to participate in, members collected $1,000 for a windmill to supply electricity to the new orphanage school. The ministry also collected and packed 501 shoeboxes full of donated items. These were sent to Samaritan's Purse in December 2010 and distributed to orphans and needy children around the world. We now have a year-round collection of empty shoeboxes and supplies from local businesses going on, as well as continued collection of supplies to be shipped to the orphanage in Africa each year in the fall.

Several days after he was forced to retire, the assistant pastor opened a non-denominational community church. He had come to my husband and me and asked if we would serve with him. We prayed about it for almost two months and have had many talks with him and others to see if this is another way God wants us to branch out and serve Him besides our own non-denominational teaching and missions ministry. My husband was asked to preach and teach and be part of the pastoral ministry in the new church and I was asked to coordinate the Kid's Bible Club. We feel that God was calling us to do this and we therefore have made this commitment recently.

True to His promise, God did turn our heart-breaking situation into exciting opportunities to serve Him and to partner with others. We believe that He moved us and many others out of the church building and brought us more in contact with the community and with people of other denominations through what has happened. It was more than we had imagined!

By the way, one week after the pastor "got rid of" the secretary and the assistant pastor, the denomination's area bishop finally stepped in and made him resign. Sadly, this happened after the new pastor had ruined just about every ministry of the church and had driven out most of the members. Now that church awaits an interim pastor and then another pastor in two years. I believe that just as God caused our heart-breaking situation to work together for our good, He can also Romans 8v28 what happened in this church and turn it around for His glory!

- Suzanne (Indiana, USA)
April 2011

The psalmist sings: "You have turned my mourning into joyful dancing. You have taken away my clothes of mourning and clothed me with joy, that I might sing praises to You and not be silent!" (Psalm 30v11-12, NLT).

Father God, I know that You are turning my sorrow into dancing, my Valley of Achor into a door of hope. I choose not to give in to fear and discouragement because of Your Romans 8v28 faithfulness! I consider my life as cherem, the old destroyed and the new devoted and totally consecrated to my Lord and Saviour, Jesus Christ. Help me to stay faithful to Him despite my circumstances. In Jesus' name, amen.

Week 49: Two for the Road

We proclaim to you what we have seen and heard, so that you
also may have fellowship with us. And our fellowship is with the
Father and with His Son, Jesus Christ. (1 John 1v3, NIV)

One of the most common words used by Christians is 'fellowship'. In the original Greek of the above verse, the word for fellowship is *koinonia*, the bond of mutual interest and devotion that binds individuals to each other. According to the verse above, the Christian has *koinonia* with other believers as well as with God Himself. To understand Christian *koinonia* better, we need to go back to the Old Testament animal sacrifice called the *shelem*[1] (peace offering, also called fellowship offering) in Leviticus chapters 3 and 7[2]. The offerer would lay his hand on the head of the animal to symbolise the transfer of his sins to the animal which would be his substitute or sin-bearer. The animal would then be slaughtered and its blood would be sprinkled by the priest on the sides of the bronze altar. The fat of the animal would be presented to the Lord and burned on the altar while the breast and the right thigh would be given to the priest. The rest of the animal would then be returned to the offerer for his meal. The peace offering was different from other Old Testament offerings in that it was the only sacrifice in which the offerer could eat part of the animal in a meal. He could do this with people he invited. During the three annual festivals in Israel[3], thousands would be offering this sacrifice and sharing in a communal meal[4].

The sacrifice was called *shelem* or peace offering because the offerer would feel not only forgiven by God and at peace with Him (and God with the offerer) by virtue of the sacrifice, but would also feel God's favour, resulting in inner peace and wholeness (*shalom*) for the person. Peace with God results in peace with others; this was what the meal symbolised. The peace offering was also called fellowship offering because on the basis of the sacrifice, the offerer would find fellowship with God, with the priest and with those who came to celebrate with him.

---

[1] The word *shelem* (peace offering) is related to the word *shalom*. See Week 45.
[2] There are 3 main classes of offerings prescribed in Leviticus: offerings to deal with sin (guilt offering which requires restitution, or sin offering if without restitution), offerings to show devotion and consecration to God (burnt offering and grain offering), and offerings to show fellowship or communion (peace offering, which includes thanksgiving and freewill offerings).
[3] The three annual festivals are the Feasts of Unleavened Bread (which starts with Passover), Pentecost and Tabernacles.
[4] At the dedication of the Temple, King Solomon offered 22,000 cattle and 120,000 sheep and goats as *shelem* (1 Kings 8v63, NIV).

Jesus is the ultimate Sin-Bearer, the Lamb of God who gave Himself as the *Shelem* for the propitiation (appeasement) of God's anger toward man's sin. The person who receives Him as his or her Substitute not only experiences peace with God and inner peace, but also receives God's favour because of the *koinonia* that now exists between the person and the Lord. Since Jesus died to bring peace between God and man and between man and man, peace and *koinonia* with God manifest in peace and *koinonia* with the community of believers called the Church or the *Ekklesia* (1st footnote, Week 44). Jesus' sacrifice was so perfect it only had to be done once and for all people who would receive Him as their Sin-Bearer. We celebrate this in the 'communion meal' (*koinonia* also means communion) or the Lord's Table which reminds us of our unity with God and with other believers.

Koinonia within Christ's *Ekklesia* connotes sharing. In the original Greek, Paul actually uses the word *koinonia* to refer to the material blessings (financial contribution) which Gentile believers were sharing with the Jewish believers in Jerusalem[5], just as the Jewish believers had shared spiritual blessings with the Gentiles (through the preaching of the gospel by the apostles and the first believers who were Jewish). Because of and for the sake of *koinonia*, each believer is expected to share what they are able to benefit others. It is in obedience to Jesus' command to "love one another"[6]. There will be people in your own local fellowship or church whom you may find difficult to get along with, but fellowship gives you the opportunity to learn to love them and to grow in Christ-likeness. Indeed, staying in Christian fellowship is beneficial for us because of the spiritual growth that comes to us through corporate worship, through the preaching, teaching and the learning together of the word of God, through opportunities for us to serve the Body of Christ, through the strength and encouragement we draw from others, and through the opportunities to practise Christ-likeness when faced with the weaknesses of other members. These are some of the blessings God bestows when believers "dwell in unity"[7].

Staying in fellowship is not only beneficial, it is also crucial. The one who is alienated from the flock becomes an easy prey for the devil who "prowls around like a roaring

---

5   Romans 15v26 (NKJV): *For it pleased those from Macedonia and Achaia to make a certain contribution* ['koinonia'] *for the poor among the saints who are in Jerusalem.* Paul's use of *koinonia* here reflects his belief that Gentile and Jewish believers would become united as the "One New Man". Ephesians 2v15, ESV: ... *that He might create in Himself one new man in place of the two, so making peace...*

6   John 13v34 (ESV): *A new commandment I give to you, that you love one another: just as I have loved you, you also are to love one another.*

7   Psalm 133v1, 3b (ESV): *Behold, how good and pleasant it is when brothers* [brethren] *dwell in unity. For there* [the 'place' of unity or harmony] *the Lord has commanded the blessing, life forevermore.*

lion looking for someone to devour" (1 Peter 5v8, NIV). This person is more likely to make a detour from the narrow road towards a path that leads away from God. If you are not in a fellowship, find one for your own sake!

Our *koinonia* with God and His *Ekklesia* has implications on marriage. The Bible says, "Do not be yoked together with unbelievers. For what do righteousness and wickedness have in common? Or what fellowship can light have with darkness?" (2 Corinthians 6v14, NIV). God does not want His child to be mismated with someone who will not walk the narrow road with him or her. The consequences that result from not obeying this command (lack of peace with God and with His *Ekklesia*, no inner peace or *shalom*, possible loss of eternal rewards, etc.) are more serious than the heartbreak that results from letting go of someone who is not a Christian.

1 John 1v3 above should remind you of *chesed* (Week 31) and the Great Commission[8]. The road may be narrow, but the Christian pilgrimage does not have to be a solitary walk. There is always room for another one! In the novel *The Pilgrim's Progress*, an allegory about a believer's journey through life on the way to heaven[9], the main character, Christian, goes on a practically solitary pilgrimage to the Celestial City. When he finally reaches it, he meets its community of happy residents. Christiana, Christian's wife who refuses to accompany him in Part 1, changes her mind in Part 2 and takes her children and other companions with her. Along the way she convinces more people to join her in the communal pilgrimage to the Celestial City. Between Christian and his wife, it is Christiana who has a richer experience of life because of *koinonia*.

Below is a story that has all the elements that characterise the Christian pilgrimage of "two for the road" – you and God, you and your local church, you and the worldwide Church or *Ekklesia*, you and your spouse, you and your family, and you and the person you bring to Jesus. Don't walk alone!

Reaching Out to Seamen

Just as the Lord's first disciples faced many tests and trials they did not understand, my wife Isobel and I certainly did. We believe God never left us when we went through difficulties, but allowed those experiences to mould us and to prepare us for our ministry to seamen. (See story in Week 24.)

---

[8] Matthew 28v18-20 (NIV): *All authority in heaven and on earth has been given to Me. Therefore go and make disciples of all nations, baptising them in the name of the Father and of the Son and of the Holy Spirit, and teaching them to obey everything I have commanded you. And surely I am with you always, to the very end of the age.*

[9] John Bunyan wrote part 1 of the novel in 1679 and added part 2 in 1684.

One of these seamen was Moses from Nigeria. Moses nearly died when an electrical shock threw him down a metal stairway to the deck below, breaking his jaw and leg in several places. When I began visiting him in hospital, he could not speak, only listen. Yet he gestured to encourage me to begin teaching him from the Bible. Eventually when he could speak, one of the first things he told me was that his accident had warned him that he was not prepared to meet his Maker. He came to know the Lord, a clear sign of this was that he began sharing the gospel with other patients and with his family when he returned home!

My story actually begins in 1967 when I worked as an electrical draughtsman for the building of the famous cruise ship Queen Elizabeth 2. One time I asked my co-worker Ralph why he avoided working on Sunday even though he would be paid double. He simply replied, "Jesus is my Lord." I doubt if he realised any more than I did, the impact that would have on me and those seamen from several countries I would minister to for the next thirty-five years. Ralph encouraged my fiancée Isobel and me to join a group of Christians who met with teenagers in cafes in Glasgow to show them the love of Jesus and to share with them the gospel. That was when God lit a flame in our hearts for evangelism, giving us thrilling experiences as we learned from the Master how to reach others.

When I met Isobel (who was already a Christian) soon after my conversion, I knew immediately she was the one God had chosen to be my wife! Soon after we got married, we moved to Southampton where I became a freelance draughtsman. I was earning good money working on ships being built there and I became excited at the possibility of working for myself and buying shops back up in Scotland. Then one night, just as we were on the brink of implementing that plan, I was suddenly wakened with the question, "Whose kingdom are you building?" I was reminded of Matthew 6v33 (NKJV): "But seek first the kingdom of God and His righteousness, and all these things shall be added to you." The inspired advice I was given by a famous gifted preacher was that if God was calling me to full-time service, as long as I kept my heart open for God to redirect me, He would find His own ways to bring us into His service and nothing would be wasted even if we went ahead with our business plan. That is exactly what happened over the next three years while we had the shops. One of them was a typical village store which we used to make contact with teenagers. There was no evangelical church for fourteen miles, yet God gave us a group of boys and girls who, as we listened to their concerns, started coming to our home for Bible study. We had no idea that God was using our experiences at this time to prepare us for another ministry a few years later.

After selling our two shops, we bought the village general store, knowing it would fail when we removed cigarettes from the shop. Nevertheless, we were willing to sacrifice the business to reach the local people for the Lord. Eventually, we sold this store at a lost, convinced that it was time for us to trust the Lord. It was then Isobel told me that a few years before we had met, she believed the Lord was calling her to full-time service when a famous preacher visited her church and gave her a prospectus from a Bible college. Because we realised we needed formal training (just as the disciples had formal training from our Lord before He sent them out on a mission), we decided to attend this college. At the time we felt a mix of excitement and apprehension about how it was all going to work out. When someone persistently asked about our financial situation, I did not expect him to reply, "Good! Now you must trust the Lord, not your money!"

Because we were struggling financially in our first year at Bible college, we found the job offer for me to work as a foreman with an electrical firm extremely tempting. God took us back to Matthew 6v24 (NKJV): "No one can serve two masters; for either he will hate the one and love the other, or else he will be loyal to the one and despise the other. You cannot serve God and mammon." The principal of the college wisely counselled us, saying that having difficulties was part of that training, not a call out of the Lord's service!

After one year in college, Isobel had to stop to care for our new baby, Elaine. I continued and we began to pray about what the Lord wanted us to do after graduation. I read about a vacancy for Port Chaplain in Southampton with a group reaching out to seamen. As we thought we would be serving the Lord abroad, we nearly turned away from it. However, we felt God's call to this job, and so after I finished Bible college, we went back to Southampton in July 1976 and joined the group. Immediately, we saw seamen from South Africa respond to the gospel and get clearly saved. This was when apartheid restricted the freedom of non-whites. Seeing them get saved was a great encouragement.

As Port Chaplain, I visited ships while they were in the Southampton docks and brought small groups of seamen from several countries into our home. There Isobel's gift of homely hospitality softened their hearts, paving the way for me to lead a Bible study, which often concluded with several praying for salvation. God also showed me ways I could reach Russian seamen every week with personal Bible teaching before the fall of communism. Later, groups of seamen from the Baltic countries eagerly came to our home for Bible study and I am still in touch with some today from Estonia and Lithuania, as well as Russia.

When the time ships stayed in port was reduced to just a few hours, Bible correspondence courses became an important aspect of the ministry to seamen. It was wonderful to see how interest in these courses spread on a ship with a large crew like the QE2, as others saw me giving out marked studies and new studies to the crew I met regularly in the mess room. This developed into a pastoral ministry as colleagues put me in contact with those seamen they met who wanted further Bible teaching. The last seven years of our ministry have been by correspondence, with Isobel writing to some of the wives of seamen. Christian translators have helped us write in other languages when that has been necessary.

Early in the 1980s, while in Southampton, I enjoyed working closely with colleagues in Hamburg. We were particularly concerned that Christian seamen were often unhappy not to have fellowship on board and seldom able to attend church. I made a point of visiting Christian seamen on their ships who had met my colleagues in Hamburg. We worked together to encourage those seamen of all ranks to gradually become like pastors and evangelists. This gave their time at sea a new significance and purpose. Eventually, regular training seminars called Church on the Oceans began to be held in the Philippines to help Christian seamen learn how to start Ship Churches without causing offence to others on board their ships. Ship Churches have also been started by other nationalities.

As a newly converted young man, I had prayed saying I was taking Jesus as Lord of my life, not fully realising that it was actually Jesus who had already taken hold of me and would have a profound effect on every aspect of my life. Yet at each stage of my transformation, He was so gentle, giving me experiences that only now as I look back over the years, I can see that they became so helpful when I went into full-time service for Him. Through our ministry, seafarers who are unlikely to attend a church in their own country are hearing the gospel in a way they would find difficult at home. They are also returning home to share their new experience of the Lord Jesus with their own family.

- David Thomson (Troon, Scotland)
March 2011

Thank You Father for sending Jesus to die for my sins, and thank You Jesus for sending the Holy Spirit to live in me, the One who will never leave me nor forsake me[10], my Friend who "sticks closer than a brother"[11]. Because of Him I know I am not alone on this narrow road. Help me to reach out to others in obedience to Your Great Commission. Help me to recognise the 'kairos' moments[12] you give me to share with them by word and deed Your love and message of salvation. Grant me the honour of presenting to You people I have led to the Lord so that I may hear Your precious, "Well done, My good and faithful servant!" Help me not to neglect koinonia with

---

[10] Deuteronomy 31v6b (NKJV): *The Lord your God, He is the One who goes with you. He will not leave you nor forsake you.*

[11] Proverbs 18v24b (ESV): *There is a friend who sticks closer than a brother.*

[12] *Kairos* is an ancient Greek word that means 'the right or opportune time'.

other believers so that I may encourage them and be encouraged by them, as we mutually build each other up in the Lord[13]. May You be pleased to answer my prayer in Jesus' name, amen!

---

[13] Hebrews 10v24-25 (NASB): *And let us consider how to stimulate one another to love and good deeds, not forsaking our own assembling together, as is the habit of some, but encouraging one another; and all the more as you see the day* [of Christ's return] *drawing near.*

Week 50: The Long and Winding Road

He changes the times and the seasons. (Daniel 2v21, NKJV)
My times are in Your hands. (Psalm 31v15a, NIV)
To everything there is a season, and a time for every matter
or purpose under heaven.... (Ecclesiastes 3v1, AMP)

The title above may remind you of the Beatles' song, but there is actually a song of the same name sang by one of the best American southern gospel tenors, Johnny Cook[1]. The song is about the "long and winding road" that "keeps on leading" us as Christian pilgrims. Indeed, the narrow road we have chosen to walk on has many turns. Sometimes the bend takes us to a time of joy when the blessings of God overtake us, and sometimes it takes us to a difficult period of disappointment, sorrow or pain. Many of the things that happen to us are consequences of our disobedience, sin or weakness, but when bad things happen despite our obedience and steadfastness as Christians, we can be perplexed over our circumstances and feel unable to take another step. We cannot tell what is around the bend ahead of us since there are many things in life that are beyond our control, but as long as we keep our focus on Jesus (Week 9) and follow His leading, we are assured of victory because the road we travel on is a Romans 8v28 road (Week 48).

What is the point of all these bends along the narrow road? Why are there happy times and sad times, easy times and difficult times for the Christian pilgrim? In other words, why are there seasons of life?

We can describe the seasons of life based on the seasons of nature. We are in springtime when God opens the door to new opportunities and new activities. We are in summer when we are experiencing rapid spiritual growth and greater effectiveness in ministry (a time of bearing much fruit). We are in autumn when we are forced to slow down or cut back on our commitments. Then there is winter, a dormant time when it seems nothing is happening and we are not bearing discernible fruit. However, the seasons of life do not come in the more predictable manner of the seasons of earth. A season of life may last quite a long time; then suddenly, one may find oneself in a new season (as when a job is lost or when a spouse dies). Life also has more seasons than the natural world. There are contrasting seasons of joy and

---

[1] The 'Long and Winding Road' was written by Johnny Cook and Mickey Mangun. Johnny Cook sang with several American groups and as a solo singer beginning in the 1970s. He died in 2000.

of sorrow, of blessing[2] and of testing[3], of successes and of failures, and seasons of gaining and seasons of losing. Although nobody likes a difficult season, it comes to every one of us, but as with the other seasons, we cannot know when it will happen unless God reveals it to us. We may not fully understand the reason for any season of life that visits us until we finally see the Lord face to face. Then we will fully know and understand[4].

The scriptures above tell us that God ordains the seasons in our lives and *every* season has a purpose. In the light of eternity, every season of life is beneficial because God uses each season to teach us something about Himself (His love, promises, faithfulness, power, etc.) and something about ourselves (the state of our commitment, the lessons we need to learn, the changes that must take place in our lives, etc.). He uses these seasons to catch our attention, to instil in us Christ-likeness and to awaken us to the realities of life and the need to examine our choices, the things that we do and the circumstances we find ourselves in. For instance, you may be going through a time of testing. Not only is this God-screened (Week 11), it is also beneficial as we have seen in Week 25. This season may be followed by a time of humbling or discipline if God decides that you need it. This period may be painful, but it is beneficial in bringing you back to unbroken fellowship with the Lord or in breaking bad habits. A season of plenty may come next – not only to bless you, but also to reveal to you your maturity (or immaturity) in the way you handle God's blessings (e.g., money). Although He does not control how you will react or respond to any season, God knows even before the season hits you and He has already determined in the counsel of heaven what He would do and how He would Romans 8v28 your mistakes and foolishness.

Asking God for hindsight about our past seasons (the lessons we need to learn) and insight regarding the current one (what He wants to teach us and how He wants us to respond) prepares us for the next season. Otherwise we may find ourselves in a season of taking practically the same test we took before, like going round the same mountain again and again! Our past experiences, if we choose to learn from them, can help us to

---

[2] Psalm 102v13 (NIV): *You will arise and have compassion on Zion, for it is time to show favour to her; the appointed time has come.* Originally, Zion was the name of the ancient Jebusite fortress in Jerusalem that David conquered. Later on, the name was applied to the temple that Solomon built and its surrounding area. Eventually, Zion referred to the city of Jerusalem, the land of Judah, the people of Israel, and God's spiritual kingdom. In the New Testament, Zion refers to the heavenly Jerusalem in Revelation as well as to the Church.

[3] Psalm 139v23-24 (NIV): *Search me, O God, and know my heart; test me and know my anxious thoughts. See if there is any offensive way in me, and lead me in the way everlasting.*

[4] 1 Corinthians 13v12b (NIV): *Now I know in part, then I shall know fully, even as I am fully known.*

finally win the victory by the grace of God[5]. It took the Israelites forty years to make the journey from Mount Horeb (where God gave the Ten Commandments) to Kadesh-Barnea at the border of the Promised Land, a journey which should have taken them just eleven days![6] Even so, those years of wandering in the desert were beneficial in the end as these taught the Israelites many things about God and prepared them for the battles to take possession of the Promised Land.

We all experience seasons of spiritual highs and of spiritual lows or times of blessing and times of testing because we all need to be sanctified. We all need to become more and more like Jesus! We will all continue to experience changing seasons until we reach the end of the road (Week 51). There may be many bends along this narrow road, but we can be advancing towards the fulfilment of our purpose individually and corporately with each other's help and compassionate understanding of what each of us is going through in our own season of life.

Below are honest stories of the seasons of life of two Christians who are still struggling, like many of us, but holding on to Jesus. If you are currently in a difficult season, do not give up on yourself or Jesus. He ultimately makes all the seasons of our lives beautiful in His time!

Mary's Story

My name is Mary. I'm at university here in Lancaster. I'm training to be a primary school teacher working with kids with special needs.

When I was little, I believed in God and heaven. I used to say that when I get to heaven, the first thing I'll do is count all the cars! However, I never really thought much about God and what He's really like until I was about eleven. At this time the church which I attended got a new youth worker who invited the kids to youth events. At the age of twelve, I did a Bible study course called 'What Would Jesus Do?'. It challenged the young people to look at some of the claims Jesus made about Himself and how He lived when He was on earth, among other things. Through studying the life of Jesus and looking at how He lived and served others, I began to see how sinful I was and so unlike Jesus. A desire to live just like He did was birthed in me and I decided to follow Him.

---

[5] Deuteronomy 11v2a (GNT): *Remember today what you have learned about the Lord through your experiences with Him.*

[6] Deuteronomy 1v2 (AMP): *It is [only] eleven days' journey from Horeb by the way of Mount Seir to Kadesh-barnea [on Canaan's border; yet Israel took forty years to get beyond it].*

I very quickly realised that this was no easy task, that this wasn't something I could do in my own strength, but with God's help. I also began to realise that there wasn't anything I could do to make God love me any more or any less because it wasn't about what I did or didn't do, but it was about what Jesus had done for me.

Through spending time with other Christians and doing Bible studies with them, reading the Bible and praying by myself, I began to grow as a Christian. However, I often forgot that it was all about Jesus and not what I did. Working with kids and young people, I used to feel a lot better if the talks I did at Kids Club went well. If they didn't, I felt like a failure and thought that God would quickly stop loving me if I didn't do better.

When I was nineteen, my sister became very ill with anorexia. Unable to accept that this was outside my control, I felt like a complete failure because I couldn't make her better. This led to a lot of negative feelings towards myself, a lot of self-hatred. I blamed myself for my sister's illness and the fact that I couldn't make things better for her led me to self-harm.

At that time I was working at a Christian holiday centre. Although it was a safe environment with supportive people, it took me a long time to be honest with my colleagues and other people around me. I was too scared to confide in anyone, fearing I would be judged and be told to sort out my life before God could use me to serve Him. I now know this is not true. In the course of time, God gave me a mentor to whom I disclosed the real extent of what was going on in my life.

Although I struggled a lot with letting God take control and allowing Him to be Lord of my life instead of me, I learned a lot during this time about how to deal with tough situations by putting my trust completely in the God who created me and loves me just as I am. I also learned so much about God's grace and faithfulness and that He loves me regardless of what I do and how much I hurt Him. I was and still am in awe of His faithfulness and of the fact that He is always there for me no matter what I've done to upset Him.

I am thankful to God for my time at this holiday centre as it allowed me to grow so much in my faith and trust in God. I learned how faithful, how forgiving and full of grace He is! He blessed me with so many supportive Christian friends who really helped me. Being in the centre also made me more excited about Jesus and the sacrifice which He made for us, and I wanted to go and live for Him more and more.

When I eventually went to university, I had the desire to share how much Jesus meant to me with those I lived with. I met some amazing friends who became my family away from home. With their encouragement, I am becoming more confident in my ministry with kids and young people at Christians Alive, my church in Lancaster. I am grateful for them and for how God provides for me at university, as well as how He reveals Himself to me as I try to live for Him day by day.

I still often forget that I have a relationship with God not because of what I do, but because of what Jesus did for me at the cross. I pray that God will remind me daily of His grace and love for me and that I will learn to grow more and more like Jesus. There are times I fail as a Christian, but I know God's grace is holding me tight.

The battle with self-harm is one I continue to face, but I also know God is faithful in that. I wrestle with why God allows my sister to still struggle with anorexic thoughts and why an all-loving God allows so much hurt in this messed-up world. I still blame myself if people close to me get hurt and I can't fix it. But I know I am a Christian not because I live a perfect life and have all the answers; I am a Christian because I worship a God who does! I know He is the hope in all these situations. I know He carries me and lets me feel His closeness in the tough times. I am learning to trust Him and to give all the hurt to the God who can fix it.

I recognise that I don't have all the answers and that I'm ill-equipped to fix people's hurt. But I also know that God will use me to show His love in situations. I am sure that through Him I will find the strength and comfort to keep going when it's hard and people around me are hurting. I need to be reminded daily that it is by God's grace we are on this earth and for His purpose we live. I'm learning to trust in Him and His plans. In everything He will be glorified!

- Mary (Lancaster, England)
August 2011

I Have Hope for the Future!

I have good memories of childhood with loving parents and a fairly comfortable middle class English family. Nonetheless, I was a bit of a loner at school, had anxious feelings of not quite fitting in and a tendency to get depressed even at an early age.

I became a Christian, but wasn't prepared to make Jesus Lord of my life. I had relationships with girls that ended in emotional turmoil and I found myself battling with quite severe depression along with manic highs. Then Mum and Dad's divorce because of Dad's adultery rocked my already shaky life. I tried several jobs, including the Police Force and sales but failed in them all. The best move I did was to do a year at a Christian healing centre where I met my wife and got serious about God. I went off to Bible college then got married and found a job as youth worker at an Anglican church.

My moods however did not cooperate. They would fluctuate from highs to extreme lows with suicidal thoughts. I struggled against being with people unless they also suffered from depression. Misery loves company! My lows would be followed by highs during which I would not sleep for some days. In this period I would take on lots of work to try to make up for the time I previously wasted, as if I could single-handedly save the world!

In 1998 I ended up in a mental hospital following a manic episode. Our eldest child was just a baby at this time and it was therefore a terrible time for my wife who has always been an incredible support, a woman of mighty faith. For the next two years, life was turned upside down. I was hospitalised several times and was put on anti-psychotic drugs. To top this, we were burgled (everything including tea bags!). I felt lost! My friends who stuck with me were also sufferers like me. We could not help each other, but this gave me more compassion and a realisation that many people are worse off than me. My wife and I felt the best way forward was to move house, and so we moved to be close to my wife's parents in Lancaster.

I couldn't understand why these things were happening. Reflecting on Matthew 21v44[7], I came to understand that these trials were part of my breaking process which had given me the desire to change, to resist the devil, to submit to Christ's total lordship and to trust Him to turn things around. Then God started to do just that. He connected me with Christian ministries[8] which helped me focus on my relationship with God. In Lancaster, God got me an admin job at the Prison and I ended up working with drug addicts and those suffering with depression, a job in which my own experience is proving helpful.

More than ever, I am putting my trust in God for my total healing which is a process I'm going through. My wife and I have four beautiful children and life is good most of the time. I still get cyclical bouts of deep depression, but I'm learning to cope better and accept help. There is no more mania or psychosis. I have hope for the future!

- Eddie (Lancaster, England)
August 2011

Part of the refrain of Johnny Cook's song goes like this: "The long and winding road keeps on leading me. Up ahead I see a sign pointing straight ahead to victory!"

---

[7] Matthew 21v44 (NIV): *Anyone who falls on this stone* [Jesus, the "cornerstone"] *will be broken to pieces; anyone on whom it falls will be crushed.*

[8] One such ministry was Ellel Ministries (ellel.org) in Ellel near Lancaster.

My Father in heaven, thank You that the seasons of my life are in Your hands and that there is a purpose for every one of them. Thank You that You were with me in all the seasons that passed, especially in the difficult and painful ones. In the times when the load was too heavy for me to carry and I thought I could not walk any farther, you carried me![9] Wherever the bend in the road will take me, I know You will never ever leave me or forsake me. Direct my steps as You have promised[10]. Help me never to deviate from the path You have set before me. It may be long and winding, but lead me on, My Saviour. Although I cannot see the end of the road, I know that because of Jesus I will see the sign that says "victory". Someday I will reach the Celestial City, and this narrow, long and winding road will turn to gold! Thank You, Jesus!

---

[9]   Remember 'Footprints in the Sand' in the story in Week 2?

[10]   Psalm 37v23-24 (AMP): *The steps of a [good] man are directed and established by the Lord when He delights in his way [and He busies Himself with his every step]. Though he falls, he shall not be utterly cast down, for the Lord grasps his hand in support and upholds him.* What an amazing picture of God's love!

Week 51: The End of the Road

I am the resurrection and the life. The one who believes in Me will live, even
though he dies; and whoever lives by believing in Me will never die.
(John 11v25b-26, NIV)

Life on earth is a journey to eternity, whether one takes the narrow or the broad road
(Week 35). When our earthly life ends, eternity begins.

The belief in eternity is common in many cultures and religions. Even Hitler believed
in eternity which was why he used the swastika as a symbol of the Third Reich to
imply that it would be eternal[1]. The reason for this common belief is simply that the
eternal God "has planted eternity in the human heart" (Ecclesiastes 3v11, NLT). He
placed the concept of eternity[2] and the natural longing for immortality in the human
soul. Still, many ignore it by living for the here and now. Sooner or later, they will
discover that there is such a thing as an 'afterlife' in eternity. Will you spend yours
in heaven or hell?

A person who receives Jesus as his Saviour and Lord already has everlasting (eternal)
life because he already has fellowship with God. When he reaches the end of his
road, he (his soul and spirit) leaves his body and goes to heaven to be with the Lord
forever[3]. His body rots in its grave until the appointed time for its resurrection comes.
Meanwhile, he beholds God's glory and enjoys his amazingly beautiful new home
called heaven. Paul sums up how wonderful heaven will be for the believer with these
words: "No eye has seen, no ear has heard, and no mind has imagined what God has
prepared[4] for those who love Him" (1 Corinthians 2v9, NLT). Heaven is more than
you can ever imagine!

One day, the soul and spirit of the believer will get re-united with his body, albeit of
a different kind. Just as Jesus was raised from the dead, all deceased believers across
the centuries (those in the Old Testament times and those in the New Testament

---

[1]   Hitler's Third Reich or Nazi Germany only lasted from 1933 to 1945. Its symbol, the swastika,
can be seen in the ancient art of the Egyptians, Romans, Greeks, Persians, Hindus, etc. To
Hindus, Buddhists and Raelians, it is a symbol of eternity.

[2]   Even mathematics incorporates the concept of eternity in its symbol for infinity, ∞.

[3]   2 Corinthians 5v8 (NLT): *Yes, we are fully confident, and we would rather be away from these*
earthly bodies, for then we will be at home with the Lord. Death means getting away from the
body and being with God.

[4]   John 14v2 (NKJV): *In My Father's house are many mansions; if it were not so, I would have*
told you. I [Jesus] *go to prepare a place for you.*

times and afterwards) will be raised, each with a new "spiritual body"[5] which will be physical but imperishable, immortal and glorious, like Jesus' resurrection body[6]. Death, a consequence of Adam's sin, will then be forever conquered[7]. Believers who are still alive when this happens will not experience death. In an instant, their bodies will be transformed into imperishable ones at the sounding of the "last trumpet"[8]. The Old Testament prophet, Hosea, prophesied of this event: "I will deliver this people from the power of the grave; I will redeem them from death. Where, O death, are your plagues? Where, O grave, is your destruction?" (Hosea 13v14, NIV). Many believe this will happen at "the rapture", the "catching away" of God's people which Paul refers to in 1 Thessalonians 4v16-17 (NIV): "For the Lord Himself will come down from heaven, with a loud command, with the voice of the archangel and with the trumpet call of God, and the dead in Christ will rise first. After that, we who are still alive and are left will be caught up (i.e., be "raptured") together with them in the clouds to meet the Lord in the air. And so we will be with the Lord forever."[9] The Bible tells us that the catching away ("rapture") of the "saints" (the New Testament term for all believers[10]) will happen soon after the sounding of the "last trumpet".

What is the "last trumpet" and when will it sound? Because Israel's sacred feasts recorded in the Old Testament were prophetic, some theologians believe that the Feast of Trumpets (later known as *Rosh Hashanah* or Jewish New Year's Day) pointed to this future event. On the days leading to the Feast of Trumpets, the *shofar* (ram's horn) would be blown daily as a reminder of the coming feast[11]. On the feast day itself, the last *shofar* call would be made and Israel would gather in a sacred assembly.

---

5   1 Corinthians 15v42-44 (NLT): *Our earthly bodies are planted in the ground when we die, but they will be raised to live forever. Our bodies are buried in brokenness, but they will be raised in glory. They are buried in weakness, but they will be raised in strength. They are buried as natural human bodies, but they will be raised as spiritual bodies.*

6   Philippians 3v21 (NIV): *…. who, by the power that enables Him to bring everything under His control, will transform our lowly bodies so that they will be like His glorious body.* See Luke 24 and John 20 to get some idea about Jesus' resurrection body.

7   Isaiah 25v8 (NIV): *He will swallow up death for ever. The Sovereign Lord will wipe away the tears from all faces; He will remove His people's disgrace from all the earth. The Lord has spoken.*

8   1 Corinthians 15v51-52 (NIV): *We will not all sleep* [die], *but we will all be changed – in a flash, in the twinkling of an eye, at the last trumpet.*

9   The word 'rapture' in this context is from *rapiemur*, the word that appears in the Vulgate, the 4th century Latin translation of the Bible. It is from the verb *rapio* which means to catch up or to take away. Many believe that when "the rapture" happens, Christians all over the world will vanish in an instant because they are taken away to heaven by God.

10 For example, Romans 8v27 (ESV): *And He who searches hearts knows what is the mind of the Spirit, because the Spirit intercedes for the <u>saints</u> according to the will of God.*

11 The *shofar* is traditionally blown each morning for the entire month preceding *Rosh Hashanah*.

Revelation 8 speaks of seven angels, each with a trumpet. When they blow their trumpets one after the other, a series of apocalyptic events happen on earth. These theologians believe that the seven angels and their trumpets refer to the 'Seven Year Tribulation' that will visit the earth[12], and the Feast of Trumpets (the sounding of the last *shofar,* apparently by God Himself based on 1 Thessalonians 4v16 which speaks of "the trumpet call of God", and Zecchariah 9v14[13]), to the rapture and assembly of the saints either in the middle of the seven-year period ('mid-tribulation rapture') or at the end of the seven years ('post-tribulation rapture').

Other theologians argue that because God promised to rescue His people from "the wrath to come", the rapture will happen before the tribulation period ('pre-tribulation rapture')[14]. They believe that the trumpets of Revelation 8 are for unbelievers, not for believers. They also point out that since Revelation 19 mentions the "wedding supper" of the Lamb (Jesus, the Lamb of God) and His Bride (the Church), then we must look into the Jewish wedding customs in Bible times to get an idea of when the rapture will happen. Traditionally, the Jewish groom would fetch his bride and would take her to his father's house. On the first night in this house, the marriage would be consummated and the guests, who would already be gathered in the house

---

[12]   Bible scholars teach us that this 'Seven Year Tribulation' period will likely commence when a coming charismatic world leader but false messiah, the ultimate Antichrist, signs a peace treaty with Israel and its Arab enemies. In the middle of this time frame, however, he breaks his covenant with Israel and proclaims himself God. The first half of the period will be marked with natural disasters and hardships which intensify in the second 3 ½ years, the future time dubbed as 'The Great Tribulation' when God pours out His judgments on a sinful world. Christians who are on earth at this time will suffer intense persecution, and may even be put to death. The apocalyptic events of this unprecedented period of earth's history are prophesied in the book of Revelation chapters 6 to 19.

[13]   Zechariah 9v14 (NKJV): *Then the Lord will be seen over them, and His arrow will go forth like lightning. The Lord God will blow the trumpet...*

[14]   1 Thessalonians 1v10 (ESV): *... and to wait for His Son from heaven, whom He raised from the dead, Jesus who <u>delivers us from the wrath to come.</u>* Also Romans 5v9 (NIV): *Since we have now been justified by His blood, how much more shall we be <u>saved from God's wrath through Him!</u>* Opponents, however, of the pre-trib rapture belief point out that the Greek word for 'wrath' in these verses is *orge* (as in Revelation 19v15: *... He treads the winepress of the fierce wrath/'orge' of God*) and not *thumos* (as in Revelation 16v1: *... pour out the seven bowls of the wrath/'thumos' of God into the earth*). The *thumos* of God is His chastening that is meant to bring repentance, while His *orge* is His final punishment of and vengeance on the unrepentant. (This is clear in Romans 2v5: *But because of your hard and impenitent heart you are storing up <u>orge</u> for yourself on the day of <u>orge</u> when God's righteous judgment will be revealed.*) According to them, God will first pour out His *thumos* at the beginning, and then His *orge* at the end of the tribulation period. They say that true believers of course will not experience God's *orge*, but they may be on earth when the bowls of God's *thumos* are poured out.

of the groom's father for the wedding supper, are informed of the consummation. The wedding guests would then feast for seven days. The pre-tribulation believers argue that Jesus will have to come to earth to fetch the Church and bring her to heaven (His Father's house) with Him. There in heaven, there will be a wedding party for one week-year or seven years. At the end of the seven years, Jesus and the Church will return to earth to establish Christ's millennial rule. The rapture according to this argument will take place before and not at the middle or at the end of the tribulation period.

The three groups seem to agree, however, that at the end of the tribulation period, Jesus will return to earth with His raptured and glorified saints to defeat the Antichrist and his massive armies[15]. The Antichrist and his "false prophet" who will deceive many through the miraculous signs he will perform on behalf of the Antichrist and in the power of satan[16], will be captured and thrown into the 'lake of burning sulphur' or hell (*Gehenna* in the Greek text). Satan himself will be bound, thrown into the Abyss ('bottomless pit') or *Hades* (Greek) and will be locked up there for a thousand years. During this glorious millennial period, the survivors of the tribulation period will be ruled by the believers (those who turned to Christ before and during the tribulation period and who have proven themselves able to take on the task during their lifetime on earth) under the headship of Jesus. After a thousand years, satan will be released and he will incite those who have half-heartedly bowed the knee to Jesus to rebel against Him, but fire will come down from heaven and destroy them. Satan will finally be thrown into *Gehenna* where he will stay forever with the Antichrist, false prophet and all the demons. Those whose names are not listed in God's Book of Life[17], including those who had died and are in *Hades,* will be judged for their sins and then thrown into *Gehenna*[18] where they will be separated from God forever[19].

Finally, the recorded events in the Bible will reach the end of the road with a second Genesis, the creation of a new heaven and earth. The Celestial City will come down from heaven, the "New Jerusalem" with golden streets and walls decorated with

---

[15] See this week's 12th footnote. The Antichrist is the first beast of Revelation 13v1-8.

[16] The "false prophet" is the second beast of Revelation 13v11-17.

[17] See 2nd footnote of Week 33.

[18] These events are prophesied in Revelation 20. *Hades* is a temporary holding place for those who will ultimately be thrown into *Gehenna*. Luke 16v23 implies that *Hades* is a place of torment. Revelation 19v20 (NIV) describes *Gehenna* as a "fiery lake of burning sulphur". It is a place of eternal suffering and torment.

[19] 2 Thessalonians 1v9 (NIV): *They will be punished with everlasting destruction and shut out from the presence of the Lord and from the glory of His might.* Hell is essentially the eternal separation from God. The Bible calls this eternal separation the "second death". See 2nd footnote of Week 33.

precious stones![20] But what really makes it an awesome place is that the throne of the triune Godhead will be there in the city with His people[21]. There will be no more sadness, suffering, evil and sin. The pilgrim's narrow road leads into eternal Eden[22] where time will come into full circle, and a new glorious age without end begins!

Below is a story of a man who had been traumatised by his experience of war. Late in his life, he received a revelation that God loved him and he gave his life to Jesus. He reached the end of life's road not long after this. Of course, this was not the end of Norman!

Never Too Late

At aged twenty, my father, Norman, faced the full horrors of the First World War. At the Battle of Somme (1 July to 18 November 1916), the suffering of the men increased daily. Cold, mud, lice and sleepless nights in the trenches were as sapping of the will as the terror of the enemy beyond the parapet. In that fateful battle, a shell burst very close with a brilliant flash and Norman felt a sharp pain in his face before losing consciousness. A piece of shrapnel had penetrated through to his mouth.

But the worst pain and sorrow he was always to carry deep down was the awareness that of his 250 closest comrades, only thirteen survived that night. He counted himself as one of the unlucky thirteen, "for I would have given anything to have gone with the rest". Strangely, he carried the burden of guilt: "Why me? Why should I and not they have been spared?"

Six months later, Norman was back at the frontline again. On 26 June 1917 the Germans attacked in dense fog. My father and his mates were surrounded by German soldiers. Hands raised and dispirited, they surrendered and were transported deep into the heartland of Germany where Norman's job was to shovel forty tons of coke a day to fire the furnaces for making munitions to be used against our own men.

Following his repatriation, he lost his first wife to encephalitis and soon after came the death of his mother. My mother, his second wife, and the family they nurtured together were some kind of consolation, but we were always aware that Norman bore

---

[20] Based on some scriptures in the Old Testament, there are Christians who say that the New Jerusalem will appear earlier, in the millennial reign of Jesus, as they believe He will be ruling from this place.

[21] Revelation 21 talks about the new heaven and new earth and the New Jerusalem.

[22] Genesis 2v8 (NIV): *Now the Lord God had planted a garden in the east, in Eden, and there He put the man He had formed.* The story of man in the Bible begins in the Eden of Genesis and ends in the Eden of Revelation.

within himself a deep and incurable bitterness. The faith of his childhood and youth was gone forever. There were long periods of sternness and brooding silence.

Towards the end of their lives, my parents came to live with my wife and me. Soon afterwards, my mother died of cancer. My father was still with us when we moved to take over a failing church in Halifax, West Yorkshire. By then, Norman was also suffering from stomach cancer. Soon after our arrival, the Reverend Trevor Dearing brought a 'Prayer, Praise and Healing Mission'. I watched with disbelief as before our eyes people went home pushing the wheelchairs on which they had depended.

My impulse was to lay hands on my father in the Trevor Dearing fashion, but never in all those years had we ever discussed personal faith. One day during early morning prayers, I asked the Lord to give me courage to broach the subject of healing with my father. But I still knew I couldn't! Yet that very day when I took Norman his cup of tea, he was rocking back and forth in his chair with pain, and suddenly he said, "David, I've been trying to pray about this thing, but I don't know how. Can you help me?"

I knelt before his chair and took his hands. My wife stood behind and put her hands on his shoulders. I simply let the Holy Spirit have His way with my words. I listened to God telling my dear father that all his life He had loved him and sought to bring comfort and healing for all he had suffered, but until now the way had been blocked. Norman streamed with tears, looked up at me and said almost accusingly, "All these years you never told me God loved me!" And for the first time since I was a child, we embraced!

His healing was not immediate, but every night he demanded a time of prayer before he got into bed. In the days that followed, the full trauma of the war disturbed his dreams as he relived the horrors of that experience sixty years back, as though it had to be expunged. One day he asked me to look at his feet. For ages he had been unable to cut his toenails. I fetched a bowl of warm water and as I washed his feet, we both wept till our tears fell into the water.

He was admitted to hospital and every day for seventeen weeks I watched him shrink into a little withered old man. Meanwhile the Prayer, Praise and Healing Mission was gathering momentum. A number of churches had come together to plan healing services. A monthly service would be held at each church in rotation. One was due on the evening I visited my father who was in much distress, begging me not to leave him.

When the time for ministry arrived that evening, the minister invited anyone who needed healing for themselves or someone by proxy to come and receive the laying on of hands[23]. I asked the minister to pray that Norman would die soon in peace. With some misgivings, he laid hands on me and prayed exactly that.

The day after, when I arrived at the hospital, Norman was for the first time sitting in a chair out of bed and seemed quite cheerful. The next day he met me at the ward, leaning on two sticks. He was reportedly asking for two breakfasts and putting on weight!

A week later, the hospital allowed him to come home. We were promised they would keep a bed in case he needed to return. While he had been away, we had made one of the large downstairs rooms in the house into a chapel for meetings and a small group gathered there early every day for prayer. I took Norman in there and he sat in silence for a while before the tears came again.

"I'm only thinking," he said, "what I've missed for seventy-eight years!" Then he looked out of the window and saw that the lawn was somewhat overgrown. Before his illness he used to cut the grass. "You've let that get in a mess," he observed. "Just start up my old Flymo[24] and I'll see what I can do."

This seemed just too incredible! Less than a couple of weeks ago my father lay dying. Hadn't I asked for him to die in peace? Did the Lord have such a sense of humour?

But mow the lawn he did, and what's more, while that fine summer weather persisted, he was out there every day forking and weeding and trundling the weeds off in his barrow.

A month or so into this miraculous return, we were due to hold the healing service on our own premises. He agreed that he would come if he didn't have to say anything. But that same afternoon he seemed very tired and decided to stay at home. "I feel that the Lord may call me home soon. Do you think so?", he asked. I answered that if that should be the Lord's will, there was nothing whatever to be afraid of.

"By gum, you're right!", he exclaimed in his old familiar way. "And when I'm gone, there's something I'd like you to do for me. Just go on loving each other the way He loves me. It's grand!" In fact, his talk all the while since he came home had been of Jesus and His love.

---

[23] Acts 28v8 (NKJV): *Paul went in to him and prayed, and he laid his hands on him and healed him.* According to Hebrews chapter 6, the laying on of hands is one of the basic practices of the Christian faith. It is done for healing, for deliverance from evil spirits, for impartation of spiritual gifts, as a sign of the call to service or ministry, etc. See also 4th footnote of Week 9.

[24] A brand of lawnmower

On the Sunday morning while we were at worship, one of our young church members sat with him and reported that Norman was reciting whole passages by heart from St. John's Gospel, which he must have remembered from his school years. Much against his will, I took him back to hospital where he lapsed into a coma. Towards midnight on the third day came the news that his breathing had changed, indicating he had not long to live. I went and sat by his bed for a couple of hours. Then all at once he turned his palms upwards on the bed cover, opened his eyes wide to smile at me, closed them and walked into heaven.

I came home and climbed quietly into bed beside my wife. Before I put out the light, I let my Bible fall open (it was the Living Bible version) and there I read, "Those who believe in Me, though they die like anyone else, will live again. Only believe and a whole lifetime past gives way to a new life in Jesus" (John 11v25). Then I remembered what we had prayed for my father – that he should die in peace. The only way we can die in peace is in the knowledge that God loves us far beyond what words can ever express.

God had answered my prayer for my father at the right time.

- David Ellis (Grange-over-Sands, Cumbria, England)
April 2011

Pilgrim, if you have not received Jesus into your life as your Saviour and Lord, it is not too late to do so now. But do not wait any longer to make the decision. The end of your road may come without any warning!

Because of Jesus, I know Father God that death is not the end for me, but the beginning of life more amazing than I can imagine. I don't know when this will come, nor if I will still be alive when Jesus comes again to claim His Bride. Should You decide for Him to return while I am still alive on earth, prepare me for the difficult time I may have to go through. Protect me from getting offended[25] at You because of the persecution and trials that will come my way before I see Him face to face. I want to be able to say with Paul, "For to me, living means living for Christ, and dying is even better" (Philippians 1v21, NLT). By Your amazing grace, I can! I praise You, Lord!

---

[25] Remember *skandalon*, Week 41.

Week 52: You Have to Be There!

.... and the name of the city from that day shall be: THE
LORD IS THERE. (Ezekiel 48v35, NKJV)

The Christian pilgrim has a glorious future. He will go to heaven when he dies. He will receive a new and imperishable body at the "first resurrection"[1]. He will receive rewards for the things he did for the Lord during his lifetime. He will rule and reign with Jesus. He will walk the golden streets of the New Jerusalem, and he will behold God's beauty and glory forever and ever! However, he still has to face the present reality of life on planet earth, its challenges and pressures which inevitably bring suffering and pain.

The Old Testament book of Job is the story of a man who was beset by trials and suffering. He lost his children, his possessions and then his health. Why would God allow a string of severe trials to come his way? Job's friends Eliphaz, Bildad and Zophar tried to make Job confess of sin for they were sure that was the reason. Job insisted he had no unconfessed sin, but he wanted to make sense of his suffering. Then God reminded Job of His awesome power. Despite the fact that He did not really give the reason for the trials, Job finally sees that man must in faith accept God's plan for his life, including suffering.

Like Job, we want to know the reason behind our suffering. We can ask God for insight regarding this. However, on this side of eternity, His reason for allowing our trial may be beyond our understanding, as it was for Job. Yes, God allows our trials, but satan must first have His consent before he can attack us (Week 11). The book of Job shows us that God sets limits to what the devil can do[2]. It is Him who decides on

---

[1] Daniel 12v2 (NIV) indicates there will be two kinds of resurrection of the dead: *Multitudes who sleep in the dust of the earth will awake: some to everlasting life, others to shame and everlasting contempt.* Revelation 20v4b-5 (NIV) says about believers who have died: *They came to life and reigned with Christ a thousand years. (The rest of the dead did not come to life until the thousand years were ended.) This is the first resurrection.* The "first resurrection" is the resurrection of all deceased believers, including those who will die during the Seven-Year Tribulation: *And I saw the souls of those who had been beheaded because of their testimony for Jesus and because of the word of God. They had not worshiped the beast* [the Antichrist] *or his image and had not received his mark on their foreheads or their hands* (Revelation 20v4, NIV). After a thousand years, there will be a "second resurrection", this time of all whose names are not written in the Book of Life, before they are cast into *Gehenna*. This resurrection is connected with the "second death". See 2nd footnote, Week 33.

[2] For example, Job 2v6 (NIV): *The Lord said to Satan, "Very well, then, he is in your hands; but you must spare his life."*

the kind, the time, the duration and intensity of satan's afflictions. Whatever specific reasons God may have for allowing these, we can be sure that He is using our trials to prepare us for our roles in Jesus' Kingdom in the near future, during His millennial reign, and beyond that. These roles require that we grow in Christ-likeness. Job was a man of exemplary character, but even he needed growth. Perhaps God wanted to deal with his fear[3] and self-righteousness[4] and perhaps it was only through a succession of drastic pruning of Job's character flaws that He could achieve this. In the end, Job emerged from his experience with a deeper understanding of God, of himself and of human nature. As a result, he became more humble, more compassionate, more forgiving and fully surrendered to God[5]. With his fire-forged character, he could be trusted by God to handle double the earthly blessings and riches he had before.

The book of Job should remind us that God is working on us. When He looks at a Christian, He sees his real identity, the person he can become if fully surrendered to Jesus. The Holy Spirit goes about His work of producing the character that is consistent with that identity (sanctification). Impulsive Simon was called Peter by Jesus to reveal to him his real solid-as-a-rock identity[6]. In the Gospels and in the book of Acts, we can see Peter's transformation as the leader of the fledgling Church after Jesus' ascension to heaven. You, too, have a real identity that was birthed in God's mind before you were born on earth. That identity is God's precious and eternal treasure and inheritance for you, but you have to fight for it by overcoming all you need to overcome to receive the 'white stone with a new name' written on it[7]. That new name is your real identity. You began to commit yourself to discovering and becoming the real you when you received Jesus into your life, but the only way you can find out who you were born to

---

[3] Job 3v25 (NIV): *What I feared has come upon me; what I dreaded has happened to me.* Literally, "I feared a fear." Ungodly fear gives the enemy the right to attack us.

[4] Job 32v1 (ESV): *So these three men ceased to answer Job, because he was righteous in his own eyes.*

[5] After hearing God's discourse about His mighty power, Job says regarding his complaining attitude: *Therefore I despise myself and repent in dust and ashes* (Job 42v6, NIV). Job's friends were pathetic comforters who presumed to know the reason behind his suffering. Yet, in obedience to God, Job prayed for them and the turning point for him came: *After Job had prayed for his friends, the Lord restored his fortunes and gave him twice as much as he had before* (Job 42v10, NIV).

[6] John 1v42 (NIV): *Jesus looked at him and said, "You are Simon son of John. You will be called Cephas" (which, when translated, is Peter).* Cephas (Aramaic) and Peter (Greek) both mean 'rock'.

[7] Revelation 2v17 (NLT): *To everyone who is victorious .... I will give to each one a white stone, and on the stone will be engraved a new name that no one understands except the one who receives it.* Receiving this stone is a sign that the person has finally overcome his weaknesses, especially the greatest one, all known only to God and the person. The "new name" on the stone will confirm it and that he has finally become the person he was born to be!

be and become that person is to stay connected and surrendered to Jesus so that He can continue to impart to you the character that goes with that identity.

It may be that your human relationships, country of birth, job, background, education or sexuality holds a major claim on your identity. However, the one thing that has the most legitimate and most important claim on your identity is God's vision for you. Your transformation into your real identity, as defined by the Creator, is the *sine qua non* to true fulfilment and security, not human relationships, nationality, job, background, education, or sexual orientation. He alone knows who you really are, the one you can become. Jesus suffered horribly to make it possible! Are you willing to surrender completely to Him and make Him the focus of your whole being so that you can become the person whose name is inscribed on the white stone? Then expect and be prepared for the pruning! Determine to get better and not bitter because of the trials that God must allow to see His vision of the real you fulfilled. Even in your frustration and bewilderment at the trials that will come to effect the transformation, you can declare with God's grace Job's profound statements of trust: "I know that my Redeemer lives[8]. Though He slays me, yet will I trust in Him[9]. And when He has tried me, I shall come out as gold![10]"

Last week's reading mentions the New Jerusalem, a heavenly symbol of the Bride of Christ. There are those who believe that it is the same city described in the Old Testament book of Ezekiel (chapters 40 to 48) because of the parallels between the two. There are also theologians who believe that Ezekiel's vision was that of the rebuilt Jerusalem and its temple (with the animal sacrifices performed to symbolise and commemorate Christ's death) which will appear during the millennial reign of Jesus, whereas the New or Heavenly Jerusalem or Zion of Revelation 21 will be like a satellite hovering above Ezekiel's temple, perhaps with a space-time portal between the two. We will have to wait to see who is right! What is more relevant to all Christian pilgrims who are going through tough times is Ezekiel's last statement in his book, "The name of the city from that day shall be: THE LORD IS THERE."

In your suffering, trials and afflictions, remember that our God is *Jehovah Shammah*, "The Lord is There"![11] As you go through the painful process of pruning[12] and

---

[8]   Job 19v25, NIV

[9]   Job 13v15, KJV

[10]   Job 23v10, ESV.

[11]   Jesus is in and with His people, individually and corporately, and where Jesus is, Yahweh/ Jehovah is there also because *"All of God lives fully in Christ"* (Colossians 2v9, NCV). Jesus is *Jehovah Shammah*. He is there with you!

[12]   John 15v1-2 (NIV): *I am the true vine, and My Father is the gardener. He cuts off every branch in Me that bears no fruit, while every branch that does bear fruit He prunes so that it will be even more fruitful.*

becoming who you were born to be, remember that He is *Jehovah Shammah* who knows you intimately (*yada* – Week 5) and feels what you feel because He Himself had walked this earth and suffered[13]. He has good plans for you[14]. He promised never to leave you nor forsake you[15]. He promised He will Romans 8v28 all your problems (Week 48). When your faith is tested, when the rubber hits the road and you feel like crying, "You have to be there!", God is there with you for He is *Jehovah Shammah*.[16]

May the testimony of our last storyteller give you great encouragement to keep on soaring, keep on running, and keep on walking until you reach the Celestial City and receive the precious white stone with your new name on it. It is waiting for you!

When The Rubber Hits the Road

People believe things for all sorts of reasons. Faith in a Divine Being is no different in that sense. But my own faith in God, as a lad growing up in the West Midlands, a church-goer, a believer in God, rests on experience.

Up to the age of sixteen I had never been tested regarding what I believed. Not really. The hardships of life had either evaded me, or they were forming an orderly queue, ready to hit in the coming years. Then, on 21st December 1988, something happened that would change our family and my life forever.

My nineteen year-old sister, Helga, had been home for just a week before Christmas, and was heading back that afternoon to the USA. We had struggled and struggled for years, fought like cat and dog (her being the aggressive cat!), and for the first time in years, that week I experienced a loving, caring sister. On the departure day I didn't want her to go back to her gap-year au pairing job in New Jersey. But I needed to do some Christmas shopping, so I headed into Birmingham, determined to get back before my sister left for the airport.

---

[13] Hebrews 4v15 (NIV): *For we do not have a high priest who is unable to sympathise with our weaknesses, but we have One [Jesus] who has been tempted in every way, just as we are – yet was without sin.*

[14] Jeremiah 29v11 (NLT): *For I know the plans I have for you," says the Lord. "They are plans for good and not for disaster, to give you a future and a hope."*

[15] Deuteronomy 31v6 (ESV): *Be strong and courageous. Do not fear or be in dread of them, for it is the Lord your God who goes with you. He will not leave you or forsake you.*

[16] The source of the inspiration for the title of this week is Susan Boyle's song, 'You Have to Be There' (from her album 'Someone to Watch over Me'), a song which can speak to anyone going through a tough time. It is a shorter version of the one written by Abba's Benny Andersson and Björn Ulvaeus for the musical 'Kristina'.

Later that afternoon, I returned home, having totally forgotten that Helga was due to leave for the airport at 2 PM. She had gone.

Afternoon turned into evening, and I sat upstairs watching something on the old TV set. Suddenly the program that I was watching was interrupted with a news flash. A plane had come down over a town in the Scottish Borders. The cameras showed dark mounds of rubble and earth, silhouettes of walled structures that were houses just an hour previous, with flames rising behind them. I shuddered and experienced that momentary grief that anyone with half a heart has in such circumstances – a deep sadness for the unknown families of those affected. Sympathy, but no empathy. I remember thinking, "Some families are going to have a miserable Christmas and New Year...."

Downstairs the phone rang. It was Auntie Winnie (I say auntie, but everyone in the church and in our neighbourhood in those days was an auntie or uncle). My dad picked up the phone. "Did Helga get away okay today?" she asked. "Yes, I think so. Why?" answered my dad. "It's just that I've seen a news flash on the telly about a plane coming down....."

I don't know how long it took from the time of that phone call, but dad called me downstairs, and the surreal began. We turned on the TV downstairs. Sure enough, the same news item that I had seen minutes before was running. Sitting together on the sofa, my dad, mum and I learned that Pan Am Flight 103, Heathrow to JFK, Boeing 747, Clipper Maid of the Seas, had come down over Lockerbie in the Scottish Borders. It was my sister's flight. Our lives would never be the same.

In the coming days and weeks, many facts were established. Bodies strewn over the beautiful borders countryside were recovered, along with parts of the plane and people's luggage. Memorial services were attended by politicians and dignitaries; private funerals and wakes took place in the US, UK and other lands. Every day for weeks and months, the tabloids and the television were fascinated and saturated with the fall-out of this event.... and it still runs even today.

There are many things that I could mention from that time. I could write of the nightmare of the local farmers, daily discovering remains of corpses, of watches still ticking whilst lives had ceased. I could write a book about the kindness of strangers that we experienced through the grieving and shock that we and other families underwent.

But most importantly, I want to tell you of the unbelievable, tangible sense of God's presence in my darkest hour. In OUR darkest hour. We found that, when everything around us seemed to point only to tragedy, to grief, to questions of "Why?", and at that moment when we were faced with such an injustice that God COULD have prevented, the Good God that I had grown up hearing about was there! On that first night, once the many friends and church family members had come and gone through our doors, we prayed as a family. We didn't understand; we were scared and confused, but we in effect said, "God, this is the time we need to know You're real, and that You're with us."

He came. He enveloped us in a kind of bubble, an almost tangible, peaceful place in which He allowed us to experience deep grief minus the despair. I can't describe it to you as a reader, but all sense of hatred, revenge and unforgiveness just dissipated in this amazing bubble of God. He had us. And He was not going to let us wallow and quit the journey that we had started with Him.

The months and years since the tragic loss of my sister have been filled with proof of God's goodness. As a family we were encouraged within days of the tragedy by the words of the apostle Paul in Romans chapter 12 verse 21, "Do not be overcome by evil, but overcome evil with good" (ESV). Here was an opportunity to use our moment in the world's spotlight to see something of immediate and eternal worth emerge. As a result of my sister's death, here are just a few of the things which we have had the privilege of being involved in.

In 1993 a children's home in Santiago, Luzon (Northern Philippines) was built with donations we received after the funeral. There are currently eighteen abused and abandoned children being loved, educated and restored in that home, and 118 children have passed through over the years. Local authorities have estimated that over 50% of them would not have survived without this project.

In 2004 in a place called Ooty, Tamil Nadu in India, another children's home was built. Thirty-two orphaned and destitute girls are being cared for and educated there as I write this. Without this home, they would not have a future.

In the Himalayan north of Pakistan there is now a hostel for girls who would otherwise lack the protection and education that they desperately need.

In Libya (the homeland of the man convicted for the bombing of Pan Am flight 103), a home for children who are mentally or physically handicapped now possesses a top-of-the-range Landrover ambulance, enabling the staff to get the children to hospital with ease, and to take them on pleasure trips. Some of these children had never been to the seaside before, just a few miles down the road.

Many other faith-based and humanitarian projects around the world have been enhanced through our personal tragedy. And many hundreds, maybe thousands of people, have invited Jesus into their lives because they heard and saw what he had done for us as a family.

On a personal level, this is the miracle of my God's goodness to me: I have not been overcome by unforgiveness and anger. Instead, I have been able to walk on from that evening before Christmas in 1988, free from bitterness, able to forgive, and wanting to make a difference in the world.

As I journey on through this short span of time we call life today, my life still encounters tragedy. Just a few months ago, we lost my wife's brother very suddenly to cancer. We are not immune just because we trust in an all-powerful and loving God. But I know this: whatever comes, He has me. And I wouldn't swap that for anything.

- Marcus Mosey (Lancaster, England)[17]

September 2011

Mighty God, my everlasting Father, I admit that there are many things in my life that must change, habits that must go and mindsets that must be replaced by the renewing of my mind by Your word. I know You are good and that You have a good plan for my life. I submit to Your pruning. Do what You need to do in my life so that I can become the person I was meant to be. Impart to me the character that I need to complete all the assignments You have planned for me to do and to fulfil Your purpose for my life. Grant me Your grace to abide in Jesus especially through the trials and tough seasons of life. Help me to keep on believing that You are indeed Jehovah Shammah, even through the times when You seem to be distant and silent[18], times when I can't seem to soar like an eagle above the storm, times when I feel too weary to run another mile and do what You have called me to do, and times when I feel like fainting as I walk the long and winding road because the battle for my future is intense.

Father, I choose to believe in You and in Your promises. I choose not to give in to fear, but to persevere in prayer and obedience so that I may receive the white stone with my new name on it, that I may hear Your "Well done, My good and faithful servant", and that I may win a crown that I can place at my Saviour's feet. I choose

---

[17] Marcus is the senior pastor at Christians Alive Church in Lancaster, www.christians-alive.org.uk

[18] In Psalm 42, David expressed his frustration at God's apparent silence: *Why have You forgotten me? Why do I go mourning because of the oppression of the enemy?* (Psalm 42v9, ESV). However, he remembered his experiences with God and encouraged himself in the Lord: *Why are you cast down, O my soul, and why are you in turmoil within me? Hope in God; for I shall again praise Him, my Salvation and my God* (42v11, ESV). God is never distant and silent. During the times when He seems silent and inactive, He is giving us the opportunity to see His provisions and answers with the eyes of faith and to listen to 'the still small voice' (1 Kings 19v12, KJV). We only need to open the word of God to 'hear' Him speak.

to persevere in prayer and obedience so that I may be able to help others soar like spiritual eagles, run like athletes for Jesus, and walk like pilgrims on earth on their way to the Celestial City. By the faith that Jesus gave me, I know I can! Thank You that You have committed Yourself to complete the work You began in my life. I recommit and rededicate my life to You, for You are my Lord, my Saviour and my God. Praise Your holy name!

Those who hope in the Lord will renew their strength. They will soar on wings like eagles; they will run and not grow weary; they will walk and not be faint (Isaiah 40v31, NIV).

And now I commend you to God and to the word of His grace, which is able to build you up and to give you the inheritance among all those who are sanctified (Acts 20v32, ESV).

Appendix 1

The Names of God in the Bible[1]

The names or titles of God in the Bible carry special significance. They are summary statements embodying His character, attributes, ministry as well as His promises. Blessed be the name of the Lord!

A. The Names of the Triune God and/or God the Father:

Elohim – the very first name of God that appears in the Bible, in Genesis 1v1: "In the beginning, *Elohim*....." It is the plural form of *El*, "Strong One" or "Majesty". Therefore, the name implies the mystery of the plurality and unity of the Holy Trinity, the three-in-one God (Deuteronomy 6v4[2]).

El Elyon – God Most High (Genesis 14v18-20)

El Roi – the God Who Sees (Genesis 16v7-8)

El Shaddai – the All-Sufficient One, the Pourer of Blessings, the God of More-than-Enough, God Almighty (Genesis 17v1)

El Olam – the Eternal or Everlasting God (Genesis 21v33)

Adonai – "the Lord" in Hebrew in the Old Testament (Genesis 15v1-2), *Kurios* (Greek) in the New Testament (Matthew 3v3)

YHWH (Yahweh) – "I Am Who I Am", or "I Am" as the shorter form (Exodus 3v14), the Self-Existent and Unchangeable One. The Latinised form, *Jehovah,* appears in English Bibles and is more familiar to non-Jews, but *Yahweh* is probably the correct pronunciation of *YHWH.* (See 8th footnote, Week 16.)

Jehovah/Yahweh Jireh – God is Provider (Genesis 22v7-8, 14)

Jehovah/Yahweh Rapha – God is Healer (Exodus 15v26)

---

[1] This appendix is not an exhaustive list of both the names or titles of God and of Bible references.

[2] Deuteronomy 6v4 (KJV): *Hear, O Israel: The Lord our God* ['Yahweh Elohim'] *is one Lord.*

Jehovah/Yahweh Nissi – God is my Banner (Exodus 17v15), my Confidence and Strength in battle

Jehovah/Yahweh Tsidkenu – God is my Righteousness (Jeremiah 23v6)

Jehovah/Yahweh Mekoddishkem – God is my Sanctifier (Exodus 31v13)

Jehovah/Yahweh Shalom – God is my Peace (Judges 6v24)

Jehovah/Yahweh Sabaoth – the Lord of Hosts (1 Samuel 1v3), Sovereign over all powers, my Captain and Deliverer

Jehovah/Yahweh Raah – the Lord is my Shepherd (Psalm 23v1)

Jehovah/Yahweh Shammah – the Lord is There, the Abiding Presence (Ezekiel 48v35)

Father – a New Testament revelation that Almighty God becomes our personal Father when we are adopted into His family through faith in His Son, Jesus. This is why Jesus called Him *Abba* (Mark 14v36), an Aramaic word for Daddy.

Other figurative titles of God include *Ancient of Days* (Daniel 7v9), *Refuge* (Psalm 9v9), *Rock* (Psalm 19v14), *Fortress* (2 Samuel 22v2), *Shield* (Genesis 15v1), *Refiner* (Malachi 3v3), *King* (1 Samuel 12v12) and *Judge* (Genesis 18v25). Another one is *My Exceedingly Great Reward* (Genesis 15v1, NKJV). He is!

B. The Names of God the Son:

Son of God (Psalm 2v7, Matthew 16v16), *Son of the Most High* (Luke 1v32), *Only Begotten Son of God* (John 3v16)

Holy One (Psalm 16v10, Acts 3v14)

Jesus or Yeshua (short for *Yehoshua* which is Hebrew for Joshua), "Yahweh (I Am) is Salvation" (Matthew 1v21, Luke 2v21)

Immanuel – "God with Us" (Isaiah 7v14, Matthew 1v23)

Saviour (Luke 2v11), *Saviour of the World* (1 John 4v14, John 4v42)

Ha-Mashiach/Masshiach/Massiah (Greek *Khristos*) – the Messiah, the Christ, the Anointed One (Daniel 9v25, John 1v41, John 4v25-26)

Jesus Christ or *Yeshua Ha-Mashiach/Masshiach/Massiah* (Matthew 1v1, 18; Acts 2v38)

Rose of Sharon and *Lily of the Valley* (Song of Songs 2v1)

Chief Cornerstone (1 Peter 2v7, Ephesians 2v20)

King (Zechariah 9v9), *King of Kings* (Revelation 19v16), *King of Israel* (Mark 15v32)

Great High Priest (Hebrews 3v1)

Wonderful, Counsellor, Mighty God, Everlasting Father, Prince of Peace (Isaiah 9v6)

Judge (Acts 10v42)

Son of David, Son of Abraham (Matthew 1v1), *Son of Man* (Matthew 8v20)

Bridegroom (Matthew 9v15)

Master and *Rabbi* or *Teacher* (Matthew 23v8)

Lamb of God "who takes away the sin of the world" (John 1v29)

Just or *Righteous One* (Acts 7v52)

Lord (Matthew 7v21), *Lord of Lords* (Revelation 17v14), *Lord of Glory* (1 Corinthians 2v8)

Deliverer (Romans 11v26)

Rock (1Corinthians 10v4)

Beloved (Ephesians 1v6)

Our Peace (Ephesians 2v14)

Our Righteousness, Holiness and Redemption (1 Corinthians 1v30), *Sun of Righteousness* (Malachi 4v2)

Head of the Church (Ephesians 4v15)

Mediator (1 Timothy 2v5) and *Advocate* (1 John 2v1)

Appendix 1

Author or *Pioneer of our Salvation* (Hebrews 2v10)

Lion of the Tribe of Judah (Revelation 5v5). The lion, a symbol of kingship and power, was the ensign of the tribe of Judah to which Jesus was born.

Faithful and True One (Revelation 19v11)

Holy Servant of God (Acts 4v27)

Horn of Salvation (Luke 1v69). Horn in the Bible symbolises strength.

The Wisdom of God, the Power of God (1 Corinthians 1v24)

Word of Life (1 John 1v1)

I Am (John 8v58); *I Am the Light of the World* (John 9v5); *I Am the Resurrection and the Life* (John 11v25); *I Am the Way, the Truth and the Life* (John 14v6); *I Am the Gate* or *Door* (John 10v9); *I Am the Bread of Life* (John 6v35); *I Am the Good Shepherd* (John 10v11); *I Am the True Vine* (John 15v1); *I Am the Alpha and Omega, the First and the Last, the Beginning and the End* (Revelation 22v13); *I Am the Bright Morning Star* (Revelation 22v16); *I Am the Almighty Who Is and Who Was and Who Is to Come* (Revelation 1v8)

God (John 20v28), the True God and Eternal Life (1 John 5v20), *Great God and Saviour* (Titus 2v13)

C. The Names of God the Holy Spirit:

Spirit of God – Ruach Elohim (Genesis 1v2, Exodus 31v3), *Spirit of the Lord – Ruach Adonai* (Judges 3v10, Ezekiel 11v5)

Spirit of God's Lordship, of Wisdom, of Understanding, of Counsel, of Might, of Knowledge, of the Fear of the Lord (Isaiah 11v2) – the "sevenfold Spirit of God" (Revelation 1v4, 5v6), referring to the sevenfold work of the Holy Spirit.

Spirit of Holiness (Psalm 29v2, Romans 1v4)

Holy Spirit – Ruach Hakkodesh (Psalm 51v11), *Pneuma Hagion* (Ephesians 1v13)

Spirit of Judgment (Isaiah 4v4)

Spirit of Grace (Hebrews 10v29), *of Grace and Supplication* (Zechariah 12v10)

Spirit of Truth (John 14v17, 1 John 4v6)

Comforter, Helper, Advocate, Counsellor (John 14v16, 26)

Holy Spirit of Promise (Ephesians 1v13)

Spirit of Glory (1 Peter 4v14)

Spirit of Sonship or *Adoption* (Romans 8v15) – Jesus is God's only begotten Son whereas Christians are God's adopted children by grace and this is confirmed to us by His Spirit.

Spirit of Life (Romans 8v2, Revelation 11v11)

Spirit of Faith (2 Corinthians 4v13)

Spirit of Wisdom and Revelation (Ephesians 1v17), *Spirit of Prophecy* (Revelation 19v10)

Spirit of the Father (Matthew 10v20)

Spirit of the Son (Galatians 4v6), *Spirit of Christ* (Romans 8v9)

Eternal Spirit (Hebrews 9v14)

God (Acts 5v3 and 4) – the Holy Spirit is regarded as God Himself

Appendix 2

I Believe What the Bible Says About Me[1]

I am what I am by the grace of God (1 Corinthians 15v10), the great "I AM" (Exodus 3v14).

I am not my own; I have been bought with the precious blood of Christ. Therefore, I belong to God (1 Corinthians 6v19-20).

I am a new creation, a new person (2 Corinthians 5v17). I have been redeemed and forgiven (Ephesians 1v7).

I am a child of God (John 1v12, Romans 8v16). I have been chosen by Him and have been adopted as His child (Ephesians 1v4-5).

I am a joint heir with Christ. I share His inheritance with Him (Romans 8v17).

I am a recipient of God's lavish grace (Ephesians 1v6, 8).

I am a chosen one of Jesus, appointed by Him to bear good fruit (John 15v16).

I am one of God's chosen people, dearly loved by Him (Colossians 3v12).

I am a friend of Jesus (John 15v15) and I am His disciple (John 13v35).

I am a worshipper of God and I serve Him (Luke 4v8).

I am seated with Christ in the heavenly realm because I am united with Him (Ephesians 2v6) and one with Him in spirit (1 Corinthians 6v17).

I am a branch of the "true vine" who is Jesus (John 15v1, 5), and I am a blessing to the world (Genesis 12v2).

I am God's workmanship, created in Christ to do the good works that He planned for me to do (Ephesians 2v10).

---

[1] This appendix is not an exhaustive list. The Bible says so much more about who you are in Jesus Christ.

I am a temple of the Holy Spirit of God who dwells in me (1 Corinthians 3v16, 6v19).

I am the light of the world (Matthew 5v14) and the salt of the earth (Matthew 5v13) because Jesus lives in me (Galatians 2v20).

I am righteous and holy in God's sight because of Jesus who bore my sins (2 Corinthians 5v21).

I am one of God's saints, the "faithful in Christ Jesus" (Ephesians 1v1).

I am a member of Christ's Body (1 Corinthians 12v27), the Church, who is His Bride (2 Corinthians 11v2, Revelation 19v7).

I am one of God's living stones in His spiritual temple, one of His holy priests who offer spiritual sacrifices that please Him (1 Peter 2v5).

I am a slave to righteousness and not a slave to sin (Romans 6v18).

I am a stranger on earth. Earth is not my real home for I am a citizen of heaven (1 Peter 2v11, Philippians 3v20).

I am God's ambassador on earth who has been sent with the message of reconciliation between Him and people through Jesus (2 Corinthians 5v19-20).

I am a member of a chosen race, a royal priesthood, a holy nation, a people created as God's own possession (1 Peter 2v9, 10).

I am an enemy of the devil and I resist him by standing firm in the faith of Jesus (1 Peter 5v8-9; Galatians 2v20).

I have been crucified with Christ. I consider myself dead to sin, but alive with the life that Jesus gives me (Galatians 2v20). I no longer live for myself but for Him (2 Corinthians 5v15).

I have been buried, raised, and made alive with Christ (Colossians 2v12, 13).

I have been consecrated (set apart) for God and therefore He hears when I pray (Psalm 4v3).

I have been rescued from satan's kingdom and transferred to the Kingdom of God by Jesus who purchased my freedom with His own blood (Colossians 1v13).

I have been "justified" by the blood of Jesus, "just as if" I had never sinned. I have been made right with God and therefore, I have peace with Him (Romans 5v1).

I have direct access to God through the Spirit (Ephesians 2v18). I approach Him with boldness, freedom and confidence (Ephesians 3v12) and receive from Him mercy and grace in time of need (Hebrews 4v16).

I have been given a spirit of power, love and self-discipline (2 Timothy 1v7).

I have been blessed with every spiritual blessing in Christ (Ephesians 1v3).

I can do all things God wants me to do because Jesus gives me the strength that I need (Philippians 4v13).

Appendix 3

The Supernatural Gifts of the Spirit

But the manifestation of the Spirit is given to each one for the profit of all: for to one is given the word of wisdom through the Spirit, to another the word of knowledge through the same Spirit, to another faith by the same Spirit, to another gifts of healings by the same Spirit, to another the working of miracles, to another prophecy, to another discerning of spirits, to another different kinds of tongues, to another the interpretation of tongues. But one and the same Spirit works all these things, distributing to each one individually as He wills. (1 Corinthians 12v7-11, NKJV)

God gives all believers gifts, talents and abilities (Week 21). These include "spiritual gifts"[1] which give evidence that the Holy Spirit is working in and through us (hence, "the manifestation of the Spirit"). Jesus sent the Holy Spirit to equip His church with these spiritual gifts (and other gifts) so that we can help build His church and continue His ministry on earth. Although these spiritual gifts are not defined in the Bible, we can glean from various scriptures what they may mean. These nine spiritual gifts given in the passage above are the following[2]:

(1) Word of wisdom – a wise word, instruction or direction inspired by the Holy Spirit regarding a specific situation. One example is Joseph's advice to Pharaoh as to how to prepare for the coming seven years of famine (Genesis 41v14-40).

(2) Word of knowledge – information or facts supernaturally revealed to the speaker. It may come through a dream, a vision (mental picture), impression or a word from the Lord. One example is in Acts 5v1-10 in which Peter reveals that Ananias and Sapphira had lied to the Church and to the Holy Spirit regarding a piece of land that they had sold (Week 46.)

---

[1] 1 Corinthians 12v4 (NLT): *There are different kinds of spiritual gifts, but the same Spirit is the source of them all.* The original Greek word here for 'gift' is *charisma*, 'gift of grace'. For this reason, spiritual gifts are also called 'charismatic gifts'. *Charisma* is from *charis* = grace. See Week 39.

[2] These gifts are not easy to differentiate. One may classify a message as a word of wisdom, but another may say it is a prophecy. What has transpired may be to someone a gift of faith, to another, of healing, and to another, the working of a miracle.

(3) Gift of faith – an unusual faith for an unusual time, faith to face a difficult situation with unwavering trust in God's word and His ability to meet a specific need. One example is the raising of Dorcas from the dead by Peter in Acts 9v36-41. Another is the story of Daniel in the den of lions (Daniel 6).

(4) Gifts of healings – given to restore physical, mental and emotional health to people through the power of God. The double plural may refer to different kinds of infirmities and the various ways God may decide to heal by His power working through a person. There are many examples in the Gospels and in the book of Acts.

(5) Working of Miracles – the supernatural power to perform in obedience to God something against the laws of nature. We see many examples of the working of miracles in the life of Jesus, as when He fed the 5000 with 5 loaves of bread and 2 fish (John 6v1-13), and when He walked on water (John 6v16-21).

(6) Prophecy – the supernatural ability to receive and convey a hindsight, insight or foresight message from God (Week 12) for the purpose of edification, encouragement or comfort of the recipient, or for giving direction or warning. There are many examples in the Bible, such as those found in the prophetic books of Isaiah, Daniel and Revelation. A specific example from the book of Acts is the prediction of a famine by Agabus in Acts 11v27-30.

(7) Discerning of Spirits – the supernatural ability to sense the presence of angels or demons or to discern a person's motivation and the source of his message or action, whether it was the Holy Spirit, a demonic spirit or the human spirit. Because satan can counterfeit the spiritual gifts of the Holy Spirit in order to deceive people (e.g., the miracles of the future Antichrist and his prophet – see Week 51 and Revelation 13) and in the light of Jesus' warning in Matthew 24 regarding deceiving 'signs and wonders'[3], this gift is very important to the Church.

(8) Gift of tongues – a Holy Spirit-inspired utterance in an unlearned human language or in a heavenly language unknown to humans and spoken usually to God and not to man (1 Corinthians 14v2), as in prayer or in worship. In Acts 2, we read that the Christians who were gathered at Pentecost spoke in tongues when the Holy Spirit came upon them[4].

---

[3] Matthew 24v24-25 (NLT): *For false messiahs and false prophets will rise up and perform great signs and wonders so as to deceive, if possible, even God's chosen ones. See, I have warned you about this ahead of time.*

[4] Acts 2v4 (NIV): *All of them were filled with the Holy Spirit and began to speak in other tongues as the Spirit enabled them.*

(9) Interpretation of tongues – the supernatural interpretation (a declaration of the meaning) of an utterance in a tongue using a language the hearers can understand. Paul says in 1 Corinthians 14v13 (NIV): "Anyone who speaks in a tongue should pray that he may interpret what he says."

Paul tells us in 1 Corinthians 14v1 that we should "eagerly desire spiritual gifts". However, spirituality or Christian maturity is not measured by the possession of these gifts. We can glean this from the first letter of Paul to the Corinthian church of his day. Although the church was endowed with spiritual gifts[5], it was immature and unspiritual[6].

A charismatic gift of the Spirit is the Spirit's manifestation through a believer, but the fruit of the Spirit is the measure of one's spirituality and character. What is the "fruit of the Spirit"? The Amplified Bible tells us in Galatians 5v22-23 that "the fruit of the [Holy] Spirit [the work which His presence within accomplishes] is *love, joy* (gladness), *peace, patience* (an even temper, forbearance), *kindness, goodness* (benevolence), *faithfulness, gentleness* (meekness, humility), *self-control* (self-restraint, continence)." These nine character traits all appear in the fruit of having the Holy Spirit living in us and transforming or sanctifying us to become more like Jesus.

Let us desire to move in the gifts of the Spirit, but more than this, let us desire to see the fruit of the Spirit mature in our lives.

---

[5] 1 Corinthians 1v4-7 (NIV): *I always thank God for you because of His grace given you in Christ Jesus. For in Him you have been enriched in every way – in all your speaking and in all your knowledge – because our testimony about Christ was confirmed in you. Therefore you do not lack any spiritual gift as you eagerly wait for our Lord Jesus Christ to be revealed.*

[6] 1 Corinthians 3v1-3 (NLT): *Dear brothers and sisters, when I was with you I couldn't talk to you as I would to spiritual people. I had to talk as though you belonged to this world or as though you were infants in the Christian life. I had to feed you with milk, not with solid food, because you weren't ready for anything stronger. And you still aren't ready, for you are still controlled by your sinful nature. You are jealous of one another and quarrel with each other. Doesn't that prove you are controlled by your sinful nature? Aren't you living like people of the world?*

Appendix 4

Our Spiritual Weapons

Put on the full armour of God, so that when the day of evil comes, you may be able to stand your ground, and after you have done everything, to stand. Stand firm then, with the belt of truth buckled around your waist, with the breastplate of righteousness in place, and with your feet fitted with the readiness that comes from the gospel of peace. In addition to all this, take up the shield of faith, with which you can extinguish all the flaming arrows of the evil one. Take the helmet of salvation and the sword of the Spirit, which is the word of God. (Ephesians 6v13-17, NIV)

We have an enemy and he is the devil. Because of him, we have to fight spiritual battles that come to us in the form of temptation, illness, relational conflict, financial pressure and persecution. We cannot therefore deny that spiritual battles exist, nor refuse to fight them. Since these battles are spiritual in nature, we need to use spiritual weapons. The passage above implies that we have been given these weapons which form the "full armour of God" – "full" (or whole) in the sense that all these elements are to be used together for offence and defence, and "of God" because He is the real source of the armour[1].

The passage above gives us the individual elements of this full armour:

1. Belt of truth –

Paul, the writer of the passage, was actually referring to the armour of a Roman soldier ready for battle. The first thing the soldier would put on was his leather belt. To this he would attach other pieces of the armour, including the sword. As 'Christian soldiers', we need to buckle the "belt of truth" around our waist. This means that we need to be firmly established in the foundational truth about who God is and who we are in Christ as revealed in the word of God (Appendix 1 and 2). This belt therefore helps us to see things from God's eternal perspective (Week 6) and protects us from satan's lies.

2. Breastplate of righteousness –

---

[1] Zechariah 4:6 (NASB): *"Not by might nor by power, but by My Spirit," says the Lord of hosts* ['Jehovah/Yahweh Sabaoth' – see Appendix 1].

The breastplate provides protection for the Roman soldier's vital organs like the heart, lungs and stomach. Isaiah 59v17 says that God Himself puts on righteousness as His breastplate[2]. So must we! Because our own righteousness is like "filthy rags"[3], then God invites us to put on His righteousness, not ours. This is why He is called *Jehovah Tsidkenu* ("God is My Righteousness" – see Appendix 1). Christ's righteousness imputed on us (8th footnote, Week 45) is our protection against the accusations of satan, "the accuser of the brethren"[4]. You know you have put on God's breastplate when you are keenly aware that you have become righteous in God's sight because of Christ's righteousness, and the more you believe it, the more you act it out. "For as he thinks within himself, so he is" says Proverbs 23v7 (NASB). Righteous thoughts produce righteous deeds! There will be times when you will be complacent, take off this breastplate and succumb to satan's lies and temptations, but you must put it back on again by confessing your sins and asking God for forgiveness[5].

3. Sandals of the gospel of peace –

The Roman soldier's leather sandals protected his feet from the rugged terrain. The iron hobnails beneath the thick soles also provided good traction so that he could be surefooted during battle. The saying in Bible times about breaking someone's sandals or shoes, a metaphor for defeating an opponent[6], shows the importance of the soldier's footwear. Our spiritual footwear is the good news ('gospel') about Christ's finished work on the cross to redeem us from satan and to place us in a right standing or relationship with God, the news that brings inner peace (*shalom/eirene* – Week 45). This right relationship is established and characterised by *chesed* (Week 31) which constrains us to obey the Great Commission to reach out to others with the same gospel of peace. These sandals are therefore associated with our 'readiness' to share the good news[7], the same good news that help us to stand our ground[8] (not to be complacent regarding sin) against satan and his demonic cohorts.

4. Shield of faith –

---

[2]   Isaiah 59v17 (ESV): *He* [the Lord] *put on righteousness as a breastplate...*
[3]   Isaiah 64v6 (AMP): *For we have all become like one who is unclean [ceremonially, like a leper], and all our righteousness (our best deeds of rightness and justice) is like filthy rags or a polluted garment...*
[4]   Revelation 12v10
[5]   1 John 1v9 (NKJV): *If we confess our sins, He is faithful and just to forgive us our sins and to cleanse us from all unrighteousness.*
[6]   Isaiah 5v27 (NKJV): *... nor the strap of their sandals be broken...*
[7]   Isaiah 52v7 (NASB): *How lovely on the mountains are the feet of him who brings good news.*
[8]   Psalm 18v33 (NLT): *He makes me as surefooted as a deer, enabling me to stand on mountain heights.*

The Roman soldier's shield was made of layers of bonded wood strips covered with leather. The leather would be drenched in water before the soldier went to battle to enable the shield to put out the fire of the enemy's flaming arrows. Our God-given faith soaked in the water of God's word[9] quenches the fiery darts of satan and his cohorts. It is faith that is <u>not</u> built on myths and legends, but on truth proven by reasoning and supported by evidence, like the evidence in the form of testimonies of the many storytellers in this book who share their experiences of the reality of God in their own lives[10]. We learn to use our shield of faith to its fullest potential by acting on the revelations we have received from God through His word (*logos* and *rhema*, Week 8). We stay alert and uncompromising through worship and prayer. We also make it a point to be in fellowship with other believers for mutual encouragement, edification and exhortation, just as the Roman soldiers would interlock their shields together to form a virtually impregnable tortoise shell formation[11].

5. Helmet of salvation –

The Roman soldier's helmet was made of bronze or iron and was worn to protect the head. Our helmet of salvation guards the battleground of the mind which satan loves to bombard with temptations, lies, doubts and discouraging thoughts because he knows that mental strongholds rule our emotions and shape the way we think and act (Week 43). Paul calls this helmet "hope of salvation"[12] to imply that we have the blessed hope (joyful and confident expectation) of God's continuing work of salvation in our life. That is, we believe that He has justified us, is sanctifying us and will one day glorify us with new resurrection bodies (Week 51). The knowledge of this truth and of the truth about God and our identity in Jesus (Appendix 1 and 2) demolish demonic strongholds or mindsets and transform the way we think. As a result, we learn to take God's eternal perspective of our circumstances and to act accordingly. The helmet of salvation, therefore, helps us to learn to think and act like Jesus.

---

[9] Ephesians 5v26 (ESV): ... *that He might sanctify her* [the Church], *having cleansed her by the washing of water with the word* [of God].

[10] Have you read the book *Who Moved the Stone* written in 1930 by Albert Henry Ross (under the pseudonym Frank Morison)? He set out to refute the claims of Jesus by examining the events of the crucifixion and the resurrection, but instead ended up writing the book because, as he said, "It was the strangeness of many notable things in the story which first arrested and held my interest. It was only later that the irresistible logic of their meaning came into view." *Who Moved the Stone* relates the journey of the author from doubt to belief and from agnosticism to faith through his own examination of the events of Good Friday and Resurrection Sunday.

[11] In a tortoise shell formation, 27 soldiers - 6 in front and 7 in each of 3 rows - would interlock their shields. The ones on the outside would hold their shields vertically, and the ones inside would hold their shields up to form a roof.

[12] 1 Thessalonians 5v8 (AMP): *Therefore, let us be sober and put on ...... for a helmet the hope of salvation.*

6. Sword of the Spirit –

The Roman sword called *machira* was unique during biblical times in being short (24 inches in length) and double-edged. The Romans used it to conquer the world! Its proper use in battle for both offence and defence required extensive practice. Ephesians 6 tells us that our spiritual sword is the "living and active, sharper than any two-edged sword" word of God[13]. Not only is it able to defend us from the lies, accusations and temptations of the enemy, it is also able to reveal to us if our thoughts and actions originated from our born-again spirit (hence, Spirit-inspired) or from our worldly flesh or "soul"[14]. Used offensively, we can pray, declare and even sing the word of God as our sword against satan's attacks. "My Assignment" in Week 23 and the story in Week 26 are examples of using God's word offensively. The amazing story in 2 Chronicles chapter 20 of the victory of King Jehoshaphat and his army against the armies of Moab and Ammon is an example of fighting our battle by singing praises to God[15]. Memorising verses from the Bible[16], waiting on God for His *rhema* word regarding what we are praying for, and acting in obedience to what He says enable us to use this sword effectively.

Paul tells us to "put on" this full armour of God. In another scripture, he tells us to "put on Jesus"[17]. Jesus is the truth[18]; He is our righteousness and holiness[19]; He is the Good News and our Peace[20]; He is the author and perfecter (or 'finisher') of our faith[21]; He is salvation[22]; and He is the living Word of God (Week 8). Therefore, to "put on the full armour of God" is to "put on Jesus" and to "put on Jesus" is to think

---

[13] Hebrews 4v12 (ESV): *For the word of God is living and active, sharper than any two-edged sword, piercing to the division of soul and of spirit, of joints and of marrow, and discerning the thoughts and intentions of the heart.*

[14] Ibid.

[15] They sang "Praise the Lord for His *chesed* endures forever!" from Psalm 106v1 and Psalm 136v1.

[16] Psalm 119v11 (NLT): *I have hidden Your word in my heart, that I might not sin against You.*

[17] Romans 13v14 (NKJV): *But put on the Lord Jesus Christ, and make no provision for the flesh, to fulfil its lusts.*

[18] John 14v6 (NIV): *Jesus answered, "I am the way and the truth and the life. No one comes to the Father except through Me".*

[19] 1Corinthians 1v30 (NIV): *It is because of Him that you are in Christ Jesus, who has become for us wisdom from God – that is, our righteousness, holiness and redemption.*

[20] Ephesians 2v14 (NIV): *For He Himself is our peace...*

[21] Hebrews 12v2 (NKJV): *... looking unto Jesus, the author and finisher of our faith, who for the joy that was set before Him endured the cross, despising the shame, and has sat down at the right hand of the throne of God.*

[22] *Yeshua*, Jesus' Hebrew name, means 'Yahweh/God is salvation' or 'God saves'.

and act the way He would by the grace and power of the Holy Spirit living in us. Regarding the situations that we face, let us ask ourselves, "What would Jesus do?"

We face spiritual battles every day, so every day, let us put on the full armour of God. Let us put on Jesus because the battle is won "not by might nor by power, but by My Spirit, says the Lord of hosts" (Zechariah 4v6, NASB).

Appendix 5

List of Contributors of Stories

The following contributors own the copyrights to their respective stories. This list is arranged alphabetically by first name:

- **Abdulahi** (Lagos, Nigeria) – Wk. 4 "A Man Finds the Right Way"
- **Alcestis (Bing) Llobrera** (Butuan City, Philippines) – Wk. 32 "Our Labours and Prayers Do Bear Fruit"
- **Arthur** (Lancaster, England) – Wk. 12 "In the Right Place at the Right Time"
- **Ave** (Kingston, Jamaica) – Wk. 25 "My Special Son Vaughn"
- **Barbara** (Lancaster, England) – Wk. 17 "The Story of the Olive Branch"
- **Barbara** (Malaga, Spain) – Wk. 18 "My Challenge from God"
- **Bart** (Alblasserdam, The Netherlands) – Wk. 15 "A Promise Fulfilled"
- **Berit Skaare** (Ilula, Tanzania) – Wk. 21 "Great Needs, Great Possibilities" and Wk. 27 "The Airport Angel of Indiana"
- **Christina** (Lancaster, England) – Wk. 10 "I Will Be with You!"
- **Christine** (Kendal, Cumbria, England) – Wk. 35 "Christine's Story"
- **Corazon** (Manchester, England) – Wk. 38 "Blood in the Wardrobe"
- **Daria Tsai** (Kaohsiung, Taiwan) – Wk. 44 "He Stirred My Nest"
- **David Ellis** (Grange-over-Sands, Cumbria, England) – Wk. 19 "The Christ of Wanchai" and Wk. 51 "Never Too Late"
- **David Thomson** (Troon, Scotland) – Wk. 24 "Often Things are not What They Seem" and Wk. 49 "Reaching Out to Seamen"
- **Derek Van Ryckeghem** (Winnipeg, Canada) – Wk. 40 "Here Am I, Lord!"
- **Desi Maxwell** (Lisburn, Northern Ireland) – Wk. 16 "Lord of Life, Send My Roots Rain"
- **Dolly Antonio** (Montalban, Rizal, Philippines) – Wk. 39 "Not a Reject"
- **Eddie** (Lancaster, England) – Wk. 50 "I Have Hope for the Future!"
- **Elisabeth** (Bromölla, Sweden) – Wk. 42 "He Restores My Soul"
- **Evelyn** (Fort Worth, Texas, USA) – Wk. 14 "Burdened by God's Love"
- **Gareth** (Lancaster, England) – Wk. 3 "Gareth's Story"
- **Gayle Haffner** (Davison, Michigan, USA) – Wk. 46 "An Angelic Visitation"
- **Gill Linder** (Cockermouth, Cumbria, England) – Wk. 33 "My Neighbour Miss Wood"
- **Grahame** (Lancaster, England) – Wk. 43 "The Long Road to Recovery"
- **Haide** (Lancaster, England) – Wk. 9 "Don't Look at the Situation and Circumstances", Wk. 15 "Rainbow Connection" and Wk. 23 "An Assignment"

317

- **Heather** (Lancaster, England) – Wk. 25 "Consider It All Joy"
- **Helen** (Lancaster, England) – Wk. 36 "His Light Invaded My Darkness"
- **"Intercessor"** (Lancaster, England) – Wk. 30 "Confession of an Intercessor"
- **Jayeel Cornelio** (Göttingen, Germany) – Wk. 28 "Doing a PhD for God"
- **Jeannie** (Vancouver, British Columbia, Canada) – Wk. 23 "God Answered My Prayers for Libya"
- **John Mosey** (Arnside, Cumbria, England) – Wk. 13 "God Doesn't Only Talk to Big Shots"
- **Joyce** (Houston, Texas, USA) – Wk. 34 "My Husband Became an Alcoholic"
- **Kathi** (Minnesota, USA) – Wk. 6 "It was Important to Him"
- **Linda Greenfield** (Ontario, Canada) – Wk. 46 "My Friend was Shot"
- **Marcus Mosey** (Lancaster, England) – Wk. 52 "When the Rubber Hits the Road"
- **Maria-Corazon** (Manila, Philippines) – Wk. 7 "Sleepless in Seattle"
- **Mary** (Lancaster, England) – Wk. 50 "Mary's Story"
- **Matti** (Espoo, Finland) – Wk. 5 "A Bed from Heaven"
- **Muriel** (Guangzhou, China) – Wk. 2, "A Chinese Girl's Conversion"
- **Nathan Mejica** (Manila, Philippines) – Wk. 20 "The Story of Shepherd of the Hills Children's Foundation"
- **Owen** (Lancaster, England) – Wk. 1 "Welcome Home, Owen!"
- **Peter and Fiona Collins** (Lancaster, England) – Wk. 8 "Something Happened to our Baby"
- **Ron** (Malaga, Spain) – Wk. 31 "A Changed Life" and "My First Visit to the Underground Church in China"
- **Rosemary** (Lancaster, England) – Wk. 37 "God Gave Me Love for My Father" and Wk. 41 "Rosemary's Car Crash"
- **Samantha Glasgow** (Trinidad and Tobago) – Wk. 47 "Jesus, the Way Maker"
- **Samson** (Kitwe, Zambia) – Wk. 26 "The Night Peter was Set Free"
- **Shannon Lee** (Taipei, Taiwan) – Wk. 45 "Shannon's Story"
- **Shirley** (Houston, Texas, USA) – Wk. 3 "Sharing the Good News" and Wk. 11 "Shirley's Story"
- **Suzanne** (Indiana, USA) – Wk. 48 "He Causes All Things to Work for Good"
- **Vic** (Bislig, Surigao del Sur, Philippines) – Wk. 22 "Pastor Vic's Story"
- **Vivienne** (Lancaster, England) – Wk. 6 "A Praying Woman"
- **Y.A.L.** (Lancashire, England) – Wk. 29 "Susan's Reluctant Intercessor"

And they overcame him because of the blood of the Lamb and because of the word of their testimony. (Revelation 12v11, NASB)

Index

Readers' Comments

Here are comments posted on Amazon by some readers of *God's Eagles, Athletes and Pilgrims*:

A hefty resource

"*God's Eagles, Athletes and Pilgrims* by Haide Sanchez is a hefty resource, chock full of material that is invaluable to both new believers and seasoned saints. It is worthy to be used as a manual to refer back to, time and time again. Working around the true life stories provided by individuals, she has applied and brought out scriptural truths to educate, build up and establish believers in the truth." (posted by Gill, 20 Mar. 2014)

Time to Fly with Eagles!

"I would strongly recommend this devotional book especially to new Christians to help lift their expectations of God in their daily lives. I have bought three copies as gifts. Brilliant!" (posted by sapling, 17 Dec. 2012)

Encouraging, inspiring, thought-provoking with a solid theology base

"It is rare to find a book that speaks to your soul, mind and spirit with every story, every introduction -- this is one of them! The Lord has used this book tremendously to speak His words of truth at pivotal moments when I needed to hear exactly the words I was reading on these pages. It is a page turner-- but I found myself purposely slowing down so that I didn't finish it too quickly - wishing it was a non-ending book. What an encouragement to hear the testimonies of people all over the world. God is alive and very active everywhere!" (posted by Evelyn Bitencourt, Washington DC, 6 Mar. 2013)

Encouraging read

"The stories in this book are incredible. It is so encouraging to read about God working in people's real lives, many of whom are going through similar things to myself. The scripture and devotional sections are edifying and uplifting and gave me strength to face each day." (posted by hgscott, 30 Dec. 2012)

Absolutely brilliant devotional

"This is an absolutely brilliant devotional. It has helped me to refocus on the plans and purposes of God in my life. All the different testimonies helped me to expect more from God, trusting that He will fulfil His plans for me to prosper me and not to harm me, plans to give me hope and a future (Jeremiah 29:11). Also the Appendices have been very valuable in helping me to think about myself the way God sees me, as His child, an heir to the throne of God! I am sure this book will bless you too, whether you are just interested in becoming a Christian or whether you have become mature. It is full of stories about the greatness and goodness of God and helps us put our circumstances into eternal perspective." (posted by Bastiaan T., 9 Dec. 2012)

Awesome, insightful, timely

"Ms. Sanchez has created one of the most interesting devotional books I have ever read. As busy people, we don't always have opportunity to read separate daily devotions, and this one geared to one per week is very helpful. At a time when we are being blasted on overdrive by new information (like a daily separate devotional thought), this WEEKLY allows for several days to reflect and develop topical thoughts to a deeper level for personal application.

One of the special applications of Sanchez's research involves GLOBAL stories/ testimonies from real people of our decade. Another aspect is that the contents involves input from a wide swathe of Christian denominations. That our generation is finally seeing heavenly inspired cross-denominational input and application is further proof that God sees the heart rather than labels, nationality or economy. Having published myself in 2011, I can say that this book covers everything a reader would want in terms of quality." (posted on 15 Jan. 2013 by Gayle Haffner, author of *Hands With a Heart: The Personal Biography of Actress ZaSu Pitts* c.2011, Biography First Place, International Book Awards)

The Reality of a Walk with God

"Haide has done an excellent job with this devotional. For a new Christian it will encourage and challenge in just the right proportion. For a mature believer it will re-affirm their experience of living the Christian life and will reflect their own relationship with God." (posted by sapling, 19 Feb. 2013)

Printed in the United States
By Bookmasters